Secondary
Education

Secondary Education: School and Community

WILLIAM VAN TIL

Coffman Distinguished Professor Emeritus of Education / Indiana State University

HOUGHTON MIFFLIN COMPANY   BOSTON
Dallas   Geneva, Illinois   Hopewell, New Jersey
Palo Alto   London

*For the youngest
of the Van Til family—
Linda, Justin, Laura, Desiree, Ross—
for whom secondary education
is still ahead*

Library of Congress Catalog Card Number: 77-76861
ISBN: 0-395-25751-4

CREDITS
Photographs on pages 5, 19, 95, 184, 268, and 346 courtesy of
Indiana State University—Audio-Visual Center.

Contents

To the Reader ix
To the Professor xi
Acknowledgments xiii

Part 1. The Setting of Secondary Education

CHAPTER 1. CRITICISMS OF SECONDARY EDUCATION IN THE 1970s 3

The Compassionate Critics 4
The Alternative School Movement 10
Back-to-Basics Movement 13
Secondary Education Through School and Community 18
Arriving at Your View of Secondary Education 26
Discussion 28   Involvement 29   Further Readings 30

CHAPTER 2. THE SOCIAL CRISIS AND SECONDARY EDUCATION 32

Evolution of the Social Crisis 32
Persistent Social Problems 34
Teaching Students During Social Crisis 50
Discussion 53   Involvement 54   Further Readings 55

CHAPTER 3. VALUE OPTIONS OF YOUTH 57

Value Confusion 58
Life Styles and Value Patterns 60
Social Developments Affecting Value Options 73
Role and Responsibility of Educators 74
Discussion 76   Involvement 78   Further Readings 78

CHAPTER 4. CHARACTERISTICS OF YOUNG PEOPLE 80

Adolescence 81
Sex Roles in Adolescence 85
Social Class 89
Ethnic Groups 94
The Three D's 104
Teachers and Young People 113
Discussion 113   Involvement 115   Further Readings 116

Part 2. The Story of Secondary Education

CHAPTER 5. DEVELOPMENT OF SECONDARY SCHOOLS 121

Old World Beginnings 122
The Emerging American Nation 125
Reorganization of Secondary Education 131
Some Statistics on Secondary Education 144
Discussion 146   Involvement 147   Further Readings 148

CHAPTER 6. CONFLICT OVER THE GOALS OF SECONDARY EDUCATION 150

Early Spokesmen for Useful Goals 151
Social Forces Influence Educational Goals 155
Goals of Progressive Education 161
Twentieth-Century Conceptions of Goals 163
Discussion 176   Involvement 178   Further Readings 179

CHAPTER 7. THE SECONDARY SCHOOL PROGRAM TODAY 181

Science 183
Mathematics 186
Social Studies 189
English Language Arts 194
Physical Education, Health, and Recreation 197
Modern Foreign Languages 199
Music 202
Art 205
Home Economics 207
Industrial Arts 209
Business Education 211
Vocational Education 213
Discussion 216   Involvement 217   Further Readings 218

Part 3. The Quest for Better Secondary Education

CHAPTER 8. SEARCHING FOR BETTER CONTENT 223

What Should Secondary Schools Teach? 225
Major Clusters of Content 232
Possible Curricular Organization 245
Discussion 246   Involvement 248   Further Readings 249

CHAPTER 9. WIDENING THE ENVIRONMENT 251

Expansion of Secondary School Plants 252
Relationships of Schools and Communities 265
The Changing Setting 280
Discussion 281   Involvement 282   Further Readings 283

CHAPTER 10. IMPROVING THE ORGANIZATION 285

Interdisciplinary Approaches 287
Individualized Instruction 299
Guidance 306
Toward Better Organization 310
Discussion 311   Involvement 312   Further Readings 313

CHAPTER 11. USING VARIED PERSONNEL 315

Teachers 315
School Board Members 330
Secondary School Principals 338
Community Members 345
Discussion 350   Involvement 352   Further Readings 353

Part 4. The Future of Secondary Education

CHAPTER 12. THE YEAR 2000: SECONDARY EDUCATION THROUGH
THE SCHOOLS AND THE COMMUNITY 359

Futurism 359
Speculation on Future Secondary Education 364
Education in the Year 2000: Three Possible Futures 383
Discussion 392   Involvement 394   Further Readings 394

Index 397

To the Reader

When a reader first picks up a book, the first question apt to arise in his or her mind is: What is this book about? The title of this book reveals its subject matter in five words, *Secondary Education: School and Community*.

The content is divided into four parts. Part One deals with the broad setting of secondary education. Part Two tells the story of secondary schools, their past and present. Part Three describes the quest for a better secondary education than now exists in America. Part Four speculates on secondary education in the future, an education that may take place through both schools and communities.

In more detail, the setting, covered in the first four chapters, reviews such questions as these:

> What are the major criticisms of American secondary education today?
>
> What are the persistent social problems in the United States and the world that secondary education must take into account?
>
> What are the value options and choices confronting our young people?
>
> In what ways are adolescents similar to each other and yet different as to sex roles, social class, ethnic backgrounds, and special problems?

In telling the story of secondary schooling, the next three chapters report on such questions as these:

> How did secondary schools come about in the world and in America?
>
> What conflicts took place over the goals of American secondary education?
>
> What are the recent developments in today's secondary schools?

In describing the quest for better secondary education, the following four chapters consider these questions:

What should secondary schools teach and what should young people of secondary school age learn?

What is the best combination of schooling and community participation in secondary education?

Would more stress on interdisciplinary study, individualized instruction, and guidance contribute to a better organization of secondary education?

What kinds of teachers, school board members, principals, and community participants does secondary education now need?

In speculating on the future, the closing chapter asks:

What might the secondary education of the future be like if it took place, as now appears likely, in both schools and community, through both schooling and community participation?

W.V.T.

To the Professor

Secondary Education: School and Community is a text for undergraduates who plan to teach in secondary schools. The book is designed for use by professors teaching such courses as principles of secondary education, problems in secondary school teaching, teaching in the secondary school, foundations of secondary education, the American high school, junior and senior high school education, and—most simply—secondary education.

Because of the strong emphasis on curriculum, some professors will also find the book useful in graduate level courses such as secondary school curriculum, curriculum development, the high school curriculum, and junior-senior high school curriculum. The book should also be helpful in the in-service education of teachers with its up-to-date overview of secondary education.

If secondary education continues to expand beyond the school walls, additional readers should also be reached by this book—the new partners in secondary education. These are the paid paraprofessionals and teacher aides, the volunteers from our communities who provide work experiences and action-learning for the young, and the informed citizens who want secondary education to contribute significantly to young lives and to American society as a whole.

A guide to some uses of the book is available from the publisher. But some broad suggestions as to possible teaching approaches may prove helpful to you now.

You may wish to focus your course on the dozen questions listed in "To the Reader." These are the central concerns of the twelve chapters. Or you may wish to build your instruction around the questions you select from those appearing at both the opening and the close of Chapter One.

You may wish to engage in some discussions and other classroom interaction with your students based upon the suggestions at the close of each chapter in the Discussion section. These suggestions include some direct uncomplicated questions calling for a brief response from students; most of the suggestions, however, call for more sustained discussions. So use them selectively and don't feel guilty if you use only a few. As you long ago learned, it is quality rather than coverage that counts in class discussions.

The suggestions in the Involvement sections at the ends of chapters invite student participation going beyond classroom talk. Again, some suggestions call for relatively brief student activities. but most necessitate substantial student time investment in trips, surveys, questionnaires, interviews, reports, debates, work with groups, essays, speakers at class sessions, and so on. Again, careful choice among Involvement activities to select those appropriate to your individual setting and situation will be necessary. Try at least some suggestions or devise your own, because the new generation of secondary educators must learn how to participate and to become involved in both school and community. In addition, individuals might be encouraged to undertake Involvement activities appropriate to your situation and locale.

Further Readings sections end each chapter. The very large majority of the selected references are from books published in the 1970s. Some are mentioned in the footnotes; most are additional sources of information. You may want to make total class or individual assignments from these lists. You may want to encourage some individuals to supplement their learning through independent unassigned readings. Outstanding students may also want to read some of the equally important articles and books referred to in the footnotes.

Good teachers always update whatever materials their classes use. *Secondary Education: School and Community* is no exception to this observation, and will require your updating. The last textual changes and additions were made in mid-1977.

My hope is that this book will help you in your own effective teaching, and that it proves to be a useful resource. But I have taught long enough to know that the most important factor in teaching is not the textbook. It is you, the teacher.

W.V.T.

Acknowledgments

I owe much to my predecessors and contemporaries in secondary education. Despite the use of footnotes and suggested Further Readings, my intellectual debt is to so many people and is so great that it never can be fully repaid.

Thanks to leaders in secondary education who read the outline and prospectus and helped me to improve the proposal and thanks to still other leaders who read and advised on the manuscript: Jean D. Grambs, University of Maryland; Richard D. Kimpston, University of Minnesota; and John F. Ohles, Kent State University.

Thanks to many of my Indiana State colleagues who teach in the dozen broad fields of the secondary school curriculum and to Professor Robert O. Williams for their help with the chapter on "The Secondary School Program Today."

Thanks to my research assistants at Indiana State University, Robert Morris, currently Assistant Professor, Auburn University, and Mary Ross, University Fellow, Indiana State University, and thanks to secretaries Ruan Fougerousse and Sherri Morris. Thanks to Dean David T. Turney for his support.

I also want to thank the Association for Supervision and Currculum Development, the John Dewey Society, and the National Society of College Teachers of Education for entrusting their presidencies to me and enabling me to learn much in the process.

Thanks are due especially to *The Condition of Education*, 1976 and 1977 editions, a United States government publication, whose data appears throughout the text. There, these sources are briefly cited. To give full credit, they are: Mary A. Golladay, *The Condition of Education: A Statistical Report on the Condition of Education in the United States together with a Description of the Activities of The National Center for Education Statistics* (Washington, D.C.: U.S. Department of Health, Education, and Welfare's Education Division and National Center for Education Statistics, U.S. Government Printing Office, 1976), and Mary A. Golladay, *The Condition of Education: A Statistical Report on the Condition of Education in the United States*, 1977 edition.

Warm thanks to the National Society for the Study of Education for permission to draw freely upon *Issues in Secondary Education*, the 1976 yearbook of the Society, which I edited.

As always, a special thanks to my wife Bee, my first mate and my best editor since our cruise down the Danube River.

Part 1.
The Setting
of Secondary
Education

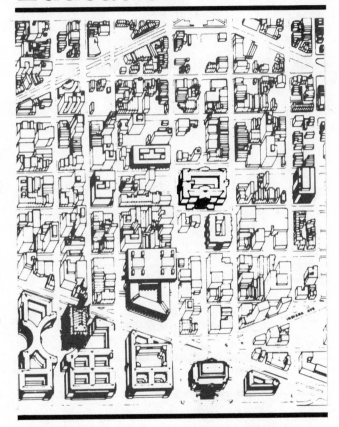

1.

Criticisms of Secondary Education in the 1970s

Many Americans are concerned about secondary education today. They are examining and debating its value. Naturally, secondary schooling has long been discussed in school board and parent-teacher meetings, over the coffee cups in faculty rooms, and in teacher education courses, magazines, and professional books. But now books for the general reader contain discussions on secondary education. Reports by scholarly commissions and committees supported by governmental and philanthropic organizations analyze high school education and recommend alternative transitions to adulthood. Television and radio programs popularize the charges and findings of the authors of such publications through panel discussions, news programs, documentaries, and talk shows. So vigorous critical commentary on secondary education reaches a broad general public today. Debate about secondary schooling is no longer the monopoly of professionals and a few concerned laypeople.

Here are some questions about secondary education being discussed in the United States today. Try your hand—or rather your head—at them:

What kind of secondary education is needed? What types of senior high schools, junior high schools, and middle schools are wanted for students between the ages of twelve and eighteen? Should secondary schooling be supplemented by out-of-school educational experiences, such as work? Is secondary school really necessary? . . . for everybody?

What should the goals of secondary education be? What is secondary education supposed to do for the United States of America in its third century? What is education for, anyway? . . . to meet the needs of learners? . . . to orient them to the society in which they live? . . . to help them make choices and clarify their values? . . . to supply them with knowledge?

What should secondary education teach? What programs should be provided? . . . for whom? What methods should be used? . . . with whom?

Where should secondary education take place? In schools? . . . comprehensive or vocational or alternative? In the community? . . . through jobs or public service activities?

How should secondary education be organized? . . . in the form of required academic courses? . . . through problem-centered learnings? . . . through multiple choices and options? . . . through action-learning beyond the school walls?

Who should staff, administer, and attempt to improve secondary education? Classroom teachers? . . . what kind of teachers? Professional administrators? . . . what type of leadership? Community people? . . . how great a role and voice?

Answers vary widely. Secondary education is in ferment, and criticism of secondary schools is increasing rapidly.

Some criticisms of secondary education are part of a wider objection to aspects of American education; such criticisms embrace both elementary and secondary education. Other criticism applies especially to secondary schools.

To provide perspective on criticisms of secondary education today, we will first describe a criticism of both elementary and secondary education that arose in the troubled 1960s and has extended into the 1970s: the view of a group of compassionate critics. Their criticism contributed to the development of alternative schools. We will then look at a view strongly opposed to that of the compassionate critics, that of the back-to-basics advocates who renewed criticism of both elementary and secondary schools in the mid-1970s. We will next consider the criticisms of secondary education in particular that were initiated during the mid-1970s by a series of reform reports. The proposed reforms were fostered by community-oriented committees and commissions. Currently, educators are attempting to adapt their programs to school-community reform proposals.

Let's listen to what contemporary critics are saying about secondary education in America.

THE COMPASSIONATE CRITICS

SUPPORTERS OF NEEDS-ORIENTED EDUCATION

Take the compassionate critics, a phrase which describes a loosely organized group of young educators who write about

FIGURE 1.1 *A Needs-oriented Education.* *These young people are participating in a class responsive to their interests.*

American education. They say that education today, including both secondary and elementary education, is dull, lifeless, and meaningless. They urge an education that is exciting, alive, and responsive to the needs and interests of young people (see Figure 1.1): therefore they wage a vigorous attack on traditional education. Listen, for instance, to James Herndon's satire in *How to Survive in Your Native Land:*

Flax is what school is all about. In my own old-fashioned geography books I went to various countries in the company of Bedouin and Greek and Turkish kids and the thing that most remains in my mind now about those imaginary kids is that they always grew flax. I myself put flax on my maps alongside corn and wheat and coal; I wrote down flax to answer questions about the products of countries. I never knew what flax was, but I knew that if I kept it in mind and wrote it down a lot and raised my hand and said it a lot, I would be making it. . . .

I think you could live your entire life in America and never see or even hear of flax, never know about it or need to know about it. Only in the school, . . . could you learn about flax. . . .

. . . It showed the school who among the students was willing and able to keep flax in mind, to raise his hand and say it aloud, to write it down, and put its name on maps. So that in the cumulative records of each child the teacher could write down for the next teacher the information that

Child reads flax, writes down flax and says flax.	Leader.
Child sometimes remembers flax.	Nice kid.
Child can't remember flax.	Child is black and/or deprived.
Child digs flax, but inadvertently says "chili-dog" instead.	Brain-damaged?
Child don't dig flax a-tall.	Reluctant learner.[1]

Or consider the proposals of Postman and Weingartner in *Teaching as a Subversive Activity:*

1. Declare a five-year moratorium on the use of all textbooks. . . .

2. Have "English" teachers "teach" Math, Math teachers English, Social Studies teachers Science, Science teachers Art, and so on. . . .

3. Transfer all the elementary-school teachers to high school and vice versa. . . .

4. Require every teacher who thinks he knows his "subject" well to write a book on it. . . .

5. Dissolve all "subjects," "courses," and especially "course requirements". . . .

6. Limit each teacher to three declarative sentences per class, and 15 interrogatives. . . .

7. Prohibit teachers from asking any questions they already know the answers to. . . .

8. Declare a moratorium on all tests and grades. . . .

9. Require all teachers to undergo some form of psychotherapy as part of their in-service training. . . .

10. Classify teachers according to their ability and make the lists public. . . .

11. Require all teachers to take a test prepared by students on what the students know. . . .

12. Make every class an elective and withhold a teacher's monthly check if his students do not show any interest in going to next month's classes. . . .

---

[1] James Herndon, *How to Survive in Your Native Land,* Simon and Schuster, New York, 1971, pp. 117–118.

13.   Require every teacher to take a one-year leave of absence every fourth year to work in some "field" other than education. . . .

14.   Require each teacher to provide some sort of evidence that he or she has had a loving relationship with at least one other human being. . . .

15.   Require that all the graffiti accumulated in the school toilets be reproduced on large paper and be hung in the school halls. . . .[2]

Postman and Weingartner also proposed that certain words generally used in education should be prohibited. Their taboo words included *teach, I.Q., test, disadvantaged, gifted,* and *dumb.*

The books of John Holt are the most widely read of the writing by the compassionate critics, *How Children Fail,* 1964; *How Children Learn,* 1967; *The Underachieving School,* 1969; *What Do I Do Monday?,* 1970; *Freedom and Beyond,* 1972; *Escape from Childhood,* 1974; *Instead of Education: Ways to Help People Do Things Better,* 1976. In *How Children Fail,* an opening gun in the campaign by the compassionate critics, Holt described the assumptions of traditional schools that he regarded as invalid:

> Behind much of what we do in school lie some ideas, that could be expressed roughly as follows: (1) of the vast body of human knowledge, there are certain bits and pieces that can be called essential, that everyone should know; (2) the extent to which a person can be considered educated, qualified to live intelligently in today's world and be a useful member of society, depends on the amount of this essential knowledge that he carries about with him; (3) it is the duty of schools, therefore, to get as much of this essential knowledge as possible into the minds of children. Thus we find ourselves trying to poke certain facts, recipes, and ideas down the gullets of every child in school, whether the morsel interests him or not, even if it frightens him or sickens him, and even if there are other things that he is much more interested in learning.
>
> These ideas are absurd and harmful nonsense. We will not begin to have true education or real learning in our schools until we sweep this nonsense out of the way. Schools should be a place where children learn what they most want to know, instead of what we think they ought to know. The child who wants to know something remembers it and uses it once he has it; the child who learns something to please or appease someone else forgets it when the need for pleasing or the danger of not appeasing is past.[3]

Even a moderate critic of the schools added his condemnation to the chorus. In his widely read *Crisis in the Classroom,* a 1970 best-seller on education, Charles E. Silberman said;

> Most of all, however, I am indignant at the failures of the public schools themselves. "The most deadly of all possible sins," Erik Erikson suggests, "is the

---

[2] Neil Postman and Charles Weingartner, *Teaching as a Subversive Activity,* Delacorte Press, New York, 1969, pp. 137–140.

[3] John Holt, *How Children Fail,* Pitman, New York, 1964, pp. 174–175.

mutilation of a child's spirit." It is not possible to spend any prolonged period visiting public school classrooms without being appalled by the mutilation visible everywhere—mutilation of spontaneity, of joy in learning, of pleasure in creating, of sense of self. The public schools—those "killers of the dream," to appropriate a phrase of Lillian Smith's—are the kind of institution one cannot really dislike until one gets to know them well. Because adults take the schools so much for granted, they fail to appreciate what grim, joyless places most American schools are, how oppressive and petty are the rules by which they are governed, how intellectually sterile and esthetically barren the atmosphere, what an appalling lack of civility obtains on the part of teachers and principals, what contempt they unconsciously display for children as children.[4]

HIGH SCHOOL STUDENT DISSENTERS

High school students also added their testimony. For instance, in Montgomery County, Maryland, students brought a petition to the school board that began

. . . it is quite safe to say that the public schools have critically negative and absolutely destructive effects on human beings and their curiosity, natural desire to learn, confidence, individuality, creativity, freedom of thought and self-respect.[5]

They supported a complete rescheduling of the curriculum, voluntary seminars organized by the students, student involvement in choosing teachers, and the elimination of letter grades.

When John Birmingham was seventeen years old, he wrote *Our Time Is Now: Notes from the High School Underground*, in which he condemned irrelevance of school courses. Of curriculum he wrote:

Curriculum is an area where a lot of reform is called for by the underground. The main criticism is of irrelevant courses. Too many courses are tailored to deal with the world as it was ten years ago, and too many teachers refuse to relate the subject matter to today. A wide variety of courses is offered, but not the right ones. Courses in music appreciation are offered at most schools, but how many schools offer courses in rock music? The curriculum in high schools today has virtually ignored the culture of the students it is educating. Rock is having a tremendous effect on the life-styles of young people in the world today; it is communicating to them. Yet many teachers will insist that it is not a serious kind of music, not to be studied.[6]

---

[4] Charles E. Silberman, *Crisis in the Classroom*, Random House, New York, 1970, p. 10.
[5] Ronald Gross and Beatrice Gross, eds., *Radical School Reform*, Simon and Schuster, New York, 1970, p. 147.
[6] John Birmingham, *Our Time Is Now: Notes from the High School Underground*, Praeger, New York, 1970, pp. 204–205.

Two teachers collected student protests against their education in *The High School Revolutionaries*. One student wrote of his school:

No matter how good the teacher may be, no matter how many books he may have published, he is not going to be able to teach anything if his students don't come to class. It's almost impossible to get the kids to come to class now, and once they're in class the situation is so bad that instead of learning anything or even being in a neutral situation they have an adverse reaction to anything that is being taught to them.

I think the educational system from top to bottom, from kindergarten to college, is in pretty bad shape.[7]

A Scarsdale, New York, student wrote:

For a student, grades can become an obsessive force in life. All our activities in school revolve around our grades. However, few students actually believe they are an accurate measure of someone's intelligence or capabilities. Teachers often say they indicate a student's "performance." They picked the right word. Attaining high grades in school is usually just a matter of performing or acting out the role of dutiful student with a straight face. . . . The parents are almost all excessively concerned with their child's grades, and some will punish or reward their kids according to their quarterly standing. All of them encourage and even push their kids into working for a higher grade whether that means learning anything or not.[8]

High School, edited by Ronald Gross and Paul Osterman, is an anthology largely about high school students who repudiate the education they are receiving. In their introduction, the editors wrote:

The American high school is the most absurd part of an educational system pervaded by absurdity.

In elementary school, children clearly need some adult supervision to protect them from present dangers. In higher education young adults usually have enough freedom so that they can, if they choose, experiment and enjoy the pleasures and prospects of life. But high school. . . .

The students are old enough to take care of themselves, old enough to reject the illegitimate authority of adults, old enough to love and fight and truly learn. To see these formidable creatures docilely submit to the indignities and boredom of the average high school is intolerably sad. . . .

Boredom, irrelevant curriculum, uninspired teaching, and rigid authoritarianism pervade the nation's high schools. These are usually at the heart of student protest and most educational criticism. Pressing further, to ask why society has created such institutions, leads to a deeper level of analysis. Schools are designed for distinctively adult needs—social stratification and socialization—and their inhumanity and destructiveness are really by-products of these purposes.[9]

---

[7] Marc Libarle and Tom Seligson, eds., *The High School Revolutionaries*, Random House, New York, 1970, pp. 4–6.
[8] *Ibid.*, p. 20.
[9] Ronald Gross and Paul Osterman, eds., *High School,* Simon and Schuster, New York, 1971, pp. 9, 19–20.

Some critics of contemporary schools have not been content with verbal jabs. Encouraged by the views of the compassionate critics and the student dissenters, they have fostered alternatives to the traditional schools in which they formerly taught and that they now totally reject.

PRIVATE ALTERNATIVE SCHOOLS

In the 1960s the alternative schools were largely pri vate schools, dependent for support on tuition and philanthropy, and often operating on a financial shoestring. As free-lance writer Bonnie Barrett Stretch says in her article, "The Rise of the 'Free School'":

Their variety seems limitless. No two are alike. They range from inner-city black to suburban and rural white. Some seem to be pastoral escapes from the grit of modern conflict, while others are deliberate experiments in integrated multicultural, multilingual education. They turn up anywhere—in city storefronts, old barns, former barracks, abandoned church buildings, and parents' or teachers' homes. They have crazy names like Someday School, Viewpoint Non-School, A Peck of Gold, The New Community, or New Directions—names that for all their diversity reflect the two things most of these schools have in common: the idea of freedom for youngsters and a humane education.[10]

Many privately financed alternative schools were often short-lived; according to one estimate, the typical private alternative school closed eighteen months after it opened its doors. But the private alternative schools represented a challenge to "the educational establishment," as critics called the public school system.

Joel Denker described such a school enrolling thirty full-time students whose average age was seventeen and who were taught by five full-time teachers plus volunteers:

We offer "classes" in a variety of areas ranging from creative writing and drama to utopian American radicalism. (We have a bulletin board where anyone who wants to get a course going puts up a time for a meeting; times of various local events—lectures, dances, films, government meetings, etc.—also appear.) These core courses, which meet once or twice a week, are intended to complement rather than serve as substitutes for the direct involvement that is central to the school. We aim to explode the classroom, to create the feeling that learning is more than a formal academic exercise, that to be worth anything it must be organically related to the person's most immediate needs and concerns. Students have done a variety of things this year: Several of the kids are working in apprenticeships with local

---

[10] Bonnie Barrett Stretch, "The Rise of the 'Free School'," *Saturday Review*, June 20, 1970, p. 76.

artists—a metal sculptor and welder and a potter, for example. A trip to Baltimore to attend the trial of the Catonsville Nine got us involved in a demonstration protesting the mockery of justice in federal court and in picketing the courthouse. We went to the City Council to hear a friend protest against its avoidance of the police issue and heard the city fathers spend forty minutes discussing the questions of civilian escorts for funeral processions. During the fall, classes frequently met in Rock Creek Park and most every weekend we camped out on some land in the Shenandoahs, the site of an old mission. A friend of ours has purchased land there so that we have access to it. [11]

One well-known independent school supported by private donations was Harlem Prep in New York City. The chairperson of the English department of the school and a graduate of the school collaborated on a description of the program:

After a period of consulting on the principles on which Harlem Prep's curriculum would be based, courses of study were drawn up. The subjects which were taught included basic mathematics, algebra, geometry, trigonometry, analytic geometry and calculus, writing skills, comparative literature, reading skills, speech, drama, mass-media analysis, creative writing, African studies, Egyptology, Caribbean studies, political science, sociology, contemporary problems of democracy, comparative economics, biology, chemistry, physics, logic, film-making and video recording, art and music.

The orientation of the courses was toward the development of skills and knowledge, the stimulation of intellectual curiosity, the development of individual research techniques, the development of standards of evaluation, and the development of tolerance to accept different opinions, criticisms, and evaluation from others. Traditional subjects were taught with a view toward applying their theories to contemporary social problems; wherever possible, interdisciplinary approaches were used. In all areas individual assignments and research projects were provided. [12]

Harlem Prep attempted to prepare future leaders who would not flee from the ghetto but who would return to it to render service. Some of its graduates entered colleges and universities across the nation.

PUBLIC ALTERNATIVE SCHOOLS

When American public secondary schools are under fire, they often respond by concessions and adaptations. So, as the 1970s opened, in response to the criticisms of the compassionate critics and the dissenting students, and as a counter to private alternative schools, a number of public school systems incorporated the idea of alternatives or options into their practices. These practices did not revolutionize the usual elementary and high schools attended by the large majority of students,

---

[11] Gross and Osterman, *High School*, pp. 193–194.
[12] Ibid., p. 275.

but they did include new options in the form of alternative schools. The public alternative school movement became one of the notable educational developments of the decade; school systems of the late 1970s continue to increase their options.

Best known of the alternatives offered by public secondary schools is the Parkway Program of the Philadelphia public schools. As described by John Bremer, "There is no schoolhouse, there is no separate building; school is not a place but an activity, a process. We are indeed a school without walls. Where do the students learn? In the city. Where in the city? Anywhere and everywhere." [13] Thus students in the program may go to art classes in museums, economic seminars in banks, auto mechanics "classes" in service stations, and leather-making classes in little leather shops. [14] In *The School Without Walls*, Bremer and von Moschzisker say:

> Once inside the program, however, every member of the unit, student and teacher alike, belongs to a basic social group called a tutorial. Each tutorial is made up of about sixteen students, one of the full-time, certified teachers, and one of the university interns. People are assigned to a tutorial by lottery. The selection is random but compulsory. . . .
>
> . . . the tutorial has, as its academic function, the development of the so-called basic skills. Originally the tutorials were to focus on language and mathematics, but some units found that much time had to be spent on personal and group problems, and so while language was continued, social studies replaced mathematics. . . . Every student's time is spent in regularly scheduled courses taught by the faculty, interns, businessmen, parents, students, librarians, curators, and individual volunteers. Each instructor brings to the course whatever interests him in his field of expertise. The students choose their own courses in consultation with their parents. . . .
>
> To summarize, a student in the parkway program must belong to a unit, or community, of about one hundred and sixty people, and within that community he must belong to a tutorial group. Beyond that, he may belong to a number of courses of study, to one or more management groups, to *ad hoc* groups for this or that purpose, and he may attend town meetings. In addition, he can elect to work independently. [15]

Across the continent in California, the Berkeley public schools developed twenty-four alternative public schools in the early 1970s that enrolled more than a fourth of Berkeley's school population. Some of these schools were large and some were small; some were held in regular public school buildings and others met in former factories, churches, and stores. Their programs were varied as their titles. Lincoln housed an environmental studies program. Model A emphasized basic skills. On Target was

---

[13] John Bremer, *The Parkway Program*, Philadelphia Public Schools, Philadelphia; 1970, p. 4.
[14] James D. Greenberg and Robert E. Roush, "A Visit to the 'School Without Walls': Two Impressions," *Phi Delta Kappan*, May 1970, p. 482.
[15] John Bremer and Michael von Moschzisker, *The School Without Walls*, Holt, Rinehart and Winston, New York, 1971, pp. 23–25.

geared to job-awareness experiences. The School of the Arts emphasized drama, dance, and music. The work of College Prep is self-explanatory, as is the orientation of West Campus Work Study. Some schools emphasized multiethnic studies; others stressed the identity of specific groups such as Casa De La Raza, Black House, and New Ark (for students of Asian background). [16]

Some school systems adopted the "school without walls" model. For instance, the Chicago public school system included the Chicago Public High School for Metropolitan Studies, known as Metro. Some cities included schools emphasizing independent study through independent study kits. As one example, New York City's John Dewey High School stressed learning for mastery within a flexible modular schedule. [17] On the other hand, the Portland, Oregon, public schools developed a problem-centered program in John Adams High School. General education in this school emphasized contemporary and historical issues and problems; the school was characterized by wide student participation in school government and frequent study programs within the community. [18]

In general, the first alternative schools within public school systems stressed a high degree of freedom, student choice, and openness. However, supporters of alternative schools within U.S. public school systems increasingly advocated a variety of options rather than exclusive emphasis on the types of schools encouraged by the compassionate critics.

BACK-TO-BASICS MOVEMENT

SUPPORTERS OF FUNDAMENTAL EDUCATION

A criticism of secondary school education diametrically opposed to that of the compassionate critics and the dissenting students gained momentum in the mid-1970s. The back-to-basics critics believe that the American schools are not sufficiently traditional. Their advice is to stress the three R's and the academic curriculum even more heavily than the usual school program does. In addition, by an ingenious twist, the back-to-basics advocates are using the new options and alternatives for their own purposes. They are fostering and supporting fundamental or traditional schools as possible alternatives or options for students.

Their fundamental and traditional alternative schools are not only dedicated to the three R's and the academic subjects; they also stress order,

---

[16] Diane Divoky, "Berkeley's Experimental Schools," *Saturday Review,* October 1972, pp. 46–51.
[17] Sol Levine, "The John Dewey High School Adventure," *Phi Delta Kappan,* October 1971, pp. 108–110.
[18] Alan L. Dobbins, "Instruction at Adams," *Phi Delta Kappan,* May 1971, pp. 516–519.

discipline, patriotic inculcation, and traditional morality. They are nostalgic for the past. For instance, *Newsweek* of October 21, 1974 reports on the reaction of an alternative public school, the John Marshall Fundamental School. The news magazine describes John Marshall as

a bastion of tradition-oriented education. Letter grades, regular examinations, strict dress codes and detention for delinquents are integral parts of the school's conservative program. Both the faculty and the student body are expected to present "an outstanding image" in dress and deportment. The curriculum is strict and basic; it features computational arithmetic (i.e. the old math), reading drill in standard phonics and rigorous homework requirements from kindergarten on. At lunchtime, teachers and volunteer parents move about the cafeteria correcting table manners. There are no graffiti on the Marshall walls; in their place hang framed patriotic sentiments and didactic homilies ("Happiness is Manners"). A 35-page school handbook spells out the Marshall goals in jargon-free clarity: "Traditional education, order, quiet, and control." [19]

Or consider the description of another "traditional" school from *U.S. News & World Report* of October 28, 1974:

At Myers Park, children are taught good manners and patriotism along with such things as arithmetic and penmanship.

Rules of deportment are posted in classrooms. The children must have a pass to leave the room. Running about the corridors, noisy conduct, speaking without first raising a hand are not permitted.

"Thoughts for the Day" are transmitted over the intercom system. Some recent examples: "Let all things be done decently and in order" . . . "An error gracefully acknowledged is a victory won."

Grades are strictly defined. Report cards evaluate work habits, effort and achievement. [20]

Many sponsors of back-to-basics programs are reacting against developments in American life during the 1960s and early 1970s. These years of turmoil and stress were marked by civil rights marches, protest against the Vietnam War, assassination of national leaders, and youth revolt. The use of drugs accelerated; sexual restrictions broke down; crime increased; a counter-culture emerged. The new problems and new life styles spread beyond the cities into suburbs, small towns and rural areas.

Schools were inevitably influenced by the turbulent 1960s and early 1970s. For instance, young people protested classroom and administrative practices that seemed to them restrictive. Social problems entered into classroom discussions. Books that used frank and bold language appeared

---

[19] *Newsweek*, October 21, 1974, p. 87. At John Marshall Fundamental School there are 1,700 students enrolled and more than 1,000 on the waiting list. In the same community 550 students are enrolled in a K–12 open school with a waiting list of 515. The schools are in Pasadena, Calif.

[20] *U.S. News & World Report*, October 28, 1974, p. 96. The applications for admission to Myers Park outnumber the spaces more than two to one. The school is in Charlotte, N.C.

in libraries or on reading lists. The compassionate critics urged an education based on student needs and interests.

Some parents felt that the life styles of their families were threatened by the new developments. They feared that modern schools placed insufficient emphasis on the three R's, that discipline had broken down, that books employing profanity and obscenity were becoming required reading, that their children were being exposed to views of rebels, dissenters, and troublemakers from minority groups.

Parental uneasiness often took the form of rejecting curriculum materials and textbooks used in schools. In some communities, parents regarded certain books used in schools as "dirty," anti-Christian and anti-American, and subversive of the authority of home and church. One such situation developed in 1974–1975 in Kanawha County in which Charleston, the capital of West Virginia, is located. A school board member, supported by fundamentalist ministers and church groups, and by the executive board of the local council of parents and teachers, attacked some of the recommended texts and supplementary books. In the fall, 20 percent of the students absented themselves from school. Violence erupted; a school and a board of education building were dynamited.

The National Education Association (NEA) sent a ten-member inquiry panel to Kanawha County. The NEA group recommended that parents be consulted and involved in the education process as advisers and not as censors. But the group also urged that there be no limitation by state legislatures of teachers' rights and responsibilities to select educational materials. The school board had recommended that some alternative elementary schools focus on the three R's; the NEA report cautiously approved this but warned that such alternative schools might increase separatism and isolation of the mountain people in the county. In Kanawha County there had been no citizen participation in selection of textbooks during the four years prior to the crisis. When, during the crisis, the board of education authorized citizenship input, it took the form of censorship. Following the crisis, Kanawha County sought for some balance between citizen and professional input in the selection of textbooks and supplementary materials. Bills were introduced in the West Virginia legislature to assure citizen involvement in textbook selection.

A historian of education, Franklin Parker, summed up the protest in West Virginia:

Kanawha County provides insight into our time—that people feel helpless, voiceless, and afraid of rapid change. They are put off balance by the concentrated troubles of our times. Kanawha County parents struck back at the schools through textbooks in the same way the English Luddites sabotaged the spinning jenny and French peasants once threw wooden shoes to disrupt textile machinery. As the Bible is accepted as the perfect guide, so having McGuffey and similar safe textbooks was comforting and secure.

People see the school as a last bastion of community control and the textbook as its ultimate symbol. The angry ones cannot burn Washington, but they can attack what is theirs, their own schools. Textbooks, which in every age mirror the morality, social relations, and political consensus of the time, reflect these same things now. But the status quo in America is not peace and plenty but wrenching change and the frustration of unfinished challenges.[21]

Not all back-to-basics supporters are fundamentalist mountain people. Some are sophisticated suburbanites who attempt to create a homogeneous community of influence within which their children can be reared, can learn the family value system, and can be insulated from the complexities of the cities. They have come to recognize how difficult it is to shape their children. Consequently, many are now depending on schools to shape young people in the directions that their parents prefer.[22]

Parents' concern for the welfare of their children has been sharpened by frequent mass media reports of declining test scores in the mid-1970s and by varied interpretations of the causes and meaning of the reported declines. To study suggested interpretations and to determine the causes of the fourteen-year decline in verbal and mathematical Scholastic Aptitude Tests scores, the College Entrance Examination Board appointed a blue ribbon study panel, headed by Willard Wirtz, former Secretary of Labor, which included national leaders in evaluation among the twenty-one members.

Late in 1977 the panel reported that the decline was largely a result of an increasing number of minority background, poor, and academically inferior students applying for college entrance and of the difficulty schools experienced in handling the special needs of these students. In addition, more women, whose math scores have been traditionally lower than men's, began applying to colleges. The panel related two-thirds to three-fourths of the decline in the seven years before 1970 to the notable extension and expansion of educational opportunity in the United States. Factors contributing to the decline since 1970 appeared to the panel to include the growth of elective courses, diminished attention to basic skills, widespread television viewing, changes in the role and responsibility of the family, social developments affecting student motivation (such as the Vietnam war, political assassinations, and Watergate), and an apparent diminution in student motivation in taking tests.

The back-to-basics movement is not new in American education. It has occurred, for instance, in such eras of anxiety as the Joseph McCarthy period, 1949–1954,[23] and years when some liberal arts professors were

[21] Franklin Parker, *The Battle of the Books: Kanawha County,* Phi Delta Kappa Educational Foundation, Bloomington, Ind., 1975, p. 33.
[22] William Van Til, William E. Brownson, and Russell L. Hamm, "Back to Basics—with a Difference," *Educational Leadership,* October 1975, p. 12.
[23] Robert C. Morris, *Era of Anxiety: An Historical Account of Right Wing Forces Affecting Education During the Years 1949 to 1954,* unpublished doctoral dissertation, Indiana State University, Terre Haute, 1977.

especially critical of schools, 1954–1960. The present movement is similar, yet different. Many contemporary back-to-basics proponents accept yesterday's assumption that the schools have somehow abandoned the three R's and must now "return" to them. Yet, as an article in the October 1975 *Educational Leadership* pointed out, there are some differences between former and present campaigns:

The root concerns of many who are calling for a return to the basics in schools grow out of the current condition of our uneasy society. The "back to basics" proponents long to return to an earlier and simpler society.

These concerns about the present and nostalgia for the past have resulted in a "back to basics" drive with a difference. First, the new "back to basics" advocacy is not an internal conflict within the educational establishment. We have had many of these professional swings of the pendulum during the 20th century. This movement, however, is essentially a grass roots challenge by parents spearheaded by non-school professionals—ministers, politicians, and leaders of community groups. Second, this is a movement without a singular thrust and without organized and identifiable leadership. Its concerns are many: textbooks, patriotism, discipline, morality, skill development—and it has assumed a variety of modes of operation: legislation, propaganda, intimidation, and harassment. Third, this back-to-basics call is meeting with success in state legislatures and school boards. Fourth, the back-to-basics emphasis of the mid-70's is emotion-laden and tends toward axe-grinding. "Back to basics" reflects a growing frustration with bureaucracies, whether presidential, congressional, or educational. But almost all institutions other than schools are beyond the reach of most citizens. Yet all can vent their anger and frustrations against schools, for the school seems to be physically "next door" and its people are known or knowable.[24]

In the March 1977 issue of *Phi Delta Kappan* on back to basics, educational journalist Ben Brodinsky wrote:

What *do* back-to-basics advocates want? Since they have no spokesman, platform, or declaration of principles, we must fall back on a composite. Here is what, at various times and in different places, back-to-basics advocates have demanded:

1.   Emphasis on reading, writing, and arithmetic in the elementary grades. Most of the school day is to be devoted to these skills. Phonics is the method advocated for reading instruction.

2.   In the secondary grades, most of the day is to be devoted to English, science, math, and history, taught from "clean" textbooks, free of notions that violate traditional family and national values.

3.   At all levels, the teacher is to take a dominant role, with "no nonsense about pupil-directed activities."

4.   Methodology is to include drill, recitation, daily homework, and frequent testing.

5.   Report cards are to carry traditional marks (A, B, C, etc.) or numerical values (100, 80, 75, etc.), issued at frequent intervals.

---

[24] Van Til, Brownson, and Hamm, "Back to Basics," pp. 8–9.

6.   Discipline is to be strict, with corporal punishment an accepted method of control. Dress codes should regulate student apparel and hair styles.

7.   Promotion from grades and graduation from high school are to be permitted only after mastery of skills and knowledge has been demonstrated through tests. Social promotion and graduation on the basis of time spent in courses are out.

8.   Eliminate the frills. The *National Review*, a conservative journal, put it this way: "Clay modeling, weaving, doll construction, flute practice, volleyball, sex education, laments about racism and other weighty matters should take place on private time."

9.   Eliminate electives and increase the number of required courses.

10.   Ban innovations (a plague on them!). New math, new science, linguistics, instruction by electronic gadgets, emphasis on concepts instead of facts—all must go.

11.   Eliminate the school's "social services"—they take time from the basic curriculum. "Social services" may include sex education, driver education, guidance, drug education, and physical education.

12.   Put patriotism back in the schools. And love for one's country. And for God.[25]

SECONDARY EDUCATION THROUGH SCHOOL AND COMMUNITY

Scholarly reports by committees and commissions also help shape the future of secondary education. Such reports are often sponsored by prestigious governmental agencies, philanthropic foundations, and educational organizations. For instance, *The Cardinal Principles of Secondary Education*, a report sponsored by a governmental commission in 1918, had a substantial impact on educational thought following World War I.[26]

In the mid-1970s, committees and commissions on the secondary education of American youth have made numerous reports. Naturally, each differed to a degree from the others. But there were common elements. In general, the reports of the mid-1970s criticized contemporary secondary schools. They called them too big and too much alike. They reported that school programs were not sufficiently individualized and personalized and that the students had few options and choices. Since almost all secondary schools divide students according to grade levels (such as seventh graders, freshman, seniors, and so on), youths are restricted to contacts and experiences with young people of approximately the same age and are segregated from older or younger people. In general, the reports urged many

---

[25] Ben Brodinsky, "Back to the Basics: The Movement and Its Meaning," *Phi Delta Kappan*, March 1977, p. 522.
[26] Commission on the Reorganization of Secondary Education, *The Cardinal Principles of Secondary Education*, Bulletin No. 35, U.S. Bureau of Education, Washington, D.C., 1918.

FIGURE 1.2 *Community-oriented Education. These young people are learning about land survey.*

more options for youth, such as work experience and community participation, in smaller schools in which age segregation is reduced.

The reports of the mid-1970s went beyond urging less dependence on look-alike comprehensive schools. They not only suggested greater dependence on alternatives and options in smaller schools in which learning opportunities cut across grade-line levels, they also urged extension of new ways of helping youth make the transition to the adult world. In particular, they advocated opportunities for young people to go to work and to participate in community life, rather than simply to attend school (see Figure 1.2). Committee members believed that this was especially important for young people who do not want to be in school and who resist the customary programs of secondary schools. As they saw it, secondary schools too often serve as custodial institutions for students who do not want to attend them. The community should educate such young people on the job and in service projects, through the efforts of business, labor, governmental agencies, and community education centers.

The most commented-upon report was that of the Panel on Youth of the President's Science Advisory Committee, *Youth: Transition to Adulthood,* sometimes called Coleman II. The report was prepared under the leadership of James S. Coleman, who had earlier prepared a seldom-read but widely reported survey for the U.S. government in 1966 entitled *Equality of Educational Opportunity.* The first report, sometimes called Coleman I, concluded that family background is much more responsible for a young person's performance in school than is schooling; the report claims this is true even when education is well financed.

Coleman II was especially critical of comprehensive high schools. At one point, the report said:

This proposal (for school diversity and student choice) goes directly against the trends in American education toward comprehensive schools. The specialized schools of the past were eliminated in one community after another. . . . Comprehensive schools seemed to have advantages of mixing students, allowing easy transfer from one curriculum to another, and in general, providing a democratic equality of opportunity and treatment. But these supposed advantages have been negated in many locales. Comprehensive schools drawing from black lower class neighborhoods or white upper middle class areas are very different. By specializing overtly in student body, they specialize covertly in curriculum. The comprehensive school becomes a narrow school, vainly trying to be like the others, but passively specializing around neighborhood input.[27]

The panel that produced *Youth: Transition to Adulthood* believed that schools are limited to teaching cognitive (intellectual) skills and knowledge and to passing on the cultural heritage. The community, panel members believed, must assume the responsibility of helping young people learn to hold jobs and take part in community improvement. Schools alone cannot help youth learn to live in the "real world," according to the committee. *Youth: Transition to Adulthood* said:

Schools are the principal formal institutions of society intended to bring youth into adulthood. But schools' structures are designed wholly for self-development, particularly the acquisition of cognitive skills and knowledge. . . .

In short, when non-cognitive activities are created for youth as ways of developing personal qualities important to a satisfactory adult life, the incorporation of them within schools places an enormous strain that is often resolved by a reversion to student role for youth and to teacher role for adults. The prospects of success for such activities appear far greater when carried on outside the school.

Examining both sides, we feel that the benefits of incorporating non-cognitive activities into school are far fewer than those from organizing them outside schools.[28]

---

[27] Report of the Panel on Youth of the President's Science Advisory Committee, *Youth: Transition to Adulthood,* University of Chicago Press, Chicago, 1974, p. 153.
[28] Ibid., pp. 146, 143.

A commission supported by the Kettering Foundation made thirty-two recommendations, two of which proved especially controversial. *The Reform of Secondary Education: A Report to the Public and the Profession* was prepared by a committee headed by a former high school principal and present foundation staff member, B. Frank Brown. The report was sympathetic to expanded work opportunities and the development of interdisciplinary studies in such fields as career education and international education. Commentary on the report focused on the recommendation that the school-leaving age be lowered to fourteen, thus making only the first eight years of education compulsory. Even though the report recommended that each citizen be entitled to fourteen years of tuition-free education beyond kindergarten, some interpreted the recommendations as hostile to the tradition of free and universal education through the high school years. If the commission recommendations were adopted, attendance at senior high school would be completely voluntary. Even attendance at junior high school would be voluntary, at least at the ninth-grade level, since the majority of young Americans are in the ninth grade when they reach the age of fourteen. Still, the commission saw its recommendations as adding to the "rights" of students:

To the rights the courts have already secured for American students, the Commission would like to add another: the right not to be in formal school beyond the age of fourteen. Compulsory attendance laws are the dead hand on the high schools. The liberation of youth and the many freedoms which the courts have given to students within the last decade make it impossible for the school to continue as a custodial institution and also to perform effectively as a teaching institution. The harm done to the school by the student who does not want to be there is measured not only by the incidence of vandalism and assault but also by a subtle and continuous degradation of the tone of the educational enterprise.[29]

THE EDUCATION OF ADOLESCENTS

A National Panel on High School and Adolescent Education organized by the U.S. Office of Education contributed to discussion of the work of secondary education through papers prepared by participants and a chairperson's digest. The panel recommended education for adolescents in five curricular domains: personal values, citizenship, the arts, the humanities, and technics or career education. The panel advocated education in these realms through a two-to-four-hour day of attendance in high schools, "society's only universal institution for the educa-

---

[29] National Commission on the Reform of Secondary Education, *The Reform of Secondary Education: A Report to the Public and the Profession*, McGraw Hill, New York, 1973, p. 133.

tion of the intellect,"[30] supplemented by joint participation of adolescents and adults in participatory education through the community. Specifically, the panel's report, *The Education of Adolescents,* called for the establishment of community art centers, a community career education center plus vocational education through increased work experience, and education in the operations of government through participation in governmental agencies. The panel also supported alternative schools emphasizing such areas as journalism or the arts in response to the special needs of the student.

In 1976, the published report of the panel made the following recommendations:

1. That the unattained practice and inadequate concept of the comprehensive high school be replaced with the more practical goal of providing comprehensive education through a variety of means including the schools. . . .

2. That educational programs be inaugurated for the joint participation of adolescents and other interested and qualified adults in the community—pedagogical programs which may be designated Participatory Education (learning by doing what is socially useful, personally satisfying, and health-supporting for the individual and the community). . . .

For educating in the arts the Panel recommends creation of a community arts center closely associated with the high school. . . .

The Panel recommends the creation of a community career education center. . . .

The Panel recommends that adolescents, in addition to the academic study of the social sciences and their methodology, should be involved in government—in all appropriate agencies within the larger community. . . .

3. That small, flexible, short-term, part-time schools be established and made available to all who are qualified and interested. . . .

4. That compulsory daily attendance be reduced from all-day sessions to an academic day of 2–4 hours. . . .

5. That the basic role of the high school as society's only universal institution for the education of the intellect be reemphasized. . . .

6. That a community guidance center be established, which would house such qualified personnel as counselors, psychologists, social workers, and technicians in the construction, administration and analysis of tests and other evaluative procedures who now work in the high school and other agencies. . . .

7. That local educational agencies understand that all the preceding recommendations are to be considered as working hypotheses to be rigorously tested through small-scale adaptations, careful monitoring, and ruthless evaluation. . . .

8. That recognition be given to the fact that adult and adolescent citizen participation in planning and reviewing change in education is vital to the installation and maintenance of needed reform. . . .

---

[30] John Henry Martin, "Chairman's Digest," U.S. Department of Health, Education, and Welfare, Office of Education, Panel on High School and Adolescent Education, April 1974, p. 23.

9.   That the Federal Government through the U.S. Office of Education and the National Institute of Education sponsor research to provide local education agencies with the technical support needed for programs of change. . . .

10.   That Federal support and State review be provided for the costs of planning and evaluation of programs designed to bring adolescents and adults together for learning and work. . . .

11.   That Federal funds be provided to establish a national recruitment training and technical support program for operational planning teams to be established at the local level. . . .[31]

OTHER COMMUNITY-RELATED PROGRAMS

Lively discussion followed the publication of the reports by the teams headed by Coleman, Brown, and Martin. Practitioners in secondary education found themselves in agreement with many of the proposals in the reports, yet in disagreement as to a fundamental strategy for the improvement of the education of youth. Should community organizations and agencies educate youth independently of schools? For instance, the National Association of Secondary School Principals (NASSP), which had been in the forefront of the movement to interrelate secondary schools and communities, had called for schools to take the lead in learning through the community. NASSP activity preceded the three reports described above.

A NASSP project, *American Youth in the Mid-Seventies*, strongly recommended action-learning as another avenue for growing up and making the transition from adolescence to adulthood. The project was particularly impressed with the action-learning opportunities for high school students in voluntary public service. In a report to American secondary school principals in the *NASSP Bulletin*, the project reported, after a study of three representative U.S. communities, that "schools, hospitals, waste recovery projects, day care centers, sanitarians, and other local agencies described hundreds of volunteer jobs waiting to be filled by young people." It reported too, that

there would be enough jobs to provide every 15- through 20-year old in the area surveyed with almost three hours of service-learning opportunities a week, some in jobs that require only a few hours each week, others in full-time work for a half year or more. Instead of working part-time over a six-year period, one-half of all young people in America could work full-time for a school year as a part of growing up."[32]

The report noted that educational institutions could provide the most opportunities for such service but added that

---

[31] National Panel on High School and Adolescent Education, *The Education of Adolescents*, U.S. Department of Health, Education, and Welfare, Washington, D.C., 1976, pp. 10–19.
[32] Robert J. Havighurst, Richard A. Graham, and Donald Eberly, "American Youth in the Mid-Seventies," *NASSP Bulletin*, November 1972, p. 7.

in just the past few years, the opportunity for action-learning in other areas has increased extraordinarily: in work connected with environmental protection, in lead-based paint detection and removal, in water and air pollution control, in the reprocessing of waste products. In still other fields such as probationary work, drug rehabilitation, and recreational programs, well-prepared young people have shown that they can do as well as their elders.[33]

But the report also noted that some public service employers wanted volunteers only if money and personnel were provided for their supervision.

A conference sponsored by the National Association of Secondary School Principals brought together political, union, and educational leaders to foster action-learning. The introduction to the conference report stresses that

action-learning is learning from experience and associated study that can be assessed and accredited by an educational institution. . . . Part-time action-learning programs will usually complement formal study in a school or college. Full-time assignments may involve guided study on the job."[34]

The NASSP took the position that action-learning should be closely associated with study in schools and colleges, rather than a transition to adulthood quite independent of the schools as suggested by the Coleman II report.

Another conference emphasizing action-learning was held under the cosponsorship of Educational Facilities Laboratories and Institute for Development of Educational Activities, Inc. *The Greening of the High School*, a report on the conference by Ruth Weinstock, describes promising action-learning projects or proposals. For instance, Boston proposes a meshing of the school system with the city's resources; the plan calls for students from kindergarten to high school to spend at least half their school year studying in the city. In Connecticut, students made a study of food prices, developed an "Earth Platform" concerning the environment, and focused on bills in the state legislature establishing statewide bicycle paths and imposing a deposit on throwaway containers. Las Vegas established "Five O'clock High," which operates from late afternoon through early evening for students who prefer to go to school at night. Syracuse, New York, proposed a plan by which a student could earn a high school diploma through academic studies, through participation in occupational, social, and political activities, or through a combination of these two approaches. With the cooperation of a group of corporate executives, organized in the Economic Development Council (EDC) of New York City, students at

---

[33] Ibid., p. 12.
[34] National Association of Secondary School Principals, *American Youth in the Mid-Seventies*, Washington, D.C., 1972, introduction.

James Monroe High School, located in the inner city, are employed by the EDC's member companies, work with volunteers from the companies who tutor at the school, and participate in a communitywide medical examination program in conjunction with a college of medicine.[35]

Emphasis on using the community ran through ten regional meetings sponsored by the National Association of Secondary School Principals prior to a national conference in Denver in 1976. At the meetings a publication on major issues emphasized the importance of school-community relationships.[36] The 1976 conference was cosponsored by the U.S. Office of Education and the NASSP. The report on the conference was titled *New Dimensions for Educating Youth*. In an overview to the report on general session addresses and workshops, editor John Chaffee, Jr., comments that four interrelated themes emerged at the national conference: "'dejuvenilize' secondary schools; increase community involvement; change the school environment; shift the curriculum focus."[37]

Of "dejuvenilizing" secondary schools, Chaffee writes:

The term was used by U.S. Commissioner of Education Terrel H. Bell, but the concept permeated a substantial number of sessions. To some it meant more student involvement in planning the curriculum or governing the school. To others it meant providing youth with more opportunities to deal with people of all ages, to break down the isolation of the youth subculture. Basically, it came down to finding ways of treating students more like adults, of making school more relevant to their lives today and not something to be regarded only as preparation for some unknown future.[38]

Of increased community involvement, Chaffee indicates that the conference discussed many specifics:

Greater use of readily available community resources, both inside the school and by having students involved in outside community activities, was routinely discussed in many sessions. Suggestions included: requiring all students to participate in some form of nonpaying community work or service, soliciting community input in planning the school curriculum, and using community resources more effectively in teaching such subjects as social studies and the arts and humanities. In short, break down the walls that too often have isolated so many schools—and their students—from their communities.[39]

---

[35] Ruth Weinstock, *The Greening of the High School*, Educational Facilities Laboratories, New York, 1973, pp. 35–47.
[36] Scott D. Thomson, chairman, *Secondary Schools in a Changing Scoiety: This We Believe*, Task Force on Secondary Schools in a Changing Society of the National Association on Secondary School Principals, Reston, Va., 1975.
[37] John Chaffee, Jr., James P. Clark, eds., *New Dimensions for Educating Youth*, U.S. Department of Health, Education, and Welfare, Office of Education, Denver, Colo., and National Association of Secondary School Principals, Reston, Va., 1976, pp. 1–2.
[38] Ibid., p. 1.
[39] Ibid.

ARRIVING AT YOUR VIEW OF SECONDARY EDUCATION

SUMMARY OF CRITICISMS OF CURRENT SECONDARY EDUCATION

To sum up, the 1970s proved to be a period of vigorous criticism of secondary education and a time of adaptations by secondary educators based on their own commitments and on the concerns expressed. The decade began with a continuing condemnation of schools by the compassionate critics that was carried over from the late 1960s. During the past ten years, the public has been reading books about education with such titles as *Our Children Are Dying, Death at an Early Age, How Children Fail, The Naked Children, The Angel Inside Went Sour, How to Survive in Your Native Land, The Way It Spozed to Be, The Underachieving School, Teaching as a Subversive Activity, Crisis in the Classroom, The Halls of Yearning, Young Lives at Stake, The Lives of Children.*

In response to such criticisms, individuals and groups established private alternative schools; many of them were short-lived. In the early years of the 1970s, public school systems responded to the criticisms and the resultant private alternative schools and a number of school systems developed options in the form of public alternative schools. The tax-supported alternatives were varied but tended to stress openness, freedom, and student choice. This type of publicly supported option developed rapidly during the mid-1970s and into the later years of the decade.

A counter criticism of the compassionate critics emerged in the mid-1970s. The back-to-basics proponents believed that rather than being too rigid, the schools were not structured enough. Through coalitions of parents and community leaders, they urged that school boards and administrators "return" to the three R's, strict discipline, and subjects that they regarded as basic. Some back-to-basics proponents utilized alternative schools for their own purposes.

Meanwhile, a series of reports calling for reform of the high schools was published in the mid-1970s. The reports represented the views of influential official groups appointed by governmental and philanthropic agencies. In general, they called for a secondary education through both school and community. Organizations of educators such as the National Association of Secondary School Principals responded favorably to a greater partnership of school and community, though the educators wanted to be sure that secondary schools maintained a significant role in the relationship. In the mid and late 1970s schools experimented with expanded work experiences and community participation.

As the decade of the seventies closes, the questions with which we opened this chapter are urgent:

What kind of secondary education is needed? What types of senior high schools, junior high schools, middle schools are needed for students between the ages of twelve and eighteen? Should secondary schooling be supplemented by out-of-school educational experiences, such as work? Is secondary school really necessary? . . . for everybody?

What should be the goals of secondary education? What is secondary education supposed to do for young Americans? Indeed, what is it supposed to do for the United States in its third century? What is education for, anyway? . . . to meet the needs of learners? . . . to orient them to the society in which they live? . . . to help them make choices and clarify their values? . . . to supply them with knowledge?

What should secondary education teach? What programs should be provided? . . . for whom? What methods should be used? . . . with whom?

Where should secondary education take place? In schools? . . . comprehensive or vocational or alternative? In the community? . . . through jobs or public service activities?

How should secondary education be organized? . . . in the form of required academic courses? . . . through problem-centered learnings? . . . through multiple choices and options? . . . through action-learning beyond the school walls?

Who should staff, administer, and attempt to improve secondary education? Classroom teachers? . . . what kind of teachers? . . . Professional administrators? . . . what type of leadership? Community people? . . . how great a role and voice?

THE TOTAL SETTING

Such questions cannot be answered without a broad examination of the *total setting* in which American secondary education exists. To ignore the setting of social realities, values, and needs of young people is to doom oneself to teaching blindly and ignorantly. Thus, the next three chapters discuss the total setting of American secondary education.

Secondary education today takes place in a time of social crisis. Chapter 2 deals with five major social problems in today's social crisis—international relations; overpopulation, pollution, and energy; racism and sexism; economic problems of production and consumption; governmental roles and responsibilities.

Within the social setting, young people of secondary school age encounter conflicting value options. Chapter 3 deals with five options as to values that face young people—the work ethic, the counter-culture, privatism, socially responsible individualism, activist protest.

Adolescents have both needs in common and characteristics derived from their variety of backgrounds. Chapter 4 deals with adolescence in general; sex roles during adolescence; social-class factors; ethnic group

influences; and deviations from the accepted patterns through delinquency, dropping out, and drugs.

The answers to the questions we have raised in this chapter rest with the
American people, aided by the education profession. As an informed
professional, you can contribute to wise decisions on vital questions. You
can prepare yourself to be a secondary educator whose ideas and specific
practices are well founded.

DISCUSSION

1.   What comments on the nature and value of secondary education have you
personally heard from your family, friends, or neighbors? What comments on the
nature and value of secondary education have you read recently? What comments
on secondary education have you seen or heard recently on television or radio?

2.   What is your preliminary response to some of the questions on secondary
education at the beginning of the chapter?

3.   What is the point underlined in James Herndon's satire on flax?

4.   As a class, talk over Postman and Weingartner's proposal. What criticisms of
education lie behind these exaggerated proposals? Do you find yourselves in
agreement on some?

5.   What is John Holt's major objection to traditional education? What approach
does he suggest in its place?

6.   Does your experience support Charles E. Silberman's characterization of public
schools? What has been your own experience with respect to the atmosphere of
schools you have attended?

7.   In what ways do you agree or disagree with the dissenting students who are
quoted? Most of them wrote in the 1960s; do you think secondary students today
would agree or disagree with their hostile views of schooling?

8.   Why were many private alternative schools short-lived? What problems and
handicaps did the private alternative school movement face?

9.   On the other hand, why did public alternative schools experience greater
success?

10.   What appear to be the several types of public alternative schools? Does one
type seem more promising to you than another?

11.   What is the viewpoint of the back-to-basics movement?

12.   How can we account for the reemergence of a back-to-basics movement at this
particular time in American society?

13.   How would a protester against textbooks in Kanawha County defend his or
her position? What might an opponent of the protesters say in response? Is there a
lesson to be learned from this "Battle of the Books"?

14. What are some of the differences between the present and former back-to-basics campaigns?

15. What are the general agreements among the reform reports of committees and commissions on secondary education in the mid-1970s?

16. What position does *Youth: Transition to Adulthood* take on comprehensive schools? . . . on the role of schools? . . . on the place of cognitive and noncognitive activities?

17. What is the view of members of your class group on the recommendation in *The Reform of Secondary Education* that the school-leaving age be lowered to fourteen? What can be said in support of and in opposition to compulsory education?

18. Should the amount of time students give to high school attendance be reduced, as recommended by the U.S. Office of Education report? Does the community center idea seem to you desirable and workable?

19. In what ways does the National Association of Secondary School Principals agree or disagree with the reform reports on secondary education of the various committees and commissions?

INVOLVEMENT

1. Make arrangements to visit the high school from which you graduated, if it is nearby. If it is not, arrange to visit a high school in the community in which you are attending college. Bear in mind that you should go first to the office of the principal in order to obtain permission to visit.

2. Determine through conversation what school in your locality comes closest to the ideas of the compassionate critics. Make arrangements to visit this school.

3. Each class member might read a book by one of the compassionate critics and report individually or through panels on the experiences and views of the writer.

4. Interview a cross-section of secondary school students on what they think of their schools. Note any common elements.

5. If an alternative school, private or public, exists within reasonable travel distance, visit it. Share your experiences through discussion.

6. Determine which secondary school in your locality comes closest to a back-to-basics program. Visit the school and compare its atmosphere, program, methodology, and so on, with that of previous schools visited.

7. Visit the local senior high school in order to learn how the school relates to the community through work experience or community participation. Look for both new programs and already established programs, such as distributive education.

8. Hold a series of classroom discussions in which you compare and contrast what you observed through your visits. Try to generalize on your observation. Avoid hasty conclusions or too early partisanship.

"Bring Back 'the Basics,' Board Members and Administrators Say Loud and Clear." *The American School Board Journal* 161 (August 1974), 31–35. A report of a survey conducted by the *American School Board Journal* during the National School Boards Association annual convention in 1974.

Cawelti, Gordon. *Vitalizing the High School: A Curriculum Critique of Major Reform Proposals.* Association for Supervision and Curriculum Development, Washington, D.C., 1974. An excellent perceptive examination of the major community-oriented reform reports of the 1970s.

Chaffee, John, Jr., and James P. Clark, eds. *New Dimensions for Educating Youth.* U.S. Department of Health, Education, and Welfare and National Association of Secondary School Principals, Denver, Colo., Reston, Va., 1976. A readable report of a conference on secondary schools that emphasizes challenges to secondary education and suggests possible settings, programs, and reforms.

Fantini, Mario D. "Back to Basics, One Alternative." *Teacher* 93 (September 1975), 33–34. A criticism by one of America's most innovative educational reformers of the counter movement calling for reemphasis on the fundamentals.

Herndon, James. *How to Survive in Your Native Land.* Simon and Schuster, New York, 1971. A poignant book that describes the author's experience while teaching in a suburban junior high school.

Kozol, Jonathan. *Free Schools.* Houghton Mifflin, Boston, 1972. Advocacy of the "free school," a special type of alternative school responsive to the needs and wishes of people in neighborhoods. A radical conception of schooling as a tool for the development of a new society.

Libarle, Marc, and Tom Seligson, eds. *The High School Revolutionaries.* Random House, New York, 1970. An original collection of essays by the high school students who were involved in student protest against the schools and society in the 1960s.

National Commission on the Reform of Secondary Education. *The Reform of Secondary Education: A Report to the Public and the Profession.* McGraw-Hill, New York, 1973. A series of recommendations for changes in secondary education, including changing the required age for compulsory attendance at schools.

National Commission on Resources for Youth. *New Roles for Youth in the School and the Community.* Citation Press, New York, 1974. Describes how the school and the community can foster community experiences for the best untapped resource in the country and the community—youth.

National Panel on High School and Adolescent Education. *The Education of Adolescents.* U.S. Department of Health, Education, and Welfare, Washington, D.C., 1976. A report that calls for a reduction of student time spent in school and for an expansion of community educative agencies.

Nevin, David, and Robert E. Bills. *The Schools That Fear Built: Segregationist Academies in the South.* Acropolis, Washington D.C., 1977. A reviewer for the *Washington Post* commented that "the values by which the academies operate are discipline, traditional methods of learning, and religious indoctrination."

Passow, Harry. *Secondary Education Reform: Retrospect and Prospect*. Teachers College Press, New York, 1976. A lively and helpful discussion of recent reports that stress community participation by secondary school students. An appraisal and some speculation on the future of reform in secondary education.

Postman, Neil, and Charles Weingartner. *Teaching as a Subversive Activity*. Delacorte Press, New York, 1969. A vigorous and provocative book that is certain to stir equally vigorous reactions on the part of the reader. A new approach to education is suggested and traditional conceptions are mercilessly criticized.

Report of the Panel on Youth of the President's Science Advisory Committee, *Youth: Transition to Adulthood*. University of Chicago Press, Chicago, 1974. Focuses on the age period from fourteen to twenty-four and raises questions about the institutions that bring youth into adulthood and proposes changes in those institutions.

Simpson, Elizabeth Leonie. *Humanistic Education: An Interpretation*. Ballinger, Cambridge, 1976. A survey commissioned by the Ford Foundation on theory, classroom practices, teacher training, and curriculum development in the field of humanistic education. Six broad methodologies are characteristic: the small group experience, simulation exercises and educational games, language as a major symbol system, planned environment—contextual learning, use of the body, and expression through the arts.

Van Til, William, William E. Brownson, and Russell L. Hamm. "Back to Basics— with a Difference." *Educational Leadership*, October 1975, pp. 8–10, 12–13. An interpretation of the contemporary back-to-basics movement as an expression of nostalgia and a repudiation of rapid social change.

Weber, G. "Back to the Basics in Schools: Here's the Case for Pushing the Current Trend Into a Landslide." *American School Board Journal* 162 (August 1975), 45–46. Argues that public education is justified only when it provides a sound basic education for all students—the bright, the average, and the slow. Contends that the first essential in social and vocational development is competence in the basics.

2.

The Social Crisis and Secondary Education

Basic questions confront educators today. Can education help humanity? Can education contribute to human survival? Can education illuminate social realities and aid in solving pressing social problems?

For secondary educators, these questions are especially relevant. Can the secondary level of education, with its massive apparatus for teaching and learning, with its schools enrolling so many young people within the American population, with its potential for community cooperation and utilization, help young people to cope with today's social realities in a time of social crisis?

A necessary first step for secondary educators is gaining an understanding of both the threat and the promise inherent in today's social crisis. So in this chapter, current social problems in the United States in its world setting are described along with some possible approaches to these problems. The discussion also indicates how the problems relate to the present lives of American young people of secondary school age.

EVOLUTION OF THE SOCIAL CRISIS

Change came slowly in many earlier historical ages. The lives of human beings followed the patterns established by their fathers and mothers, who in turn had followed the patterns of *their* fathers and mothers. Ancient Egypt, for instance, was a stable society; for centuries generations of slaves labored to build the pyramids, while peasants along the Nile cultivated the same land that their ancestors had.

With the Industrial Revolution, the pace of change quickened in the Western world. The European nations reached for new resources and lands through exploration and exploitation. Science fostered new technology. The lives of men and women in industrial lands differed from their parents' and still more from their grandparents'.

Though well aware by the late nineteenth century that they were living through a period of swift change, Western people were confident that they could control and direct social developments and could solve social problems. The Victorian age in England was a time of optimism. The United States at the turn of the century lived in what Henry Seidel Canby described as *The Age of Confidence*. Many read Mark Twain's humorous works, but few took seriously the deep pessimism of his *Pudd'nhead Wilson*. The dominant view was that humankind was engaged in an upward evolution from its primordial beginnings. Progress was regarded as natural, inescapable, inevitable. The poet William Ernest Henley expressed it well: "I am the master of my fate; I am the captain of my soul."[1]

Change accelerated in the twentieth century. Turbulent events shook the former confidence and optimism of the Western nations. Possibly the disillusionment can be dated from August 3, 1914, the day that World War I was apparent. That night, Edward Grey, Viscount of Fallodon, stood at his window in the British Foreign Office watching the London lamplighters and said sadly, "The lamps are going out all over Europe; we shall not see them lit again in our lifetime."[2] At the close of that war, the British novelist H. G. Wells said, "Human history becomes more and more a race between education and catastrophe."[3] In the closing years of World War I, the Bolshevik Revolution broke out and shook the world. A "changeless" Mother Russia was transformed from a czarist empire to a communist state.

In America disillusionment with crusades for a better world set in. Ernest Hemingway spoke for a postwar view in the 1920s when he quoted Gertrude Stein before opening his novel, *The Sun Also Rises:* "You are all a lost generation." In England, an expatriate American, T. S. Eliot, summarized a world view through the title of his influential poem, *The Waste Land*.

The Great Depression of the 1930s was a further blow to the confidence of the advanced civilizations. Failure of banks, mounting unemployment, and spread of poverty graphically showed how economically interdependent human beings had become in an industrialized, free-enterprise society. Americans not only found themselves highly dependent on the actions of their fellow citizens, but they also discovered that when a bank failed in Vienna, Austria, the world's banking system shuddered and faltered and world economies were convulsed.

---

[1] William Ernest Henley, *Poems*, Charles Scribner's Sons, New York, 1926, p. 119
[2] John Bartlett, *Familiar Quotations*, 14th ed., Little Brown, Boston, 1968, p. 863.
[3] H. G. Wells, *The Outline of History*, Garden City Publishing, Garden City, N.Y., 1920, chap. 41.

Full recovery from the Great Depression was achieved only through World War II, which dwarfed the earlier world war in its destruction and casualties. When the first atomic bomb leveled Hiroshima, the potentiality of nuclear power to destroy the world was demonstrated. In the postwar era, more and more nations acquired destructive nuclear capability. A Cold War between the United States and the Soviet Union developed. There were frightening regional confrontations.

The Third World, the underdeveloped nations, threw off many of the remaining shackles of colonialism and imperialism. New African and Asian nations demanded a place in the sun in a time of a revolution of rising expectations. The world's population climbed; in the underdeveloped lands, population rises were sharpest. The gap between the rich and the poor increased. Meanwhile, evidence mounted that the developed nations could not indefinitely continue their prodigal usage of a disproportionate share of the world's energy. Global resource bases are not infinite or inexhaustible; there are limits to growth.

Blacks demanded an end to racial discrimination in the United States, which experienced some long hot summers of racial turmoil. A war in the quagmire of Vietnam dragged on; a fraction of the youth population took to the streets in militant protest. Feminists struggled against subordination of women. A sexual revolution affected long-established practices concerning marriage and the family.

In the late 1970s, Americans found themselves in a national and world setting characterized by a formidable catalogue of social problems—the continuing threat of nuclear war, the population explosion, the reality of regional famines, the energy crisis, a deterioration of the ecology even to the biosphere, the persistence of racism and sexism, faltering economies, governmental corruption and ineffective bureaucracies, often intolerable lives in the inner cities, and myriad similar threats.

So the world of the late 1970s is no longer marked by the serene confidence in progress that had characterized Victorian England or America at the turn of the century. The world in which we now live is worried and shaken. In this age of anxiety, some observers have concluded that the future of humankind on this small planet is dim. Others believe that humanity will survive, even prevail, but not without severe struggles against formidable problems.

PERSISTENT SOCIAL PROBLEMS

INTERNATIONAL RELATIONS

Problems and Responses The threat overshadowing human survival today is war. A doubter might react to this statement by pointing out that humankind has engaged in warfare throughout the ages, yet the human race has survived and has even multiplied. But such a response does not take into account the fantastic increase in destructive power that has accompanied scientific and technological development. Nuclear bombs and airborne missiles are a far cry from clubs, arrows, and rifles. Such instruments of death dropping from the skies can exterminate entire cities and whole populations through the fallout that accompanies nuclear explosions, whereas the trench warfare of the World War I era and swift movement of panzer divisions characteristic of World War II were necessarily restricted to the destruction of opposing military forces in limited geographic areas. In an age of overkill, both warring and neutral nations would be destroyed, for a new world war would necessarily be a total war. Since World War II, humankind has confined its hostilities to regional wars fought with a constantly more destructive technology, although fragile, mutual agreements have kept it from employing nuclear warheads as yet. The mutual restraint rose out of recognition that the holocaust of World War III could prove to be the earth's last war. This is the ominous setting in which the quest for peace proceeds.

Guided by the assumption that peace can be achieved and maintained by agreements among sovereign nations, the United States attempts to enter into compacts with world powers and mediate disputes among smaller powers. For instance, during the 1970s the United States sought detente with the Soviet Union and the People's Republic of China, and achieved some degree of success. Agreements as to strategic arms limitations have been reached. In 1975 Secretary of State Henry Kissinger achieved an agreement between Israel and Egypt in the oil-rich, explosive Middle East. In 1977 Cyrus Vance, acting for President Jimmy Carter, brought American disarmament proposals to Moscow; the Soviet Union rejected them. Negotiations continue still. Some think that agreements among independent sovereign powers to refrain from hostilities is the only realistic approach to maintaining peace. Others regard this option as too risky since it depends upon the fallible calculations of leaders whose primary concern seems to be their own national interests.

Some believe that establishment of international government is necessary to achieve enduring peace. According to this view, a world government equipped with an international peace-keeping force must replace the sovereignty of contending national states. Opponents call proposals for international government utopian and unachievable. They can foresee no possible situation in which the developed nations would give up their present power. But the quest for a world state goes on through such eloquent spokesmen as Norman Cousins, who made the case for world government in *Modern Man Is Obsolete*.

To still other students of international affairs, the closest that the nations of the world will come to international cooperation to reduce warfare is through an international organization made up of the nations of the world, not through a world government. So they call for more dependence upon a world organization such as the United Nations, rather than heavy reliance, as at present, upon mediation by the independent world powers.

The U.N. organization, which was created in the aftermath of World War II, grew slowly in popularity among the citizenry of the United States, despite the persistence of conservative nationalistic opposition. In mediating small regional disputes, the U.N. enjoyed some success; in mediating larger conflicts, such as the Vietnam War, which involved the national interest of major powers, the U.N. was markedly less successful. In the 1970s the internal conflicts between the underdeveloped nations, largely the Third World countries of Africa, Asia, and South America, and the developed nations, largely industrialized, capitalist nations of Europe and North America, grew sharper. The *have-not* nations, sometimes with the support of developed socialist nations, called for greater financial aid from the West than the *have* nations were willing to grant. In 1975 the U.N. passed a resolution declaring Zionism to be racism; the United States regarded the action as anti-Semitic. In the mid-1970s, the American delegation to the U.N., led by Daniel P. Moynihan, adopted a harder line on disagreements with the U.N. majority. Moynihan's successor, William Scranton, employed a more conciliatory style yet maintained the hard line. President Carter's new ambassador to the United Nations, Andrew Young, a black who had been a congressman from Georgia, expressed strong opposition to racism and his vigorous support of black majority rule in Africa; his bluntness was appreciated by many representatives to the U.N., though resented by some.

Relationship to Young People The quest for peace is difficult. Yet the alternative, war among the nations, is potentially catastrophic. The problems of war and peace are of high importance to American youth. Wars are primarily fought by the young, who are drafted during wartime and often conscripted for training during peacetime. Youth is well aware of this relationship to war. The nearest the United States has ever come to a youth uprising occurred in the late 1960s when many young people protested American participation in the Vietnam War. Their agitation contributed to the decision of Lyndon B. Johnson not to be a candidate again for the presidency and added to the turmoil of the Nixon years.

Rather than lock the barn after the horse is stolen through protesting wars already under way, many perceptive young people of secondary school age are aware of the necessity of serious and comprehensive study of international relations. This does not involve study of the nature of war in our times alone. Consideration of possible constructive ways of establishing and maintaining peaceful relations is also needed. Understanding the cultures of varied peoples of the world and how to achieve mutual understanding is essential. Acquaintance with representatives of the various culture groups in the United States as well as travel abroad to understand people with whom Americans share the planet should help. Deliberate and reflective participation by youth will be required.

International education is a formidable undertaking for secondary educators. Yet if survival receives high priority, stress on international relations through secondary education programs is a necessity.

OVERPOPULATION, POLLUTION, AND ENERGY

Problems and Responses One of the difficulties faced by humankind today is that the social problems affecting survival—overpopulation, pollution, and energy use—are interrelated. The complex of value decisions concerning the ecology and environment of our planet, the accelerating population growth, and the availability of energy resources do not provide human beings with relatively simple value choices; rather, it involves dilemmas. A dilemma is a predicament as to possible alternatives that seemingly defies a satisfactory solution and presents hard choices.

The advocates of dealing with overpopulation remind us rightly that this problem (or any other social problem, for that matter) cannot be solved without taking into account factors related to excess population. Consider the acceleration in world population growth reported by Paul Ehrlich in *The Population Bomb.* By about the year A.D. 1650, there were 500 million people in the world. By 1850, two hundred years later, there were 1 billion people. Only eighty years later in 1930, there were 2 billion people. Just forty-five years later, in 1975, the world population reached the 4 billion mark.[4] The best current estimates are that by the year 2000, the population of the world will be approaching 7 billion people. Not only does the population of the earth steadily double, it now doubles in fewer and fewer years.

Meanwhile, scientific developments have expanded the span of life, reduced death through childbirth, and conquered childhood diseases with the help of drugs. Since we value human life, such scientific developments are recognized as praiseworthy. Yet part of the dilemma is that scientific death control, when not accompanied by birth control, results in more mouths to be fed.

Population grows fastest in the relatively underdeveloped regions of Africa, Asia, Latin America, and Oceania. A 70 percent increase during the last twenty-five years of this century is anticipated in these four regions. The population of Africa alone will double between 1975 and 2000. Only a 19 percent increase is anticipated for North America, Europe, and the Soviet Union, relatively developed areas.[5] As the Population Reference

---

[4] Paul R. Ehrlich, *The Population Bomb,* Ballantine, New York, 1968, p. 18.
[5] Population Reference Bureau, "Between the Lines," *1975 World Population Data Sheet,* March 1975. Courtesy of Population Reference Bureau, Inc., Washington, D.C.

Bureau says, "In general, the poorest countries with the highest birth, death, and infant mortality rates, the lowest average length of life, and the youngest populations have the lowest levels of food supply. The reverse is true for the wealthier countries."[6] By the year 2000, 82 percent of the world's population will live in Africa, Asia, Latin America, and Oceania— the regions that now have food shortages.

To many people in the Western world, the answer to famine and squalid living conditions in lands beset by food shortages and to uncomfortable crowding in the urban areas of the developed countries is to urge population policies involving responsible planned parenthood and to increase food production through a successful "Green Revolution." However, some in the Western world resist birth control on religious grounds. Most of the underdeveloped nations are not persuaded that high birth rates are detrimental to their national purposes. Many Third World leaders believe that the essence of the global problem is not population. To them, the social illness stems from a disproportionate utilization of the world's resources by the developed nations.

As the industrial cities of the world expand, their growing humanity pollutes the air, the land, and the water. In rural societies, a high degree of harmony with nature was achieved through the ecological cycle; people grew crops, fed animals, and returned wastes to the soil as organic matter. Nature cooperated through photosynthesis. In industrial societies, natural resources are depleted in the productive process and waste products flow into the streams, lakes, and seas from the factories; into the air through the exhaust of automobiles, trucks, planes and through the belchings of smokestacks; and onto the land in the form of slag heaps and strip-mine spoil banks.[7]

The ecological protest of the past thirty years has been motivated less by a concern for beauty than by the recognition that we are poisoning the only environment we have, threatening our health and irretrievably destroying the heritage of our children and our children's children. Rachel Carson dramatized in *Silent Spring* an American rural environment ruined by pesticides that impartially destroyed both harmful insects and healthy living things.[8] Barry Commoner in *The Closing Circle* portrayed our society as relying heavily on synthetic fibers, plastics, detergents, pesticides, and fertilizer technology, thus producing a load that nature simply cannot bear.[9] Noel Mostert in *Supership* depicted the destruction of the life of the oceans of the world through oil spills from mammoth tankers.[10] Some scientists warn that the layer of ozone ten to twenty miles above the earth

---

[6] Ibid.
[7] Barry Commoner, *The Closing Circle*, Alfred A. Knopf, New York, 1971.
[8] Rachel Carson, *Silent Spring*, Houghton Mifflin, Boston, 1962
[9] Commoner, *Closing Circle*.
[10] Noel Mostert, *Supership*, Alfred A. Knopf, New York, 1974.

that shields the land from excessive ultraviolet radiation is threatened by oxides of nitrogen from giant planes, by gases from refrigerator systems, and even by aerosol cans.

In the late 1960s preserving the environment became a requisite for the survival of the planet. The response of many American people was hearty and swift. Legislation was introduced; voluntary clean-ups, both superficial and fundamental, were instituted. New standards were established for automobile emissions; environmental lawsuits were undertaken. Organizations and governmental bodies multiplied: Friends of the Earth, state and city committees for environmental information, conservation foundations, university centers, the federal Environmental Protection Agency, the Federal Radiation Council, the Federal Water Control Administration, U.N. conferences on the human environment, the U.N. Scientific Commission on the Effects of Atomic Radiation. But the crusade for the environment naturally encountered resistance from those who benefited economically from things as they were. Government regulations were condemned as governmental interference and the virtues of free enterprise and unfettered choices by the public were extolled. The environmentalists were scoffed at as doomsday prophets.

The major setback, however, to environmentalists came from the third in the complex of interrelated problems. The question of the uses of energy in a world where there wasn't enough to go around became paramount. The reduction of oil imports from the Arab nations resulted in turned-down thermostats, line-ups of cars at the gas pumps, and speed limits reduced to fifty-five miles an hour during the winter of 1974. A recession decreased job availability; some workers saw environmental controls as threats to their jobs.

In this setting, the environmental crusade clashed with the nation's urgent energy demands. Faced with choices between maintaining living standards and protecting the environment, legislative and executive bodies often opted for living standards. For instance, in the mid-1970s the Alaskan oil pipeline was authorized; higher emission standards for automobiles were delayed; lawsuits against pollution by factories consumed considerable time before their resolution; compromise strip-mining legislation was defeated; flights by the noisy giant Concorde SST plane were authorized. Yet the Environmental Protection Agency persisted and reported progress.

The gravity of the energy crisis was brought home to the American people in 1977. Addressing a joint session of the United States Congress, President Jimmy Carter said on April 20, 1977:

We have to deal with the greatest domestic challenge our nation will face in our life time. We must act now—together—to devise and to implement a comprehensive national energy plan to cope with a crisis that otherwise could overwhelm us. . . . The heart of our energy problem is that our demand for fuel keeps rising more quickly than our production, and our primary means of solving this problem is to reduce waste and inefficiency.

President Carter called for an effort that would be the moral equivalent of war.[11]

An aspiration of socially conscious Americans—to maintain for themselves a high national standard of living while helping less developed nations to reach the levels of the developed countries—seemed less achievable than formerly thought in decades prior to the 1970s.

The problems of overpopulation, pollution, and energy use are interrelated, and the direction to take to resolve these dilemmas is apparent: check population growth, preserve the environment, and conserve energy. The direction involves simplifying life styles, reducing materialistic acquisition, and eliminating waste.

Relationship to Young People Young people are often more aware of this complex of problems than are their elders. Many are conscious that unless the problems are met, they will come home to roost with their generation. Consequently, many young people are ready to give thought to the relation of the population explosion to their own planning concerning marriage, career, and family. They have already demonstrated their concern for the environment through participation in clean-up campaigns and environmental crusades in many communities. They have been critical of overly materialistic strivings on the part of their parents.

Because of such concern, the overpopulation, pollution, and energy cluster of problems can be made meaningful to secondary school youth. That the problems are related to the survival of humankind make their inclusion in secondary education imperative.

RACISM AND SEXISM

Problems and Responses What is meant by race? By racism? *Race* means a "human population distinguished as a more or less distinct group by genetically transmitted physical characteristics."[12] Despite the categorizations of human populations into separate races, all human beings belong to the same species, *Homo sapiens.* The word *race* is inappropriate if applied to national, religious, geographic, linguistic, or cultural groups. Nor can the biological criteria of race be equated with such characteristics as intelligence, personality, or character.[13] Yet racism is widespread in our world. Racism is "the assumption that psycho-cultural traits and capacities are determined by biological race and that races differ decisively from one another which is usually coupled with a belief in the

---

[11] *Washington Post*, April 21, 1977, p. A21.
[12] *American Heritage Dictionary of the English Language*, Houghton Mifflin, Boston, 1969, pp. 1074–1075.
[13] William H. Harris and Judith S. Levey, eds., *The New Columbia Encyclopedia*, Columbia University Press, New York, 1975, p. 2263.

inherent superiority of a particular race and its right to domination over others."[14] In the Republic of South Africa, racism takes the form of apartheid, an official policy of racial segregation to promote and maintain white domination. In many nations of the world, racism takes the form of anti-Semitism against Jewish people. In the United States, despite the Constitution and twentieth-century Supreme Court decisions, racism persists and results today in discrimination directed especially against blacks, Hispanics, and Native Americans, along with other minorities.

Racism is disastrous to individuals and society. Through racist attitudes and policies, individual persons are subordinated, discriminated against, and segregated because of genetic characteristics or social factors that are beyond their control. Individual potentialities are stifled; lives are warped; people are denied equal chances for opportunities, whether educational, vocational, civic, or cultural. Racist attitudes and policies destroy the unity of nations and cause antagonisms to develop between minorities and the majority. The suppression of minorities results in destructive conflicts marked by hatred, hostility, and violence. The resultant combat often takes the form of civil disorder, rioting, lawlessness, and crime.

To build better relationships among Americans of different skin colors, religious preferences, and national origins, programs were developed to combat segregation and to foster integration. To desegregate is to stop separating or isolating minority group members from others. To integrate is to unite and unify through bringing about mutual acceptance of all in desegregated settings. A group may be physically desegregated yet may not demonstrate the quality of full acceptance of persons as individuals that characterizes truly integrated relationships.

Racial segregation prevailed virtually unchanged in the United States until World War II. Throughout the South and often in the North, Jim Crow laws forced blacks to attend separate schools and colleges, to sit in the back of buses or in special sections of railroad cars or in special galleries in theaters, and to use separate waiting rooms and toilet facilities. Segregation even prevailed in jails, hospitals, and churches. In 1896 the *Plessy* v. *Ferguson* decision of the Supreme Court upheld the constitutionality of so-called separate but equal accommodation laws.

Civil rights groups, the intercultural education movement, outspoken blacks, and liberal whites all pointed to the inconsistency between discrimination and defense of democracy in wartime. These forces encouraged progress in desegregation during World War II. President Franklin D. Roosevelt created a Fair Employment Practices Committee (FEPC) in 1941 and "no discrimination" clauses were included in government contracts. In 1948 President Harry S. Truman issued a directive to end segregation in the

---

[14] Philip Babcock Gore, ed., *Webster's Third New International Dictionary*, G. & C. Merriam, Springfield, Mass., 1968, p. 1870.

armed forces. In 1954 the Supreme Court in the crucial *Brown* v. *Board of Education of Topeka* case ruled that segregation in public schools was inherently unequal and thus unconstitutional. The Civil Rights Act of 1964 included a provision barring the use of federal funds for segregated programs and schools. In 1965 a Voting Rights Act was passed. By the mid-1970s only 12 percent of black students in the United States were in completely segregated schools. The problem of removing school segregation had moved North.

Desegregation of schools was more readily achieved within American society than was the goal of integration marked by full acceptance of individuals as persons. Adults organized groups and led protests, sometimes violent, against the physical desegregation of schools. In the mid-1970s, busing to achieve desegregation particularly outraged residents of all-white neighborhoods. Intercultural education programs often did not accompany school desegregation efforts. The economic gap between blacks and whites persisted. Progress came slowly and grudgingly. Some blacks became disillusioned with the possibility of achieving desegregation and integration within their lifetimes. Other blacks persisted in their belief in the importance of the desegregation-integration strategy, despite admitted setbacks and difficulties.

Black militants developed a black power approach, which emphasized the establishment of black identity. Black power advocates believe that before a group can play a significant role in American society, it must first close ranks and achieve its own solidarity. The minority group can then bargain from a position of strength. Thus the sponsors of black power called for black people to lead and support their own organizations and to develop black control of communities in which blacks live through decentralized boards of education, black administrators, and black teachers. The new black strategy stressed awareness of being black.

Critics of the black power and black identity approach rejected it as yet another form of "separate but equal" that risked a return to separatism. They regarded the new strategy as a temporary gain of power for some black leaders in local communities that imperiled a long-range commitment to full equality and shared participation for black people in the larger national community. The more bitter opponents of black power even condemned it as a form of racism.

Blacks were not the only group caught up in the question of the preferable strategy to adopt to achieve human rights in the United States. Mexican-Americans, Puerto Ricans, and Native Americans faced similar perplexities as to strategies: a full share in participation in American life versus maintenance of group identity in an ethnic pluralism.

Women, though numerically the majority in the United States, called attention to parallels between their own status and that of minority group members. Feminist leaders pointed to the subordinate roles assigned women throughout American and indeed world history. Women had to wage campaigns for equality as did minorities. In 1848 a general declaration of women's rights was proposed at a Seneca Falls, New York, meeting by Elizabeth Cady Stanton, Lucretia Mott, and others. Their declaration of independence demanded full legal equality, full educational and commercial opportunities, equal pay, and the right to vote. A National American Woman Suffrage Association unified in 1890 two groups working for votes for women. The right to vote was sought by the woman suffragists who achieved their goal through the Nineteenth Amendment to the U.S. Constitution in 1920.

Half a century later, the feminist movement for political, social, and educational equality for women focused on efforts to pass still another constitutional amendment, the Equal Rights Amendment, which states simply: "Equality of rights under the law shall not be denied or abridged by the United States or by any State on account of sex." Although Congress passed the amendment in 1972, the struggle to get the proposed amendment ratified by thirty-eight states continued in the mid-1970s. The women's liberation movement, through the National Organization for Women (NOW), the National Women's Political Caucus, and other groups, also campaigned for abortion reform, federally financed child-care centers, equal pay for equal work, and occupational upgrading— in general for the removal of all barriers to education, influence, and power for women. Education frequently drew fire since those engaged in the campaign believed that the enemy, sexism, was entrenched in stereotypes in textbooks, in curriculum, and in guidance procedures.

Critics of contemporary feminism sometimes regard some of its more vigorous exponents as abrasive in their attitudes to homemakers, indifferent to legislation to protect working women from high-risk occupations or excessive working hours, and inclined to concern themselves with somewhat more specialized issues such as the defense of lesbianism. When state-level equal rights amendments failed in New York and New Jersey in 1975, commentators reported that among those who heavily contributed to the defeat were women who were offended by what they saw as excesses of the women's liberation movement.

Relationship to Young People   Issues related to racism and sexism are real and important to contemporary high school youth. If the young person happens to be a male and black, Hispanic, Native American, or of other minority background, he knows from personal experiences and from associates the reality of discrimination. If the young person happens to be male and WASP (white, Anglo-Saxon, Protestant), he knows that he will steadily encounter and interact with people whose background characteristics differ from his own. Often he recognizes that the quality of his existence will be heavily influenced by the quality of his relationships with others in his community and in the wider society. If the young person happens to be female, she encounters similar problems related to her racial or ethnic background. In addition, she is also personally involved in a complex of perplexities related to career versus homemaking, marriage versus remaining single, rearing children versus childlessness, and so on. Members of her family and the young males with whom she associates in high school also become involved in her decisions.

ECONOMIC PROBLEMS OF PRODUCTION AND CONSUMPTION

Problem and Responses The economic system of the United States is complex. Basically, the American economy is a capitalist system, yet it also includes socialized aspects. Capitalism is characterized by private ownership of property and the means of production. The capitalist system is obvious in the United States where families aspire to own their own homes and stockholders own corporations. Yet capitalism in the United States is not unregulated. One need only recall the variety of regulatory agencies of government intended to supervise practices and curb excesses in industry, trade, and transportation.

In addition, socialized institutions exist in the American economic system. Socialism is characterized by collective or government ownership and management of property and the means of production. In the United States such institutions as the national parks, national forests, and the public schools are owned collectively by the people. Yet, unlike the pattern in nations that are basically socialist, many public utilities and natural resources are not owned collectively or managed by the government in the United States. Certainly, the U.S. federal government does not assume responsibility for all economic planning and direction as does the Soviet Union's centralized government.

The American economy is a form of capitalism, characterized by some degree of regulation and modified by coexisting socialist institutions. The system is sometimes called a mixed economy. Its advocates, however, usually refer to it as the free-enterprise system and they value its competitive aspects more highly than its cooperative ones.

All economic systems have their problems and the American economic system is no exception. One major problem is disproportionate distribution of economic rewards. In 1970 the average income received by a family in the top 5 percent of the income distribution was twelve times higher than the average income of a family in the poorest 20 percent of the income distribution. A family in the poorest fifth of the income distribution received about one-fourth of the average income of American families, while a family in the top fifth received three and a half times the average income of American families.[15] Six percent of the people owned 57 percent of the

---

[15] Arthur B. Shostak, Jon Van Til, and Sally Bould Van Til, *Privilege in America: An End to Inequality?* Prentice-Hall, Englewood Cliffs, N.J., 1973, p. 29.

nation's wealth (that is, the value of its assets). Seventeen percent of the people owned 75 percent of the nation's wealth.[16] Critics term this condition a maldistribution of income and wealth. They point to its consequences, a struggle for existence by the poor and relative economic ease for the rich, accompanied by inequalities in education, health, housing, and job opportunities.

A second problem is the recurrence of prosperity and recession or depression. The American economy, unlike centrally planned economies, is subject to the swing of business cycles. In periods of prosperity, employment is high, industry produces at near capacity, consumers buy confidently, and business is brisk. In periods of recession, unemployment rises, industry cuts back production, consumers are cautious, and business declines. In periods of depression, unemployment is widespread, industry closes some plants, consumers are unable to buy and are restricted largely to necessities, and business is bad. In recent years, regulatory and control devices administered through governmental agencies, such as fiscal and taxation policies and governmental employment programs, have reduced the extremes of the cycle. For instance, by the mid-1970s the United States had not had a great depression crisis since the 1930s. But the cyclical characteristics of the economy persist, creating difficulties for long-range planning by individuals and organizations.

Complicating the economic situation today is the persistence of inflation, whether the economy is in a prosperity boom or a recession decline. In recent decades, the prices paid by consumers have steadily increased. The conventional economic wisdom has held that in periods of recession characterized by unemployment, the "natural forces" of the market would cause prices to fall and inflation to dwindle and disappear. But in the economic recession of the 1970s, both increased unemployment and rising prices have been apparent. The economists coined the term *stagflation* to describe the combination of economic stagnation and inflation. Some theorized that power of big business and big labor resulted in rigidities in the economic system that made it impossible for natural forces to prevail. Despite rising production, unemployment was at 7.1 percent in August 1977. The jobless rate for whites was 6.1 percent, and for blacks 14.5 percent. Meanwhile, inflation continued.

Consumer problems also characterize the American economy. The free-enterprise system puts heavy stress on production; consumers often have to fend for themselves—the tradition of "let the buyer beware." Consuming is still a highly individualistic matter; consumers are not well organized and are not able to exert economic power as are business enterprises and labor unions. The consumer usually receives insufficient information for self-protection. Advertising is primarily geared to the interests of the seller, not the buyer.

---

[16] Ibid., pp. 18, 19.

Despite these problems, the American form of economic organization has enjoyed remarkable success. The combination of freedom to innovate, a substantial resource base on the North American continent, and an energetic and expanding work force have contributed to a standard of living in the United States that is high even when compared to smaller nations with more manageable economies such as Sweden and West Germany. Indeed, today some observers believe that a problem of the United States may be too much success! It may not prove possible in the decades ahead for the United States to maintain its present high degree of energy utilization while allowing the extensive pollution that accompanies high industrial production. In 1973 the United States, with 4.5 percent of the world's population,[17] used 29.8 percent of the world's energy.[18] Much depends upon whether new forms of energy can be developed and current levels of pollution reduced. Experimentation and innovation also goes forward to attempt to solve or reduce the four problems mentioned earlier: maldistribution of income and wealth, the extremes of the business cycle, continuous inflation, and consumer problems.

Relationship to Young People Economic problems of production and consumption affect young Americans of high school age. As part of their transition from adolescence to adulthood, they want to play a role in the economic system both to acquire experiences in the real world and to earn spending money. Yet the economic system is geared primarily to adult wage earning. Though adults give lip service to youth participation in production, youth employment in practice is often regarded as an expendable rather than a necessary matter.

Consequently, adolescents frequently cannot find sufficient after-school or vacation work, particularly in periods marked by downturns of the business cycle. Adolescents who drop out of school also encounter difficulties in finding jobs. This is especially the case with minority group American youth. Youth unemployment is usually markedly larger than adult unemployment, and unemployment among black, Hispanic, and Native American youth is generally double that of other young people. The problem is particularly severe for minority group young people who drop out of school temporarily or permanently during the high school years. In August 1977 unemployment among black teen-agers reached 40.4 percent.

Sociologists have pointed out the existence of a youth culture in American society. The youth culture includes distinctive goods and services that young people value highly and urgently want to buy. For instance, youth's priority purchases are stereos, rock records and cassettes, citizen band

---

[17] U.S. Bureau of the Census, *Statistical Abstract of the United States*, 96th ed., Washington, D.C., 1975, p. 836.
[18] U.S. Bureau of the Census, *Statistical Abstract of the United States*, 97th ed., Washington, D.C., 1976, p. 550.

radios, used cars, and distinctive clothing; and services valued highly by youth include sports events, discotheques, dance bands, and concerts by youth-oriented musical groups. Yet young people, like the rest of American society, find that the prices of goods and services important in their culture steadily rise with continuous inflation. They are provided with little help, aside from the opinions and gossip of people of their own ages, in respect to wise consumption.

Consequently, economic problems of consumption and production are important to young people at the secondary school level even though they are not yet full-time wage earners or family heads. Problems of maldistribution of income and wealth, extremes of the business cycle, continuous inflation, and consuming goods and services do affect their daily lives. The American secondary school should not be blind to their involvement and concern.

GOVERNMENTAL ROLES AND RESPONSIBILITIES

Problems and Responses   It is not enough to simply say that the U.S. government should do something about such persistent social problems as war, the pollution-overpopulation-energy interrelationship, racism and sexism, and economic problems. One must also consider the possible roles and responsibilities of government. Matters relating to government thus necessarily become a fifth cluster of persistent social problems in today's social crisis.

Government should do for the welfare of the citizenry what individuals cannot do independently for themselves, say the sages. The Preamble to the U.S. Constitution states:

We the people of the United States, in order to form a more perfect union, establish justice, insure domestic tranquillity, provide for the common defense, promote the general welfare, and secure the blessings of liberty to ourselves and our posterity, do ordain and establish this Constitution for the United States of America.

The rest of the Constitution spells out these goals.

Government began small in the United States. Indeed, many of those who worked toward a new nation were troubled by the possibility of too much government authority and thus specified what the government should *not* do through the Bill of Rights. These first ten amendments to the Constitution were proposed and ratified by the states as their first order of business after the adoption of the Constitution. Ensuing U.S. history has been marked by conflicts over the proper roles of governments and individuals, and over the proper allocation of responsibilities to persons, localities, states, and the federal government.

With the increasing complexity of life in an industrial society, the U.S. government grew larger and larger. The federal government in particular attempted to cope with the persisting social problems cited in this chapter.

For instance, consider some of the governmental approaches used to meet problems of the economic system such as maldistribution, the business cycle, inflation, and consumer protection: taxation, regulation, fiscal policy, and legislation. Here are some illustrations of widely used approaches.

A progressive income tax instituted through the Sixteenth Amendment to the U.S. Constitution in 1913 has the potentiality to deal with the problem of disproportionate distribution of income and wealth. Although present income-tax laws provide many loopholes for the rich and opportunities for favoritism for the few, the device of taxing the rich more heavily and the poor more lightly (even to the extent of creating a "negative" income tax through which money would be remitted to the poorest people) could be used for a broad distribution of national income and wealth. The potentialities increase through an allied policy for redistributing income provided by government benefits to low-income groups through health programs, educational support, welfare payments, housing provision, and unemployment insurance.

Believers in individual initiative, however, warn of the danger of "killing the goose that lays the golden eggs" through high taxation on individual enterprisers and governmental benefits to low-income people. They fear that high taxation will reduce incentive for all Americans, whatever their income level. At the opposite economic pole from the enthusiasts for individual initiative are some socialists who believe that the rich, who hold the power and control the purse strings, will not allow income taxation to be sufficiently progressive or governmental benefits to be extensive enough to achieve a redistribution of income in the United States. A third view is that of a sizeable segment of the American public, which regards the combination of a reformed progressive income-tax system without loopholes or favoritism with a program of governmental benefits that supplements income but does not eliminate incentives to employment as a workable approach to the income-distribution problem.

Another tool is government regulation to cope with recession and depression. Rather than accept Adam Smith's fatalistic conclusion that business cycles must develop in accordance with natural forces guided by "the invisible hand," the U.S. government frequently intervenes in the business cycle to reduce the impact of downturns upon the citizenry. Financial and commercial depressions in America once grew out of speculative and fiscal crises. The development of reserve banks, such as the Federal Reserve System of the early twentieth century, sharply reduced such crises through controls on loans and investments with resulting stabilization of economic conditions. For instance, in the Great Depression, which began in 1929, no central bank in the Federal Reserve System failed. Today depressions and recessions affect industry more directly than they do finance or commerce.

Governments also mount job-training, unemployment and welfare programs to blunt the impact of depression or recession. In an attempt to avert or stem economic downturns, they spend public funds for large-scale public works programs. The theory behind such actions is that spending in the private sector will then take place, and that private enterprise stimulated by such pump priming will find it profitable to produce.

The federal government attacks problems of inflation. It relies largely on fiscal policies such as raising or lowering interest rates. Increases or cuts in income taxes are also used for deflationary or inflationary purposes.

Legislation and agencies protecting the consumer date from the late nineteenth century when journalistic novelists, such as Upton Sinclair, who wrote *The Jungle* about the meat-packing industry, exposed unhealthy conditions in food-related industries. Agencies such as the Food and Drug Administration had their origins in the work of such muckrakers. Today a consumer movement under the leadership of Ralph Nader attempts to extend protection of the consumer.

But all such activities, however benign their purposes, must be supported by taxpayers; a popular contemporary proverb advises us that there is no such thing as a free lunch. Thus storms of controversy steadily rage over governmental programs and priorities. In broad terms, liberals believe that the social needs of the populace for health, housing, education, welfare, and other social requirements have priority over military spending and business subsidies, whereas conservatives tend to frown on welfare-related spending yet support spending for the military establishment. In broad terms, liberals assume that a substantial governmental bureaucracy will be required to administer governmental programs, whereas conservatives regard bureaucrats as wasteful tax-eaters and campaign for a marked reduction in the size of governmental agencies.

Supporters of expanded governmental activities with respect to the general welfare often point to urban blight, pollution, inadequate health care, insufficient provisions for old age, and inadequate educational facilities and staffing as illustrations of the necessity for governmental investment in human beings. Opponents of government expansion point out that deficit spending cannot be extended indefinitely and point to the critical financial situation in which New York City found itself in 1975 as a clear example of the shape of things to come.

Relationship to Young People Problems related to government can be dramatized for people of high school age. Their lives and those of their families are closely related to the various theoretical positions concerning government. Young people will inherit the social ramifications of decisions being made today, and increasingly they are conscious of this. That youth can be involved in political action related to government policies was demonstrated when the vital interests of the young were affected during the period of the Vietnam War of the 1960s and early 1970s. At that time youths spoke up, often loudly through street protests. Yet a considerable number also involved themselves in support of peace candidates for office. A concomitant development was the acquisition of the right to vote at age eighteen. When the draft was no longer a problem for American youth and the armed forces returned to recruiting and voluntary enlistment, youth political participation diminished. But the potential remains.

TEACHING STUDENTS DURING SOCIAL CRISIS

Young people of high school age are necessarily shaped by their prior experiences, in which the family usually plays a particularly significant role. According to their family orientations, secondary school students often bring with them to school varying positions on the social crisis. To the conservative student, the status quo frequently appears, if not totally desirable, at least necessary. Conservatives point out ways in which contemporary Americans are better off than their ancestors. They warn us that we should not be alarmed by our problems. They believe that too much social experimentation may worsen rather than better the social situation.

Faced with the social crisis, the liberal secondary school students will often inherit from their family backgrounds a preference for change. They opt for significant evolutionary development, rather than advocate standing pat or fostering revolution. They see social problems as formidable but within the control of humankind if we work hard within the current social framework. Thus liberal secondary students often place faith in a variety of reforms and modifications within the present system.

Secondary school students from families with a radical orientation will probably see the solution to social difficulties in the adoption of a totally different system. They see no more hope in tinkering with what they regard as a fundamentally rotten system than they do in supporting a vicious status quo. Their presentation of a persuasive new vision is usually stronger than their description of the daily operation of their projected ideal.

What is the secondary school teacher's role with respect to conservative, liberal, or radical secondary school students, shaped as they are by parental and other influences? Some educators believe that the teacher's right and responsibility in today's social crisis is to indoctrinate the view that the teacher supports personally. However, most educators believe that indoctrination of fixed answers by teachers denies the mission of education to develop independent thought by individuals. Thus they believe that in school situations in which evidence is considered and consequences are judged, students should be encouraged to use their own intelligence in making decisions about ideas. They believe that teachers who impose their favorite views confuse their proper responsibilities as citizens to freely and actively advocate their viewpoints with their responsibilities as teachers, which revolve around cultivating reflective thought by students.

There is another dimension in the thinking of students with respect to the social crisis. As a function of their personality characteristics, students may lean toward an optimistic or a pessimistic interpretation of the current social crisis.

To optimistic students the promise is bright for possible solutions to problems in the social crisis. Such students usually express high faith in the potentiality of technology to resolve many social dilemmas. For instance, in regard to the overpopulation-pollution-energy complex of problems, optimistic students look to technology to develop new sources of energy while at the same time utilizing the by-products of the industrial process to reduce pollution to a minimum. Thus a continually expanding population will be feasible. Similarly, the optimistic student points to past triumphs of humankind over social evils.

To students who lean toward pessimism, the grim likelihood is for catastrophe for humankind. They see the dilemmas of the human race as insoluble; build-ups of power by nations or groups betoken coming devastation; and present inabilities to cope presage a coming social breakdown. For instance, again in relation to the overpopulation-pollution-energy complex of problems, pessimistic students see limitations to our growth; the pollution of the land, sea, and air as inescapable; and overpopulation as inevitable. Similarly, pessimistic students point to past catastrophes that have blighted the experiences of humankind.

Again, some may see the role of education as encouraging either optimism or pessimism or, indeed, some presumed golden mean between extremes. However, educators who view reflective thought by students as the proper goal of education view the educator's major responsibility as thorough and uncompromising acquaintance of learners with social realities accompanied by vigorous appraisal of social consequences of alternative possible actions.

Our description above of the five persistent problem areas by no means constitutes a complete description of the social crisis of our times. The reader can supply many unmentioned manifestations of the contemporary social crisis whether in the form of additional problems or offshoots of the major problems. Certainly, these manifestations will include problems related to health care, slums, crime, law and justice, urban blight, drug abuse, corruption in government and business, and civil liberties (see Figure 2.1). In addition, new social problems, now unanticipated, will necessarily arise in time. Whatever the teacher's subject specialization might be, he or she must be aware of and informed on social problems. The persistent problem areas discussed in this chapter—international relations; overpopulation, pollution, energy; racism and sexism; economic problems of production and consumption; government roles and responsibilities—and the

FIGURE 2.1 *Relationships of Social Realities to Secondary School Students Today.*

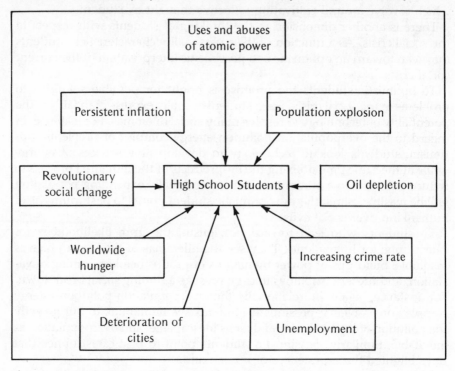

emerging problems are inescapable. In these last decades of the twentieth century, the content of the subjects and broad fields of the secondary school curriculum often relate to such social realities.

To cite only a few of the many possible examples, language arts teachers acquaint students with literature from many world cultures by men and women of varied ethnic, racial, religious, and social-class backgrounds. Science teachers help students understand problems of population, conservation, and energy. Physical education teachers meet problems of racism and sexism in their daily work with students in the gymnasium or on the playing field. Any vocational or career education program necessarily involves an understanding of the nature of production. As to governmental roles and responsibilities, a fundamental mission of social studies teaching is citizenship education.

Foreign language instructors teach languages so that people can communicate and achieve understanding of the language and customs of people both in other countries and in our own pluralistic nation. In the area of economic problems, mathematics and home economics teachers help educate consumers in their classes. Business education teachers help students to recognize and avail themselves of opportunities in the business world that have opened for minority group members and for women. Industrial arts teachers help students understand the role of technology in our productive process. Music and fine arts teachers acquaint young people with the creative work of people of all nations and cultural backgrounds.

Not only does the content of the curriculum relate to social realities. So do the concerns of students, as this chapter has demonstrated. Students are not wrapped in cotton and insulated from the real world. They encounter social realities through daily out-of-school experiences in their homes and the community, through magazines, books, radio, records, and television. In informal relationships with students, through questions raised in class, through casual conversations in the corridor, through sessions for counseling and guidance, teachers frequently find themselves dealing with aspects of the social crisis.

The secondary teacher who is unacquainted with social realities is obsolete in today's secondary schools. With awareness of the social realities of the broader society, teaching and relationships with students take on wider meaning and greater relevance.

DISCUSSION

1. Illustrate the differences in the pace of change between early civilizations and twentieth-century civilizations.

2. What are some of the major social problems facing Americans in the late 1970s? In your opinion, which are the most threatening of these problems? Why is war a more menacing problem in the last half of the twentieth century than it was in earlier times?

3. What are some of the theories as to how peace might best be maintained and wars avoided? What are some of the assumptions underlying these views?

4. In what ways are students of secondary school age affected by problems of war and peace? Why is study of international education necessary in secondary school programs?

5. How are the problems of overpopulation, pollution, and energy interrelated?

6. What are the major proposals to deal with the above cluster of problems? Which seem most workable to you?

7. How have young people demonstrated their concern for problems of overpopulation, pollution, and energy? What would you advocate that young people do to help in the solution of such problems?

8. What are race and racism?

9. What is the history of the issue of racial segregation and the campaign for integration? Is there a difference between integration and desegregation?

10. What are the two major strategies advocated by contemporary blacks? Do other minorities face comparable conflicts as to strategy?

11. What is the meaning of sexism?

12. What is the history of the feminist movement? What is the present status of the struggles for equality for women?

13. Illustrate how young people are affected by the problems of racism and sexism. Gather illustrations from class members who are themselves of varied backgrounds.

14. What are some of the major problems of the American economic system? What is the case for and against the economic system currently used in the United States?

15. How does the economic system influence young Americans of high school age?

16. What is the function of government? What approaches are used by government in dealing with social problems? How would you appraise these approaches—for instance, desirable and workable, or undesirable and unworkable? What is the case for and against expanded governmental activities?

17. How are the lives of young people affected by government?

18. What is the secondary school teacher's role with respect to the ideas of conservative, liberal, or radical students? With respect to pessimistic or optimistic students?

19. Illustrate how the subject area that you propose to teach in secondary education relates to social realities discussed in this chapter. Illustrate further with social realities not dealt with extensively in this chapter.

20. After reading the questions with which Chapter 1 ends, have you changed your position on any of these questions? Why have you? Indeed, why haven't you?

INVOLVEMENT

1. Consider carefully the relationships between today's social problems and the broad field of the curriculum that you know best. Differentiate between those social problems to which your field of specialization can make a major contribution, those to which your field can make a minor contribution, and those that bear no relationship to your field.

2. Think through your own position with respect to issues of war and peace. Consider carefully whether you are ready to join groups with programs dealing with international relations. If you are ready, identify yourself with such a group.

3. Inform yourself further on problems of overpopulation, pollution, and energy. Inform yourself on activities in connection with these problems on your own campus and in your own community. If you have a commitment, join with other

like-minded people in groups working for population control, pollution control, energy conservation, and so on.

4.   Explore problems of racism and sexism in conversations with family and friends. Increase your sensitivity as to possible positions people take. Experiment with being a conscious force to work against racism and sexism through your conversations, attitudes, and actions.

5.   If ready to do so, identify yourself with a group working against racism and/or sexism.

6.   Conduct an informal survey in your class, neighborhood, or community on attitudes toward busing.

7.   Improve your knowledge of economic problems through reading regularly a newspaper that carries substantial domestic and international economic news, such as the *New York Times, Washington Post,* or *St. Louis Post-Dispatch.*

8.   Become active in a political party of your choice. In an election year, actively support candidates of your choice.

9.   Visualize teaching situations in which discussion of the five social problems emphasized in this chapter might come up. Determine for yourself whether the preferable response would be avoidance, expression of your own views, encouragement of open discussion by students, or some other choice.

10.   Write an essay on education and society that includes your reasoning on how education is affected by society and how society is affected by education.

11.   Compare and contrast views of class members on how best to deal with the contemporary social crisis. Emphasize particularly a discussion of the role of education in coping with contemporary social problems.

FURTHER READINGS

Banks, James A. *Teaching Strategies for Ethnic Studies.* Allyn and Bacon, Boston 1973. A comprehensive book of strategies and resources for teachers working with a variety of American ethnic groups.

Brown, Lester R. *In the Human Interest.* W. W. Norton, New York, 1974. A book on overpopulation that calls for immediate action in terms of family planning and the satisfaction of basic social needs of people in all countries.

Buergenthal, Thomas, and Judith Torney. *International Human Rights and International Education.* U.S. National Commission on UNESCO, Department of State, Washington, D.C., 1976. An assessment of teaching for global interdependence with suggestions for improved teaching about war, peace, and international relations.

Cabrera, Y. Arturo. *Emerging Faces, The Mexican-Americans.* Wm. C. Brown, Dubuque, Iowa, 1971. Discusses relevant issues directly concerning Mexican-Americans in today's society.

Calderwood, James D., John D. Lawrence, and John E. Maher. *Economics in the Curriculum.* John Wiley, New York, 1970. New and effective ways of teaching economics.

Galbraith, John Kenneth. *Economics and the Public Purpose.* Houghton Mifflin, Boston, 1973. An analysis of the total economic system that concludes that "left to themselves, economic forces do not work out for the best except perhaps for the powerful." The case for relating economics to public purposes is made.

Harrison, Barbara Grizzuti. *Unlearning the Lie: Sexism in School.* Liveright, New York, 1973. An account of the Woodward School, Brooklyn, New York, where a score of feminists struggled to provide their children with an alternative to sexist education. The author describes curriculum changes, evolving social awarenesses, new teaching methods, and ways of relating to children.

Heilbroner, Robert L. *An Inquiry into the Human Prospect.* W. W. Norton, New York, 1974. A statement of the major difficulties faced by humankind today. Heilbroner envisions catastrophe unless fundamental changes in society come about.

Henderson, George, ed. *Education for Peace: Focus on Mankind.* Association for Supervision and Curriculum Development, Washington, D.C., 1973. A yearbook to inform on the issues of war and peace, to encourage teaching young people about them and to help individuals improve their effectiveness as educators for peace.

Nelson, Jack L., ed. *Patterns of Power: Social Foundations of Education,* 2nd ed. Pitman, New York, 1974. An anthology on social foundations of education stressing the school; poverty, racism, and inequality; education in turmoil; and teaching in a mass society.

Sieber, Sam D., and David E. Wilder, eds. *The School in Society.* The Free Press, New York, 1973. Studies in the sociology of education that stress the social system of education but include some writings on broader societal issues.

Stacey, Judith, Susan Bereaud, and Joan Daniels, eds. *And Jill Came Tumbling After.* Dell, New York, 1974. A collection of current literature on sexism and how schools can work against sex discrimination.

Stent, Madelon D., William R. Hazard, and Harry N. Rivlin, eds. *Cultural Pluralism in Education: A Mandate for Change.* Appleton-Century-Crofts, New York, 1973. A strong argument for cultural pluralism and attendant cultural diversity that includes discussions of ethnic studies, bilingual education, and teaching materials to help young people take pride in their cultural backgrounds. Though the contributors are themselves of varied backgrounds, all agree on the importance of cultural pluralism.

3.

Value Options of Youth

Not only do young people of secondary school age today live in a time of social crisis, they also live in a period in our history marked by a range of value options. Both their elders and their contemporaries hold to a variety of views on what is right and wrong, desirable and undesirable. An assortment of life styles are current and available.

This was not always so. Puritan youth of early New England encountered a single code of values that dictated a harsh, rigid, and authoritarian morality. Although some might stray from the straight and narrow prescribed path, as did Hester Prynne in Hawthorne's *The Scarlet Letter,* young people did not meet anyone who doubted the rightness of the path and the wrongness of straying from it.

In the new American nation, the value options of the nineteenth-century youth were broader, yet still limited. Young people could stay in the community in which they were born and be guided by the conventions of family, religion, neighbors, and townspeople. Or young persons could pack their bags and move west, where they would encounter new people in a harder, more adventurous, and riskier life on the frontier.

Life became much more complex in the United States with the rise of the large cities and the decrease of the rural population. Schools grew larger and more distant from a youth's home. Wage earners increasingly worked away from home, then away from neighborhoods, then beyond the boundaries of the community. At first, unmarried young women, then childless wives, and eventually mothers left their homes daily to work for pay, first in the new factories, then in the offices, and eventually in virtually every occupation and profession that employed males. Recreational opportunities sprang up throughout the cities and multiplied. In the complexity of the new cities, the value options encountered by American youth increased.

By the twentieth century the American mosaic was made up of people of varied races, religions, nationalities and social classes. People's occupations, recreations, organizations, clubs, homes, vacations, travels, interests, and life styles multiplied. Despite technological developments encouraging uniformity, pluralism became a fact in American life, and the possible value options proliferated.

Simultaneously, the older monolithic sanctions weakened. Massachusetts Bay Puritanism was no longer the only religion; a variety of religious beliefs (including both the denominations of Christianity and other world religions and their offshoots) became available. Moral codes, which were dependent on the homogeneity of the small-town population and which were enforced by unified public opinion, weakened in the face of the new heterogeneity. Nationalistic patriotic beliefs that formerly bound together many American citizens became less mandatory; they were diluted by internationalism and a new interpretation of what was involved in being a loyal American. Long-established beliefs were challenged by new interpretations about how a person might live.

VALUE CONFUSION

Widened value options were often accompanied by greater value confusion. Value confusion was compounded for many contemporary high school students by social developments within their lifetimes. Consider the following developments during the life span of the 1978 high school graduate. Note particularly the value implications for youth—implications that some national and local leaders had feet of clay, that corruption was the norm, that the ends justify the means:

In 1960 a U-2 aerial reconnaissance plane spying for the United States over the Soviet Union was shot down.

In 1960 some contestants were arrested for perjury in connection with a fixed television quiz program.

In 1961 civil rights Freedom Riders were attacked and beaten in Alabama.

In 1962 the Cuban missile crisis brought the Soviet Union and the United States to the brink of war.

In 1963 President John F. Kennedy was assassinated.

In 1964 the undeclared war in Vietnam was escalated by the United States.

In 1965 Malcolm X was shot.

In 1965 there was violence against civil rights workers in Alabama.

In 1965 there were race riots in the Watts district of Los Angeles.

In 1967 Israel and the Arab nations fought the Six-Day War.

In 1967 a major antiwar demonstration took place in Washington.

In 1967 there were riots by blacks in Cleveland, Newark, and Detroit.

In 1968 Reverend Martin Luther King, Jr., was assassinated in Memphis.

In 1968 it was announced that crimes of violence in the United States had increased 57 percent since 1960.

In 1968 Robert F. Kennedy was assassinated in Los Angeles.

In 1968 riots and charges of police brutality marked the Democratic convention in Chicago.

In 1968 Czechoslovakia was invaded by Soviet and Warsaw Pact troops.

In 1969 Senator Edward Kennedy was in political trouble because of the incident at Chappaquiddick Island, Massachusetts.

In 1969 inflation became a worldwide problem.

In 1969 the Charles Manson "family" killed actress Sharon Tate and others.

In 1969 Lieutenant William Calley, Jr., was tried on murder charges for the massacre of civilians at My Lai, Vietnam.

In 1969 Supreme Court Justice Abe Fortas resigned after disclosure of dealings with a convicted financier.

In 1970 four students were killed by the National Guard at Kent State University, Ohio.

In 1971 fighting in Indochina spread to Laos and Cambodia.

In 1971 Lieutenant William Calley, Jr., was found guilty of premeditated murder in the My Lai massacre in Vietnam.

In 1972 the Watergate affair began with a break-in at the Democratic National Headquarters.

In 1972 George Wallace was shot and partially paralyzed.

In 1972 Clifford Irving concocted a Howard Hughes "biography."

In 1972 Arab terrorists killed Israeli Olympic athletes and hostages in Munich.

In 1973 Vice President Spiro Agnew resigned and pleaded *nolo contendere* to income-tax evasion.

1974 President Richard Nixon resigned after the House Judiciary Committee recommended impeachment by the House of Representatives.

In 1974 President Gerald Ford granted former President Nixon a pardon for any criminal offenses committed while in office.

In 1975 the CIA was charged with complicity in the assassination and attempted assassination of foreign leaders.

In 1975 the FBI was charged with harassment of Reverend Martin Luther King, Jr., and improper activities against other American citizens.

In 1976 three members of Congress became involved in widely publicized sex scandals.

In 1976 surveys showed that the majority of Americans believe that neither Lee Harvey Oswald nor James Earl Ray acted alone in the assassination of President John Kennedy and Reverend Martin Luther King, Jr.

In 1977 a congressional committee conducted a new investigation into these assassinations.

In 1977 President Jimmy Carter's proposals for reductions in gasoline usage encountered strong opposition from various vested interests.

In 1977 some members of Congress were accused of being improperly influenced by South Korean agents.

The impact of such events has resulted in a widespread cynicism among Americans. Faith in leaders and institutions is at a low ebb. Young people of secondary school age, born in the early 1960s and attending secondary schools in the 1970s, are especially affected. To teach about values in American schools today is a difficult task.

LIFE STYLES AND VALUE PATTERNS

The consequences of such events make it highly important for secondary educators to be aware of the major value directions encountered by American youth today. Although the value options are numerous and varied, it is still possible to group them into five broad categories. The remainder of this chapter will consider the life styles and value patterns of those who choose (1) the work ethic, (2) the counterculture, (3) privatism, (4) socially responsible individualism, (5) activist protest. Still other ways of categorizing life styles and value patterns of youth are also possible.

THE WORK ETHIC

The work ethic as a life style arrived in America early. The Pilgrims brought it with them when they settled in Plymouth, Massachusetts, in 1620 and established the first permanent settlement in the New

World. Unlike the gold-seeking explorers and adventurers who preceded them to America, the Pilgrims intended to put down roots in the New World, to build their houses and churches and schools and remain permanently. The passengers on the Mayflower were mostly "freemen" who paid their own way. There were only a few servants among them. They were largely artisans, farmers, and laborers. With the settlement of the Massachusetts Bay Colony almost ten years later, middle-class people from England joined the migration along with professionals, scholars, and a few wealthy merchants. They were followed to the New World by others from England who came as indentured servants. Peasants who could find no place in England and who hungered for their own pieces of land across the ocean joined the growing migration. Commitment to work was a common denominator of most settlers of the area that became the royal colony of Massachusetts in 1691.

Emphasis on work was deeply embedded in the religious tradition of the Puritan newcomers. A forefather of Puritanism was John Calvin of Geneva, Switzerland. Calvin lived in a world that was moving from an agrarian medieval economy into a commercial and industrial era. He accepted the emerging capitalist system and encouraged trade and production. Calvinism regarded thrift, sobriety, industry, and responsibility as essential to the achievement of the reign of God on earth. The Puritans of New England echoed the Calvinistic view that all people had a spiritual calling to advance the kingdom of God on earth through their vocational calling. Thus, work was given a religious justification.

This religious conviction of the necessity of work was reflected in the first law concerning education in the New World, that of the General Court of the Massachusetts Bay Colony in 1642. The Court,

taking into consideration the great neglect of many parents and masters in training up their children in learning, and labor, and other employments which may be profitable to the Commonwealth [ordered that the chosen men of every town] shall have power to take account from time to time of all parents and masters, and of their children, concerning their calling and employment of their children, especially of their ability to read and understand the principles of religion and the capital laws of this country . . . and they shall have power . . . to put forth apprentices the children as such as they shall (find) not to be able and fit to employ and to bring them up . . . and they are to take care of such as are said to keep cattle (or) be set to some other employment . . . as spinning, . . . knitting, weaving tape, etc.[1]

A Massachusetts father wrote to his son who was enrolled at Harvard College during the 1670s:

Remember therefore, that though you have spent your time in the vanity of childhood, sports and mirth, little minding better things, yet that now, when come

---

[1] Law of 1642 reprinted in *Records of the Governor and Company of the Massachusetts Bay*, William White, Boston, 1853, vol. 2, pp. 6–7, 203.

to this ripeness of admission to the college, that now God and man expects you should put away childish things; now is the time come, wherein you are to be serious, and to learn sobriety, and wisdom in all your ways which concern God and man.[2]

Although other Protestants who established additional colonies in the New World were not as insistent as the Puritans, they also followed this work ethic. When, in 1920, pioneering sociologist Max Weber looked back at the intimate connection between the ascetic work ideal fostered by Calvinism and the rise of capitalist institutions, he titled his major book *Protestant Ethic and the Spirit of Capitalism*. In addition, neither Catholicism nor Judaism has been exempt from emphasis on the importance of hard work as an integral responsibility of humankind.

In addition to the sanctions of religion, the work ethic was strongly fostered by the physical setting of the New World and later of the new nation. Hard work and frugality were necessary wherever people chose to settle, on the sea coasts, in the western wilderness, in the growing towns, on the frontier, or in the emerging industrial cities. The surrounding environment was such that the Americans simply could not survive without working. The free-enterprise spirit nurtured the work ethic. Those who were able to combine hard work, shrewdness, and good luck received substantial economic rewards. In over one hundred books for boys, Horatio Alger chronicled the hard work and exemplary lives of his heroes, people who struggled successfully against poverty and adversity and inevitably gained wealth and honor. Teachers and clergy, politicians and businesspeople, the rich and the poor—all united in singing the praises of hard work and its complementary virtues of honesty, responsibility, thrift, steadiness, and loyalty. Not until the twentieth century did substantial doubts appear as to the adequacy of the work ethic as a sufficiently worthy conception of life goals.

So powerful is the heritage of the work ethic that it is little wonder that it remains a dominant life style in America today. Work is central in the lives of a substantial segment of Americans. For them, leisure and family relationships are subordinate. In addition to economic rewards, their status and prestige are bound up intimately with their occupations.

Consequently, many young people of secondary school age take for granted the desirability of the work ethic and its constellation of related values. They are serious and dedicated in their preparation for participation in the adult world of work. To them, the primary purpose of schools is to prepare a person for a job.

Obviously, there is much that is admirable about the work ethic. Its

---

[2] "A Letter from the Reverend Mr. Thomas Shepard to His Son at His Admission into the College," reprinted in *Publications of the Colonial Society of Massachusetts* 14 (1913), 192–198.

supporters rightly point out that a stable, productive society requires people who are hard working, thrifty, energetic, innovating, and responsible in order for improvements in the standard of living to be forthcoming. Although advocates of the importance of work recognize the roles of natural resources and geographic location in the growth of the American economy, they believe that the work ethic made the greatest contribution to the economic development of the United States. They add that interpersonal relationships go more smoothly and comfortably in a land in which people are dedicated and responsible in their work, as well as thoughtful and frugal in their spending. To the supporters of the work ethic, the well-trained, self-disciplined, productive, and thrifty worker or enterpriser represents the true American ideal.

Critics of the work ethic believe that it is not sufficiently encompassing to constitute a totally desirable pattern. They point to some of its outcomes they regard as negative. They say, for instance, that the work ethic leads to a consuming materialism in which only the earning of money is regarded as important and in which human beings are judged simply by their material possessions. They believe that the work ethic ideal is much too narrow, leaving out of consideration the human being as a creator, as enjoyer of leisure, as active participant in social improvement. They believe that the work ethic leads to competitive excesses rather than to cooperation, to selfishness rather than to altruism, to concern for the individual (and perhaps the person's immediate family) rather than to a wider concern for the welfare of humankind. In literature they point to such supporters of the work ethic as Sinclair Lewis's George F. Babbitt, J. P. Marquand's George Apley, or Budd Schulberg's Sammy. Historians portray the intellectual and cultural limitations of the American millionaires of the Gilded Age and more recent eras.

THE COUNTER-CULTURE

The counter-culture looks at life in the opposite way from the work ethic. Counter-culture life styles emerged in America in the 1960s, though the word *counter-culture* itself did not find its way into dictionaries until the 1970s. Essentially, the counter-culture approach to life rejects the values associated with the work ethic and substitutes freedom, mobility, self-expression, and searching for "highs." Critics quickly add that the freedom of the counter-culture is actually license, the mobility is homeless rootlessness, the self-expression means "anything goes," the supposed highs come from drugs and sexual deviance.

The expression *counter-culture* is new, but similar life styles date back at least to rebellious movements of the nineteenth century, when it was called Bohemianism. Believing that Gypsies came from the central European area of Bohemia, the French called the footloose Gypsies Bohemians. In the nineteenth century the term *Bohemians* was used to describe penniless and supposedly carefree writers, poets, journalists, artists, actors, and sculptors, who lived unconventional lives in attics and cafés. Bohemians include such literary figures as Villon, Byron, Baudelaire, Poe, and Wilde. In America a typical center of Bohemia was Greenwich Village in New York City during the late nineteenth and early twentieth centuries. Other Bohemians congregated in San Francisco, Carmel, and Taos in the West, Chicago in the Midwest, and Boston and Philadelphia in the East.

In the 1950s the counter-culture was presaged by the beat generation, people who frenetically and restlessly pursued new sensations and experiences. The beat generation rejected traditional social and artistic forms and sought expression in multiple intense experiences and eastern religions such as Zen Buddhism. Their major spokesmen included the poet Allen Ginsberg and the novelist Jack Kerouac, whose *On The Road* was a testament of the movement. San Francisco became a center for the beat generation.

In the 1960s those who followed the beat life style were often called hippies. Hippies were constantly on the move in search of new contacts. They startled Americans who practiced the work ethic by their long hair, beards, unconventional clothes, and general physical disarray. They rejected the Establishment as life-denying. An outstanding novelist who described hippie values was Ken Kesey, who wrote *One Flew over the Cuckoo's Nest* in 1962. Years later, the book was made into an outstanding film that won four major Academy Awards in 1976. Although the hippie era had passed into history, its anti-Establishment viewpoint still commanded a substantial audience.

Increasingly, observers of American society recognized the similarities among the Bohemians, beat generation, and hippies. All represented a life style running counter to the culture, one that substituted rebelliousness for conformity, wandering for steady work, minimum worldly goods for accumulation, free spending of limited income for thriftiness and frugality, unconventionality for convention. A counter-culture had emerged. Charles A. Reich, a proponent of the counter-culture, described it optimistically in *The Greening of America*. [3] His thesis was that a new life style had developed not simply for the minority of young rebels with whom it was identified but also for the large body of Americans. The new pattern was proposed as a replacement for the dying work ethic. Reich himself left his law professorship at Yale to take up a counter-culture life style in San Francisco. To Reich, the gray tone of a work-oriented society was being replaced by a movement toward a greener America characterized by joy in living, love of other people, creative expression, and high mobility. As Reich saw it, the hedonists were taking over from the Puritans. Theodore

---

[3] Charles A. Reich, *The Greening of America*, Random House, New York, 1970.

Roszak supplied historical support to the thesis with his *The Making of a Counter Culture*. [4]

The evidence of a subculture was apparent on university campuses, along highways, in communes, and in city neighborhoods and resort towns in which members of the counter-culture congregated. Some of the ways of the counter-culture also influenced a wider group of Americans. Increasingly seen in conventional social and work environments were beards and luxuriant hairstyles, casual clothes, the use of marijuana, credit cards as a replacement for hard cash. Some young workers on the automobile assembly lines resented and rejected overtime work, despite the additional income involved. Sexual experimentation and living together outside of marriage increased. The gay liberation movement expanded. Unconventional vacation resorts prospered. Some Americans combined conventional patterns at work with unconventional swinging life styles as private individuals. The antibourgeois values of artists were often imitated by people who were not notably creative.

To some who speculated on the impact of the counter-culture on American life, the results appeared to be greater freedom, a better balance between work and leisure, more openness, greater tolerance, more respect for individuality and creativity, more love for other members of small groups. To others, the wider influence of the counter-culture seemed a threat to a productive society, a rising standard of living, and an accumulation of savings to foster capital investment and to provide reasonable family and retirement security. They asked, in effect, "In a society marked by the counter-culture ethic, who is going to take care of the store?" Proponents of the counter-culture responded flippantly that those who asked the question were. They reminded their critics that counter-culture ways had a long distance to go before they could possibly replace the prevailing work ethic.

The counter-culture ethic waxed in the relatively prosperous era and in the climate of youth and black dissent that prevailed in the late 1960s. But the counter-culture waned in the recession-troubled early years of the 1970s. Yet it persisted as one of the value options available to American youth. The free, uninhibited, hedonistic, emotion-oriented life style of the counter-culture enlisted not only runaways but also the many who stayed home yet adopted the ethic, with modification, in their hedonistic life styles.

PRIVATISM

The least conspicuous of the value options for American adults and youth is privatism. Yet privatism is widespread in America. Indeed, some regard it as the prevalent American pattern of living.

[4] Theodore Roszak, *The Making of a Counter Culture: Reflections on The Technocratic Society and Its Youthful Opposition*, Doubleday, Garden City, N.Y., 1969.

Private is defined by the *American Heritage Dictionary of the English Language* as "secluded from the sight, presence, or intrusion of others; of or confined to one person; personal; not available for public use, control, or participation; belonging to a particular person or persons, as opposed to the public or the government." *Privatism* is a word coined by sociologists to describe a pattern of living characterized by these phrases. Privatism is characterized by absorption with one's self, one's immediate surrounding, one's immediate family, and one's close friends or social circle.

Privatism is, however, also characterized by apathy and indifference toward social institutions, whether governmental or business or union or social service. Persons who live by the privatism ethic do not participate in voluntary social action or in the workings of local, state, or national government. To the extent that they think about and have an attitude toward such activities it is often one of suspicion and hostility. As they see it, social organizations exist to take from them rather than to contribute to their lives. "They" are inefficient and corrupt and out to do them in. Indifference to social institutions does not mean that privatists stay away from occasions attended or watched by large numbers of other people, such as professional football games and movies, popular television programs, or a variety of spectacular events. They attend or watch, but as spectators.

Privatism grows out of some socially healthy values, for instance, love of family and loyalty to friends. It is individualistic, self-reliant, and self-sufficient in nature. At its best, privatism has resulted in the creation of magnificent art products, literary masterpieces, enduring friendships, and lively interaction in social circles. But at its worst, privatism has resulted in narrow selfishness, the ignoring of the needs of other human beings, indifference to social welfare, and callousness toward those who do not belong to the self-limited group. At its worst, it can lead to bigotry, intolerance, indifference, or apathy toward all outside the small magic circle.

Privatism is particularly widespread in America today because of mistrust of such social institutions as government and business. Privatists point to corruption and inefficiency and wash their hands of their own responsibility. As they see it, governments make wars, favor others, and tax them heavily. Business raises its prices, destroys the environment, and exploits them as workers and consumers. All a person can do in response is, like Voltaire's Candide, attempt to cultivate one's own garden.

The youth dissent of the 1960s usually took one of two forms. It usually was represented either by counter-culture life styles or by political activism through demonstrations and other mass means. Both types of dissent involved youth coming together in groups to register their disagreement with the ways of society. Disillusioned with the failure of such action to fundamentally change or reform American society, many young people later turned inward rather than outward. They turned to privatism. Some found their satisfactions through highly personalized, rather than socially reformist, forms of religion. A contemplative procedure, transcendental meditation, was studied and practiced by many. Some turned to the cinema; for instance, attendance at motion pictures increased. Others found their satisfaction in the arts; for instance, shops devoted to a variety of hobbies flourished. Still others, less intellectually oriented, found their satisfactions in drinking with chosen companions or following favorite teams avidly on television. To many, the activities of leaders in government, industry, or the world of temporary celebrities were something to laugh at with Bob Hope, Johnny Carson, or Archie Bunker.

SOCIALLY RESPONSIBLE INDIVIDUALISM

A fourth possible option for contemporary youth and adults is socially responsible individualism. As the phrase implies, this ethic combines individuality with a social orientation. Socially responsible individualists recognize their own uniqueness, follow their own interests, and develop their own personalities. But, simultaneously, they recognize the dependence of human beings upon each other and the need for workable social institutions to improve the total society and to make life better for humankind.

The ethic of the socially responsible individual is based upon the democratic heritage. Democracy has a long history, and over the years its philosophic meaning has changed as democratic forms have evolved. The idea of democracy was originated by the Greeks, who recognized that humankind had a choice with respect to government. People might be governed by a single ruler, a selected group, or a special class of people; or the people might share in the activities of government. For instance, citizens might participate in self-government through being members of the assembly. They might take turns in assuming executive duties. They might serve as jurors and thus pass judgment on the misbehavior of fellow citizens or help resolve conflicts that arose among the citizenry. This form of government, quite different from the aristocracy advocated by philosopher Plato, became known as democracy.

As conceived in the city-state, Athenian Greek democracy had its obvious limitations. For instance, taking turns at governing can work only in a small community. Too, Athenian democracy was limited in scope; it applied only to the minority who were free citizens in a city in which the majority were slaves or noncitizens. Later experimentation with democracy in Italian cities or religious communities was often characterized by similar limitations. Early attempts at democracy frequently succumbed to aristocracies, tyrannies, and elites.

As societies grew larger and more complex after the Middle Ages, nation-states replaced dependence upon the medieval walled cities. If democracy was to be a workable form of government in a large national society, representation of the people had to replace individual participation. Thus, the idea developed of the citizenry taking part in governing through their elected representatives. Whole populations could participate through naming a smaller number of people to act on their behalf.

The idea of representation was used in the busy city of Rome. It expanded during the feudal era when kings, in search of advice, selected representatives from influential groups such as the clergy, nobility, and burghers. But kings early on claimed that they ruled by a supposedly divine right and they appointed representatives out of beneficent generosity. Representation of the people had to be justified by critics of absolute monarchies.

As early as the thirteenth century, King John of England was compelled by the barons to recognize their feudal rights. Later interpretation of the Magna Carta stressed that its vaguely worded provisions also protected the rights of subjects of the kings and the rights of communities. The Magna Carta became a symbol of the supremacy of constitutions over kings and was frequently cited by opponents of the arbitrary power of monarchies.

In the seventeenth century the English philosopher Thomas Hobbes claimed that people had entered into a contract whereby they gave up their original liberty to live in anarchy without government in return for the order and safety provided by the organized state. The English philosopher John Locke maintained that in such a contract the monarch must reflect the will of the people. The French philosopher Jean Jacques Rousseau argued that the general will of the people provided the way of establishing rights and duties, privileges and responsibilities, of all involved in governance. The American statesman Thomas Jefferson wrote with his colleagues certain inalienable natural rights into the Declaration of Independence of the new American nation.

We hold these truths to be self-evident: that all men are created equal, that they are endowed by their Creator with certain unalienable rights; that among these are life, liberty, and the pursuit of happiness. That to secure these rights, governments are instituted among men, deriving their just powers from the consent of the governed; that whenever any form of government becomes destructive of these ends, it is the right of the people to alter or to abolish it, and to institute new government, laying its foundation on such principles, and organizing its powers in such form, as to them shall seem most likely to effect their safety and happiness.

In this way the ideas of a contract involving reciprocal obligations, and of natural rights such as life, liberty, and the pursuit of happiness, were invoked to support the British parliamentary system, the French Revolution, and the American Revolution. Representative government became a hallmark of Western democracy.

Certain aspects of democracy, especially individualism and liberty, were encouraged by frontier conditions in the new United States. Restrictions on voting were reduced over the years as poor people joined propertied people in voting, blacks joined whites, women joined men, and youth at age eighteen joined adults in the right to exercise the voting franchise. However, in an increasingly urban, industrialized America, emphasis on individualism and liberty was modified by new stress on the companion democratic values of working together for common purposes and fostering the common welfare of all the people.

In the twentieth century people animated by the democratic spirit aspired to social, educational, and economic equality as their predecessors had aspired to political democracy two hundred years earlier. Increasingly, democracy became conceived not simply as a governmental form but as a social philosophy applicable to economic, industrial, and educational institutions.

The democratic way of life underlies the current life style of socially responsible individualism. The practitioners of this life style usually attempt to reconcile two aspects of the democratic way of life: the individualistic, libertarian aspect and the social, shared-interest aspect. Consequently, socially responsible individualists see themselves as individual persons free to make decisions, to adopt distinctive patterns that represent individual talents or interests, to agree or disagree with majorities. Simultaneously, socially responsible individualists see themselves as intimately bound up with the lives of others, sharing responsibility for the general welfare, recognizing with John Donne that "no man is an island," attempting according to their lights to improve the surrounding society. Thus the life style combines individuality with deep concern for the lives of others. Socially responsible individualism includes social and political sensitivity and awareness, along with being creative, productive, and unique.

An advantage of socially responsible individualism is that it allows the individual to be a person, going his or her own way, doing his or her own thing occupationally and recreationally. Thus, if individuals receive much of their satisfaction from work, as do practitioners of the work ethic, they can continue these satisfactions. If they gain satisfaction from family or television or recreation, as practitioners of privatism often do, they can continue to be private persons.

Socially responsible individualism has an additional advantage as a life style. It ensures that persons have relationships to other people. In those relationships they attempt to improve life for themselves and others. Thus they are placed squarely within the life-justifying patterns fostered by the great religions of the world. They are also within the mainstream of their predecessors in world history who have attempted to improve the society in which they live. In short, they are living up to their mission as human beings.

A disadvantage of this life style is that the roles may clash. Rather than achieving a balance, such persons may lean heavily in one or the other direction. By leaning heavily in the individualistic direction, these persons' life styles may in actuality be indistinguishable from the life styles of privatism. By leaning heavily in the social responsibility direction, their life styles may depend heavily upon the satisfactions afforded by social service, yet neglect the cultivation of the individual personality. Another possible disadvantage is the frustration that socially responsible persons often encounter in contemporary society. The campaigns for social improvement in which they enlist may not succeed, or may move very slowly, or indeed may prove, in historial retrospect, to be misguided.

Socially responsible individualism was the life style of many young leaders who fought in the American Revolution and founded the new republic. Thomas Jefferson is an outstanding exemplar of the young colonial who combined distinct individualism (his interest in architecture and invention) with social responsibility (his participation in authorship of the Declaration of Independence, his founding of the University of Virginia, and his presidency of the new nation). Yet, like Americans of his time less socially responsible than he, Jefferson's vision was culture-bound; he thought blacks to be naturally inferior and he was a slaveholder.

In modern times, illustrations of socially responsible individualism are provided by many contemporary college and high school students who enlist in campaigns for consumer protection or for preservation of the environment, or who work on behalf of political candidates—while not relinquishing their individualities. Yet in the latter half of the 1970s, the acceptance of social responsibilities by the young diminished in a post-Watergate era marked by apathy, suspicion of government and business, and disillusionment with the effectiveness of social change by whatever means.

ACTIVIST PROTEST

A fifth possible life style for American youth is that of activist protest. During the late 1960s a worldwide phenomenon was apparent. In such nations as France, Germany, Japan, and the United States, a segment of the youth population took to the streets, marching, picketing, praying, and generally protesting policies of their government, economic leaders, and educational institutions. By the early 1970s, the student revolt was over as suddenly as it had begun; the protest of the activists shrunk toward nothingness.

Sociologists have attempted to account for the rapid rise and sudden collapse of activism as a life style. The simplest theory is that many young people became deeply disturbed by the increasing involvement of American military forces in Vietnam. They joined in a vigorous mass protest against the war and, in the United States, against the military draft. This theory holds that when the American forces were withdrawn from Southeast Asia and when the war ground to a halt, the student protests ended.

To put the theory bluntly, it holds that just as businesspeople organized for their vested interests, just as laborers struck for their vested interests, so American young people protested for their vested interests. Their vested interest was in avoiding the life disruption that accompanied being drafted to serve in the jungles of a faraway land. So they defended through their protests their right to live. Critics of the vested interest theory contend that it underestimates the moral idealism of youth and their outrage at what they saw as the senseless killing of Vietnamese people as well as American soldiers in an immoral and illegal war. Critics also point out that the theory does not account for the activism of women who stood no chance of being drafted.

A more complex theory about the youth revolt emphasizes that the seeds of rebellion were long generating and claims that dissent will rise again. According to this view, the youth protest of the late 1960s dates back at least to the civil rights movement of the 1950s, the rise of a New Left under the leadership of Students for a Democratic Society (SDS) in the early sixties, the mistrust of such dominant national leaders as Lyndon B. Johnson and Richard M. Nixon, the protest on the campus of the University of California at Berkeley in 1964, and the revulsion against the assassinations of John Kennedy in 1963 and Martin Luther King and Robert Kennedy in 1968.

Supporters of this view believe that underlying the youth dissent was a long-time smoldering resentment against bureaucratic institutions and corrupt values in a technology obsessed society. The flames broke out in the late sixties. In 1969 they culminated in the high schools; during that year 59 percent of American high school principals and 56 percent of junior high school principals reported protests in 67 percent of city and suburban secondary schools.[5] A high point of college protests was reached in 1970, when there was a nationwide strike on 200 college campuses. The revolt was snuffed out by threats of political repression, by recession in the economy, by exhaustion among the participants, and by a discouraged acceptance by participants of the futility of the struggle. The theory holds that since bureaucracy is still dominant, values still corrupt, and technology still supreme, youth protest will rise again after a temporary lull.

Studies of the young people who are most active in the leadership of the youth protests of the late 1960s indicate that these youths often had parents who themselves were liberal and radical in their beliefs. Rather than rebelling against their parents' values, the young dissidents were attempting to put these values into practice. To the extent that antagonism against parents was involved, it was against the degree to which their parents had attained comfortable, secure positions in a relatively affluent society and

---

[5] "Survey Finds Dissent Moving into Lower Grades," *Education USA*, March 10, 1969, p. 151.

then failed to act upon their humane values. The rebels sometimes saw their parents as suburban sellouts to middle-class comfort and immoral institutions.

The protests of the late 1960s differed from those of earlier radicals, who took a leftist position as to politics. The new student rebels mistrusted government and authority, whereas the Old Left wanted to use central government for social progress. The new dissidents stressed a participatory democracy marked by full participation by all, higher autonomy for the individual, and organization that would readily change and adjust. They did not reject work, as did many of the counter-culture; instead they insisted on meaningful and moral work.

Though the student revolt of the mid-1970s only occasionally sputtered into flame as a protest against rises in tuition or curtailment of admissions, dissent had an effect on American life. Various contemporary movements such as women's liberation, gay liberation, and prison reform movements are part of the heritage of the student activists of the late 1960s.

To the credit of the student activists is a genuine concern about the improvement of society. They recognize that improvement of society does not come about automatically but must be worked for by human beings. Activist protest is usually motivated by a high individual sense of conscience and a belief in values frequently derived from religious traditions and from a belief in the democratic way of life.

Critics of activist protest as a life style object largely to the means used. Some activists do not follow the socially accepted ground rules for bringing about change. They violate laws, as when demonstrations become violent or marchers go beyond reasonable bounds. Some activists, however, respect democratic processes and procedures as they work for democratic goals. Rather than violate the ground rules, they attempt through orderly procedures to modify them.

A disadvantage of intense identification with activist protest as a life style is that one's personal life frequently becomes subordinated to the movement. Zeal for a cause sometimes becomes fanaticism. Some, however, can experience deep satisfaction through the identification of personal living with a social cause for which they crusade.

Like the counter-culture life style, activist protest reached a peak in the late 1960s and then declined sharply. The activists attribute this to repression or threats of repression on the part of wielders of power in American society. What remains of activist protest in the late 1970s usually avoids the earlier excesses of the activists. Although activists such as Jerry Rubin and Abbie Hoffman are seldom heard from today, the more orderly yet still intense activism of Ralph Nader and his associates persists. The Nader protesters, originally concerned primarily with problems of the consumer, have expanded their scope to include a variety of governmental and social issues. Campaigns for the improvement of the environment also continue, typified by the ecological campaign against "the dirty dozen," those members of Congress who most frequently have voted against environmental protective measures. And, during the 1976 presidential election campaign, many citizens markedly increased their participation in campaigns for candidates, thus becoming, at least temporarily, more activist than formerly.

SOCIAL DEVELOPMENTS AFFECTING VALUE OPTIONS

The work ethic, the counter-culture, privatism, socially responsible individualism, and activist protest are prominent among the current life styles open to youth. Which of these options will prosper and which of them will diminish depends heavily now, as in the past, upon social developments that affect the options. This dependence can be illustrated by situations in the American past in which life styles were affected by social developments.

For instance, the early settlers soon encountered the variety of religions brought by other immigrants to the New World. Their religious traditions confronted the ideas of the Enlightenment, marked by libertarian and scientific thought. With the passage of time, a Puritan life style that was once accepted by America's early settlers lost its original hold on Americans.

Similarly, the life style of frontier individualism, which was accepted by generations going west and glorified as an independent way marked by freedom and liberty, did not prove workable in the new industrial civilization. In an urban industrial America, frontier individualism degenerated into ruthless industrial individualism marked by disregard for human welfare. Thus frontier individualism had to be modified by values that took into account the common welfare.

Similarly, a characteristic nineteenth-century view of immigration, that of the melting pot, was modified by the insistence of new Americans upon maintaining aspects of their culture that they found satisfactory. The former American view, advocated as a life style for immigrants, was that the newcomers to America should assimilate, that is, should adopt totally the American customs of the majority, whether they applied to food and clothing or to even more fundamental matters such as religion, ethics, and morality. But resistance to absorption was high. Cultural pluralism prevailed. Increasingly, the majority recognized that the newcomers would keep what they valued from their inherited traditions.

Social developments will undoubtedly affect the current life style options. The social realities sketched in Chapter 2 will certainly affect the workability of the options. Indeed, some social theorists believe that a great transformation in major industrialized nations, such as the United States, is inevitable. For instance, Willis V. Harman points out

four great dilemmas in the industrialized world. The first is the growth dilemma. On the one hand, the industrialized nations, whether capitalist or socialist, need continued economic growth if their economies are to prosper. But on the other hand, they cannot live with the consequences of that growth, such as pollution and energy depletion. A second dilemma is the need for societal control of technology. Yet controls may jeopardize the basic characteristics of a free enterprise system. A third dilemma is that it will cost industrialized nations a great deal to move toward a more equitable distribution of the earth's resources, an expenditure the industrialized nations are reluctant to make. Yet the expectations and demands of the Third World are coming so rapidly that they could only be met by a drastic lowering of the standard of living in the richer nations. A fourth dilemma is that a work role is essential to an individual's development and esteem. Yet the economy seems unable to provide enough satisfactory work opportunities.[6]

Harman believes that these dilemmas cannot be resolved within our present industrial system. He foresees a society dedicated to self-realization and an ecological ethic.

If such a transformation were to come about, the work ethic would necessarily be diminished, for high production and high consumption would no longer be basic life goals. Activist protest would probably be heard in the transition to a new social system. The counter-culture and privatism might prosper in a society that effectively utilized leisure and creativity. But, above all, socially responsible individualism would prosper. A new society of the great transformation would place heavy emphasis upon the responsibility of all to care for the environment, to conserve energy, to overcome urban decay. It would also stress individual self-realization and fully functioning self-actualizing personalities. Improvement of the environment and self-realization of individuals are among the goals of socially responsible individualism.

ROLE AND RESPONSIBILITY OF EDUCATORS

In secondary education, matters related to values arise constantly. Questions of good and bad, right and wrong, are as inescapable in secondary schools as they are in life. For instance, in the study of literature, teachers and students constantly encounter characters in situations that involve moral decisions. Despite the objectivity of the

---

[6] William Van Til, "The Nine Crucial Issues in Secondary Education," *NASSP Bulletin*, May 1976, p. 101.

scientific method, the field of science often involves judgments that are not value-free. Teachers of the social studies help students to think about an array of controversial issues, each of which necessitates value judgments. Questions involving values occur in all the broad fields of the curriculum. Similarly, value consideration enters into guidance of students, disciplinary procedures, decisions in faculty meetings, and the life of the school in general.

What is the secondary school teacher's role in the many matters that involve values? Is it to be a protagonist for one or another of the several options discussed in this chapter? Or is it to be the role of the clarifier of value alternatives who requires students to face the consequences of their value-based decisions? Educators are not in agreement in their answers to these questions.

Some educators believe it is the responsibility of education to foster and encourage the democratic way of life. Such educators say that humankind's long historical experience has led to the conclusion that democratic values are of greatest worth. Therefore, we should teach young people to live by such democratic values as respect for each individual personality, working together for common purposes commonly arrived at, fostering the general welfare, and using intelligence on issues that confront us. Consequently, we should favor those contemporary value options that best reflect democratic values, such as socially responsible individualism. In this interpretation, teachers should discourage the value options that appear to be less reflective of democratic values, such as those of the counter-culture or of privatism. For instance, the student inclined to the counter-culture's doing your own thing or privatism's isolation from others would be reminded, subtly or overtly, of the desirability of working with others, of participating in the common life, of sharing with others.

Those who would openly sponsor democratic values usually agree that a teacher does not teach fixed answers to controversial personal and social problems. They usually hold, for instance, that a teacher does not indoctrinate for the Republican party as opposed to the Democratic party, for international organization as a replacement of national states, for one or another controversial economic or political policy. However, they will contend that, as to values, the teacher must identify with and support broad democratic values. To those who take this view, it is the right and responsibility of the teacher to encourage students to support whatever policies and programs most reflect democratic values. This school of thought says that we cannot be neutral about values.

On the other hand, some educators take the position that, with respect to values, it is not the role of the teacher to favor one pattern or option, whether subtly or overtly. To those who take this viewpoint, the single greatest responsibility of the teacher is to encourage the students to think. Help the students to understand the alternatives, foster situations and discussions in which the students must clarify their value preferences, encourage the students to face the consequences of their choices—in two words, encourage thought—but do not advocate any one position on values, even the attractive democratic model. Clarification rather than imposition is the teacher's obligation. So argue those who support fostering choices among values.

With respect to the several value options discussed in this chapter, the value-clarifying teacher would not urge upon students any particular option despite his or her personal preference. The value clarifier would ask students to consider carefully the options and their consequences. But the clarifier would not urge acceptance of socially responsible individualism rather than the work ethic or any other option.

The value clarifier holds that indoctrination is indoctrination, whether it takes the form of imposing fixed answers to controversial problems or urging particular values on students. The teacher, says this view, should stay neutral as to values, however attractive. The teacher should be loyal only to the use of the method of intelligence. If it is charged that devotion to reflective thought is a value, the value clarifier usually pleads guilty. However, he or she contends that the use of intelligence as the selected key value opens up value consideration rather than closes off free exploration of value possibilities.

Just as you have a choice among the value options as to your life style, you have a choice as to whether you will advocate certain values as a teacher or will attempt to clarify values through encouraging students to apply reflective thought. The decision will not be easy. However, it will heavily influence your teaching.

DISCUSSION

1.   What were the value options of young people of secondary school age in the colonies, in the new nation, and during the nineteenth century before the Western frontier closed?

2.   Why did the range of possible value options increase during the twentieth century?

3.   Which of the many negative developments during the lifetime of today's high school student especially affected you? Which developments especially affected others in your class? Which did not affect you? Are any developments listed of which you were not aware?

4.   Do you find any evidence of cynicism or lack of faith in leaders and institutions among Americans in general? . . . among young Americans in particular?

5.   What are the life styles or value patterns that you believe to be widespread, in addition to the five discussed throughout the chapter? Describe these options fully.

6. Can you demonstrate that the work ethic is deeply rooted in American life and thus a continuing influence on the lives of many young Americans? What contributed to the persistence of this powerful influence?

7. What can be said in support of and in opposition to living by the work ethic as a life style for contemporary young Americans?

8. What is the meaning of counter-culture? What is the origin of this way of looking at the world?

9. What are the similarities among Bohemians, the beat generation, and hippies? Are there differences, too?

10. How has the counter-culture life style influenced young Americans who do not live completely by this life style?

11. What can be said for and against the counter-culture as a life style or value option? Why does the counter-culture way of living wax and wane in American life?

12. What is the meaning of privatism? What are its characteristics?

13. What is the characteristic privatist attitude toward business, government, and social institutions in general?

14. What are the pros and cons of privatism as a life style for contemporary young people?

15. What way of life supplies a basis for socially responsible individualism?

16. Discuss the evolution of the meaning of democracy. Spend sufficient time with other students in clarifying what democracy means to you today.

17. What kinds of emphases in life does socially responsible individualism attempt to reconcile?

18. What are the possible advantages and disadvantages of socially responsible individualism as a life style for secondary school age youth? . . . for Americans as a whole?

19. What are the characteristics of activist protest? How is it similar to and different from other life styles?

20. What has been found to be the characteristic background of the activist?

21. What is to be said for and against activism as a value option?

22. Why does activism, like the counter-culture option, seem to ebb and flow as a life style for young people?

23. Indicate how social developments have affected the value options of young people in the past. Speculate on possible social developments that might affect current life styles of secondary school youth.

24. What is the secondary school teacher's role in the matters that involve values? What is the case for being a protagonist of a value pattern? What is the case for being a clarifier?

25. Should the teacher indoctrinate? Is indoctrination inescapable?

INVOLVEMENT

1. Interview people of your own generation as to the possible value options of young people. Interview a few people of your parents' generation and a few of your grandparents' generation. Are there differences? Can you generalize on them?

2. Check our list of negative developments during the life span of the 1978 high school graduate with students of middle or junior high school age and students of senior high school age. Did some events have more influence on older students than younger students? Can the students think of other events in American life that had a major impact on them? Do you find any evidence of cynicism or lack of faith in leaders and institutions?

3. Select someone whom you know well and try to describe in writing his or her life style. Use many specifics. Compare your essay with that of others.

4. As a class, develop a questionnaire as to life styles and value options. Include questions that would tend to place a person in one or another category according to the individual's response. Try the resultant questionnaire on students not in your class and on secondary school students.

5. Develop, as a class group, a list of additional indications of the influence of the counter-culture life style on secondary school students.

6. Develop a list of works of fiction that deal with life styles. Plan a panel through which individual class members share with the group as a whole the life styles of fictional characters about whom class members have read.

7. From your reading of current newspapers and magazines, select individuals currently in the news who seem to best exemplify one or another life style. Compare your selections with those of others in your class.

8. Set up role-playing situations through which the value options of secondary school age young people can be dramatized.

9. Role play a classroom situation in which a value option is encountered. Role play it with an emphasis on indoctrination by the teacher. Play it again with an emphasis on clarification. Discuss thoroughly similarities and differences in the dramatized situations.

10. Bring the question of indoctrination versus clarification of value options into family discussions or discussions among your friends. Get a variety of viewpoints. Attempt to defend whatever viewpoint you have tentatively adopted for yourself.

FURTHER READINGS

Bressler, Leo, and Marion Bressler, eds. *Youth in American Life: Selected Readings.* Houghton Mifflin, Boston, 1972. Examines the American way of life by analyzing various aspects of the American experience of youth from 1620 to the present.

Casteel, J. Doyle, and Robert J. Stahl. *Value Clarification in the Classroom: A Primer.* Goodyear Publishing, Pacific Palisades, Calif., 1975. An attempt to spell out value clarification through the technique of value sheets. This highly focused book emphasizes what students and teachers do with respect to value clarification and describes materials and activities that contribute to value clarification.

Keniston, Kenneth. *The Uncommitted.* Dell, New York, 1970. A study of alienated youth who have rejected the values and dominant life styles of our society.

Keniston, Kenneth. *Young Radicals: Notes on Committed Youth.* Harcourt Brace Jovanovich, New York, 1968. The best single book on student activists, their backgrounds, struggles, and commitments.

Lerner, Max. *Values in Education.* Phi Delta Kappa, Bloomington, Ind. 1976. An examination by a major scholar of American life, the author of *America as a Civilization,* of the role of values in American schools and society.

National Association of Secondary School Principals. *The Mood of American Youth.* National Association of Secondary School Principals, Reston, Va., 1974. A reappraisal of the attitudes and viewpoints of contemporary youth. An attempt to bring educators up to date on the way young people look at the world in the mid 1970s.

Neff, Walter. *Work and Human Behavior.* Atherton Press, New York, 1968. A readable, comprehensive analysis of the human values of work and the relationship of work to the individual and society. Though Neff writes from a psychiatric background, he postulates needed changes in education and occupational training.

Pawley, Martin. *The Private Future.* Random House, New York, 1974. An analysis of contemporary social trends leading to privatism with an attendant loss of the sense of community. A powerful and frightening description of the consequences of withdrawal from relationships with others.

Reich, Charles A. *The Greening of America,* Random House, New York, 1970. A widely read advocacy of the counter-culture as a life style. The author sees a new "consciousness" emerging that will contribute to "the greening of America."

Roszak, Theodore. *The Making of a Counter Culture: Reflections on the Technocratic Society and Its Youthful Opposition.* Doubleday, Garden City, N.Y., 1969. A sympathetic historian describes the background and development of the counter-culture movement.

Terkel, Studs. *Working.* Pantheon, New York, 1974. To quote from the subtitle: "People Talk About What They Do All Day and How They Feel About Doing It." The mystique, boredom, and satisfactions of work described by those who work.

Work in America. Report of a special task force to the Secretary of the U.S. Department of Health, Education and Welfare, Washington D.C., 1973. A report on education and the world of work in a society in transition. Excellent overview.

Yankelovich, Daniel. *The New Morality: A Profile of American Youth in the 70's.* McGraw-Hill, New York, 1974. A research project utilizing survey data to describe trends in values and attitudes, to compare the views of youth who attend college and those who do not, and to provide profiles of special groups in the youth population.

4.

Characteristics
of Young
People

In the United States, the period of secondary education is coterminous with the period in the life span
that psychologists have termed adolescence. Adolescence has been defined in biological terms as the time
between puberty (the stage at which the individual
becomes physiologically capable of sexual reproduction) at twelve or thirteen years of age and full physical adulthood at the age of seventeen or eighteen.
Recent research indicates that today puberty arrives
even earlier than age twelve or thirteen. Since the
characteristic sixth grader in a middle school is eleven
or twelve and the characteristic high school senior is
seventeen or eighteen, secondary education and
adolescence occupy approximately the same span.

To teach people effectively, one must know something of their characteristics. Thus the secondary
school teacher should understand adolescence, the
life stage of young people of secondary school age. A
major task of the teacher is to meet the needs of the
learner. Obviously, if the teacher is to meet the
learner's needs he or she must understand the
learner's characteristics.

Consequently, this chapter on the characteristics of
young people deals with adolescence, stressing
similarities among adolescents as reported by students of adolescent psychology. But differences are
important too. The chapter then considers sex roles of
young people and social-class factors influencing
their characteristics. Their experiences stemming
from their multicultural backgrounds are described;
to illustrate, the growing-up experiences of blacks,
Mexican-Americans, and "new ethnics" from European backgrounds are selected from among the many
possibilities. The chapter concludes with the characteristics of young people who deviate from the norm
through delinquency, dropping out, or drug abuse.

When a person mentions adolescence, listeners often react predictably and think immediately of adolescence as a stormy, tumultuous period marked by rebellion, conflict with parents, irrationality, irresponsibility, strange clothes and behavior and speech, and storm and stress. Though he doesn't know it, the man in the street owes this picture in his head to G. Stanley Hall,[1] who pioneered the concept of adolescence, and whose two-volume, 1,375-page book *Adolescence* (first published in 1904) popularized the storm and stress interpretation of postpuberty.

However, many psychologists today are skeptical of the interpretation of adolescence as a period in which the turmoil of storm and stress is necessarily biologically built into the individual's development. Indeed, Albert Bandura regards it as a myth not supported by his own studies of middle-class families of adolescent boys.[2]

Contemporary psychologists, such as Robert E. Grinder, believe that the cultural influences of the times in which the adolescent lives are more important in an adolescent's development than G. Stanley Hall thought.[3] In other words, modern psychologists point out that a student of adolescence must also take into account such cultural influences as the family, social-class factors, the values of the surrounding society, and the nature of the times in which the individual comes to adolescence. Studies of adolescence should not be devoted to research on physiological functions alone, although biological aspects must also be considered.

Until we have more evidence, it's sensible to assume that the adolescent period has the potentiality for problems and stresses for the young person, but that personal and cultural circumstances can either create such pressures or reduce them. Whatever the sources, the behavior of adolescents is important to the secondary school educator. Yet, despite the plausibility of generalizations, an educator must keep in mind the inescapable fact that people are individuals and will not always behave in accordance with the generalizations.

COMMON ELEMENTS

With these warnings in mind, let us consider some of the insights of psychologists and sociologists into the behavior of American adolescents as a whole. In broad terms, adolescence is a time of many changes. On the one hand, the adolescent wants new emotional experiences and looks for new understandings, but at the same time tries to

---

[1] G. Stanley Hall, *Adolescence,* 2 vols., D. Appleton, New York, 1925.
[2] Albert Bandura, "The Stormy Decade: Fact or Fiction?" *Psychology in the Schools* 1, (July 1964), 224–231.
[3] Robert E. Grinder and Charles E. Strickland, "G. *Stanley Hall and the Social Significance of Adolescence,"* *Teachers College Record* 64 (February 1963), pp. 390–399.

defend against possible undesirable consequences of new experiences and understandings. The adolescent has hopes and ideals and longings and passions, although older people often do not regard these as of high importance. It is little wonder that the emotions of the adolescent are often mixed.

Parents and family often seem to the adolescent to unnecessarily restrict the young person's freedom. The adolescent wants to reach out beyond the home. In adolescence, friendships can be intense and attachments to others of similar ages strong. The adolescent is often idealistic, hoping to reform undesirable conditions and to achieve significant things. The young person, limited in experience, tries to make up his or her mind based on the behavior of specific individuals encountered in person or through reading or television viewing. The adolescent will often overgeneralize from a few cases.

Psychologists agree that the primary concern of adolescence is developing and making sure of some relatively stable picture of one's self. The individual asks: "Who am I? What am I? Where am I going? What should I do with my life?" The individual has to test his or her picture of himself or herself against others. So the adolescent has to learn to relate to others, with all of the difficulties that involves.

In his widely read textbook, *The Psychology of Adolescence*, John E. Horrocks describes six major points of reference from which one may view adolescent growth and development.

1. Adolescence is a period when the "individual becomes increasingly aware of self." Adolescents test themselves against reality. In time, they achieve greater self-stabilization, developing individual self-concepts and concepts of others. They learn the roles that are most likely to fit these concepts.

2. Adolescents seek status. They try to be emancipated from submissive acceptance of the authority of their parents. Consequently, there is often a struggle against adults. Adolescents particularly struggle against relationships that subordinate them because they are young, inexperienced, and unskilled. They aspire to be economically independent and explore possible vocational interests in the process.

3. Group relationships become highly important to adolescents. They want very much to be recognized by people of their own age. They need to have status. Consequently, they often want to conform to the ways of people of their own generation. Their interest in sex grows and their emotions and activities become correspondingly complex and conflicting.

4. Meanwhile, adolescents are developing and growing physically. Their bodies are changing and with this, their motor patterns. Adolescents have to revise their former images of their bodies. During adolescence, individuals attain physical maturity.

5. Simultaneously, intellectual capacities expand and develop. In a school-centered society such as ours, adolescents meet academic and intellectual requirements. They are often urged to learn things for future use, but they often see no real function for the skills and concepts urged upon them. They try to understand their surrounding environment in terms of the experiences and knowledge they encounter.

6. Adolescents develop values and appraise them. They search for values that a person might live by. They try to harmonize these ideals with their own pictures of themselves. They often find conflicts between their ideals and what seem to them to be reality.

As Horrocks points out, adolescents are handicapped in that they frequently face situations for which they are unprepared due to inexperience. Adults often ask them to accept patterns of behavior although they are not emotionally or socially ready to do so. They find that important people in their lives, such as parents or teachers or peers, hold to differing and sometimes opposite values. Meanwhile, they have no status upon which they can fall back. Many demands are made on them. They encounter taboos and restrictions. Their frustrations in such circumstances may take the form of aggression or withdrawal.[4]

Robert E. Grinder in another widely read book, *Adolescence,* emphasizes the importance of society with which the individual adolescent must come to terms. Society expects adolescents to learn to participate effectively in its workings. It expects them to develop relationships so that they become competent members of society. So people are continually evaluating, directing, and prescribing for adolescents. Youth always has to take into account the expectations of others as they develop their own competencies and arrive at their self-concepts. The significant people in their lives usually try to "adjust" adolescents.

Grinder regards the life-adjustment approach of many educators and psychologists as

anachronistic in a society where concepts of adulthood, maturity and sociocultural status quo may be incompatible or nonfunctional. Modern societies are unstable, structural changes occur unpredictably, many interpersonal relationships are only temporarily expedient, and adults of different persuasions may be equally effective as citizens. Each generation of adolescents, both individually and collectively, must consider which aspects of society, and which standards of adulthood, should be reaffirmed and which should be challenged.[5]

Edgar Z. Friedenberg also believes that adolescents should reaffirm or challenge aspects of society and standards of adulthood. In *The Vanishing*

[4] John E. Horrocks, *The Psychology of Adolescence,* 4th ed., Houghton Mifflin, Boston, 1976, pp. 4–5.
[5] Robert E. Grinder, *Adolescence,* John Wiley, New York, 1973, p. 3.

Adolescent, Friedenberg points out that if adolescents are to learn who they really are, what they feel, and if they are to achieve humane relationships with others, they must learn to question their culture.[6] Erik Erikson's *The Challenge of Youth* suggested that youth must test extremes before firm decision making.[7] These extremes may represent rebellion and even delinquent or self-destructive tendencies. Adults can help by sanctioning and respecting a moratorium or delay period in adolescence while adolescents test themselves before reaching a commitment. What is important to Erikson is that there be a formation of the individual's identity in adolescence rather than prolonged identity confusion in the young individual.

But identity formation and the avoidance of prolonged identity confusion is hard for adolescents to achieve in a society marked by sharp inconsistencies and even hypocrisy. Perceptive adolescents often recognize that adults do not always practice what they preach. Frequently, adults exhort young people about desirable ideals and yet practice in their own daily living the exact opposite of what they advocate.

Recognizing the importance of the psychological self and the social society, Kenneth Keniston, writing primarily of late adolescence and early adulthood, says that

perhaps the central issue during youth is the *tension between self and society.* In adolescence, young men and women tend to accept their society's definitions of them as rebels, truants, conformists, athletes, or achievers. But in youth, the relationship between socially assigned labels and the "real self" becomes more problematic and constitutes a focus of central concern. The awareness of actual or potential conflict, disparity, lack of congruence between what one is (one's identity, values, integrity) and the resources and demands of the existing society increases. The adolescent is struggling to define who he is; the youth begins to sense who he is and thus to recognize the possibility of conflict and disparity between his emerging selfhood and his social order."[8]

Consequently, Keniston reports an ambivalence toward both self and society on the part of young people. A central problem of youth is how self and society can be made more congruent. In the attempt to reconcile the self

---

[6] Edgar Z. Friedenberg, *The Vanishing Adolescent,* Beacon Press, Boston, 1959.
[7] Erik Erikson, ed., *The Challenge of Youth,* Anchor, New York, 1965, p.4.
[8] Kenneth Keniston, "Prologue: Youth as a Stage of Life," in *Youth,* eds. Robert J. Havighurst and Phillip H. Dreyer, The Seventy-fourth Yearbook of the National Society for the Study of Education, University of Chicago Press, Chicago, 1975, p. 9. A term frequently used to describe secondary school students is *youth.* The word has been variously defined, but today it refers to people from age fifteen through twenty-four, with the added qualification "more or less." So it covers only part of the secondary education age range and continues beyond the customary age span for secondary education into adulthood. *Youth,* when used in this chapter, will be applied only to the ninth through twelfth grade students in high school rather than to the typical middle or junior high school student.

and the world, young persons probe and venture and foray. Sometimes they feel estranged and sometimes they feel able to change or achieve things. They may try to break out of their established prescribed roles. They may value movement rather than staying put. They may see adults as people who are static and are not fully "alive." They may find sanctuary in solidarity with other youths in subcultural groups. They may join others and identify with them, in effect sharing their identities.

Many common elements in the lives of adolescents are readily apparent. For instance, they include the struggle for emancipation from great dependency upon parents. They involve the establishment of personal and sexual identity. They include the development of a personal, moral, and ethical code. They also involve deciding on an individual career and life style.

DIFFERENCES TOO

In addition to common elements among adolescents differences are also obvious. To cite one clearcut example, there are differences among young, middle, and older adolescents. Adolescence is made up of a series of stages. They influence, for instance, affectionate relationships with others. During early adolescence, the age range from twelve to fifteen, young people usually move from dependence upon the family to closer relationships with members of the peer group. Young persons who are in a middle stage of adolescence move into new relationships with individuals of the opposite sex. In late adolescence, individuals move toward integrating themselves into the adult society; as they do, they develop further the capacity to care for and love others.

SEX ROLES IN ADOLESCENCE

Differences in the area of sex roles in adolescence have long been taken for granted. Yet, in the 1970s, many of these long-assumed differentiations are rapidly disappearing. The traditional sex roles of men and women, and with them the traditional roles of boys and girls in American society, are experiencing notable changes.

The traditional pattern in the development of adolescence in American life was marked by a split along sex lines. Boys went one way toward their roles as adult men and girls took another path to their roles as adult women. Specifically, the boy was called upon to make vocational choices and to prepare for work. Adolescence for him was a time to try to tie preferences, talents, and experiences into whatever vocational roles were opened to him by his surrounding society. Once having established some identity through the world of work, the boy then moved toward exploring deeper relationships with girls, learning to give and receive love, and eventually marrying.

On the other hand, the traditional role for the girl in adolescence was closely tied to interpersonal relationships. Her role was to become a wife and mother. Traditionally, entrance into vocations was not a primary expectation for a girl. True, she might work briefly before marriage or might return to work following childbearing and the rearing of children. But earning a family's living was the responsibility of a husband-to-be. In the traditional system, the girl was to establish her identity through her relationships with her husband and her children. Even if a woman did work, it was primarily to help her family achieve its goals rather than to prove herself. Thus, as Elizabeth Douvan has pointed out:

In the traditional system, . . . development from adolescence on looked very different in males and females. The concerns, interests, and values of the sex groups were demonstrably different, with males focusing on individual achievement and work preparation and females on social relationships, social leadership, preparation for marriage, and family roles.[9]

But a number of changes have taken place that have affected the roles of women and that are increasingly affecting, in addition, the roles of men. One change had its beginnings in the nineteenth century and continues uninterruptedly today. To put it simply, women are now being educated; the former male monopoly of the eighteenth century has been broken. Just about the same number of girls graduate from high school today as do boys. True, more males go to college than do females, but the rise of the percentage of women registrants in colleges is sharp. With their increased education, many young women have decided that traditional homemaking is not enough for them. The isolation that comes with raising young children was to many young women too limiting. Many women wanted more opportunities to use their minds and to develop skills and interests cultivated by their education. Thus the education of woman became a force in breaking down the traditional sex roles.

Effective birth control technology, such as the pill, came on the scene in the mid-twentieth century. A woman could choose whether or not she wanted to become a mother. In the past, a woman could hardly avoid motherhood and still be considered a complete person by society. In fact, if she did not become a mother, she was expected by society to at least play a maternal role, such as that of a teacher or a nurse. Today, given the choice, some young women decide to have no children even if they plan to marry.

---

[9] Elizabeth Douvan, "Sex Differences in the Opportunities, Demands, and Developments of Youth," in Havighurst and Dreyer, *Youth*, p. 29.

Although the majority of women follow the more usual goals by marrying and having children, or by combining motherhood and a career, the traditional role does not have the full sway that it had in the period before the development of effective birth control technology.

In the 1970s still another major contributor to the reduction of differentiation in sex roles in adulthood, and thus in the preparatory adolescent patterns, has been the contemporary women's movement. Women's liberation has struck a responsive chord in many women. Some older reform-minded women have tended to stress changes in the laws, such as the Equal Rights Amendment, but many of the younger women have also challenged the present division of home and occupational responsibilities. They have called for greater sharing and coresponsibility rather than separate roles. They have advocated sharing household responsibilities, baby care, and economic support. To many, being the key person in family interpersonal relationships was no longer a sufficient destiny.

The breakdown of the traditional sex differentiations is having a substantial effect upon the lives of adolescents. The traditional assumptions still exist, but now many adolescent girls are being encouraged to achieve the same kinds of individual vocational and career goals long associated with boys. Individual development rather than future maternal relationships is seen as of highest importance. Since this has been a long time coming, many girls in adolescence are readily adapting to the new situation.

The changes in traditional sex roles for the girl also have sharp implications for the boy. Adaptation to these changes is often difficult. The older expectation of the adolescent boy stressed ruggedness, toughness, control of emotions, and similar attitudes related to what had been conceived to be a masculine role. Today the boy is called upon to suppress or overcome some of these characteristics and is asked to become ready to share formerly female household tasks, such as caring for babies, and to express emotional warmth toward others. The shift away from the earlier masculine ideal may require adjustment on the part of adolescent boys, especially working-class youth.

Meanwhile the debate goes on among scholars as to whether differences in sex roles are heavily biological or whether they are largely social. Some hold that the male is "built" for strength, achievement, and masculine identification, and that the girl is "built" for dependence, homemaking, and female identification. Those who hold to the social interpretation stress that many of these assumptions are based not on nature of the sexes but the way we rear children and adolescents. They believe that the more American society moves away from traditional role differentiation, the more the supposed biological differences will diminish. Career differences will disappear; preferences for certain school subjects will become more equal; aptitudes will become more equivalent; responses of adolescents of both sexes will grow more alike (see Figure 4.1).

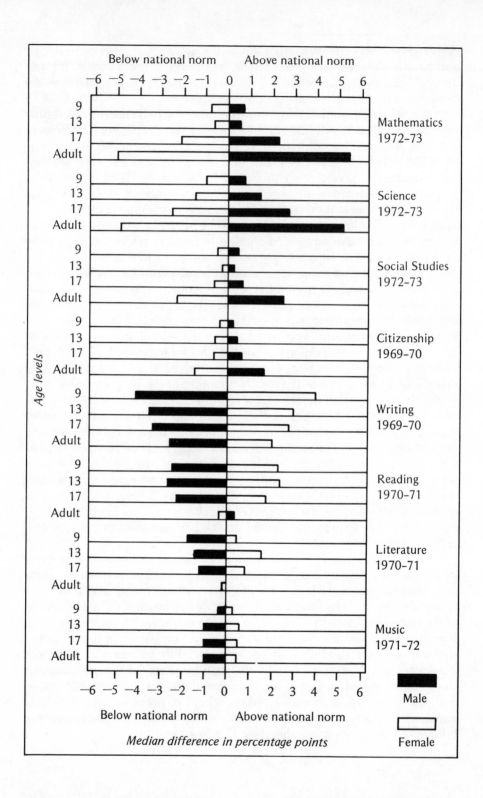

Though the argument about nature versus nurture goes on with respect to biological versus social influences on sex roles in adolescence, an additional dimension as to dissimilarities in adolescence is clearly recognizable as sociological. Adolescent behavior patterns are clearly influenced by social-class factors. Dissimilarities in adolescents stem partly from social-class experiences that have characterized their varying backgrounds.

In their efforts to describe social classes in America, sociologists have studied a variety of American communities. For instance, W. Lloyd Warner studied Morris, Illinois, to which he gave the pseudonym of Jonesville, and Newburyport, Massachusetts, which he called Yankee City.[10] August B. Hollingshead also used Morris, Illinois, as his laboratory; he called the community Elmtown in his report on the experiences of young people influenced by social-class factors.[11] Celia Stendler studied a working-class community that she called Brasstown.[12] A black scholar of social class, Allison Davis, reported on a southern community he called Deep South.[13] Robert J. Havighurst and associates described River City, along the Mississippi River.[14] Arthur Vidich and Joseph Bensman reported on the life of Springdale, a small town.[15] Herbert Gans studied a new housing development for his account of the life of Levittowners.[16] Patricia C. Sexton reported inequalities of opportunities in Big City in the Middle West,[17] and

---

[10] W. Lloyd Warner and Leo Srole, *The Social Systems of American Ethnic Groups*, Yale University Press, New Haven, 1945; W. Lloyd Warner and Paul S. Lunt, *The Status Systems of a Modern Community*, Yale University Press, New Haven, 1942; W. Lloyd Warner, *Democracy in Jonesville: A Study in Quality and Inequality*, Harper Brothers, New York, 1949.

[11] August B. Hollingshead, *Elmtown's Youth: The Impact of Social Classes on Adolescents*, John Wiley, New York, 1949.

[12] Celia Stendler, *Children of Brasstown: A Study of Their Awareness of the Symbols of Social Class*, doctoral thesis, Columbia University; published as a University of Illinois Bulletin, vol. 46, no. 59, 1949.

[13] Allison Davis, *Deep South*, University of Chicago Press, Chicago, 1941.

[14] Robert J. Havighurst, Paul Hoover Bowman, Gordon P. Liddle, Charles V. Matthews, and James V. Pierce, *Growing Up in River City*, John Wiley, New York, 1962.

[15] Arthur Vidich and Joseph Bensman, *Small Town in Mass Society*, Princeton University Press, Princeton, 1958.

[16] Herbert Gans, *Levittowners: Ways of Life and Politics in a New Suburban Community*, Pantheon, New York, 1967.

[17] Patricia C. Sexton, *Education and Income*, Viking Press, New York, 1961.

FIGURE 4.1 *Achievement in Subject Areas.*

[a] A major source of reliable information on a nationwide basis is the data collected, analyzed, and reported by the National Assessment of Educational Progress (NAEP), which reports on the knowledge, skills, understandings, and attitudes of Americans in four age groups: 9, 13, 17, and 26–35.

SOURCE: *The Condition of Education*, U.S. Government Printing Office, Washington, D.C., 1976, p. 43.

with Brendan Sexton, described the values of members of the working class in *Blue Collars and Hard-Hats.* [18]

Such social-class studies use income, occupation, place of residence, quality of housing, education, and other factors in determining an individual's social class. The resulting categories sometimes run as high as nine or as low as two. One useful division frequently used by sociologists is a sixfold category that takes the three standard groupings of upper, middle, and lower and then divides each into two divisions. Thus the upper upper class is assumed to be made up of long-established, influential, and prosperous families. The lower upper class consists of families who may be equally prosperous but who have not been as prestigious or as long established. The upper middle class is made up of managerial and professional families who live in comfortable homes and who are often active in the community. The lower middle class consists of families who earn their living from white-collar jobs and who live in smaller houses and in ordinary neighborhoods. The upper lower class is made up of working class families whose wage earners usually work with their hands and whose houses are small and clean but not in the best neighborhoods. The lower lower class are the people who, justly or unjustly, are condemned by society as shiftless and careless and who live in badly kept, deteriorating housing.

Such studies necessarily include insights on adolescents. They demonstrate that the experiences of young people differ as they grow up within families in the various social classes. Consider, for instance, the differing experiences of adolescents in the six-class division described above. Upper upper adolescents from the long-established, prestigious families not only have the benefits stemming from being well fed, housed, and clad, but are also carefully trained for influential roles in life through clubs, private schools, and travel. They are taught the currently popular social skills, whether they be dancing, tennis, or etiquette, through tutors and special instruction. Their families give considerable forethought to the colleges that their children will attend; indeed, some babies are enrolled at particular prep schools or colleges at birth (see Figure 4.2). Upper upper adolescents are taught that they have a secure and privileged place in American society. Precedents and assurance surround them. Their quest for identity

---

[18] Patricia C. Sexton and Brendan Sexton, *Blue Collars and Hard-Hats*, Random House, New York, 1971.

FIGURE 4.2 *College Plans of High School Seniors. Educational plans of high school seniors are closely related to family income level.*

SOURCE: *The Condition of Education*, U.S. Government Printing Office, Washington, D.C., 1976, p. 77.

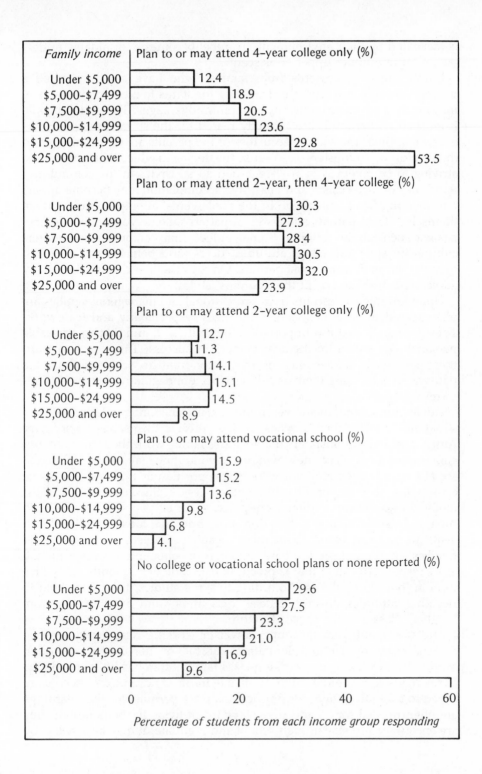

Family income	Plan to or may attend 4-year college only (%)

Under $5,000 — 12.4
$5,000-$7,499 — 18.9
$7,500-$9,999 — 20.5
$10,000-$14,999 — 23.6
$15,000-$24,999 — 29.8
$25,000 and over — 53.5

Plan to or may attend 2-year, then 4-year college (%)

Under $5,000 — 30.3
$5,000-$7,499 — 27.3
$7,500-$9,999 — 28.4
$10,000-$14,999 — 30.5
$15,000-$24,999 — 32.0
$25,000 and over — 23.9

Plan to or may attend 2-year college only (%)

Under $5,000 — 12.7
$5,000-$7,499 — 11.3
$7,500-$9,999 — 14.1
$10,000-$14,999 — 15.1
$15,000-$24,999 — 14.5
$25,000 and over — 8.9

Plan to or may attend vocational school (%)

Under $5,000 — 15.9
$5,000-$7,499 — 15.2
$7,500-$9,999 — 13.6
$10,000-$14,999 — 9.8
$15,000-$24,999 — 6.8
$25,000 and over — 4.1

No college or vocational school plans or none reported (%)

Under $5,000 — 29.6
$5,000-$7,499 — 27.5
$7,500-$9,999 — 23.3
$10,000-$14,999 — 21.0
$15,000-$24,999 — 16.9
$25,000 and over — 9.6

0   20   40   60

Percentage of students from each income group responding

is facilitated by their environment. To rebel becomes a formidable under-taking for any upper upper adolescent.

Lower upper adolescents from families who have newly acquired a degree of wealth and who are struggling for status to accompany the new income are also characterized by economic advantages. The young people from such backgrounds are carefully reared for the social struggle. How-ever, sometimes the social insecurities of the parents are communicated to their children. Youngsters often sense the degree to which their parents are striving to be accepted in well-regarded social circles in the community. Attributes of materialism and obsessive accumulation may become appar-ent to young family members. In the adolescents' attempt to differentiate themselves from parents and parents' patterns, some young people rebel against such family patterns. Some, indeed, may embrace the counter-culture life style and adopt attitudes, dress, and behavior calculated to disturb their more conformist parents. On the other hand, of course, many adolescents learn to accept their parents' styles.

Upper middle adolescents from professional and managerial families are often reared in an atmosphere that prizes respectability and teamwork. They are taught that it is important to be well liked, and that an agreeable personality is useful for the achievement of success. They too may learn these lessons in adolescence or they may come to scorn parental life patterns, condemning them as self-serving, unimaginative, or overly con-formist.

Adolescents from the lower middle class encounter relatively fewer social ambitions in their families, which perceive themselves as ordinary Americans. In an atmosphere that includes family work about the yard and garage, and doing all of one's own housework, they may be less inclined to social striving. They may not value social position as highly as the social classes described earlier. Possibly they are less inclined to regard upward mobility as a desirable course. They may mistrust people who appear to them to be social climbers. This does not imply that lower middle adoles-cents are not concerned about their vocations. Indeed, along with their families, they often see the basic function of schooling as prevocational. They respect education that is practical; *theoretical* is frequently a negative term in their vocabularies. According to some studies, they often hold to negative attitudes toward rebels, dissenters, and intellectuals from "higher" classes in the social structure.

The adolescent from the upper lower or working-class family may be circumscribed by cultural limitations of his or her home. Although scholarships do exist, the working-class family often has little knowledge of the roads to higher education available for its children. Adolescents are urged to take jobs whenever physical maturity permits, for their earnings are often needed for an adequate standard of living in the family. If they are encouraged to stay in high school and graduate, it may be less for the

FIGURE 4.3 *Occupations of Young Males, by Educational Attainment.   The percentages of young males in white-collar jobs increases for groups with higher educational attainment.*

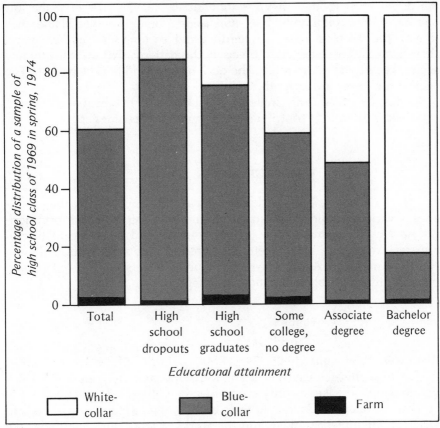

SOURCE: *The Condition of Education,* U.S. Government Printing Office, Washington, D.C., 1976, p. 114.

abstract benefits of an education and more for vocational reasons (see Figure 4.3); high school graduation in our society is frequently assumed to be a dividing line between "good" or "poor" jobs. Cultural limitations of the homes of working-class adolescents may also include limited family conversation, an overuse of television, and a lack of travel or vacation opportunities. Toughness, realism, autonomy, even fatalism may be valued.

Of all the adolescents' experiences, growing up in the lower lower class home is the most difficult. As a member of a family regarded with little respect in society, the adolescent is seen this way too by others in the community. Sometimes these include policemen and workers for social agencies and, unfortunately, teachers who rely too heavily on gossip or anecdotal records. So lower lower adolescents are regarded with substantial doubt even though they, as individuals, may not deserve the low opinion of their community. But, quite aside from undeserved blame, they face another problem—they can hardly avoid learning some of the ways of their families. These are often precisely the patterns that the surrounding society regards as undesirable. The deck of cards in life is heavily stacked against the lower lower youth.

So despite adolescent similarities pointed out by the psychologists, social-class groupings contribute to dissimilar adolescent experiences.

ETHNIC GROUPS

Class backgrounds also influence heavily the experience of various ethnic groups in the culturally pluralistic mosaic of American society. The illustrations we offer are limited by space to blacks, Mexican-Americans, and the ethnics of recent European origin, although Native Americans, Asian-Americans, Puerto Ricans, and WASPs could provide other possible illustrations (see Figure 4.4).

BLACKS

In 1977, of an American population of 216,123,000,[19] there were approximately 25,379,000 blacks. In the adolescent age range, twelve to eighteen inclusive, there were approximately 4,071,000 black young people.[20] Like majority group members, these adolescents went to schools, developed relations to their friends, interacted with parents and teachers, attempted to move into the world of work, and had their own fashions, speech patterns, and modes of behavior. But the specific nature of their adolescent experiences was different from that of white adolescents. For one thing, blacks still live largely among blacks, despite campaigns for integration. Second, blacks are usually poorer than whites, despite campaigns for equal economic opportunity (see Table 4.1). So black adolescents are influenced as they grow up both by their black experience and by their social class status.

There is a higher proportion of economically poor black youths than white youths, and the former usually come into the job market earlier than

---

[19] U.S. Bureau of the Census, U.S. Department of Commerce, *Population Estimates and Projections*, Series P-25, No. 648, U.S. Government Printing Office, Washington, D.C., March 1977.
[20] U.S. Bureau of the Census, U.S. Department of Commerce, "Projections of the Population of the United States: 1975 to 2050," *Current Population Reports*, Series P-25, No. 601, U.S. Government Printing Office, Washington, D.C., 1975, pp. 39, 43.

FIGURE 4.4 *A Musical Interest.* *One young person in the American culturally pluralistic mosaic.*

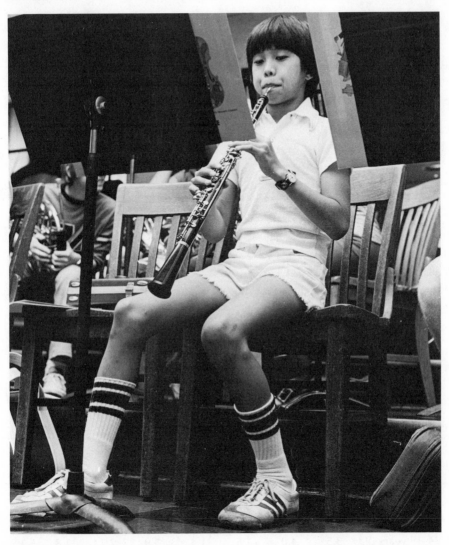

the latter. Similarly, black youths usually drop out of school earlier (see Table 4.2).

Despite desegregation of many American schools, black young people have been largely separated from whites through residential patterns and persistent societal segregation practices, customs and manipulations. They enter the job market highly aware of a historical tradition of discrimination and restriction and often find that they are still among those who are left

TABLE 4.1 *Median income in 1973 of families, by sex and race of head and place of residence, 1974*

SEX OF FAMILY HEAD	MEDIAN FAMILY INCOME		
	Central cities	Suburban rings	Nonmetropolitan areas
All families			
Total	$11,343	$14,007	$10,327
White	12,332	14,214	10,712
Black	7,517	9,019	5,771
Families with male head			
Total	12,759	14,717	10,870
White	13,224	14,847	11,176
Black	10,641	11,025	6,641
Families with female head			
Total	5,357	7,069	5,247
White	6,490	7,429	5,632
Black	4,176	4,829	3,780

SOURCE: U.S. Department of Commerce, Bureau of the Census, *Current Population Reports,* series P-23, no. 55, "Social and Economic Characteristics of the Metropolitan and Nonmetropolitan Population: 1974 and 1970," U.S. Government Printing Office, Washington, D.C., 1975, p. 15.

TABLE 4.2 *Percentage of high school dropouts among persons 14–24 years old, by race and sex, 1967 and 1974*

	1967				1974			
	Black		White		Black		White	
AGE	*Male*	*Female*	*Male*	*Female*	*Male*	*Female*	*Male*	*Female*
1	2	3	4	5	6	7	8	9
Total, 14 to 24 years old	23.9	21.8	11.6	13.1	16.3	18.1	11.0	11.0
14–15 years old	3.5	4.0	1.5	1.4	3.9	2.1	1.8	1.9
16–17 years old	11.7	14.6	7.0	9.4	8.3	12.6	9.4	9.1
18–19 years old	30.6	22.0	15.4	16.3	26.9	20.2	17.4	13.9
20–24 years old	42.6	26.1	18.8	19.0	23.6	27.7	13.6	14.5

NOTE: Dropouts are persons who are not enrolled in school and who are not high school graduates.
SOURCES: U.S. Department of Commerce, Bureau of the Census, *Current Population Reports,* series P-23, no. 46, and series P-20, no. 278.
From W. Vance Grant and C. George Lind, *Digest of Educational Statistics,* 1975 ed., National Center for Education Statistics, U.S. Department of Health, Education, and Welfare, U.S. Government Printing Office, Washington, D.C., 1976, p. 59.

out. Proportionately, they are more frequently unemployed than are whites. This is not to deny that many blacks are improving their social-class status. But it is to say that most blacks today live out their lives as low-income people. Once a rural people, today blacks predominantly live in the cities. Many whites leave the central cities for the suburbs and blacks move into leftover deteriorating housing.

The black adolescent in the ghetto community is not only segregated from white adolescents; he or she is also separated from the black middle class and its aspirations since, as the black middle class moves up, it attempts to leave the ghetto. So the people whom ghetto adolescents emulate may include the people who have "made it big" in the ghetto, sometimes through illegal activities that seem to the young people bold and daring. To achieve a socially healthy identity while handicapped by the total surrounding is a difficult task for black adolescents in the ghetto. Although black adolescents of the middle classes encounter more constructive role models, even they have to relate their ambitions and goals to what white society currently sanctions. Whatever the black adolescent's class background, he or she encounters persistent institutional racism.

During recent decades, another broad difference between black and white adolescents has been apparent. The pacesetters among black youth have been active in movements for civil rights and blackness; they have not been identified with the counter-culture movement.

Black youth have often been involved in the civil rights movement; in the 1950s and 1960s, their concern was largely for equal rights and the achievement of integration. Indeed, some historians date the beginning of the contemporary civil rights movement to the black college students from North Carolina who sat at a lunch counter at a Woolworth store, asked for service, and would not move when they were refused it. Black young people have participated in boycotts, sit-ins, pray-ins, freedom rides, picketing, rallies, and voter registration drives. They have marched with A. Phillip Randolph, Martin Luther King, and Roy Wilkins. They have supported movements sponsored by the National Association for the Advancement of Colored People (NAACP), the Southern Christian Leadership Conference (SCLC), the Congress of Racial Equality (CORE), and the Student Non-Violent Coordinating Committee (SNCC).

Unfortunately, though understandably, some black young people have been participants in the urban rioting that characterized some of the summers of the 1960s and the racial disturbances that followed the tragic assassination of Martin Luther King. Most of the looting and burning that was the manifestation of anger and rebellion was done by young ghetto residents; black leaders of all ages who had worked for desegregation tried valiantly to stem the violence.

But a mood of disillusionment with civil rights struggles for desegregation and integration shifted youthful allegiances to black power, awareness, and identity. In the late 1960s and into the 1970s, many leaders among black adolescents and youth have been active in emphasizing blackness. They have advocated solidarity among blacks through campus unions, high school clubs, black studies programs, rap sessions, and black sororities and fraternities. They have worn their symbols of togetherness such as dashikis, Afros, and distinctive clothes styles. They have talked together of the black experience and the black heritage and they have supported black novels, plays, art creations, and soul food. Their proud slogan continues to be "Black is beautiful."

In recent years, many black adolescents have segregated themselves from whites. In the face of persistent racism, they have decided to go it on their own. Despite the growing number of black officials, typified by recent black mayors of Newark, Cleveland, Atlanta, Detroit, and other cities, black youth is somewhat skeptical of change through the political process. Black youth, eighteen to twenty-four, voted less frequently in the 1972 national election than did blacks over twenty-four.

Many young blacks are also skeptical of the strivings of black middle-class members, whom they sometimes condemn as Uncle Toms, Oreos, and members of the black bourgeoisie. Yet, despite scoffing at the white and black middle classes, some young blacks are moving up the social ladder. The open admissions policies of colleges of the early 1970s enabled some young blacks to move into managerial and professional study programs. A combination of affirmative action programs and their own demonstrated abilities have enabled a growing number to move into roles in the business system and professional world. Though some black young people reject integration as a goal, many support the breaking of color lines, whether by the older black generation, typified by Jackie Robinson, Marian Anderson, Thurgood Marshall, Kenneth B. Clark, and Edward Brooke or by a generation closer to their own ages, typified by Julian Bond, Arthur Ashe, and Andrew Young.

Largely because youth leaders were engaged in the early struggle for civil rights and in the later struggle for black identity and power, and because the majority of their followers among black young people were engaged in a struggle for economic survival, black adolescents and youth have played almost no part in the counter-culture movement during the past decade. Apparently, communes, rock religious productions, acid trips, Woodstock festivals, and a "greening of America" held few charms for black young people, whether leaders or followers. They left such matters to a segment of white American adolescents and youth from the middle or upper classes.

Contemporary black adolescents vary widely in personalities and characteristics. They include many young people in the lower classes, a growing number in the two middle classes, and a few in the upper classes. They range in social views from total alienation to total assimilation; most are somewhere in between. Some may aspire to live like Superfly or Shaft, and others may aspire to be like Martin Luther King or Thurgood Marshall.

Some may be resigned, others militant; some may be uneducated, others scholarly; some may welcome cooperation with whites, others reject relationships with majority group members.

Yet all have in common that they experience their adolescence as blacks in an America in which the black person is one in about nine of the American people. All have in common that they grow up in one of the social classes at a time in American life in which an economic gap persists between the incomes of most blacks and most whites.

MEXICAN-AMERICANS

More than half of all Americans whose original language was Spanish are Mexican-Americans. The remainder of the Hispanic-Americans are largely Puerto Ricans, Cubans, and people from Central and South America. Though the 1975 census indicates that Hispanic-Americans number 11.2 million, the actual number is substantially larger. This is primarily because many Mexican-Americans have crossed the border into the United States without following the established procedures of the Immigration and Naturalization Service. In 1976 the Community Relations Service of the U.S. Justice Department estimated that there may be more than 8 million such immigrants who have entered the United States illegally, most of them from Mexico.[21]

Originally, Mexican-Americans settled as farmers in five southwestern states: Arizona, California, Colorado, New Mexico, and Texas. Even today 85 percent of Mexican-Americans in the United States live in these five states. But increasingly they have moved to cities within the states and to cities elsewhere. So the majority of Mexican-Americans today live and work in urban areas, such as San Antonio and Los Angeles. However, many continue to be migrant farm workers.

Like other minority groups, their work varies widely. At the top of the social-class scale are those who are businesspeople, ranchers, professional workers, and public employees. At the bottom of the social scale are migrant workers and welfare recipients. But, like blacks, the larger proportion are poor people.

Mexican-American adolescents encounter many handicaps in American society. Their native language is Spanish so they face an initial handicap of having to be bilingual if they are to make their way in American society. And the schools have often not adjusted to the reality of a Spanish-speaking population.

Mexican-American adolescents are also bicultural. They recognize that the society that surrounds them is dominated by customs different from

---

[21] "Official Urges National Assessment as Hispanic-American Population Rises Sharply," *New York Times*, April 9, 1976, p. 13.

those of Mexico. Mexican-American young people are greatly influenced by two cultures. They live among the Anglos, as they call majority group residents of the United States, yet they bring into Anglo society the ways that many families learn in Mexico. Conflicts between the ways of the two cultures complicate the lives of adolescents.

For instance, the traditional role of the father in the Mexican family is that of head of the family. He represents his family in the outside world and feels that he carries responsibility for the family's honor. Any adolescent's behavior is seen as reflecting directly on the father. Traditionally, the Mexican father values masculinity even to the extent of living by *machismo,* a deep-seated belief in masculine superiority and male sexual prowess and privileges. The mother's traditional role has been that of submission as she works for the welfare of her husband and her children. She is expected to have an especially close relationship with her daughter. Warm love for the mother on the part of her children is taken for granted in the Mexican family. Though the father is the authoritarian patriarch, the mother is in actuality very influential in the day-by-day life of the Mexican family.

But the Mexican-American family, influenced by worldwide cultural changes in the late twentieth century and by the surrounding Anglo culture, faces challenges and responds with some degree of change. Today many Mexican-American women hold jobs involving a greater participation in a wider world and an increase in freedom. The adolescent boy is often threatened by this new role assumed by the Mexican-American mother; he may be particularly troubled if he takes seriously the tradition of machismo. If he rebels during his adolescence, he may in turn threaten his father's image of how a family should be run.

Complications in family relationships increase with courtship. The traditional pattern has been that courtship and marriage are controlled by the family. Courtship occurs early, usually after the girl's fifteenth birthday. During courtship, the girl is usually treated with high respect by the young male. This pattern during middle adolescence differs from the Anglo adolescent custom of dating widely, or "playing the field." It also runs counter to independent decisions as to marriage made by young men and women rather than by their families.

The necessity for bilinguality and the existence of bicultural backgrounds complicate the educational experiences of Mexican-Americans. So in the southwestern United States, Mexican-American young people drop out of school earlier than Anglo youth or nonwhite youth. This is easily understandable. Many Mexican-American children on entering the first grade do not speak English as well as the Anglo or black children for whom English is the native tongue. Partially because of language, Mexican-American children often fail during the elementary education years. Their culture is different from ways of living frequently advocated by the teachers. Anglo teachers often do not understand Mexican-American culture, including emphasis in the Mexican family on the present and relative lack of concern for the achievement in the future that many Anglos work for. The Mexican-American heritage is frequently ignored; everybody in the school is expected to live up to Anglo aspirations. As Mexican-American adolescents look around them, they often recognize that their group is being left out. They naturally assume that this is likely to happen whether they conform to the new culture or not. So as the eighth grade or high school entrance nears, they often drop out of school. Immediately pressing economic factors play a major role in the decision. They also suspect that if they stayed in they would be "guided" by the school into vocational and agricultural courses as the only tracks the school authorities think appropriate for them.

Resenting such misunderstanding, many Mexican-American adolescents think of themselves as Chicanos and express pride in their heritage, which is derived from Spanish-Mexican-Indian backgrounds. In the late sixties, some Chicano youth were active in boycotts of schools in California, Texas, and Arizona. School leaders with vision have responded not with suppression but with bilingual programs, discussion of the Mexican-American heritage, special textbooks, individualized instruction, field trips to widen cultural horizons, and a relaxation of unreasonable uniform expectancies. Such multicultural programs may reduce some of the tensions experienced by Mexican-American adolescents in growing up in a new land.

The experiences of other Hispanic-Americans is often similar to that of the Mexican-Americans. Yet their experiences differ too. For instance, since Puerto Rico is a part of the United States, currently a commonwealth, the Puerto Rican can travel legally and unrestrictedly between the island and the American mainland. New York City is frequently the Puerto Rican's first destination in the United States. The Puerto Rican's adjustment to mainland life is not complicated by the necessity to lie low out of the sight of federal authorities, which is the unhappy experience of many Mexican-American migrants. Another illustration of a differing cultural experience is that of many Cubans who came to Miami and other Florida cities after Castro came to power. While many of them are poor, some of them occupied positions of considerable status in Cuban society and find themselves underemployed with respect to their skills and talents. Such special factors influence the lives of Hispanic-American adolescents.

THE "NEW ETHNICS" FROM EUROPE

Still another of the experiences that influence the adolescent years are those of the children of families who have come from Europe within recent generations. The late nineteenth and early twentieth centuries were times of substantial migration from Europe by people from central and southern European countries such as Poland, the Austro-Hungarian Empire, the Balkans, Russia, and Italy. These groups followed mid-nineteenth-century immigration by people from Ireland, Scotland, Germany, and the Scandinavian countries.

The natural inclination of immigrant groups is to first live in the neighborhoods to which their friends and family came earlier. So ethnic neighborhoods grew up in American metropolises such as Boston, Philadelphia, New York, Detroit, and Chicago. As immigrant families became more familiar with American ways and particularly as they prospered, some left the old neighborhoods and frequently settled in new locations where others than those from the old country lived. Marriages across nationality lines in such families were common. Religious lines were crossed in marriage, though frequently with doubts and reservations on the part of families. The descendants of such marriages frequently represented a blend of many European strains. For them the melting pot theory worked well.

But not all families left the old neighborhoods. Sometimes the people who remained with the immigrant neighborhoods were those who were not economically successful. In such neighborhoods, the residents, rather than forgetting their heritages, often took pride in their national backgrounds and their American adaptations in their own communities. They lived closely with their churches or synagogues, their clubs and organizations, and their cooking and customs derived from their original Old World countries.

Some welcomed new residents to established neighborhoods with toleration and acceptance. That people of their own particular ethnic group had gotten there first was not important to them. But to some, people of other backgrounds who wanted to move into "the old neighborhood" were unwelcome. Often they were particularly unwelcome if they were of darker skin color.

What one writer, Michael Novak, has called the "unmeltable ethnics" came into the national spotlight in the 1970s. In implementing the 1954 Supreme Court decision against segregation of public schools, judges ordered busing of black students into such neighborhoods and, occasionally, busing European background ethnics into black neighborhoods (see Figure 4.5). Some residents of these ethnic enclaves already resented those who had moved up and out of their neighborhoods and into a higher economic stratum. They were angry at liberals who lived in areas unaffected by the in-migration of blacks and Spanish-speaking people; they regarded their critics as hypocrites who expected the residents of established neighborhoods to adjust to dark-skinned neighbors, yet would not themselves welcome blacks or Hispanic-American people to the suburbs. Some residents of the old neighborhoods feared that the newcomers would bring with them disruption, crime, violence, and poor living conditions. Since many residents of the old neighborhoods were already having a hard time in American life, encountering unemployment and inflation and what

FIGURE 4.5 *Interdistrict Busing: Public Opinion. Opposition to busing is relatively unchanged since 1972, as is revealed in the responses to the following question: "In general do you favor or oppose the busing of black and white children from one school district to another?"*

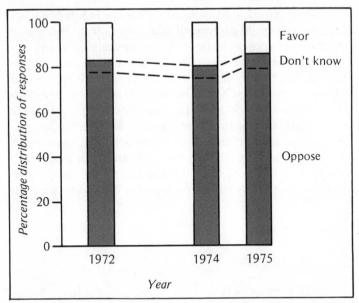

Source: *The Condition of Education*, U.S. Government Printing Office, Washington, D.C., 1976, p. 55.

appeared to them affirmative discrimination, their resistance to outsiders stiffened.

Some political candidates during the 1976 elections promised not to sanction "intrusion" by the federal government through introducing low-income housing for minority group members in neighborhoods that are largely inhabited by members of one or another ethnic group from Europe. However, the Supreme Court ruled in 1976 that the federal government could be ordered to provide low-cost public housing for minority group members in the suburbs if the government had been found to have contributed to segregation in the city through its funding of public housing. It appeared that the suburbs, as well as the old ethnic neighborhoods, soon would be required to accept low-income residents in public housing.

Inevitably attitudes related to conflicts over neighborhoods are transmitted to adolescents. In the mid-1970s the nation read about and saw via television racial disturbances by adolescents and adults in long-established Irish neighborhoods in Boston. But the nation also saw peace marches in Boston in which adolescents and adults proclaimed their faith in racial harmony and understanding and in the American tradition. (The inscription for the Statue of Liberty reads, "Give me your tired, your poor, your huddled masses yearning to breathe free . . . I lift my lamp beside the golden door.")

To portray all of Michael Novak's unmeltable ethnics as bigots or racists is a misinterpretation. Similarly, to portray all adolescents from this group as violent opponents of newcomers is false. Some undoubtedly are, but recent studies of ethnic groups have reminded us that white ethnic voters from old neighborhoods are tied by tradition to the Democratic party and generally vote for Democrats even when these candidates are highly sympathetic to the aspirations of black and Hispanic-Americans.[22] In 1972 when the Democratic candidate was the liberal Senator George McGovern, the white ethnic groups of Irish, Italian, and Slavic ancestry more often voted for this liberal candidate than did the average Democratic voter.[23] So we cannot conclude that adolescents from the families of the unmeltable ethnics are unanimously hostile to adolescents who differ from them in skin color.

THE THREE D'S

Still another way in which some individual adolescents differ from educational psychologists' descriptions of the adolescent in general is in deviations from commonly accepted social norms. For instance, some adolescents are delinquent; some drop out of school early; some are drug abusers. Obviously, there are many other behavior differences among adolescents. However, because these particular behavior differences present special difficulties for teachers, we are singling out the three D's—delinquency, dropping out, and drugs—for analysis in this chapter on characteristics of young people.

DELINQUENTS

Some adolescents grow up in ways that are troublesome to organized society. People often reject adolescents who behave in ways contrary to what is expected of the normal young person. In broad terms, such young people are described as juvenile delinquents.

A more limited definition is that juvenile delinquents are children or adolescents who commit illegal acts. However, only some who commit illegal acts are brought to court and still fewer are found guilty. So the

[22] Mark Levy and Michael Kramer, *The Ethnic Factor*, Simon and Schuster, New York, 1972.
[23] Andrew M. Greeley, *Ethnicity in the United States*, John Wiley, New York, 1974.

narrowest definition of the juvenile delinquent is a child or adolescent brought into court and judged to be guilty.

Many factors are related to juvenile delinquency. Social-class status is one important factor. The rate of juvenile delinquency is highest in the upper lower and lower lower classes. Delinquent gangs are usually made up of members of these two classes, and the most serious types of juvenile offenses are more likely to be found in these same classes.

A second factor in accounting for delinquency relates to lack of success by adolescents in schools. Most delinquents have a history of failure in school. In general, delinquents are lower in intelligence than nondelinquents as measured by today's dubious IQ scales. The combination of class status, school failure, and "lower intelligence" contribute to the high dropout rate among delinquents. The large majority of sixteen- and seventeen-year-old delinquents are dropouts. However, one should not conclude that most dropouts are delinquents. The fact is that most dropouts have no court record whatsoever.

Negative family experience is another factor relating to delinquency. Families that lack cohesion, supervision, and affection for the young person and that are characterized by overly rigid, inconsistent, or neglectful approaches to discipline contribute to juvenile delinquency.

Group action is also related to delinquent behavior. Juvenile delinquents often operate in groups and juvenile crimes usually involve accomplices. But, again, all groups are not delinquent subcultures; coming together in close-knit groups is a characteristic of adolescence in general.

A final factor is that juvenile delinquency has been primarily a male manifestation. Male delinquents far outnumber the female delinquents, whose delinquent offenses have been primarily incorrigibility, truancy, and sexual misconduct. Fighting and stealing are less common offenses among girls than among boys. Some speculate that the changing role of women in our society, which has many desirable aspects, may also have the unfortunate outcome of causing delinquency to rise among girls, whose offenses may then be more similar to those of boys.

Delinquency among adolescents involves many factors and has complex causes. Some delinquent behavior grows out of emotional disturbances. A few delinquents are extremely aggressive, uncontrollable, and even psychopathic. Some seem to be highly anxious and compulsive. Others have less serious emotional disturbances. But such personality disorders, taken as a whole, can account for only a small minority of delinquents.

Some delinquency may grow out of the conflicts and crises experienced by many adolescents as part of their normal development. The reader of this book may possibly be able to recall some of his or her experiences during adolescence that may have verged on delinquent behavior or that may have resulted in a brush with the law. However, adolescents usually outgrow this type of delinquency.

The most usual form of delinquency grows out of conflicts in young people who reject many accepted values, who are themselves rejected, and who become alienated. They fight society and its regulations. These adolescents constitute a delinquent subculture.

Some students of delinquency think that lower-class culture, which emphasizes toughness, seeking excitement, independence, and accepting a somewhat fatalistic view of life, accounts for some delinquency. Others think that disadvantaged young people are sometimes delinquent because they are unable to achieve a good economic status. It is argued that they then proceed to acquire money illegally. Still others think that rather than a lack of ability to succeed in modern society, it is lack of opportunity that makes boys come together to achieve their ends through illegal procedures. Still others think that society's failure to provide jobs and relevant schooling leads to idleness, which, in turn, leads to delinquent behavior. All agree that much delinquent behavior grows out of experiences in subcultures that foster delinquency.

DROPOUTS

There was a time in American life when dropping out of secondary school was customary and taken for granted. It was a very long time! From the days of the first academies and public high schools to the middle of the twentieth century, the majority of American adolescents dropped out of school prior to high school graduation. Only in the past three decades have those who have stayed in outnumbered those who have dropped out. In 1975 dropouts were 25 percent of high school students. Once in the majority, dropouts are now in the minority. Once the norm, today's dropouts deviate from the norm (see Figure 4.6).

As the dropout rate declines, the argument over whether those who are potential dropouts should stay in school grows. The orthodox position among educators is that such potential dropouts should continue in school at least until high school graduation. An unorthodox position, yet one that is heard today with increasing frequency, is that alternative pathways to adulthood other than schooling should be provided by American society.

The orthodox position argues that the typical dropout, who is male and usually is beyond his sixteenth birthday, is handicapping himself in life by dropping out before high school graduation (see Figure 4.7). Although he may think that he is dropping out of his own free will, he is actually dropping out because he has had negative school experiences and because he happened to be born into an upper lower or lower lower class family. In fact, more usually than not his lower-class parents before him were dropouts. So are many of his friends and relatives.

In school he usually never learns to read well. He usually ranks in the lower quarter of his class. He is frequently left back in one or more grades, so he is older than his classmates. He runs into discipline problems. He

FIGURE 4.6 *High School Graduation Rate.* *The ratio of high school graduates to the 17-year-old population has remained higher for females than for males since 1901.*

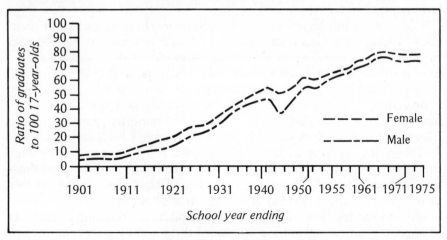

SOURCE: Mary A. Golladay, ed., *The Condition of Education*, U.S. Government Printing Office, Washington, D.C., 1977, p. 45.

FIGURE 4.7 *High School Graduation Rates, by Sex.* *The high school graduation rate has been consistently higher for females than for males.*

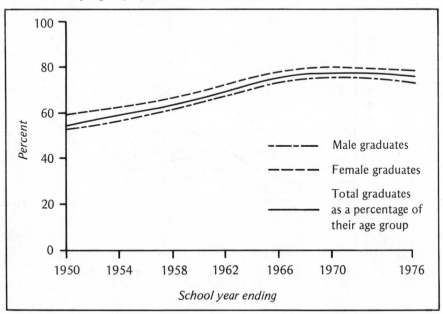

SOURCE: *The Condition of Education*, U.S. Government Printing Office, Washington, D.C., 1976, p. 34.

doesn't like school and, in turn, the school rejects him—or he thinks it does. In short, year after year while he attends classes, the school reminds him that he is a failure.

Because of factors beyond their control—poor schooling and lower social class—young people drop out of school. Thus they are shortchanged both by school and society. According to the conventional view, schools should improve their programs and retain such students, and both school and society should help people to surmount their lower-class backgrounds.

According to the prevailing view, dropouts are now quite likely to be unemployed for a period of time. If they are minority-group members, their chances of unemployment increase (see Figure 4.8). If and when they find jobs, they will be unskilled jobs for relatively low pay. All through dropouts' youth and adult life, they will have lower incomes than those who stayed in school. There is a direct demonstrable correlation between years spent in school and family income in adulthood.

The unorthodox view of dropouts is not optimistic about the possibilities of improved schooling or modification of the social-class system through

FIGURE 4.8 *Unemployment Rates for High School Dropouts. Unemployment rates for high school dropouts from 1968 to 1975 were consistently higher for blacks than for whites.*

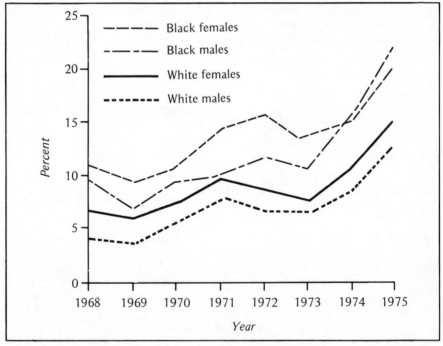

Source: *The Condition of Education,* U.S. Government Printing Office, Washington, D.C., 1976, p. 115.

schools or through governmental policies and programs. This view holds that schools are essentially cognitive institutions, and that most of the 25 percent of young people who now drop out will not reach the intellectual standards maintained by educators. As to the possibilities of staying in affecting upward mobility, this view cites research summaries by Christopher Jencks and associates to the effect that increased schooling does not contribute to equal economic opportunity. In an article, Bane and Jencks say, "The main policy implication of these findings is that although school reform is important for improving the lives of children, schools cannot contribute significantly to adult equality."[24] Since society refuses to take direct governmental action to bring about economic equality, we had best be realistic and give young people the alternative of working rather than attending school. (See Figure 4.9 for unemployment rates for college graduates.)

The unorthodox view also argues that the reasons dropouts are often unemployed are family background and individual abilities. The mere act of dropping out does not increase young persons' chances of being unemployed. The dissenting view also questions the argument that the income of dropouts is markedly less than that of employed high school graduates. At first the incomes are nearly identical. Those who think dropping out is not detrimental point out that dropouts are about as well satisfied with their jobs as are graduates. The unconventional view, however, does not quarrel with the contention that the long-range earnings of high school graduates will be higher.

Why then, ask the critics, has society given the dropouts a bad name? Let us regear the total educational system so that there are alternatives to staying in school and graduating from high school. Let us sponsor employment for those beyond sixteen—or, indeed, beyond fourteen—who want to learn through employment as an alternative route. Let us have both community and school-sponsored employment opportunities. Let us stop trying to fit square pegs into round holes. Let us stop attempting to sell education on the basis of dubious economic rewards. Reserve schools for those who want to attend and provide alternatives for youth preferring other roads to maturity and adulthood. So goes the unorthodox argument.

DRUG ABUSERS

A third deviation from the normal by adolescents is the abuse of drugs. The word *abuse* is used intentionally, because the majority of adolescents do, in fact, *use* drugs. For instance, the National Institute of Alcohol Abuse and Alcoholism concludes that 81 percent of

---

[24] Mary Jo Bane and Christopher Jencks, "The Schools and Equal Opportunity," *Saturday Review of Education*, September 16, 1972, p. 38.

FIGURE 4.9 *Unemployment Rates for College Graduates. The unemployment rate for college graduates has usually been higher for females than for males.*

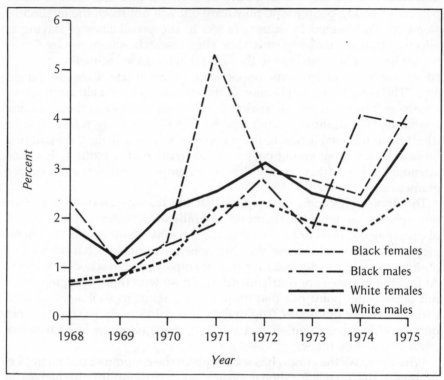

SOURCE: *The Condition of Education*, U.S. Government Printing Office, Washington, D.C., 1976, p. 115.

junior and senior high school students in the United States drink alcohol on some basis.[25] Also, a report prepared in 1976 by the National Institute on Drug Abuse on marijuana use and delivered to the U.S. Congress by the Department of Health, Education, and Welfare states that half of Americans in the eighteen-to-twenty-five-year age range have tried marijuana at least once. The institute concluded that the use of marijuana was on the rise. Their 1972 survey indicated that 48 percent of this age group had tried marijuana, and their 1974-1975 survey showed that the figure had risen to 53 percent. Their 1976 report commented,

In seven years, what was once clearly statistically deviant behavior has become the norm in this age group. While in previous years use was correlated with level of education, the percentage now reporting marijuana use is virtually identical for

[25] "Student Alcohol Abuse Demands New Solutions," *Education USA*, March 29, 1976, p. 183.

high school dropouts, high school graduates and college graduates in the similar age ranges.[26]

In 1976 the institute conducted a survey of drug usage among high school seniors in particular. (See also an opinion poll in Figure 4.10.) The Associated Press reported on November 23, 1976:

More than half of the Bicentennial class of high school seniors tried marijuana and three out of 10 were users at graduation time, according to government surveys.

The National Institute on Drug Abuse surveyed 17,000 high school seniors in 130 schools last spring and found that 53 per cent had tried marijuana, a 5 per cent increase over the class of 1975.

---

[26] "Half of Americans Age 18 to 25 Said to Have Tried Marijuana," *New York Times*, February 12, 1976, p. 20.

FIGURE 4.10 *Drug Use by Young People: Public Opinion. The majority of individuals from communities of all sizes and from all regions answered "yes" to the question: "Is the use of drugs by young people a serious problem in this community?"*

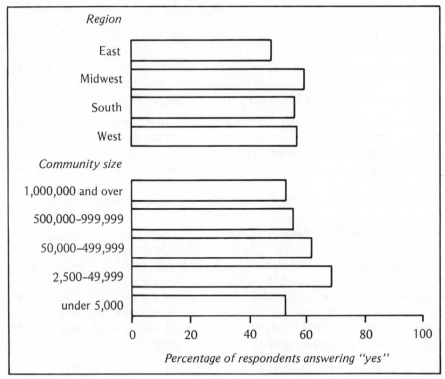

SOURCE: *The Condition of Education*, U.S. Government Printing Office, Washington, D.C., 1976, p. 57.

FIGURE 4.11   *Attendance at Programs on Effects of Drugs: Public Opinion.   A substantial majority of parents answered "yes" to the question: "Should the schools in this community require students to attend a program on the effects of drugs and alcohol?"*

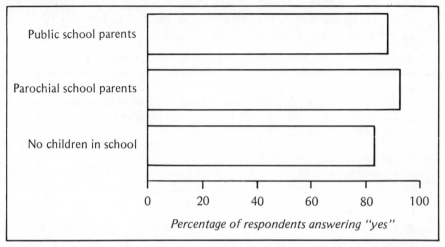

SOURCE: *The Condition of Education,* U.S. Government Printing Office, Washington, D.C., 1976, p. 57.

The survey, released today, said 32 percent regarded themselves as current marijuana users.

Although cigarettes and alcohol were used more frequently than marijuana by young adults, 57 per cent of high school seniors thought there was a serious health risk for cigarettes while only 40 per cent felt the same way about marijuana.[27]

Although cigarette smoking is not yet the norm among American adolescents there has been a substantial rise among young people during the past six years, particularly among teen-aged girls. Twenty-seven percent of girls thirteen through seventeen years old now smoke. Four out of ten smokers use at least one pack a day, according to the American Cancer Society. Seven years earlier only 22 percent of teen-age girls smoked. Only one in ten smokers used a pack or more a day. Consequently, girls today are smoking nearly as heavily as are boys.

There may be quarrels over whether or not the above youth practices as to alcohol, marijuana, and cigarettes should be tolerated or whether all use of drugs should be vigorously combated by society. However, there is no disagreement on the undesirability of abuse of drugs. Drug abusers certainly include the 28 percent of teen-agers who get drunk at least four times a year and the 5 percent who get drunk at least once a week, according to the National Institute on Alcohol Abuse and Alcoholism.[28] Nor is there any

---

[27] "Drug Use Report Issued," *Terre Haute Tribune,* November 23, 1976, p. 1.
[28] "Student Alcohol Abuse Demands New Solutions," *Education USA,* p. 183.

question that the use of hard drugs such as LSD, hashish, or heroin is socially and individually destructive. Similarly, the evidence linking heavy smoking to cancer now appears undeniable.

So the abuse of drugs is a deviation among adolescents that calls for education, attention by society, and remediation (see Figure 4.11).

TEACHERS AND YOUNG PEOPLE

A goal of American secondary education is to educate as best we can each individual young person. To do so, teachers must see each person as a distinct and, indeed, unique human being. Whether engaged in teaching, counseling, or planning learning experiences, the good teacher will attempt to help individual persons who are necessarily characterized by individual differences.

The information assembled in this chapter should help secondary school teachers of all subjects and all specializations to recognize some of the similarities among adolescents. Even more important, the foregoing descriptions of sex roles in adolescence, social-class factors, ethnic group experiences, and the three D's should provide secondary school teachers with cues to ways in which individuals differ in their needs, responses, and behavior. With such cues in mind, teachers can better adapt their subject matter, style, and methods to the individuals of varied backgrounds who will inevitably be members of their classes.

DISCUSSION

1. Define adolescence. What is the usual interpretation of adolescence by the average person? How does it differ from the viewpoint of today's experts on adolescence?

2. What are the broad generalizations on adolescence that can be derived from the writings of the experts? Do these check with your own experiences and observations?

3. How important is society in the development of the adolescent?

4. Were you a "typical adolescent"?

5. What are the major classifications of differences among adolescents?

6. What are the traditional sex roles of men and women in American society? . . . of boys and girls? What seem to be the emerging sex roles? What accounts for the change?

7. Do you approve or disapprove of traditional sex roles? In this connection, what are your basic assumptions as to the nature of human beings? . . . as to biological sex role factors . . . as to a good society?

8. According to the sociologists, what are some possible social-class groupings? Take one of these groupings and indicate the social-class differences reported by the sociologists.

9. Illustrate how young people are influenced by social-class backgrounds. Why is growing up particularly a difficult process for the lower lower young person?

10. In broad terms, how might ethnic differences influence the lives of adolescents?

11. In general, how do the lives of black adolescents differ from those of white adolescents? What social factors account for these persisting differences?

12. Are black young people more inclined to accept or reject certain value options because of their black experience?

13. What are the characteristic attitudes, viewpoints, and styles among black young people who stress black identity? Do they differ from black young people who stress integration into the larger American society?

14. In a discussion of Mexican-American adolescents, what is the meaning and importance of the concept "bicultural"? Can you illustrate? What groups other than Mexican-Americans also face the reality of biculturalism?

15. What are traditional Mexican-American patterns and customs? What patterns and customs are emerging in contemporary Mexican-American life?

16. Why is bilinguality necessary for Mexican-Americans? What blocks bilinguality?

17. What is special about the problems faced by Mexican-American students? How do they compare with problems faced by Anglos? . . . by other Hispanic background students?

18. What is the meaning of "new ethnics" from Europe? What were the experiences of late-nineteenth-century immigrants from Europe? What are some of the recent experiences of their descendants who remained in "the old neighborhood"?

19. What factors have brought "the unmeltable ethnics" into the national spotlight in the 1970s? How has government responded to problems of desegregation in established neighborhoods? How have young adolescents of various groups responded?

20. What are the behavior manifestations that present a special difficulty for teachers? Are there behavior manifestations that are less obvious and troubling yet equally as important?

21. What are some of the meanings of juvenile delinquency? What meaning do you have in mind when you use the term?

22. How is female delinquency changing?

23. What are among the causes of delinquency? What are the ways in which schools could help to reduce delinquency rather than contribute to it?

24. What are the characteristics of the usual dropout?

25.   Contrast the conventional and the unorthodox view as to the desirability and importance of dropping out.

26.   What is the evidence that the use of drugs is extensive?

27.   What is the distinction between drug use and abuse? Do you agree with those who believe that any use of a drug constitutes abuse?

28.   Why do we as teachers have to understand the characteristics of secondary school age young people? Why are individual differences among young people important to a teacher?

29.   Summarize similarities among adolescents. What factors help to account for differences?

INVOLVEMENT

1.   Through conversations with a variety of people, test the hypothesis that they usually think of adolescence as a period of storm and stress.

2.   Interview teachers on their generalizations concerning the characteristics of the students they teach. Check these against the characteristics of adolescents described by educational psychologists.

3.   Gather evidence from current newspapers and magazines as to emerging roles of women and the decline of traditional roles. Share your findings with members of your class through discussions.

4.   Talk to high school students of both sexes concerning career plans, family plans, and changing sex roles. Try to classify their responses with regard to their traditionalism or modernity.

5.   On the basis of observation and interviews, attempt to describe the social-class backgrounds of the students of the secondary school most available to you for observation. Check your tentative findings with a perceptive teacher from this school. Talk it over with a few students.

6.   Read about social-class measurement techniques as described by W. Lloyd Warner in *Social Class in America*. Try measuring the social-class status of members of your own class, then your family, and finally a cross section of secondary school students.

7.   Include in your program of school visits some schools with a large representation of minority group members. Look for both similarities to and differences from schools with fewer minority group members. Does evidence of discrimination persist in the schools you visited?

8.   Invite to class some minority group members to discuss problems of intercultural relationships. Also invite to class some minority group members to talk on matters on which they are experts and which do not relate as closely to intergroup conflicts or problems.

9.   Visit neighborhoods where people live whose backgrounds differ from the

backgrounds of most class members. Plan such visits carefully and with the cooperation of individuals living in the neighborhoods. On return, talk over your observations.

10.　Attempt to find opportunities to tutor young people of backgrounds different from your own.

11.　Invite to the class a local specialist on delinquency who can discuss views on causes, remedies, and desired interrelationships with schools. Through visits, get acquainted with institutions for the treatment of juvenile delinquents in your area.

12.　Read both fiction and nonfiction on juvenile delinquency and share insights with class members.

13.　Invite to class the individual in the local school system most familiar with the problem of dropouts.

14.　Attempt to invite to class people who take the conventional and unconventional views of the desirability of dropping out. Evaluate their views after their departure.

15.　Attempt to get a realistic picture of drug abuse in your own community. Partial insights may be supplied by judges, guidance counselors, students, and leaders of organizations concerned about aspects of the problem.

16.　Try your hand at character sketches of young people whom you know or whom you imagine. Attempt to dramatize the existence of differences among adolescents. Prepare and post a summary of some of the major similarities and differences among adolescents.

FURTHER READINGS

Bottomore, T. B. *Classes in Modern Society*. Vintage, New York, 1966. An introduction to the study of class as a sociological concept.

Conroy, Pat. *The Water Is Wide*. Dell, New York, 1974. The story of a white teacher and disadvantaged black students in the South. It has been made into a motion picture, *Conrack*.

Girdano, Dorothy Dusek, and Daniel A. Girdano. *Drugs—a Factual Account*. Addison-Wesley, Reading, Mass., 1973. An account of the historical, social, and legal impact of drugs on our society. Its presentation of physiology of the nervous system and pharmacology of selected drugs provides understanding of the drug problem.

Handlin, Oscar, and Mary F. Handlin. *Facing Life: Youth and the Family in American History*. Little, Brown, Boston, 1971. A social history of young Americans that traces the changes that have occurred in the maturation process to adulthood from colonial societies to the present.

Havighurst, Robert J., ed. *Youth*. The Seventy-fourth Yearbook of the National Society for the Study of Education. University of Chicago Press, Chicago, 1975. An indispensable book dealing with youth from ages fifteen through twenty-four. Included are theory, relationships of youth to social institutions, and a highly readable section on pluralism that includes chapters on black youth, Mexican-American youth, women, and low-income youth.

Konopka, Gisela. *Young Girls: A Portrait of Adolescent Feelings.* Prentice-Hall, Englewood Cliffs, N.J., 1973. A report on the way adolescent girls feel about their peers and their surrounding environment.

Lemasters, E. E. *Blue-Collar Aristocrats.* University of Wisconsin Press, Madison, 1975. A study of the life styles of working-class men observed and interviewed in a tavern.

Matteson, David R. *Adolescence Today: Sex Roles and the Search for Identity.* Dorsey Press, Homewood, Ill., 1975. Sex-role identification is the integrating theme for this scholarly and compassionate study of the adolescent's crises and search for personal identity within today's society. It provides a framework for understanding adolescence and refers to the views of Erik Erikson throughout.

Novak, Michael. *The Rise of the Unmeltable Ethnics: Politics and Culture in the Seventies.* Macmillan, New York, 1972. A searching look at the third generation of immigrants. Points out that the melting pot has not produced a standardized, homogeneous citizenry.

Rogers, Dorothy. *The Psychology of Adolescence,* 3rd ed. Prentice-Hall, Englewood Cliffs, N.J., 1977. Covers problems of the adolescent personality, and discusses sexuality, drugs, career education, alternative schools, and minority adolescents.

Rogers, Dorothy, ed. *Issues in Adolescent Psychology,* 3rd ed. Prentice-Hall, Englewood Cliffs, N.J., 1977. A collection of readings on issues concerning adolescents, adolescent personality development, self-actualization, peer relations, and the development of values and social consequences. Varied and provocative.

Rosaldo, Renato, Robert A. Calvert, and Gustav L. Seligmann, eds. *Chicano.* Morrow, New York, 1974. An account of the activities of young Chicanos by a variety of authorities on Mexican-American life.

Sebald, Hans. *Adolescence: A Social Psychological Analysis,* 2nd ed. Prentice-Hall, Englewood Cliffs, N.J., 1977. A new edition of a book discussing the sociological, psychological, and historical forces that influence modern adolescence. Emphasizes identity as an important factor in the growth of adolescents.

Sennett, Richard, and Jonathan Cobb. *The Hidden Injuries of Class.* Knopf, New York, 1972. Presents interviews that help the reader to understand the lives of blue-collar workers and some of the emotional wounds they experience in our society.

Sexton, Patricia Cayo. *The Feminized Male: Classrooms, White Collars and the Decline of Manliness.* Random House, New York, 1969. The author seeks, in our schools and society, the factors that feminize men. Postulates that modern men are more troubled than women by social roles and sex norms.

Stoll, Clarice Stasz. *Female and Male: Socialization, Social Roles and Social Structure.* Wm. C. Brown, Dubuque, Iowa, 1974. Written as a text for undergraduate students, this book reviews theories and findings on how sex roles are determined, perpetuated, and justified.

Part 2.
The Story of Secondary Education

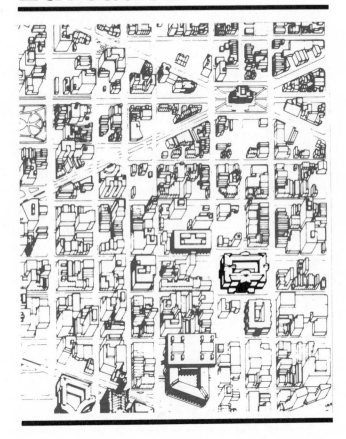

5.

Development of
Secondary
Schools

Although the origins of secondary schools on the world scene are obscure, they are worth tracing because they throw light on a conflict that has persisted throughout the history of secondary education and that continues to be sharp in the United States today. In broad terms, some conceive of secondary education as the study of disciplines or subjects that derive from a tradition stressing classical, humanistic, liberal education. They believe that the goal of secondary education is mastery of subject matter by the student in order to meet college entrance requirements. Others see secondary education as the study of disciplinary and interdisciplinary subject matter derived from a tradition stressing the social and individual uses of education. They believe that the goal of secondary education is to educate all youth for contemporary life. The emphasis in the first group has been upon such subjects as grammar, classical languages, and literary masterpieces. The emphasis in the second group has been upon such fields as the social sciences, the sciences, and vocational fields, and now includes such interdisciplinary problems as human relations, career education, international education, and the environment.

Today's secondary school teachers repeatedly encounter this conflict. On the one hand, they are urged to stress career education, regardless of the subject or field they teach. They soon learn that funds are available from the federal government to support career education. On the other hand, secondary school teachers are urged to stress college preparatory subject matter. Parents want a college prep curriculum, they are told.

On the one hand, secondary school teachers are urged by social forces and their own consciences to foster international understanding, to educate against racism, and to give attention to such new problems as the state of the ecology. On the other hand, they are urged not to depart from the textbooks that set forth in orderly and logical fashion the content of separate subject matters.

When secondary school teachers consider the most desirable curriculum for the last decades of the twentieth century, they are pressed to include new knowledge from the social sciences and sciences at a time of an explosion of knowledge. Simultaneously, they are prodded to retain instruction in Latin and not to neglect literary classics of past ages.

The secondary school teacher should provide abundant opportunity for vocational education in the secondary school curriculum, some entreat. Get them all ready for college subjects, others exhort. Make education more academic, some say. Make education more relevant, others urge.

If the teachers specialize in junior high school or middle school education, they are strongly advised to meet the real needs of preadolescents and adolescents. At the same time, they are told that they must get their students ready for high school so that the high school can get them ready for college.

Teachers encounter many other illustrations of the conflict between an older and a newer conception of education. They hear about the conflict during their own college education. They experience the conflict when they become teachers and have to make decisions on what they will stress in their own classroom teaching and on what types of programs they will support when they take part in curriculum revision. To compound the confusion growing out of this historical conflict, they are frequently told that their teaching must satisfy both of the contending views.

How did this conflict on secondary education come about? As with many of our contemporary problems, some historical background helps our understanding.

OLD WORLD BEGINNINGS

GREECE

The creative and ingenious Greeks who contributed so much to civilization probably should be credited with the beginnings of secondary education. In the seventh century B.C., elementary schools developed in Athens to teach music, letters (reading, writing, and some study of numbers), and gymnastics to boys, from the families of citizens, from the ages of seven to fifteen. When these boys reached fifteen, two possibilities emerged, and they have a familiar ring to the modern reader. The poor boys went to work and some of the rich boys went to school. A form of secondary education developed in Athens for that minority of the children of Athenian citizens who went beyond elementary education.

The precursors of secondary schools that the more prosperous boys attended were public gymnasiums, where Greek youths worked on physical exercise, participated in discussions, and attended lectures. Some centuries later the sophists, who were wandering scholars from the Greek colonies, set up two options, rhetorical and philosophical schools. These attracted many Greek young males; they left the gymnasiums behind them and joined the new schools. The rhetorical schools prepared young men for public careers through extensive training in speech, which emphasized grammar, rhetoric, and oratory. These schools helped young males to become political and social leaders in Athenian society. The philosophical schools stressed, as the name indicates, an understanding of philosophic discourse. In Athens, they grew out of the Socratic tradition and included Plato's academy and Aristotle's lyceum along with Stoic and Epicurean schools.

Bear in mind that these beginnings of secondary education were highly informal. There was no agreed-upon curriculum nor were diplomas or degrees awarded. However, the gymnasiums and later the schools of the sophists did offer the first systematic education beyond the elementary level in the historical record.

During the Hellenistic period Greek culture spread throughout the Mediterranean world. In the secondary schools marked by influence of the Greeks the emphasis on gymnastics declined. The approach of the sophists, however, flourished, and increasing numbers of boys from thirteen or fourteen to about sixteen or eighteen years of age studied with them. Indeed, there came an increase in public support and control of education. Some grammatists, as the sophists came to be called, were paid through public funds rather than through the fees that had been charged by earlier teachers. Even the origins of the profession of the school superintendent can be traced to this period![1]

ROME

Rome succeeded Greece at the center of the world stage. But the influence of the Greek tradition was powerful. During the third century B.C., when Rome instituted its version of secondary education, Roman boys were taught *Greek* grammar and literature, not *Latin* grammar and literature. This development is understandable. Greece was the world's source of culture and the Romans turned to it. The teachers of Rome often had Greek backgrounds. Although they might be slaves in Rome, they had often been leaders in the colonies from which they came. The Romans respected such teachers for their scholarship and culture. The

---

[1] Ralph L. Pounds, *The Development of Education in Western Culture,* Appleton-Century-Crofts, New York, 1968, pp. 46–51.

teachers of Roman youth were engaged in private education supported by fees. Their instruction was not controlled or supervised by the public authorities. A Roman teacher was called a *grammaticus* and later a *litteratus*.

As Rome grew more influential, the study of Latin grammar and literature developed in the secondary schools. Again, this is an understandable development. A similar change has occurred throughout the history of education: first, instruction is in the language of the civilization upon which the new nation draws; eventually, the language and literature of the new nation supplants it in the curriculum. In Rome the rhetorical school emphasizing grammar became more popular than the philosophical school; the Romans leaned toward practicality rather than toward speculation.

MIDDLE AGES TO REFORMATION

During the Middle Ages instruction emphasizing grammar persisted in church schools as religionists educated some boys for a vocation within the Roman Catholic Church.[2] With the Renaissance and Reformation, the secondary schools attempted to widen education beyond the theological outlook of the Middle Ages. They did so by bringing students into contact with the classical traditions of Greece and Rome, which were the sources of world culture that had persisted into the eras of rebirth and church reform. These languages and traditions used by educated people were the founts of knowledge, and thus humanistic scholars based the education of the young upon the classics.

A rise of the middle classes accompanied the reformation of the churches. As trade and commerce developed, the emerging European nations needed to educate the young in a more practical and utilitarian fashion than the older classical education did. Reformers urged that education use the vernacular, the ordinary everyday language of the people of the land or region, so that the common people might read the Bible and engage in trade and commerce.

Faced with the demand for a new type of education, the schools characteristically compromised, as secondary schools were to do so often in the future. In the new academies sponsored by the Protestant dissenters, the classics still persisted. Yet along with the classics came an increase in applied mathematical and scientific content. By the seventeenth century the academies sponsored by the various dissenters combined the ancient classical content with new courses taught in the vernacular languages. The new courses included geography, surveying, navigation, economics, politics, natural science, anatomy, and modern languages. Of course, not all schools taught all these newer subjects.

---

[2] Ibid., p. 91.

So the educational tradition that the American colonists inherited from Europe was a dual one. From Europe came the traditional classical curriculum that was regarded as the proper education for leaders of the church and the state. After all, the sacred literature of the Christian churches was written in Latin and Greek, and the humanists of the Renaissance and Reformation had based an education for humane people firmly upon the Greek and Roman contributions. Yet, along with the classical tradition, the colonists inherited the beginnings of a practical tradition stressing the usefulness of education for individuals participating in daily life; some secondary schools in Europe had moved toward studies based upon science and even toward "practical" studies.[3]

LATIN GRAMMAR SCHOOLS

Since the American colonies were an offshoot of Europe in general and of Great Britain in particular, the first secondary schools in the New World followed these models—European and, specifically, British schools. In 1635 a Latin Grammar School was established in Boston. The school combined what later ages would regard as elementary and secondary levels, for it enrolled students from ages seven through fourteen. The model followed was the classical model. A major purpose of the school was clear, to prepare boys to enter Harvard College. Equally clear was Harvard's role: to train young men to be leaders in the church and the state. This first college entrance curriculum in America stressed Latin, Greek, and mathematics. College admissions requirements were plainly set forth by Harvard College: "When any scholar is able to understand Tully, or such like classical Latin author [extemporaneously], and make and speak true Latin in verse and prose, . . . and decline perfectly the [inflectional forms] of nouns and verbs in the Greek tongue: Let him then and not before be capable of admission into the college."[4]

The Puritans encouraged the spread of Latin grammar schools through laws such as that of 1647, which stressed the educational goals of the colonial theocracy.

It being one chief project of that old deluder, Satan, to keep men from the knowledge of the scriptures, as in former times by keeping them in an unknown tongue so in these latter times by persuading from the use of tongues, . . . and that learning might not be buried in the grave of our fathers in the church and Commonwealth. . . . It is therefore ordered, that every township in this jurisdiction, after

---

[3] Ibid., pp. 151–153.
[4] Adapted from "New Englands First Fruits: In Respect . . . of the Progress of Learning in the College at Cambridge in Massachusetts Bay," London, 1643, p. 13.

the Lord hath increased them to the number of 50 householders shall then forthwith appoint one within their town to teach all such children as shall resort to him to write and read, . . . and it is further ordered, that where any town shall increase to the number of 100 families or householders, they shall set up a grammar school, the master thereof being able to instruct youth so far as they may be fitted for the University.[5]

Connecticut followed with similar legislation three years later, and soon public grammar schools were established in towns throughout New England. New Haven, for instance, had its Hopkins Grammar School, "the erection of the said school being principally for the instruction of hopeful youth in the Latin tongue, and other learned languages so far as to prepare such youth for the college and public service of the country in church, and Commonwealth."[6]

But America did not long remain "the new Jerusalem" of the Puritans. With substantial immigration from Europe and the development of the various colonies along the Eastern seaboard, the same demands upon schools that had developed in Europe appeared in America. The rising middle classes did not believe that the education received in the Latin grammar school was appropriate for colonies active in trade and commerce and even contemplating manufacture of products. More realistic and utilitarian secondary schools were needed. An egalitarian nation aspired to more than the education of an elite for an intermingled church and state leadership role. Common people should be educated too.

ACADEMIES

Benjamin Franklin, who always spoke eloquently for new ideas in the colonies, proposed in 1749 an academy that would break with the traditions of the Latin grammar school. Franklin, perhaps the most skillful politician of his era, phrased carefully his case for the useful versus the ornamental:

It would be well if they could be taught *every Thing* that is useful, and *every Thing* that is ornamental; But Art is long and their Time is short. It is, therefore, propos'd that they learn those Things that are likely to be *most useful* and *most ornamental*, Regard being had to the several Professions for which they are intended.[7]

Once again, secondary education straddled the fence. The academies provided a Latin classical curriculum as well as courses of studies that included the teaching of English and such vocationally oriented subjects as

---

[5] Law of 1647, reprinted in Nathaniel B. Shurtleff, M.D. (ed.), *Records of the Governor and Company of the Massachusetts Bay in New England,* William White, Boston, 1853, vol. 2, p. 203.
[6] "Code of Regulations," reprinted in *American Journal of Education* 4 (March 1858), 710.
[7] Quoted in David B. Tyack, ed., *Turning Points in American Education History,* Blaisdell, Waltham, Mass., 1967, p. 74.

agriculture, navigation, and mechanics. As the academy movement developed, a wide range of possible programs was offered. Some of the academies were little more than glorified elementary schools to teach the three R's. Some were exclusive institutions preparing students for the better colleges. Still others emphasized practical skills. The variety of possible subjects for study grew wider.

Originally the academies were for boys only. In the nineteenth century, pioneer feminist leaders, such as Emma Willard, succeeded in their campaigns to make secondary education available to girls.

Although the academies were private schools, they often received funds or land from the state governments established in the new United States after the American Revolution. Despite tuition costs and a consequent tendency of the academy to enroll the elite, quite a few American young people of farm, trade, and commercial backgrounds managed to obtain some education through the academies. By 1859 there were more than 6,000 academies in existence.[8] It was not until the 1890s that students enrolled in the new high schools were to outnumber those in the academies.[9]

HIGH SCHOOLS

The eventual replacement for the academy appeared on the scene in 1821. It was called the high school and was intended for boys twelve years of age and over who had finished their elementary education and did not intend to go on to college. When the first public high school was founded, it was called the English Classical School. The Boston School Committee argued the need for this additional school for Boston youth.

The mode of education now adopted, and the branches of knowledge that are taught at our English Grammar schools, are not sufficiently extensive or otherwise calculated to bring the powers of the mind into operation nor to qualify a youth to fill usefully and respectably many of those stations, both public and private, in which he may be placed. A parent who wishes to give a child an education that shall fit him for active life, and shall serve as a foundation for eminence in his profession, whether Mercantile or Mechanical, is under the necessity of giving him a different education from any which our public schools can now furnish. Hence, many children are separated from their parents and sent to private academies in this vicinity to acquire that instruction which cannot be obtained at the public seminaries.[10]

---

[8] Robert O. Hahan and David B. Bidna, *Secondary Education: Origins and Direction*, Macmillan, New York, 1965, p. 52
[9] Tyack, *Turning Points*, p. 353.
[10] Ibid., p. 364.

The sponsors of the English Classical School stressed mathematics, English, geography and such vocational subjects as navigation and surveying. But, to their chagrin, some of the school's teachers chose the traditional direction after the school opened. Indeed, the first high school even developed a dropout problem! The school committee noted in 1823 that seventy-six students had dropped out largely because useful and practical studies were minimized and studies not originally intended were included in the program. The Boston School Committee recommended that the school return to its original purposes, including fitting the student for "active life" and "eminence in his profession, whether Mercantile or Mechanical." As a symbolic gesture, they renamed the high school. In 1824 the English Classical School became the English High School.

Thus the first high school in America was born out of a move against an overly classical curriculum and in sympathy for practical and useful education. The state of Massachusetts followed with a law requiring the towns to establish high schools, but not until a half century later did other states follow this example.

As indicated, the high school grew out of Yankee practicality and realism. That the early lawmakers favored the functional and practical is shown by the 1827 Massachusetts law that required towns of 500 families or more to have a high school offering U.S. history, surveying, algebra, bookkeeping, and geometry. Not until a city reached 4,000 persons or more were the classics made an additional requirement. [11]

Yet so strong is our tradition in secondary education of allegiance to the classical humanistic studies traditionally required for college entrance, in addition to the individually and socially useful areas, that the new high school developed in both directions. To the high schools came both those who planned to go on to college and those who planned to go directly into employment. The resulting high school curriculum valued highly college preparatory subjects, including the classics and other more recently added requirements, yet included education more related to daily living, including vocations.

Through this combination, America avoided the dual system of education that has characterized secondary education in Europe (see Figure 5.1). Undoubtedly, the democratic ideal was furthered through avoiding one set of schools for the prosperous who were destined for college attendance and another set of schools for the people who could not afford to attend college. However, one disadvantage was profound confusion about the mission of American high schools. The conflict persists to our own time, as can be demonstrated through a visit to today's American comprehensive high schools, which include college preparatory programs and practical,

---

[11] Ibid., p. 354.

FIGURE 5.1 *Population Aged 15–18 Enrolled in Education. The education enrollment of U.S. teen-agers of both sexes is higher than that of other countries.*

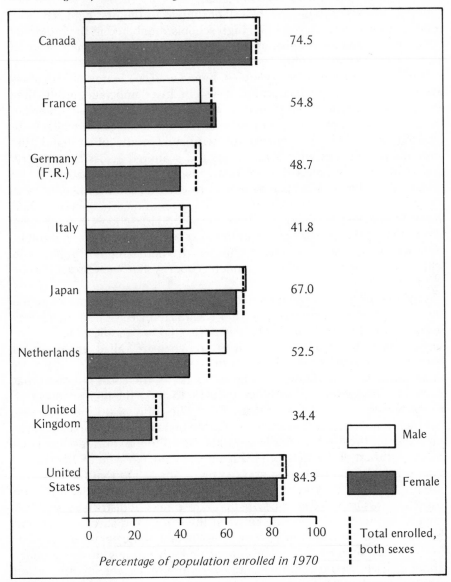

SOURCE: *The Condition of Education*, U.S. Government Printing Office, Washington, D.C., 1976, p. 170.

noncollege-prep programs stressing business, vocational education, homemaking, and other similar subjects.

In the fifty years following the establishment of the first high school in 1821, it grew slowly. In the 1850s high schools numbered in the hundreds while the academies numbered in the thousands. By 1860 there were at least 300 high schools compared to more than 6,000 academies.

The high schools had an advantage, however. They were public schools within the total American educational system. In a democratic society, they offered the promise of education to all the adolescents of all American families. In addition, many of them were located in the cities, which were growing throughout the nineteenth century. On the other hand, the numerous academies were semiprivate and scattered across the country; they flourished especially in rural areas, towns, and smaller cities.

Inevitably, the question had to arise as to whether the U.S. people, who had created a local tax-supported elementary common school system, had the additional responsibility of supporting secondary schools through taxation of the public. A half century after the establishment of the first public high school no one was quite certain as to whether or not public high schools were legally part of the common school system to be supported by public funds.

A major case in the development of secondary education came before the Supreme Court of Michigan. The 1874 Kalamazoo Decision in the case of *Stuart* v. *School District No. 1 of Kalamazoo* arrived at "a judicial determination of the right of school authorities, in what are called union school districts of the state, to levy taxes on the general public for the support of what in this state are known as high schools."[12] The court indicated that there was "no present authority in this state to make the high schools free by taxation levied on the people at large." The court heard the argument that high school instruction was not "for the benefit of the people at large" but rather for the few best able to pay out funds. But the court reasoned that the constitution of the state of Michigan provided a system of elementary schools as common schools supported by taxation, and that the constitution provided for support of the university. The court pointed out that no restriction was imposed by the state upon the power of districts to establish schools that were intermediate between the common district schools and the university. "The inference seems irresistible that the people expect that the tendency toward the establishment of high schools in the primary school districts would continue until every locality capable of supporting one was supplied."[13] So the Kalamazoo Decision was that a high school level between the elementary school and higher education levels was equally deserving of tax support.

---

[12] *Stuart* v. *School District No. 1 of Kalamazoo*, 30 Mich. 69 (1874).
[13] Ibid.

The historic decision meant that America would have the opportunity to develop a universal public secondary school system, rather than follow the European pattern of education that favored the relatively few enrolled in a selective system of college preparatory schools. The way was open for a boom in the growth of the high schools in America. By 1890 there were 2,526 public high schools in the United States.

REORGANIZATION OF SECONDARY EDUCATION

JUNIOR HIGH SCHOOLS

Having created an educational ladder made up of elementary schools, high schools, and college and universities, Americans might have been expected to rest on their educational oars. But this was not to be the case. In the early twentieth century, a combination of factors resulted in the reorganization of the educational ladder that had been assembled throughout the nineteenth century. Americans invented the junior high school.

The commonly accepted birthdate of the junior high school is the academic year 1909–10. In the autumn of 1909 Columbus, Ohio, opened a three-year school that was intermediate between elementary and high school education. In January of 1910, Berkeley, California, opened two such schools, both of them three-year intermediate institutions between elementary school and high school. Columbus, Ohio, called its school a "Junior High School"—and the name has endured until the present. Berkeley called its schools "Introductory High Schools"—and the name disappeared into the mists of history. But the Berkeley school superintendent, Frank F. Bunker, publicized the new institution energetically, and many educators first heard of junior high schools from his missionary zeal. So historians allow you a choice as to whether you regard the Middle West or the West Coast as the birthplace of the three-year intermediate school. To complicate your decision, Richmond, Indiana, has staked a claim because in 1895 an "Intermediate School" was built in that community for seventh and eighth grades for "a fuller more vital offering of work for these pupils."[14]

Why was this new institution, the junior high school, proposed toward the turn of the century? One contributing factor was the strong hand of the influential late-nineteenth-century college presidents. Their concern was not only with what they conceived to be better college preparation; they

---

[14] N. C. Heironomus, "Is This the Earliest Known Junior High School?" *The Clearing House,* May 1940, p. 518.

also wanted students to enter college earlier, graduate sooner, and begin more promptly to make their contributions through their learned professions. The prestigious President Charles W. Eliot of Harvard raised the question of shortening and enriching high school programs as early as 1873. He pushed the matter further in an address to the school superintendents of the country in 1888. Eliot was troubled that the average college graduate was nearly twenty-three years old on graduation and would not begin practicing a learned profession until approximately twenty-seven years of age. So the Committee of Ten on Secondary School Studies, under Eliot's chairmanship, recommended in 1894 pushing several of the usual high school subjects, such as algebra, geometry, natural science, and foreign languages into the elementary years. Or, suggested the committee, an alternative could be to reduce elementary education from eight years to six years and begin secondary education with the seventh grade. This second alternative meant that students would then enter college two years earlier than was then the custom.[15]

Other national committees took up the question of economy of time and the proper requirements for admission to college. The Committee of Fifteen preferred Eliot's first option and recommended algebra in the seventh and eighth years and English grammar yielding to Latin in the eighth year. The Committee on College Entrance Requirements preferred the second option and recommended in 1899 a six-year high school.

College presidents still talked of economy of time and of studying college-type subjects earlier. For instance, President William R. Harper of the University of Chicago advanced an ingenious proposal to link the elementary school with the high school and the high school with the first two years of college work to reduce precollege time by one year for all and by two years for the best students. The Committee on Economy of Time in Education, which began meeting in 1907 and completed its work in 1913, called for six years of elementary education and six years of high school education, thus supporting the early college entrance campaign. This committee also suggested a possible division of the secondary years into a four-year and a two-year school, and a special report it issued recommended the possibility of dividing the six years into two three-year segments.

As educators politely wrangled over possible reorganization of secondary education, a familiar separation of ideas as to the proper work of secondary education again emerged. To the Committee of Ten, dominated by the college presidents, secondary education was essentially preparation for college through subject matter inherited from classical, humanistic, liberal arts education.

---

[15] National Education Association, *Report of the Committee of Ten on Secondary School Studies,* American Book, New York, 1894, p. 45.

Then in 1918 the last and the most influential of the series of turn-of-the-century reports appeared, that of the Commission on the Reorganization of Secondary Education. Advocacy of a junior high school designed for the best possible present education for young people of junior high school age was clear and specific. In the report, neither economy of time nor subject matter justified simply as preparatory for college were central concerns. Instead, a program to meet the needs of the young people attending the schools was the goal. The commission wrote:

The eight years heretofore given to elementary education have not, as a rule, been effectively utilized. The last two of these years in particular have not been well adapted to the needs of the adolescent. . . . We believe that much of the difficulty will be removed by a new type of secondary education beginning at about 12 or 13. Furthermore, the period of four years now allotted to the high school is too short a time in which to accomplish the work outlined above.

We, therefore, recommend a reorganization of the school system whereby the first six years shall be devoted to elementary education designed to meet the needs of pupils approximately 6 to 12 years of age; and the second six years to secondary education designed to meet the needs of pupils approximately 12 to 18 years of age.

The six years to be devoted to secondary education may well be divided into two periods which may be designated as the junior and senior periods. In the junior period emphasis should be placed upon the attempt to help the pupil explore his own aptitudes and to make at least provisional choice of the kinds of work to which he shall devote himself. In the senior period emphasis should be given to training in the fields thus chosen. This distinction lies at the basis of the organization of the junior and senior high schools.

In the junior high school there should be a gradual introduction of departmental instruction; some choice of subjects under guidance, promotion by subjects, prevocational courses, and a social organization that calls forth initiative and develops the sense of personal responsibility for the welfare of the group.[16]

Although reports of educators of varying persuasions contribute to ferment, they stand little chance of prevailing unless their proposals are supported by the surrounding social situation. In the case of the junior high school, its justification grew out of influential social forces. One social force contributing to the development of the new junior high school was the extent to which students, frequently left back, dropped out of school in the early twentieth century. During the first decade of the twentieth century, two out of three young people never even reached the high school! Only one out of ten who entered the first grade graduated from high school.

Certainly, a variety of factors entered into children being held back one

---

[16] Commission on the Reorganization of Secondary Education, *The Cardinal Principles of Secondary Education*, Bulletin No. 35, U.S. Department of the Interior, Bureau of Education, Washington, D.C., 1918, pp. 12–13.

or more grades and eventually dropping out of school. Educators recognized that factors relating to intelligence and to economics were partially responsible. But many educators were persuaded that the blame rested with the program of the high school also. Too many pupils were encountering a curriculum designed for the minority destined for college. Too many pupils could see no connection between school learning and life. Too many students saw no relationship between their daily experiences or potential futures and what was taught in the schools. On the high school level even more than on the elementary level the content was academic and traditional, and the methods formal and sterile. Consequently, many students experienced failure and were held back. Not only did the adolescent of purportedly average or below-average ability drop out, all save the very few eventually withdrew. The earlier students left, the less prepared they were for an increasingly complex industrial, urban society.

A substantial answer, for many educators, lay in establishing the junior high school, which could emancipate itself from college domination and be socially and personally useful to the adolescent. Note the word—the *adolescent*. For the early twentieth century was a period in which G. Stanley Hall, mentioned in Chapter 4, made a major impact on the minds of psychologists and educators. Readers of his *Adolescence* (1904) drew from his work further support for establishing a new school. It was to be a separate school that employed newer methods and that made special provisions for those entering into that unique stage of life called adolescence.

Most of all, the surrounding social realities of the time supported the junior high school movement. Something had to be done about educating young people beyond the literacy promoted by the elementary school. In the new impersonal cities, the family could not fulfill its former functions as effectively as it had in an earlier agrarian society. Vocational training was needed for the new work in the city. Social problems that accompanied the rise of the factory system cried out for solution: unemployment, prejudice against blacks and immigrants, labor-capital conflict, American imperialism. Always complicating the picture was the fact that many of the early adolescents to be educated were themselves foreign born or the children of foreign-born parents. By 1910 one third of the American people were either foreign born or of foreign-born parentage. If the high schools cannot do the job, thought many educators, perhaps a new institution, the junior high school can.

So through the ferment of the various commissions, the concern for those who were left back or who dropped out, the new recognition of adolescence as a stage in development, and the changes in social setting, American education decided to try the form of organization that became known as junior high school.

The junior high school movement boomed. In 1910 only the Columbus and Berkeley junior high schools had been established, but by 1920 there were 387; by 1930, 1,842; by 1940 2,372; by 1950 3,227; by 1960 4,996;[17] by 1975 7,690.[18]

When the junior high school began, its advocates stressed vocational training for early adolescents in a separate institution. However, a social reform movement of the early twentieth century, symbolized by the presidencies of Theodore Roosevelt, Woodrow Wilson, and Franklin D. Roosevelt, struggled to change the weaknesses in urban industrial life. One of the targets of this progressive movement was child labor. With the passage of child labor laws, many adolescents stayed in school through the junior high school years. Consequently, specific vocational training moved upward into the senior high school years; vocational orientation, exploration, and guidance replaced specific job preparation in the junior high school.

Some junior high school theoreticians favored the views of the college presidents who emphasized economy of time and earlier preparation in college subjects. However, the junior high school movement freed itself sufficiently from college domination to stress instead varied individual differences of pupils, prevocational training and exploration, counseling and guidance, meeting the needs of early adolescence, bridging the gap between elementary and secondary schools through coordination rather than strict separation, and developing good citizenship. When the Department of Superintendence of the National Education Association tabulated the views on the junior high school of individual leaders and organizations between 1920 and 1927, the purposes of the junior high school were ranked in the following order:

1. Meeting individual differences of pupils—enabling pupils to follow the lines of their interest and ability;

2. Prevocational training and exploration resulting in wise choice of later school courses and life work;

3. Counseling or guidance—bringing pupils into contact with influences that should give direction and purpose to their lives;

4. Meeting the needs of the early adolescent group;

5. Bridging the gap between elementary and secondary schools—proper coordination between lower and higher schools;

6. Development of qualities of good citizenship—preparation of pupils to play a larger part in the life of the community;

7. Providing opportunities for profitable self-activity—early development of leadership, individuality, and initiative;

---

[17] William Van Til, Gordon F. Vars, and John H. Lounsbury, *Modern Education for the Junior High School Years*, 2nd ed., Bobbs-Merrill, Indianapolis, 1967, p. 42.
[18] Betty J. Foster and Judi M. Carpenter, eds., *Statistics of Public Elementary and Secondary Day Schools*, U.S. Department of Health, Education and Welfare, Washington, D.C., 1976, p. 6.

8. Retention of pupils beyond compulsory school age;

9. Continuation of common education or regular scholastic or academic training;

10. Rounding out a complete unit of training beyond the elementary grades for those who must leave school early;

11. Introduction of new subjects into the curriculum;

12. Effecting economy of time in education;

13. Stimulation of educational advancement;

14. Beginning of definite occupational training;

15. Giving opportunity for earlier preparation for college.[19]

Note the low ranking of the economy of time (12, 15) and early vocational training (14) emphases.

Broadly speaking, in our own times the major purposes of the junior high school became (1) to continue the common education needed by all citizens in the democracy and (2) to provide experiences especially suited to the diverse abilities, needs, and interests of individual young adolescents. In other words, the junior high school ideally was to provide general education and education for diversity. More specifically, the junior high school was to continue the general education of the elementary school years, including basic skills, to provide a transition between elementary and senior high school, to introduce new specific areas and specializations, to help students to discover and follow their interests and aptitudes, to help with rapid physical development, to develop social confidence, to assist in the development of values and philosophy, and to encourage self-management and leadership.[20]

Ideally, this was what junior high schools were to do, but throughout the twentieth century they have always been handicapped by their "junior" status. For instance, junior high schools have sometimes been housed in leftover facilities (fortunately, others were located in fine new buildings). Standards, policies, and regulations have often been geared to elementary and high schools. Teachers have often been drawn from either elementary or high schools and have not had specific preparation for junior high school work. Sometimes the junior high school in a school system has been regarded as a stepchild. The very name "junior" may be a handicap connoting immaturity.

Consequently, though the enrollment in junior high schools climbed steadily throughout the twentieth century, some educators of the 1960s began thinking in terms of a middle school covering a somewhat different age span as the preferable intermediate school. Perhaps it would be better,

---

[19] Department of Superintendence, *The Junior High School Curriculum*, Fifth Yearbook, National Education Association, Washington, D.C., 1927, p. 20.

[20] Van Til, Vars, and Lounsbury, *Modern Education*, p. 35.

they suggested, to substitute for the six-three-three system a five-three-four ladder with the middle school made up of sixth, seventh, and eighth grades or even fifth through eighth grades.

MIDDLE SCHOOLS

As with the junior high school, the middle school movement had mixed antecedents. Some proponents were motivated by much of the same concerns that had long animated those who advocated college preparation. In a Cold War between the United States and the Soviet Union, the Soviet Union had sent Sputnik into space in 1957. Many Americans were appalled at the possibility of their nation being second in the space race. Schools were a convenient scapegoat, and the cry rose for academic excellence and the production of specialists in science and mathematics. Some argued that a return to the four-year high school would best foster academic programs of college preparation.

Most advocates of middle schools, however, accepted the individually and socially useful view of intermediate education. Many were willing to discard the ninth grade from the intermediate institution because, as they saw it, the ninth grade had been "captured" by the senior high school pattern which requires the accumulation of a fixed number of credits (Carnegie units) in certain specific courses for admission to college. Too, they pointed to studies that showed that young people were maturing earlier today, both physically and socially. They argued that there might be greater homogeneity in the last half of the twentieth century among sixth to eighth graders than among seventh to ninth graders. Some reasoned that a fresh start in a new institution, the middle school, might result in new opportunities to deal with individual differences and the needs of adolescents, a goal only partially realized by the "junior" high schools.

One other factor helps account for the rise of the middle school in the 1960s: the civil rights drive against segregated schools. In the early 1960s civil rights leaders realistically recognized the difficulties of desegregating elementary schools in the heavily black inner-city areas of our urban metropolises. To desegregate the early elementary grades in these areas would require substantial busing or use of public transportation. However, students at the fifth- and sixth-grade levels might more readily be transported to desegregated schools well beyond walking distance of their homes. Civil rights leaders of the early sixties thus supported the middle school as a means of getting children out of all-black schools as soon as possible. This reasoning contributed to New York City's announcement in 1965 of a shift from six-three-three to five-three-four programs. The concept of the middle school was congenial to those who worked for racial integration.

However, some leaders of black communities came to regard community control by blacks as more desirable than integrated urban schools. In the debate over middle schools versus junior high schools, avoidance of segregation was mentioned less frequently as an argument for the middle school. Significantly, New York City, with the nation's largest school system, in 1976 initiated studies leading to a return to junior high school organization. The concept of the middle school had become less attractive to black leadership, which accepted a degree of black separatism in return for local community controls.

Many supporters of the middle school are squarely in the socially and individually useful tradition of secondary education. For instance, Theodore Moss in *Middle School* says:

> The overall goal of the middle school, like any other unit of the school system, is to serve the needs of the students and society. As the elementary school is concerned with children, and as the high school focuses on adolescents, the middle school is designed specifically to meet the needs of pre-adolescents.[21]

Like the junior high school, the middle school has grown. It is still too early to determine whether it will eventually replace the junior high school on the American secondary school ladder. By 1966 the middle school organization of five-three-four type was used in 3.3 percent of all school systems enrolling more than 300 pupils. Of all such systems, 1.1 percent used the four-four-four plan in 1966. The middle school organization had grown to 4.4 percent by 1966.

By 1971 there were 2,080 middle schools in the United States. By 1975 there were 3,224 middle schools. U.S. Office of Education statisticians (who group middle schools under elementary education) reported in 1975 that "the middle school, although a popular emerging classification, comprised only 5.2 percent of elementary schools."[22] Incidentally, the jurisdictional dispute between elementary and secondary education as to where the middle school belongs is lively and not resolved. In this book we group middle schools within secondary education while recognizing that its placement is a matter of controversy.

Whether the middle school dominates or supplements developments in secondary education depends largely upon the power of the forces supporting middle school education. These include college preparation advocates, modern educators willing to cede the ninth grade to the high school, research psychologists who stress the earlier maturity of the adolescent, educational reformers who want a new chance to develop a school for preadolescence, and integrationists among the blacks. It is an open question as to whether these forces, somewhat uncomfortable with each other, are potentially as influential as the forces that contributed to the development of the junior high school. As the reader will recall, the junior high

---

[21] Theodore C. Moss, *Middle School*, Houghton Mifflin, Boston, 1969, p. 20.
[22] Foster and Carpenter, *Statistics*, p. 6.

school grew out of the reports of college presidents and others who spoke for reorganization, out of the alarming prevalence of students who dropped out or who were left back, out of the vocational education movement, out of the discovery of the significance of the period of adolescence and the high degree of individuality among adolescents, and out of the social problems caused by urbanization.

EVOLUTION OF SENIOR HIGH SCHOOLS

Naturally, the organizational structure of the American high school was affected by the burgeoning growth of the junior high school since 1910 and the emergence of the middle school since the 1960s (Figure 5.2). When the twentieth century opened, a high school was by definition a four-year institution, part of an eight-year elementary school and four-year high school educational system. In 1920 "regular" four-year high schools constituted 93.7 percent of all public secondary schools. Combination junior-senior high schools constituted 5.8 percent of public secondary schools. Thus in 1920 junior high schools and three-year senior high schools constituted only .5 percent of all public secondary schools![23]

However, by 1964, prior to the development of the middle school movement, only 28 percent of all public secondary schools were "regular" four-year high schools. The large majority of public secondary schools were reorganized in structure with combined junior-senior high schools accounting for 23 percent, three-year senior high schools for 21 percent, and junior high schools for 28 percent.[24] And these figures do not include the newcomer to secondary education in the 1960s—the middle school!

By 1974, 32 percent of all public secondary schools were junior high schools. Junior-senior high schools accounted for 19 percent. Statisticians no longer separated "regular" four-year high schools from three-year senior high schools; instead, both were lumped together as senior highs and totaled about 48 percent. Vocational-technical secondary schools accounted for 2 percent. As mentioned earlier, middle schools are grouped by the statisticians under elementary rather than secondary education.[25]

When educators refer today to "a high school" without using modifiers, they may be referring to a "regular" four-year high school or a three-year senior high school or the senior segment of a junior-senior high school. A

---

[23] W. Gaumnitz and J. D. Hull, *Junior High School Versus the Traditional High School Organization*, Circular 373, U.S. Office of Education, U.S. Government Printing Office, Washington, D.C., 1953, p. 9.

[24] U.S. Office of Education, *Statistics of State School Systems, 1963–64*, U.S. Government Printing Office, Washington, D.C., 1965, p. 21.

[25] Geraldine J. Scott and Paul M. Dunn, *Statistics of State School Systems 1973–1974*, National Center for Education Statistics, U.S. Department of Health, Education and Welfare, U.S. Government Printing Office, Washington, D.C., 1976, p. 26.

FIGURE 5.2 *The Structure of Education. A range of school organizational patterns and subdivisions exists within the basic elementary/secondary and postsecondary levels.*

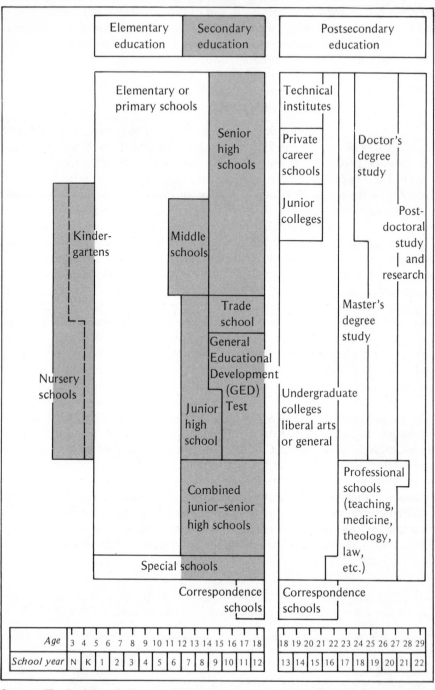

SOURCE: *The Condition of Education*, U.S. Government Printing Office, Washington, D.C., 1976, p. 14.

140   *Development of Secondary Schools*

common denominator of all three types is that each includes at least the tenth-, eleventh-, and twelfth-grade levels.

Attendance at high schools of all three types boomed during the twentieth century as the American population grew, as more and more students stayed in, and as fewer and fewer students dropped out (see Figure 5.3). In the American system of education marked by local control of schools, communities developed differing kinds of high schools. The four general kinds are comprehensive, general, specialized, and vocational.

A comprehensive high school is open to all young people of high school age who live in a community or an area within a community. The program of a comprehensive high school includes offerings for the college bound, the vocationally oriented, and those neither going to college nor specializing in a particular vocation. The comprehensive high school, usually a large school, attempts to serve all the children of the community in one school. Advocates of the comprehensive school believe that it is socially healthy for American democracy to educate together all young Americans, whatever their races, ethnic backgrounds, religious preferences, or social-class backgrounds might be. Yet the comprehensive high school is, in actuality, limited by the nature of the community itself in what it can do in bringing together young Americans of such varied backgrounds. If the community happens to be all white, Christian, and upper middle class, for instance, the comprehensive high school will not play the integrating function that some advocates of comprehensive schools support.

James B. Conant staunchly supported the comprehensive high school in his influential 1959 report to interested citizens, *The American High School Today*. He stated what he saw as the three main objectives of a comprehensive high school:

First, to provide a general education for all the future citizens; *Second,* to provide good elective programs for those who wish to use their acquired skills immediately on graduation; *Third,* to provide satisfactory programs for those whose vocations will depend on their subsequent education in a college or university.[26]

Conant, a distinguished chemist, a Harvard University president, and a holder of high public offices, specified twenty-one recommendations for school board members and school administrators, many of whom earnestly attempted to implement the recommendations during the 1960s. His report supported increased counseling, ability grouping, remedial reading, and programs for the academically talented and the highly gifted. The report rejected "tracks" such as college preparatory or vocational or commercial. Required programs for all were specified and included four years of English, three or four years of social studies, one year of mathematics, and

---

[26] James B. Conant, *The American High School Today*, McGraw-Hill, New York, 1959, p. 17.

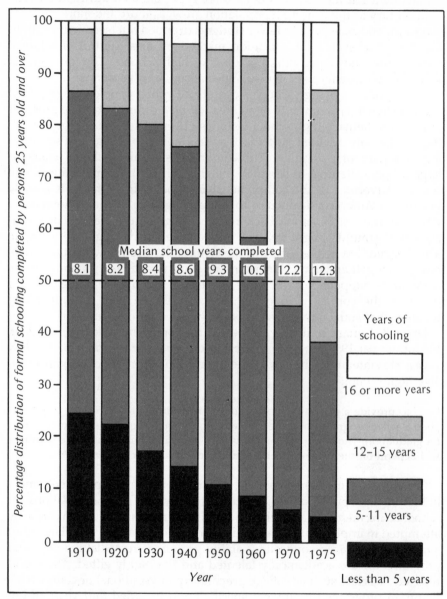

FIGURE 5.3 *Changing Educational Attainment. The distribution of adult attainment has shifted substantially in the last sixty-five years, with a larger percentage of adults obtaining a high school education or beyond.*

SOURCE: Mary A. Golladay, ed., *The Condition of Education,* U.S. Government Printing Office, Washington, D.C., 1977, p. 103.

one year of science. Conant supported strong emphasis on English composition and a developmental reading program. As to electives, he urged offering a third or fourth year of a foreign language no matter how few students might enroll; he supported diversified programs for the development of marketable skills; he described possible science electives. To accommodate the many subjects envisioned, he suggested a seven- or eight-period day with each period as short as forty-five minutes.

The report was highly prescriptive and regarded by some critics as containing insufficient justification, yet it was highly influential and contributed to a nationwide definition of the program of the large comprehensive high school. Conant wanted to eliminate small high schools with graduating classes of less than a hundred students, which he regarded as "one of the serious obstacles to good secondary education throughout most of the United States."[27]

A second kind of high school, the general high school, resembles the comprehensive high school in that it is open to all young people in a particular community or community area yet differs from it in that one particular type of educational program is stressed. Today general high schools are frequently found in upper-income suburbs that offer an essentially college preparatory curriculum. Such schools are frequently small. If youngsters want vocational education for a specific occupation that does not require college education, they usually will not find such a program in the general high school.

A third kind of high school is the specialized high school, usually found in large cities. Such a high school caters to special groups of students with special abilities and interests. Large metropolises have created schools for students talented in the sciences or in mathematics. Some have been created for future artists and musicians or fashion designers or future business leaders. A frequently cited illustration is the Bronx High School of Science in New York City. Understandably, there are relatively few specialized high schools, in part because of the cost factor.

A fourth kind of high school that developed in the twentieth century is the vocational high school. Such a school offers programs of vocational training for a variety of occupations. For instance, a student may specialize in a particular trade, industry, or business in order to become, for instance, a carpenter or automobile mechanic or welder. Vocational programs are usually introductory in nature; the assumption is made that the student will learn advanced skills, if needed, on the job. General education is also included in vocational schools, but it is often not as demanding as in the college-entrance-oriented school. Vocational schools, which are usually large, are more often found in large cities than elsewhere. Vocational or

---

[27] Ibid., p. 77.

trade schools are a minority among high schools and number in the hundreds, whereas comprehensive or general high schools constitute the very large majority of secondary schools.

SOME STATISTICS ON SECONDARY EDUCATION

The number of students and teachers involved in secondary education in modern America is impressive. Public secondary schools in 1975 were attended by 19,146,276 young people and private secondary schools were attended by about 1,400,000 young people. In 1975 in the public school sector alone there were 11,480 senior high schools, 7,690 junior high schools, and 3,224 middle schools with elementary grades only, and 4,122 schools were combined junior-senior high schools. There were also 545 vocational technical high schools.[28] In the fall of 1975 approximately 1,023,000 persons taught grades nine through twelve in public secondary schools and 93,000 in private secondary schools. For an elaboration of recent statistics, see Table 5.1.

American secondary schools have steadily increased their holding power. The dropout rate has declined. For instance, if we compare the number of high school graduates with the number of people who are seventeen years old, we find that in 1900 slightly more than six people graduated from high school for every one hundred people who were then seventeen years old, but that by 1950 fifty-nine people graduated from high school for every one hundred persons who were seventeen years old. By 1975 seventy-five people graduated from high school for every one hundred persons who were seventeen years old.[29]

All in all, in 1975 more than 21 million people were actively engaged in secondary education, whether as students or as teachers. And this does not include administrators, bus drivers, clerks, maintenance staff, and so on. The size and scope of secondary education must always be considered as one looks at the problems of American secondary schooling. Secondary education has come a long way from the classical tradition of early days. Within the individual junior, middle, and senior high schools, earnest people debate the best offerings and methods for the students enrolled. The American public joins in the discussion. Now the struggle intensifies as to how best to achieve a socially and individually useful education for our young people, regardless of whether they are bound for college, specializing in a particular vocation, or unsure of their educational and

---

[28] Foster and Carpenter, eds., *Statistics*, pp. 5–6.
[29] National Center for Educational Statistics, *Digest of Educational Statistics*, 1975 ed., U.S. Government Printing Office, Washington, D.C., 1976, p. 59.

TABLE 5.1 *Historical summary of fall survey statistics on school districts, pupils in membership, teachers, and high school graduates in public elementary and secondary day schools, 50 states and the District of Columbia, 1971 to 1975*

ITEM	FALL 1971	FALL 1972	FALL 1973	FALL 1974	FALL 1975
1	2	3	4	5	6
A. Local school districts					
Total districts	17,289	16,960	16,730	16,568	16,376
Operating	16,838	16,515	16,365	16,239	16,013
Nonoperating	451	445	365	329	363
B. Membership					
Total pupils in membership	46,081,000	45,744,000	45,429,497	45,053,272	44,838,490
Elementary schools	27,688,000	27,323,000	26,434,971	26,382,400	25,692,214
Secondary schools	18,393,000	18,421,000	18,994,526	18,670,872	19,146,276
Percentage of total membership in elementary schools	60.1	59.7	58.2	58.6	57.3
Percentage of total membership in secondary schools	39.9	40.3	41.8	41.4	42.7
C. Classroom teachers					
Total teachers, full-time and part-time (FTE)	2,063,000	2,103,000	2,133,363	2,165,538	2,203,089
D. Pupil-teacher ratio					
Pupil-teacher ratio (total elementary and secondary schools)	22.3	21.8	21.3	20.8	20.4
E. Public high school graduates	1971–72	1972–73	1973–74	1974–75	
Total graduates (day school)	2,699,000	2,730,000	2,763,314	2,823,023	
Boys	1,342,000	1,353,000	1,362,565	1,389,353	
Girls	1,357,000	1,377,000	1,400,749	1,433,670	
Other programs	29,839	34,973	40,204	36,392	
High school equivalency certificates	180,000	190,713	186,410	225,585	

SOURCE: Betty J. Foster and Judi M. Carpenter, eds., *Statistics of Public Elementary and Secondary Day Schools*, U.S. Department of Health, Education, and Welfare, U.S. Government Printing Office, Washington, D.C., 1976, p. 12.

vocational plans. How can we help them live well in our complex contemporary American society? What should be the goals of secondary education in the United States? We turn to the problem of desirable goals in the next chapter.

DISCUSSION

1. In broadest terms, what is the continuing conflict over the nature of secondary education? Illustrate some of the ways in which today's secondary school teacher encounters this conflict.

2. What were the characteristics of ancient Greek secondary education? In what ways did it resemble and differ from contemporary American education?

3. How does the shift in the language of instruction in ancient Rome illustrate a repeated development in the history of education?

4. As the Middle Ages were succeeded by the Reformation, what social changes accounted for the growing emphasis on practical and utilitarian education?

5. What were the purposes of Puritan schools? What was the program of the Latin Grammar School? Why did the academy replace the Latin grammar schools? What was the nature of the program of the early academies? How were these schools financed?

6. What accounts for the origin of the English High School? How did the curriculum of this Boston school change?

7. What are the advantages and disadvantages of a high school curriculum that combines the classical with the individually and socially useful orientations?

8. What is the importance of the Kalamazoo decision?

9. Why was the junior high school proposed early in the twentieth century? What purposes did college presidents and their prestigious committees wish the proposed junior high school to serve? How did the recommendations of the 1918 Commission on the Reorganization of Secondary Education differ from the recommendations of earlier committees? What social forces helped create the junior high school in the early twentieth century?

10. What was the extent of the problem of students being held back one or more grades and eventually dropping out?

11. How did G. Stanley Hall's work contribute to establishment of the junior high school?

12. What social problems help account for the junior high school movement? Why?

13. What were the original purposes of the junior high school? How did they change with time? Why did they change?

14. What accounts for the rise of the middle school in the 1960s and 1970s? Are the factors that account for the development of the middle school as powerful as the factors that accounted for the rise of the junior high school?

15. Essentially, what is a comprehensive high school? What accounts for its creation? What are its major objectives?

16. What was the Conant report and why was it influential?

17. What is the function of the types of high schools other than the comprehensive high school?

INVOLVEMENT

1. If you can return to the high school from which you graduated, ask several of your former teachers about the conflicts they have experienced as to what to teach. Attempt to relate this to the conflict between the older and newer conceptions of education discussed in this chapter.

2. As a class, share class members' experiences with the conflict between the classical humanistic tradition and the socially and individually useful approach. How did individual class members resolve this conflict?

3. Supplement the brief accounts of education in world civilizations with reports derived from a textbook on the history of education.

4. If a long-established public or private school exists within reasonable distance of the community in which you now reside, visit it and learn whatever you can about its original curriculum and how that curriculum persisted or changed.

5. Develop a schedule of visits to high school classes at quite different levels, ranging from middle school and junior high school through senior high school. Compare and contrast behavior, curriculum, atmosphere, and other factors. Attempt to account for differences. Can you observe in the high school evidence of both earlier and modern programs? Can you recognize in the junior high school allegiance to earlier or later conceptions of the good junior high school? Do you find that the new middle school is different from your own recollections of either elementary school or the junior high school segment of your secondary education?

6. Attempt to visit different types of high schools, including a comprehensive high school and a vocational high school. Talk over with others on the trip similarities and differences. Discuss your ideas and those of others as to advantages and disadvantages of each type of school.

7. Interview older residents of the community about secondary education when they were young. To what extent did it exist? How was the secondary education they recall different from that which you experienced? Different from that which you are currently observing?

FURTHER READINGS

Alexander, William M., J. Galen Saylor, and Emmett L. Williams. *The High School: Today and Tomorrow*. Holt, Rinehart and Winston, New York, 1971. A highly competent textbook that includes sections on the high school in American life, the curriculum of the high school, teaching in the high school, and the high school of tomorrow.

Bough, Max E., and Russell L. Hamm, eds. *The American Intermediate School: A Book of Readings*. Interstate Printers and Publishers, Danville, Ill., 1974. A discussion of curriculum direction in the emerging middle school.

Featherstone, Joseph. *What Schools Can Do*. Liveright, New York, 1976. An able journalist sets forth a constructive program of "sober progressivism" through a series of essays, ranging over a variety of topics, that appeared in the *New Republic* and other journals.

Kindred, Leslie W., et al. *The Middle School Curriculum*. Allyn and Bacon, Boston, 1976. The emerging middle school curriculum. Stresses curriculum for the middle school population and innovations that facilitate learning.

Krug, Edward A. *The Shaping of the American High School*. 2 vols. Harper & Row, New York, 1964, 1972. Discusses the shaping of the American secondary school from 1880 to 1941. The first volume discusses the early years, 1880–1920, and the second volume, 1920–1941.

National Center for Education Statistics. *The Condition of Education*. U.S. Government Printing Office, Washington, D.C., 1976. A splendid compilation of statistical materials presented through dramatic charts and tables and ranging widely over the broad field of education. Prepared by the Planning Office of the National Center for Education Statistics. The single most useful source of recent statistics for a student of education (also the 1977 edition).

Overly, Donald E., Jon Rye Kinghorn, and Richard L. Preston. *The Middle School: Humanizing Education for Youth*. Charles A. Jones, Worthington, Ohio, 1972. A book on the middle school that conceives this level as an opportunity for individualizing and humanizing instruction. Includes foundational considerations, various programs of curriculum development, alternatives as to innovations, suggestions for student involvement, and alternatives for school procedures and facilities.

Perkinson, Henry J., ed. *Two Hundred Years of American Educational Thought*. David McKay, New York, 1976. An historical overview of the American approach to education, with some emphasis on the more modern critics.

Smith, Frederick R., and C. Benjamin Cox. *Secondary Schools in a Changing Society*. Holt, Rinehart and Winston, New York, 1976. A textbook on social and professional issues facing secondary educators in a dynamic, pluralistic society. Poses hard questions and avoids easy answers.

Tyack, David B., ed. *Turning Points in American Educational History*. Blaisdell, Waltham, Mass., 1967. A lively focus on turning points in history that familiarizes the reader with individuals and major movements.

U.S. Office of Education. *Projections of Teacher Supply and Demand to 1980-81.* U.S. Department of Education, Department of Health, Education, and Welfare, Washington, D.C., 1976. A projection that indicates that competition for teaching posts is becoming stiffer and is not expected to relax until at least 1981. For new teachers, the outlook is gloomy.

6.

Conflict over the Goals of Secondary Education

The Declaration of Independence speaks of "self-evident truths." One self-evident truth in education is that teachers must have goals; that is, they must know what they are trying to accomplish. Teachers must think through the general direction in which learning should go. A journey would be meandering and aimless if it had no destination. Similarly, in our educational journeys as teachers we must have goals. One of Abraham Lincoln's favorite quotes was "without vision, the people perish."

As we have seen, secondary education in America began with the Latin Grammar School, an institution inherited from Europe and devoted to preparing students for entrance into Harvard College through a classical curriculum. The academy, however, was originated to provide practical and socially useful programs for colonial Americans. The first high school was also created to be individually and socially useful to a wide range of American young people who did not contemplate going to college. The junior high school and the middle school were invented to serve the needs of young adolescents or preadolescents. College entrance considerations continued to play a part in the programs of nineteenth- and twentieth-century secondary schools. But the major drive of American secondary education was to define and establish an education for contemporary American life that was appropriate for all youth, including those who were not bound for college.

From the earliest days of the new nation to present times, the question of what constitutes individually and socially useful education for all American youth has persisted. Many voices have been heard in the attempts to define such education for young Americans. Many thinkers have been involved in the struggle to go beyond traditionalism and to achieve an education appropriate for American democracy. Inevitably, the views of educators have been heavily shaped by the social forces that characterized their particular eras.

This chapter deals with the efforts of educators in American society to define in theory and carry out in practice a relevant education for all American youth. Although there might be growing agreement that education should be individually and socially useful, there have always been a variety of interpretations about what constitutes desirable education and consequent conflicts over goals.

EARLY SPOKESMEN FOR USEFUL GOALS

BENJAMIN FRANKLIN

In addition to his roles as a statesman, printer, scientist, and writer, Benjamin Franklin might well be regarded as the father of modern secondary education in America. Ironically enough, Franklin left school at ten years of age to help his father, a tallow chandler and soapmaker. In his *Autobiography*, Franklin reports that he acquired fair writing skills but failed in arithmetic. He was a self-educated man who took advantage of every opportunity to improve his writing through letters, abstracts, and rewriting. He practiced debating, taught himself science, learned history, and acquired knowledge of philosophy and foreign languages.

Although Franklin was a "dropout," he supported schooling for the people of the colonies in the years immediately before the American Revolution, for he mistrusted the process of informal self-education as too chancy. Since he stressed utility and valued common sense, he judged the learning of English to be more important than study of the classics, and he stressed history and science as well in his educational proposals for an academy in Philadelphia. Unlike the early settlers who identified theology with education, Franklin stressed moral behavior, not religious doctrine; he believed that living well was preferable to indoctrination in religious orthodoxy. Above all, he wanted to open up useful education to the people of the colonies, including people from humble origins such as his own, rather than to allow secondary and higher education to be reserved exclusively for the youth of prosperous families destined for the ministry and a limited range of learned professions such as medicine and the law.

When Franklin developed his *Proposals Relating to the Education of Youth in*

Pennsylvania, he specified useful approaches which he had tried in his own self-education:

All should be taught to write a *fair Hand,* and swift, as that is useful to All. And with it may be learnt something of *Drawing,* by imitation of Prints, and some of the first Principles of Perspective. *Arithmetick, Accounts,* and some of the first Principles of *Geometry* and *Astronomy.*

The English Language might be taught by Grammar; . . . The *Stiles* principally to be cultivated, being the *clear* and the *concise.* Reading should also be taught, and pronouncing, properly, distinctly, emphatically. . . .

To form their Stile, they should be put on Writing Letters to each other, making Abstracts of what they read; or writing the same Things in their own Words; telling or writing Stories lately read, in their own Expressions. . . .

To form their Pronunciation, they may be put on making Declamations, repeating Speeches, delivering Orations, etc.[1]

Franklin depended highly upon history:

But if History be made a constant Part of their Reading, such as the Translations of the Greek and Roman Historians, and the modern Histories of ancient Greece and Rome, etc. may not almost all Kinds of useful Knowledge be that Way introduc'd to Advantage, and with Pleasure to the Student? As Geography . . . Chronology . . . Ancient Customs . . . Morality.[2]

Franklin believed that history "will show the wonderful Effects of Oratory," will deal with the "Advantage of Civil Orders and Constitutions" and thus lead to "sound Politicks," and will foster the "Use of Logic." Universal history would give a connected idea of human affairs. He advocated "natural history" to provide scientific understanding. Histories of nature would be "of great Use to them, whether they are Merchants, Handicrafts, or Divines." He stated that "Natural History will also afford Opportunities of introducing many Observations, relating to the Preservation of Health, which may afterwards be of great Use. . . . While they are reading Natural History, might not a little Gardening, Planting, Grafting, Inoculating, etc. be taught and practiced; and now and then Excursions made to the neighbouring Plantations of the best Farmers." The history of commerce would also be taught and "will naturally introduce a Desire to be instructed in Mechanicks."[3]

Franklin believed not only that education should be useful; he also believed that students should enjoy school. He talked of schools as pleasant, interesting environments. He wanted the library of his academy to

[1] Benjamin Franklin, "Proposals Relating to the Education of Youth in Pennsylvania," *The Papers of Benjamin Franklin,* ed. Leonard Labaree, et al., vol. 3 (January 1, 1745–June 30, 1750), Yale University Press, New Haven, 1961, pp. 404–410.
[2] Ibid., pp. 410–412.
[3] Ibid., pp. 397–419.

contain more than books; he specified maps, globes, mathematical instruments, apparatus for experiments, prints, and machines.

The key word in Franklin's educational vocabulary was *useful*; his version of usefulness grew out of his self-education, his studies, and his times.

THOMAS JEFFERSON

Another man for all seasons who contributed to education was the versatile Thomas Jefferson, president of the United States, author of the Declaration of Independence, founder of the University of Virginia, scientist, architect, and philosopher-statesman. Jefferson's major contribution to education was his perception that education was necessary if the people of the new United States were to govern themselves and remain free. In his letters he wrote, "If a nation expects to be ignorant and free, in a state of civilization, it expects what never was and never will be."[4] He also wrote: "Enlighten the people generally, and tyranny and oppressions of body and mind will vanish like evil spirits at the dawn of day."[5] And he stated: "I know no safe depository of the ultimate powers of the society but the people themselves; and if we think them not enlightened enough to exercise their control with a wholesome discretion, the remedy is not to take it from them, but to inform their discretion."[6] In short, he supported education for citizenship in the new nation.

Jefferson wrote each of these letters when he was in his seventies. Much earlier, when he was in his thirties, Jefferson fostered a less sweeping version of education for citizenship. Rather than extensive education for all, he stressed a natural aristocracy of "genius and virtue." In 1779 he introduced a bill in the Virginia legislature for the more general diffusion of knowledge. All free (but not slave) male and female children were to be provided with three years of education without tuition charge.

At every of those schools shall be taught reading, writing, and common arithmetick, and the books which shall be used therein for instructing the children to read shall be such as will at the same time make them acquainted with the Graecian, Roman, English, and American history.[7]

Then the boy (not girl) "of best genius in the school" would be sent to one of the twenty grammar schools

---

[4] Letter to Colonel Charles Yancey, January 6, 1816, in *Familiar Quotations*, ed. John Bartlett, Little, Brown, Boston, 1968, p. 473.
[5] Letter to Du Pont de Nemours, April 24, 1816, in *Familiar Quotations*, ed. John Bartlett, Little, Brown, Boston, 1968, p. 473.
[6] Letter to William Charles Jarvis, September 28, 1820, in *Familiar Quotations*, ed. John Bartlett, Little, Brown, Boston, 1968, p. 473.
[7] Paul L. Ford, ed., *The Works of Thomas Jefferson*, G. P. Putnam, New York, 1904, vol. 2, pp. 411–426.

for teaching Greek, Latin, Geography, and the higher branches of numerical arithmetic. . . . Of the boys thus sent in any one year, trial is to be made at the grammar schools one or two years, and the best geniuses of the whole selected, and continued six years, and the residue dismissed. By this means twenty of the best geniuses will be raked from the rubbish annually, and be instructed, at the public expense, so far as the grammar schools go.[8]

Then half the "best geniuses" who were "raked from the rubbish" were to study tuition-free at William and Mary College. The other half were to become grammar school teachers. Although Jefferson's plan was highly selective, it was a step toward universal public education; indeed, the proposal was ahead of its time, and the Virginia Assembly rejected the bill.

Jefferson, devoted to the new republic to which he had contributed so much, opposed educating young Americans abroad. He feared that this experience would turn them away from the manners, morals, and habits of the new nation. Noah Webster, author of an *American Spelling Book*, which helped establish standards for American usage of the English language, also felt that a foreign education would dilute American homogeneity. Benjamin Rush, with Jefferson a signer of the Declaration of Independence, also supported like-mindedness on behalf of uniform and peaceable government. Jefferson, Webster, and Rush were among the new American patriots who called for schools primarily to teach American youth the new beliefs upon which the new republic was based. Their views encouraged both homogeneity and nationalism.

HORACE MANN

In the early national period in the United States, Horace Mann was the great advocate of universal public education. During his years as secretary of the state board of education in Massachusetts from 1837 to 1849, he campaigned indefatigably for public education for all. Mann sold American public education. Like many who sell, he struck a persistently optimistic note in his appeals for support of public education from a variety of social groups. He told the businesspeople that education had a market value, and that the more knowledge was diffused the more the wealth of the country would grow and the aims of industrialists would be served. He told reformers, already becoming troubled by slums, crime, and ignorance in the growing cities, that education would overcome vice, intemperance, disease, and other ills. He told the working men that education was the road out of poor conditions and into a fair share in the

---

[8] Thomas Jefferson, *Notes on the State of Virginia*, ed. Paul L. Ford, Historical Printing Club, Brooklyn, N.Y., 1894, pp. 185–188.

American economy. He told patriots that education would underwrite the principles of the Declaration of Independence, the U.S. Constitution, and the dream of a great republic.

Horace Mann was not alone in his campaign for universal tax-supported public education, a crusade which opened the way to the expansion of secondary education. Fellow reformers labored across the country. Public schools were not to be charity institutions but instead the finest possible schools that could be developed in a young and growing America. They would not only teach the three R's, they would also promote morality and a distinctively American way of life. They would make private education unnecessary. American education would match in merit the American experiment in government.

SOCIAL FORCES INFLUENCE EDUCATIONAL GOALS

RISE OF INDUSTRIALISM

According to the first census taken in the new nation, only one out of every twenty Americans lived in a city or its immediate surroundings in 1790. America was a rural land. Beyond the eastern seaboard and beyond the Kentucky region of the Appalachians pioneered by Daniel Boone there lay an unexplored continent.

Though the citizens of this predominantly agrarian nation might still think of themselves as Massachusetts farmers or Virginia planters or Georgian plantation owners, they had much in common. Their heritage was largely British and northern European. Americans had successfully fought a war against a European power. Now they were cementing their unity. Their Revolutionary era leaders urged upon them still greater homogeneity that their republican ideas might prevail. With Jacksonian democracy, the common people, white and male, gained still more power. In the first half of the nineteenth century Native Americans and blacks were among the Americans but were not *of* the Americans; Native Americans were people to be pushed steadily westward, and blacks were regarded as property. Patriotism, nationalism, and unity were valued in the agrarian homogeneous nation that emerged in the several decades after the American Revolution.

But in the early nineteenth century, industrialism and immigration began to change the rural and homogeneous nation. The steamboat came to the American scene in 1807, the Erie Canal in 1825, and the steam railroad in 1826. Developments in transportation and communication were accompanied by the rise of industry. Many industrial plants were built after the first American factory came into operation at Beverly, Massachusetts, in 1787.[9] With industrialism, migration to the new nation increased.

IMMIGRATION AND AMERICANIZATION

Many immigrants naturally settled in the cities where the factories were located. By the decade previous to the Civil War, there were four times as many cities in the North as in the South. Consequently, the immigrants poured into the growing Northern cities. By 1845 the Irish had become the largest national immigrant group in New York City. More Irish immigrants came to the cities of the New World after the 1845-1849 potato famine in their native land. More than half the residents of New York City were foreign born in 1855 and more than half of these foreign born were Irish.[10]

In the last half of the nineteenth century, urban growth accelerated sharply. The population of New York City increased by 50 percent every ten years during the period from 1840 to 1870.[11] But more immigrants were still to come in the early twentieth century, particularly from southern and eastern Europe. Between 1901 and 1910 more than 6 million immigrants from southern and eastern Europe arrived. Beck says:

Between 1905 and 1914—the peak of immigration—there were six years in each of which more than a million immigrants came. Except for two years during the Civil War, the flow was never less than 100,000 per year between 1845 and 1930. There were over 36 million immigrants by the time of the Great Depression.[12]

Internal migration within the country increased in the late national era as industry and urbanism grew. After the Civil War, many blacks, freed from bondage by the Emancipation Proclamation, migrated North. Throughout the nineteenth century the population as a whole participated in the westward movement. Major cities grew up in every section of the country; they were no longer confined to the industrial North.

The United States became an urban nation with a culturally pluralistic population. The descendants of the original white Protestants from Great Britain and northern Europe shared the nation with free blacks and Native Americans; with Catholics, Jews, and the unchurched; with immigrants from central, southern, and eastern Europe and from the Near East and the

---

[9] Robert H. Beck, "The History of Issues in Secondary Education" in *Issues in Secondary Education*, Seventy-fifth Yearbook of the National Society for the Study of Education, ed. William Van Til, The University of Chicago Press, Chicago, 1976, p. 41.
[10] Diane Ravitch, *The Great School Wars: New York City, 1805-1973*, Basic Books, New York, 1974, pp. 100-104.
[11] Beck, "History of Issues," pp. 40-41.
[12] Ibid., p. 52.

Orient. The initial response of those who had come to America first was predictable. Americanize the newcomers. Make them resemble us. Absorb the various foreign elements in the American melting pot.

The universal public tax-supported education for which Horace Mann campaigned was accompanied by a growth in compulsory school attendance by children. Since elementary school attendance was increasingly required, the main responsibility for Americanization fell on the elementary school. Young children from immigrant families often learned to read through the McGuffey Readers, which indoctrinated them in the ideals valued by Protestants and the political ideals valued by conservative whites who had long lived in the United States. Between 1836 and 1922, 122 million of these readers were sold; McGuffey and the curriculum of the elementary school were practically synonymous terms. High school attendance was often out of reach to many young people of immigrant descent, whose families needed whatever wages these young people could earn.

At both the elementary and high school levels, civics and American history, along with instruction in the English language, were stressed in the education of immigrants. The goal was often to Americanize immigrant children and youth. Chauvinistic people often assumed that the new immigrants were from inferior stocks. Indeed, as late as 1934, Elwood P. Cubberley, a widely read historian of education, could write:

These Southern and Eastern Europeans were of a very different type from the North and West European who preceded them. Largely illiterate, docile, often lacking in initiative, and almost wholly without the Anglo-Saxon conceptions of righteousness, liberty, law, order, public decency, and government, their coming has served to dilute tremendously our national stock and to weaken and corrupt our political life. . . . Our national life, for the past quarter of a century, has been afflicted with a serious case of racial indigestion.[13]

Cubberley recommended that national safety and welfare demand that Americans educate such people in the principles and ideals of the United States as well as teach them to use the English language as the common national tongue. As the high schools grew and as more immigrant children managed to attend them during the twentieth century, secondary educators readily followed such advice.

Only in recent decades have American educators come to appreciate the pluralism of cultures that make up the American people, and to introduce into the curriculum the study of the cultural backgrounds of the various ethnic groups that make up the American mosaic. And, as a result, only recently have adolescents of black, Mexican-American, Native American,

---

[13] Elwood P. Cubberley, *Public Education in the United States*, Houghton Mifflin, Boston, 1934, pp. 485–486.

Puerto Rican, Asian-American, and central, southern, and eastern European backgrounds had the opportunity to study their own cultural heritages and to take pride in the contributions and characteristics of their ancestors.

VOCATIONAL EDUCATION

In an industrial and urban society, there were some new necessities for Americans, whether long established or newcomers. Rather than concentrate on languages that had once served the Greeks and Romans well but that were no longer essential in an age of translations, all Americans had to be well acquainted with their own language, English, in order to work and live effectively in urban, industrial complexes. All had to learn arithmetic for a variety of transactions in which they engaged as businesspeople, workers, and consumers. And it became increasingly clear that the urban, industrial society also required that schools help people in their vocational preparation, especially at the secondary school level.

In the older agrarian society, youth learned to work within the family—the boy in the barn and the fields and the girl at her mother's elbow. In the urban, industrial society, parents could no longer teach the skills that young people needed to learn. Men worked at jobs far from their homes, where they were increasingly joined by women. Nor could the family serve other functions, such as recreation, once readily assumed in the agrarian society.

The need for vocational education through schools became particularly apparent. Businesspeople, union workers, politicians, and educators could share this perception in common. A vigorous movement toward vocational education was launched in the last quarter of the nineteenth century. A coalition of individuals and groups with vocational concerns came together in 1907 as the National Society for the Promotion of Industrial Education. The organization called for more occupational education for adolescents in the industrial environment. Federal governmental support was achieved in 1917 when the Smith-Hughes Vocational Education Act became law. Since then, vocational education programs have been supported by federal funds.

URBAN REFORM

The spread of industrialism, the growth of the cities, and the tide of immigration, key elements in the development of American society, brought with them many interrelated social problems. Industrialism was accompanied by child labor, low wages, recurrent depression, and poor working conditions. Urbanism was accompanied by slums, commercialized vice, increased crime, and organized gangs. For many people, the immigrant experience meant exploitation, fear, and loneliness in an environment characterized by poverty. To counter these realities, a social reform movement began in the 1890s and persisted into modern times. Historians have termed this program of social and political reform the Progressive movement. Broader in scope than the progressive education that owed much to it, the movement originated in the late nineteenth century and took many forms—the establishment of settlement houses, the fostering of country life, municipal reform movements, and the legislation of the Theodore Roosevelt, Woodrow Wilson, and Franklin D. Roosevelt administrations.

Among the outstanding settlement houses were Jane Addams's Hull House, established in Chicago in 1889 as a community center for the neighborhood poor, and Lillian Wald's Henry Street Settlement in New York City, first organized in 1893 as a visiting nurse service. The settlement house workers took their cues originally from the settlements begun in England. They recognized that the immigrant newcomers had left behind them organized communities that gave meaning to their lives and had come across the seas only to encounter the disorganization of life in the slums.

The settlement house workers plunged in to tackle the pressing problems they saw all about them. Among their targets were filthy neighborhoods, vandalism, disease, unemployment, and illiteracy. Their responses were programs to rid homes of vermin and to establish boys' and girls' clubs for recreation; they sponsored visiting nurses and medical clinics, vocational education, and instruction in reading. Since many schools regarded coping with such realities as beyond their scope, the settlement houses necessarily developed educational programs ranging from kindergartens for children, to clubs for adolescents, to adult education for neighborhood workers. Settlement houses became practical and realistic schools teaching English to the immigrants; sponsoring political discussions; providing instruction in cooking, sewing, and child care; and offering opportunities in music, fine arts, and dramatics.

The more perceptive of the settlement house workers recognized that they had to play a role in the larger society in addition to their day-to-day work with the immediate problems of people in the slums. Lillian Wald extended her concern for visiting nurse services into proposals for broad public health programs. Jane Addams became a leader in the woman's suffrage and pacifist movements, and served as a member of Chicago's board of education. Florence Kelley, a social worker and a Hull House resident, worked for protective labor legislation for women and children. The three were associated with the National Child Labor Committee, which promoted the establishment of a U.S. Children's Bureau. The settlement house movement had come a long way from campaigns to clean up the streets. For instance, as Hull House developed, it became increasingly a center for social reform activity. Jane Addams aspired to humanizing the conditions of industrial work.

RURAL REFORM

Not all Americans lived in the city or worked in factories. Many remained on the farm. If they were to stay with agricultural activities, country life had to be made more attractive. Reformers sponsored nature-study clubs. They created boys' and girls' agriculture clubs for a greater appreciation of country living and for encouragement of gardening, livestock care, and cooking.

Rural schools were severely criticized as overly academic and traditional. Social reformers advocated that curriculum in these schools be related to the agricultural setting and they suggested more learning in the fields, gardens, and barns. Rural teachers were urged to improve the physical setting of their schools, to make them community centers; to develop the study of agriculture, home economics, and rural ways; to help children use the tools with which farmers worked.

During the administration of Theodore Roosevelt, a Commission on Country Life was appointed that recognized the reformers' efforts. By 1914 Congress passed the Smith-Lever Act to set up a national system of extension work in agriculture and home economics.

BROAD SOCIAL REFORM

Improvement of life in the cities and on the farms necessitated broad social reforms, as the settlement house workers and country life reformers painfully learned. The Progressive movement of the turn of the century involved campaigns against municipal corruption and national efforts to establish social legislation.

City residents, who desperately needed help with their immediate problems, often sanctioned government corruption if officials helped them with their urgent needs of finding jobs or avoiding trouble with the law. In return for such favors, voters supported political machines. In the long run, the politicians profited and the people were exploited. Journalists of the Progressive era, typified by such crusaders as Lincoln Steffens and S. S. McClure, campaigned against corruption, despite being labeled "muckrakers." Municipal reform administrations sometimes prevailed temporarily over political bossism.

National legislation was passed to eliminate child labor, establish minimum wage laws, control railroad rates, support cooperative efforts by farmers, and fight monopolies. The federal government administrations of Theodore Roosevelt and Woodrow Wilson were replete with such programs; when conservatives succeeded them in power, the clock of social reform, though slowed, was seldom turned back.

When progressive education came upon the American scene in the late nineteenth century a combination of social forces in the growing American democracy was behind it. The progressive education movement grew out of the practicality of Benjamin Franklin with his emphasis upon useful education. It drew upon Thomas Jefferson's beliefs in the diffusion of knowledge in a republic so that the common people might govern themselves. It reflected Horace Mann's aspiration for schools for literate and informed citizens who were educated irrespective of class distinctions to play roles in commerce and industry and to support the principles of the great experiment in republicanism. Progressive education also grew out of the recognition that classical education was not sufficient in an increasingly industrial society that called for more preparation for work whether in cities or in rural areas, in factories or on farms. Progressive education also stemmed from the broad Progressive movement of an era that fostered social reform through settlement houses, country life campaigns, municipal reform, and broad national legislation.

As Lawrence A. Cremin, a historian of progressive education, wrote, progressive education was part of a vast humanitarian effort to apply the ideal of government by, of, and for the people and to realize the promise of American life within the new urban-industrial civilization.

First, it [Progressivism] meant broadening the program and function of the school to include direct concern for health, vocation, and the quality of family and community life.

Second, it meant applying in the classroom the pedagogical principles derived from new scientific research in psychology and the social sciences.

Third, it meant tailoring instruction more and more to the different kinds and classes of children who were being brought within the purview of the school. . . .

Finally, Progressivism implied the radical faith that culture could be democratized without being vulgarized, the faith that everyone could share not only in the benefits of the new sciences, but in the pursuit of the arts as well.[14]

FRANCIS WAYLAND PARKER

Although progressive education grew out of long-established as well as more recent forces in American life, individual educators played their roles in its theory and implementation. For instance, as early as 1875 Francis W. Parker, as superintendent of the public schools of Quincy, Massachusetts, replaced the formal textbooks with more active and realistic approaches to learning. Along with his school board, he

---

[14] Lawrence A. Cremin, *The Transformation of the School: Progressivism in American Education, 1876–1957*, Alfred A. Knopf, New York, 1961, pp. viii–ix.

recognized that though children knew the rules of grammar they could not write successful letters; though they could read their textbooks, they could not read unfamiliar material; though they knew the required word lists, they could not spell. So magazines, newspapers, and teacher-created materials entered the classroom. Geography included trips. Drawing was added to the program. Arithmetic was made practical.

When Parker later became the principal of the Cook County Normal School in Chicago he introduced other innovations to relate subjects of the curriculum to each other and to center learning on the child. For instance, communication was taught through combining spelling, reading, penmanship, and grammar. Nature study was part of science. Geography involved exploration of the surrounding area. Sharing and self-expression was emphasized in meetings of children and teachers in assemblies. Teachers were encouraged to begin where the children were and lead them into new content.[15] Rather than accept overly bookish and dictatorial atmospheres, Parker attempted to create an environment marked by creativity, discovery, spontaneity, and pleasure in school work. He wrote of his faith in the interests and abilities of teachers and students in *Talks on Teaching*.

JOHN DEWEY

The great practitioner and theoretician of progressive education was John Dewey (1859–1952). Dewey's career covered the late nineteenth century and the first half of the twentieth century. As early as 1896 he established a laboratory school in Chicago in which he tested and developed his educational ideas. Dewey saw the purpose of the Laboratory School as discovering "in administration, selection of subject matter, and the methods of learning, teaching, and discipline, how a school could become a cooperative community while developing in individuals their own capacities and satisfying their own needs."[16]

Obviously, it is difficult to summarize briefly the major educational ideas affecting secondary education of a man who wrote 18,000 pages in book form and 5,000 pages in article form, yet to understand what Dewey was thinking during the years when his educational theories were being evolved and tested in the Laboratory School, the following quotation from *My Pedagogic Creed* may possibly help. Dewey wrote in 1897:

—this educational process has two sides—one psychological and one sociological—and that neither can be subordinated to the other, or neglected, without evil results following. Of these two sides, the psychological is the basis. The child's own instincts and powers furnish the material and give the starting-point for all education. Save as the efforts of the educator connect with some

---

[15] Ibid., 131–133.
[16] Katherine Camp Mayhew and Anna Camp Edwards, *The Dewey School*, D. Appleton-Century, New York, 1936, p. xiv.

activity which the child is carrying on of his own initiative independent of the educator, education becomes reduced to a pressure from without. It may, indeed, give certain external results, but cannot truly be called educative. Without insight into the psychological structure and activities of the individual, the educative process will, therefore, be haphazard and arbitrary. If it chances to coincide with the child's activity it will get a leverage; if it does not, it will result in friction, or disintegration, or arrest of the child's nature.

—knowledge of social conditions, of the present state of civilization, is necessary in order properly to interpret the child's powers. The child has his own instincts and tendencies, but we do not know what these mean until we can translate them into their social equivalents. We must be able to carry them back into a social past and see them as the inheritance of previous race activities. We must also be able to project them into the future to see what their outcome and end will be. In the illustration just used, it is the ability to see in the child's babblings the promise and potency of a future social intercourse and conversation which enables one to deal in the proper way with that instinct.

—the psychological and social sides are organically related, and that education cannot be regarded as a compromise between the two, or a superimposition of one upon the other. . . .

In sum, I believe that the individual who is to be educated is a social individual, and that society is an organic union of individuals. If we eliminate the social factor from the child we are left only with an abstraction; if we eliminate the individual factor from society, we are left only with an inert and lifeless mass. Education, therefore, must begin with a psychological insight into the child's capacities, interests, and habits. It must be controlled at every point by reference to these same considerations. These powers, interests, and habits must be continually interpreted—we must know what they mean. They must be translated into terms of their social equivalents—into terms of what they are capable of in the way of social service.[17]

TWENTIETH-CENTURY CONCEPTIONS OF GOALS

COLLEGE PREPARATORY VIEWS

Although various social forces favored education that was useful to all American youth and relevant to the individual and to society, voices in support of an earlier tradition continued to be heard. Those who spoke for the better-known colleges were particularly vociferous. They urgently advocated preparation for college entrance as the goal of high schools, and they protested vigorously, angrily, and eloquently against departures from the standard academic curriculum.

As the high schools took over from the academies and as the colleges could no longer depend upon obtaining their enrollment from some few

---

[17] John Dewey, *My Pedagogic Creed*, E. L. Kellogg, New York, 1897, pp. 4–6.

elite academies, complaints from college administrators and faculty members increased, and so did collegiate attempts to exercise control over the secondary schools. For instance, accreditation was advocated by colleges. Checking up on high school programs was first regarded as a responsibility of college and university faculty members. Power to accredit later shifted toward secondary educators themselves, active in such organizations as the North Central Association.

The College Entrance Examination Board was created in 1900 to avoid chaos in college admissions. In its early years, the board provided a common definition of course requirements and a common set of entrance examinations based upon these requirements. As secondary educators increasingly rejected constraints on their curricula, these common requirements and examinations were replaced by Scholastic Aptitude Tests and a battery of achievement tests. Still another tool that served the college view was the development in 1909 of a standard unit called the "Carnegie unit," which represented a course given five periods each week. The Carnegie unit was widely accepted and contributed to greater standardization of high schools.

Perhaps the most powerful of the collegiate influences on secondary education curriculums were the national committees created to bring the high school programs more into line with the perceptions of the colleges. The Committee of Ten on Secondary School Studies was appointed in 1892, and its membership included a majority of college presidents. The committee ambitiously prescribed academic content in such subjects as Latin, Greek, and mathematics along with the social and natural sciences and English, which by then had become part of the high school curriculum. The committee considered itself competent to deal with the nature of every subject, the best way to instruct, how to test, and the amount of time to be given to each subject.

The fondness of the committee for the classical languages is reflected in its recommendations for Latin and Greek study. For Latin, a minimum of four years of study, five times a week, not less than forty-five minutes per period, was recommended. Latin was prescribed whether students were destined for college or for work. Although translations were readily available, the college presidents argued for Latin so that all young people might gain "an insight into the thought and feeling of people who have contributed very largely to make the life of the civilized world what it is today." Greek was to be studied for three years, with five meetings per week during the first year and four during the last two years. The committee, under the chairmanship of President Charles W. Eliot of Harvard, believed that vocational education should be indefinitely postponed, preferably until after college graduation.

Following the report of the Committee of Ten, other committees reported on concerns that were of great importance to colleges. The titles of the committees themselves testified to these concerns: Committee on College Entrance Requirements, Committee on Economy of Time in Education, and Committee upon the Articulation of High School and College. However, increasingly public school educators and professors of education played a role in the appointed committees. Greater sympathy and understanding of the point of view of secondary school educators became evident.

SEVEN CARDINAL PRINCIPLES OF SECONDARY EDUCATION

The decisive step into a twentieth century that was seeking an education related to the lives of adolescents in American society was taken by the Commission on the Reorganization of Secondary Education in its 1918 report. Unlike those who saw the high school as designed simply for college entrance, this commission's members, who developed the report often simply called the "Seven Cardinal Principles," advocated that secondary education be based on the present and prospective lives of young people. The seven cardinal principles stressed in the report were:

1. *Health.* Health needs cannot be neglected during the period of secondary education without serious danger to the individual and the race. The secondary school should therefore provide health instruction, inculcate health habits, organize an effective program of physical activities, regard health needs in planning work and play, and cooperate with home and community in safeguarding and promoting health interests. . . .

2. *Command of fundamental processes.* Much of the energy of the elementary school is properly devoted to teaching certain fundamental processes, such as reading, writing, arithmetical computations, and the elements of oral and written expression. The facility that a child of 12 or 14 may acquire in the use of these tools is not sufficient for the needs of modern life. This is particularly true of the mother tongue. . . .

3. *Worthy home membership.* Worthy home membership as an objective calls for the development of those qualities that make the individual a worthy member of a family, both contributing to and deriving benefit from that membership. . . . The coeducational school with a faculty of men and women should, in its organization and its activities, exemplify wholesome relations between boys and girls and men and women. . . .

4. *Vocation.* Vocational education should equip the individual to secure a livelihood for himself and those dependent on him, to serve society well through his vocation, to maintain the right relationships toward his fellow workers and society, and, as far as possible, to find in that vocation his own best development. . . .

5. *Civic education.* Civic education should develop in the individual those qualities whereby he will act well his part as a member of neighborhood, town or city, State, and Nation, and give him a basis for understanding international problems. . . .

6. *Worthy use of leisure.* Education should equip the individual to secure from his leisure the re-creation of body, mind, and spirit, and the enrichment and enlargement of his personality. . . .

7. *Ethical character.* In a democratic society ethical character becomes paramount among the objectives of the secondary school. Among the means for developing ethical character may be mentioned the wise selection of content and methods of instruction in all subjects of study, the social contacts of pupils with one another and with their teachers, the opportunities afforded by the organization and administration of the school for the development on the part of pupils of the sense of personal responsibility and initiative, and, above all, the spirit of service and the principles of true democracy which should permeate the entire school—principal, teachers, and pupils.[18]

DEPRESSION ERA REPORTS

The Great Depression of the 1930s heavily influenced thought about the nature of secondary education. Unemployment was widespread. The rate of joblessness was particularly high among youth. Those young people fortunate enough to be employed drew low wages in dead-end jobs. Young people had too much time on their hands and insufficient resources and opportunities to take advantage of their enforced leisure. Social problems afflicted the nation—labor conflicts, homeless people, farm protests, pervasive poverty. Meanwhile Nazism under Adolf Hitler was rising abroad. Native fascist movements developed at home. By 1933 there were 16 million unemployed, approximately one third of the available labor force in the United States.

The voices of eloquent educators were raised in protest. For instance, George S. Counts advocated social reconstructionism, a drive to bring about a better society through study and action on social problems in the schools. In 1932, in *Dare the School Build a New Social Order?* based on his address to the Progressive Education Association, Counts dramatically described the Depression era:

Who among us, if he had not been reared amid our institutions, could believe his eyes as he surveys the economic situation, or his ears as he listens to solemn [disquisitions] by our financial and political leaders on the cause and cure of the depression! Here is a society that manifests the most extraordinary contradictions: a mastery over the forces of nature, surpassing the wildest dreams of antiquity, is accompanied by extreme material insecurity; dire poverty walks hand in hand with the most extravagant living the world has ever known; an abundance of goods of all kinds is coupled with privation, misery, and even starvation; an excess of production is seriously offered as the underlying cause of severe physical suffering;

---

[18] Commission on the Reorganization of Secondary Education, *The Cardinal Principles of Secondary Education,* Bulletin No. 35, U.S. Bureau of Education, Washington, D.C., 1918, pp. 11–15.

breakfastless children march to school past bankrupt shops laden with rich foods gathered from the ends of the earth; strong men by the million walk the streets in a futile search for employment and with the exhaustion of hope enter the ranks of the damned; great captains of industry close factories without warning and dismiss the workmen by whose labors they have amassed huge fortunes through the years; automatic machinery increasingly displaces men and threatens society with a growing contingent of the permanently unemployed; racketeers and gangsters with the connivance of public officials fasten themselves on the channels of trade and exact toll at the end of the machine gun; economic parasitism, . . . is so prevalent that the tradition of honest labor is showing signs of decay. . . .[19]

During the Depression the American Council on Education, a major educational organization, appointed the American Youth Commission. The commission studied 13,000 young people in Maryland who were between the ages of sixteen and twenty-four and published *Youth Tell Their Story*. Howard M. Bell described graphically the conditions and attitudes of these representative young American people. A foreword by Homer P. Rainey summarized issues described in the study:

(1) Certainly one of the paramount problems which this study reveals is the necessity of equalizing educational opportunities. . . . (2) The second need identified by this study is that of finding employment for youth as they emerge from their school experience. . . . (3) A very large percentage of youth assert that economic security is their most urgent personal need. The problem of unemployment is very great. . . . (4) Guidance is one of youth's most pressing necessities. . . . (5) This study also reveals the lack of appropriate and adequate vocational training. . . . (6) The program of general secondary education for youth is in serious need of thorough reorganization. There is abundant evidence that the secondary schools as now operated are ill suited to a large percentage of youth attending them. . . . (7) Because of the lack of employment opportunities and the reduction in hours of labor, the matter of leisure time emerges as a social problem of real significance. . . . (8) If we are to have happy and effective citizens, it is clear that a great deal of attention must be given to health education, including social and personal hygiene. (9) Any listing of the problems raised by this study would be seriously deficient that did not bring to our notice the implications for citizenship that arise out of the attitudes which young people hold. Youth's indifference to the ballot and to other civic responsibilities and privileges is worthy of serious attention. . . . (10) These studies also reflect the need for community planning for youth.[20]

The Depression era gave impetus to those educators who advocated that American education come to grips with the social realities of the culture.

---

[19] George S. Counts, *Dare the School Build a New Social Order?* Arno Press and *The New York Times*, New York, 1969, pp. 33-34. (Originally published by John Day, New York, 1932.)
[20] Howard M. Bell, *Youth Tell Their Story*, American Council on Education, Washington, D.C., 1938, foreword.

Stress in citizenship education shifted from a placid acceptance of "the American way" toward reexamination of American institutions and social action toward improvement of American life.

Progressive education built upon its origins to reach a peak in the first half of the twentieth century, following the establishment of the Progressive Education Association in 1919. Major wings of the progressive education movement emerged. The dominant wing placed strong emphasis upon the needs and interests of young people. An influential spokesman for this general position was William Heard Kilpatrick, a philosopher of education who urged that education take its point of departure from the genuine concerns of young people and lead them into projects that involve problem solving and self-motivated activity. Another wing of progressive education, under the leadership of such social reconstructionists as George S. Counts, advocated focusing the curriculum on the real and urgent social problems of the times. Still a third wing, typified by the views of Boyd H. Bode, called on young people to use the method of intelligence as they studied the conflicts between authoritarian and democratic ways of living.

Throughout his long career, John Dewey recognized the need for a comprehensive and inclusive theory of progressive education. Two of his many contributions are particularly important in this connection: *Democracy and Education* (1916) and *Experience and Education* (1938). In *Democracy and Education* Dewey pointed out that in a democratic society marked by change, common interests must be shared by many groups as they interacted with and related to each other. In Dewey's words, "A democracy is more than a form of government; it is primarily a mode of associated living, of conjoint communicated experience."[21] In such a democracy, both the individual and society were important. Individuals should live fully, and as they made their choices should relate themselves to the broad social setting. They should combine individuality with concern for others who made up the society in which they lived. Education involves experiences. The best education added to the meaning of those experiences as individuals reconstructed or reorganized what they experienced. In this way, individuals could grow in their ability to direct their subsequent experiences. Instead of simply adapting to things as they were, people could then change the surrounding environment and share with others in associated living in a democracy.

Dewey attempted to resist misinterpretations of progressive education and to reconcile the wings of the movement. In so doing, he steadfastly

---

[21] John Dewey, *Democracy and Education*, Macmillan, New York, 1916, p. 87.

maintained that education could begin with the concerns of the individual learner and move into social concerns and issues. Such education would be characterized by reflective thought on individual perplexities, social problems, and humane values. Dewey rejected dualisms and either/or formulations. He would not be forced into a false forced choice as to the importance of individuals, society, or values. He supported a progressive reorganization of subject matter. His *Experience and Education* criticized oversimplifications by some progressive schools.[22]

THE EIGHT-YEAR STUDY

Experimentation with progressive ideas and methods began in private schools and university laboratory schools during the early twentieth century. By the 1920s and 1930s suburban and city schools were introducing progressive practices. The Progressive Education Association sought to evaluate the outcomes of progressive education. Through a Commission on the Relation of the School and College, an Eight-Year Study in thirty school systems was launched in the 1930s. Colleges agreed to cooperate by accepting students from the selected progressive schools without imposing the usual requirements. The staff of the Eight-Year Study paired 1,475 students from the progressive schools with an equal number of students from more conventional secondary schools. Each of the pairs was matched to be as similar as possible in a variety of factors such as sex, scholastic aptitude scores, home and community backgrounds, and interests. But one of the pair had gone to a progressive school and the other to a traditional school. How would the progressives fare in college as compared to their counterparts who had attended traditional schools?

In brief, the students from progressive schools did as well as the students from conservative schools in mastery of subject matter. In other important aspects of education, the students from the progressive schools were distinctly more successful than their partners in the inquiry. Specifically, the progressives earned a slightly higher total grade average and received slightly more academic honors in each year. They were also judged to possess a higher degree of intellectual curiosity and drive; to be more precise, systematic, and objective in their thinking; and to have clearer ideas concerning education. The students from the progressive schools more often demonstrated resourcefulness in meeting different situations, participated more frequently in the arts, and participated more often in most of the organized student groups. They had a better orientation toward a choice of a vocation and demonstrated a more active concern for what was going on in the world.

---

[22] John Dewey, *Experience and Education*, Kappa Delta Pi Lecture Series, Collier, New York, 1938.

Since the reports of the Eight-Year Study appeared during World War II, they drew less attention than they would have ordinarily received. This was unfortunate for the progressive education movement because the carefully developed study was a scientifically constructed and significant piece of research that conclusively refuted the contention of critics that students in progressive schools "learned nothing" and could not succeed in college.

EDUCATIONAL POLICIES COMMISSION

Many educators were favorably impressed by the demonstration through the Eight-Year Study that conventionally organized courses were not essential to success in college. Those who called for a curriculum dealing with the major personal and social problems of young people took heart. The influence of the progressive education movement was apparent in a report of the Educational Policies Commission sponsored by the National Education Association and the American Association of School Administrators. The Commission set forth in 1944 a view on the goals in education described in terms of the imperative needs of youth:

1. All youth need to develop salable skills and those undertakings and attitudes that make the worker an intelligent and productive participant in economic life. To this end, most youth need supervised work experience as well as education in the skills and knowledge of their occupations.

2. All youth need to develop and maintain good health and physical fitness.

3. All youth need to understand the rights and duties of the citizen of a democratic society, and to be diligent and competent in the performance of their obligations as members of the community and citizens of the state and nation.

4. All youth need to understand the significance of the family for the individual and society, and the conditions conducive to successful family life.

5. All youth need to know how to purchase and use goods and services intelligently, understanding both the values received by the consumer and the economic consequences of their acts.

6. All youth need to understand the methods of science, the influence of science on human life, and the main scientific facts concerning the nature of the world and of man.

7. All youth need opportunities to develop their capacities to appreciate beauty in literature, art, music, and nature.

8. All youth need to be able to use their leisure time well and to budget it wisely, balancing activities that yield satisfactions to the individual with those that are socially useful.

9. All youth need to develop respect for other persons, to grow in their insight into ethical values and principles, and to be able to live and work cooperatively with others.

10. All youth need to grow in their ability to think rationally, to express their thoughts clearly, and to read and listen with understanding.[23]

Education for All American Youth went beyond a listing of the ten imperative needs of youth; it also spelled out possible programs to deal with the needs. A program for a hypothetical rural community called Farmville was described. Similarly, a program for an urban community, named American City, was outlined. The proposed programs included a common learnings, or core, course that cut across broad fields of learning in an interdisciplinary manner to deal directly with the imperative needs the commission had specified. Common learnings courses had been tested in the experimentation of progressive schools; now the Educational Policies Commission was calling for wider adoption of these approaches in secondary schools throughout the nation.

RIGHT-WING CRITICISM

Not everyone looked favorably on the extension of progressive education. In the late 1940s and early 1950s the views of Senator Joseph McCarthy encouraged strident criticism of American education by right-wing reactionary groups. Senator McCarthy claimed that the national government, the universities, and the U.S. armed forces had been extensively infiltrated by the Communist party. Although McCarthy's charges were never substantiated and though the witch hunt he launched came to be regarded as an attack on civil liberties in America, the mood of McCarthyism was infectious. Through pamphlets and magazines and even through the *Congressional Record,* right-wing reactionary forces assailed secondary education as communistic, socialistic, radical, un-American, and antireligious. School systems that employed progressive methods were particularly singled out for attack. A classic case of the era was the dismissal of Willard Goslin as the superintendent of the Pasadena, California, public schools. Goslin had supported teaching about the United Nations, race relations, and sex education in the school system. An able journalist, David Hulburd, wrote an objective account of the case in *This Happened in Pasadena.* Following hearings and a vote of censure against McCarthy by the U.S. Senate, the assaults on the schools that had been characterized by sensationalism and unsubstantiated accusations waned markedly.

ACADEMIC CRITICS

A more rational, though angry, criticism of secondary education in the midcentury followed. A segment of the academic community continued to reject, as it had in the past, the proposals of modern

---

[23] Educational Policies Commission, *Education for All American Youth,* National Education Association, Washington, D.C., 1944, pp. 225–226.

educators for an education centered on individual and social problems of youth. The new academic critics objected in particular to interdisciplinary studies through core, or common learnings, courses and to attempts to interrelate in instruction the social studies or the sciences. The supporters of the academic view wanted history to be taught as history without considerations of geography, economics, or sociology. For instance, Arthur E. Bestor, then a professor of history at the University of Illinois, argued that study of separate subject disciplines would help young people to develop a range of intellectual powers. With the separate subjects mastered and with intellectual discipline achieved, students could then on their own coordinate their knowledge. Only then, urged Bestor, could students solve problems they might encounter. Attempts to integrate or interrelate disciplines would fail, according to Bestor; core, or common learnings, programs would by-pass a necessary stage of analysis that could be achieved, he argued, only through study of the separate subjects.

Hyman G. Rickover, who developed the nuclear-powered submarine as a naval officer, joined the debate. Admiral Rickover was particularly critical of a supposed neglect of science and mathematics in American secondary schools. In the climate of the Cold War with the Soviet Union, Rickover visualized a threat to the national survival of the United States if scientific and mathematical training was not upgraded.

Like Bestor, Rickover was highly critical of life-adjustment education, a program that had been fostered a few years earlier by the U.S. Office of Education. During a conference, Charles A. Prosser, a long-time advocate of increased vocational emphasis in education, had pointed out that American secondary schools were helpful to students bound for college and students bound for specific trades and vocations. However, said Prosser, a large middle group saw little point in their education. For them, Prosser advocated an education in the real problems they would face in life. The Prosser Resolution was adopted and life-adjustment education encouraged. Critics of the idea particularly focused on the word *adjustment*, which they interpreted, unlike Prosser, as uncritical acceptance of whatever existed. Criticism of life-adjustment education was strongly supported by the educationally conservative Council for Basic Education.

The academic criticism of progressive education was given impetus by the launching of Sputnik by the Russians in 1957. American political leaders expressed considerable alarm that the Russians were "ahead" in space technology and exploration. One broad social response was the space program of the National Aeronautics and Space Administration (NASA), which later developed the Apollo Program at a cost of $20 billion and landed men on the moon. In the same year that NASA was created, 1958, a National Defense Education Act (NDEA) was passed by Congress particularly to advance education in science, mathematics, and modern foreign languages.

PROJECTS IN THE SUBJECTS

With the help of NDEA funds, projects were established to improve teaching in a variety of subject fields. For instance, instruction in physics was reconstructed. Three versions of biology textbooks were developed. Chemistry was revised through projects. Earth science was newly emphasized. New mathematics programs were created. After a revision in 1964 of the National Defense Education Act, many social scientists and other scholars participated in the development of projects.

The projects were often developed by liberal arts specialists from colleges and universities in collaboration with secondary school teachers who were skilled in methodology. The products of the various projects were disseminated through summer workshops, textbooks, packets, and in-service training programs. A major contribution of the projects was the reduction of obsolescent material in textbooks and courses of study used in secondary schools. In the best of the projects, principles, relationships, and processes of inquiry were stressed.

Since the projects were by definition dedicated to the improvement of teaching in the separate subject fields, project programs seldom dealt with broad interdisciplinary problems such as race relations, energy and the environment, and consumer issues. Thus the life problems stressed by the progressive education movement and reflected in *Education for All American Youth* were by-passed. Specialized education flourished as a result of these projects but general education declined.

Eventually, this was recognized by some who had been most active in fostering the project approach to education. For instance, Jerome Bruner had written in 1960 *The Process of Education,* a brilliant rationale for the projects that stressed study of the disciplines so that students might understand their structure. By this Bruner meant that students must understand the major concepts in each discipline and know the methods of inquiry each used. But ten years later Bruner recognized that students needed more than expertise in subject matter areas. He proposed a dual curriculum, made up partly of the structure of the disciplines approach inherent in the projects and partly of the "immediate and compelling concerns" of students.[24]

By the late 1960s Americans could not evade the problems that beset the nation. This was the period of unprecedented youth revolt, racial disturbances, an unpopular war in Vietnam, and a style of national administration that resulted in the Watergate affair.

---

[24] Jerome S. Bruner, "The Process of Education Revisited, " *Phi Delta Kappan,* September 1971, p. 21.

COMPENSATORY EDUCATION

With the decrease in Cold War tensions, national concern increased for disadvantaged children and youth. The plight of the poor was rediscovered. Problems of the inner city were recognized. In the mid-sixties, urged by President Lyndon B. Johnson, Congress enacted an Economic Opportunity Act and Manpower Development and Training Act Amendment. Programs to compensate for the disadvantages of the poor, including many blacks and other minority group members, were created. Typical was New York City's program stressing the education of parents. It included trips to widen the "horizons" of junior and senior high school students.

To be successful in compensatory education, great emphasis had to be placed on motivating students. Consequently, emphasis on education of potential usefulness to the young moved back to the center of the stage. Relevance and meaningfulness resumed their former central roles in educational proposals and plans.

CONTINUING CONFLICT OVER CURRENT GOALS

Differing conceptions of desirable goals for secondary education persisted during the 1970s. If readers will review the discussion in Chapter 1, they will find that differing conceptions of goals underlay the major contemporary criticisms of education in the 1970s. For instance, the compassionate critics stressed the goal of meeting the needs and interests of individuals. They reflected the views of that wing of the progressive education movement that emphasized the importance of the learner and advocated a child- or youth-centered school. Many of the alternative schools which were founded on the basis of such compassionate criticism stressed freedom, informality, and openness in their programs.

A differing conception of goals for secondary education was characteristic of the back-to-basics advocates of the 1970s. They saw the goals of schools as teaching the three R's supplemented by formal teaching of separate subject matter content. Their views often reflected their predecessors who conceived secondary education as a vehicle for meeting college entrance requirements. Their way of conceiving educational goals was closer to that of the Committee of Ten than to the commission that developed the Seven Cardinal Principles of Education and far closer to the academic critics than to the progressive education movement. The alternative schools that they encouraged were for instruction in basic, fundamental, traditional education.

The third major group of critics of contemporary education focused on the high school in particular and advocated a marked increase in the use of the community in secondary education. The committees and commissions that supported reforms of secondary education in the mid-1970s stressed community-conscious schooling, new transitions to adulthood, and less time on academic instruction. The sponsors reflected earlier emphases on vocational education and community participation. Their emphasis on the socially useful was similar to that fostered by the U.S. Office of Education during the 1970s—career education. Sidney P. Marland, former U.S. Commissioner of Education, has pointed out that career education has a long and honorable ancestry, dating back to Benjamin Franklin's advocacy of more useful education. Career education advocates urged that schools orient and equip young people to earn a living in a personally significant and satisfying career field. However, they contended that more than vocational education was needed; career education should be an integral part of study by young people in all courses throughout both elementary and secondary school years.

Many other voices are heard in discussions and debates during the 1970s concerning the goals of secondary education. Some educators and citizens call for greater emphasis on the emotions in education through affective education. Some would limit education to its intellectual aspect and emphasize cognitive education. And some call for "confluent education," drawing from both affective and cognitive aspects.

The debate over whether the goal of secondary education should be general education or vocational specialization or some combination of these goes on. Tides ebb and flow in this discussion.

In the late 1970s American secondary education continues its quest for relevance. The broad general direction in which education is going is toward a useful education for all American youth, stressing individually and socially significant learning. The exact nature of such education continues to be a matter of controversy, and dissenters from the general direction persist. Yet as conflicts over goals persist, the areas of common agreement expand and the swings of the educational pendulum become less severe.

An illustration of the areas of common agreement as to goals was recently supplied by a National Education Association Bicentennial Panel. A Cardinal Principles Preplanning Committee asked forty-eight individuals, most of them widely known, whether the original Seven Cardinal Principles had retained their merit and, if so, what were the new ways in which they should be interpreted in anticipation of changing conditions in the world community. *Today's Education* reports in "The Seven Cardinal Principles Revisited":

Are the seven cardinal principles still valid? Those . . . who recall the principles with nostalgia and affection will be pleased to learn that all save a few members of the NEA Bicentennial Panel felt that the seven goals have retained their usefulness and their importance even after the passage of nearly 60 years.

At the same time, educators who see a need for new goals and directions that anticipate a millennium can take comfort from and find satisfaction in the fact that the Bicentennial Panel also felt that the old meanings attached to the cardinal principles were no longer adequate for learning and living in an interdependent human community.[25]

In Part 3 of this book, we will take up four struggles in secondary education today—for a better content, for a better setting, for a better organization, for a better staff. Varying conceptions of goals are involved in each of these four struggles. We will be better equipped to make decisions concerning these current struggles if we are well aware of the program of secondary schools today. Consequently, the next chapter deals with the major broad fields of today's secondary school curriculum, their place in the total curriculum, their commonly recognized objectives, and the trends and tendencies within each.

DISCUSSION

1. Why think about goals in education? Why must a teacher have purposes?

2. From your knowledge of history, describe the life and work of Benjamin Franklin. What contributions did he make to American life? For which of his educational contributions will Franklin probably most be remembered?

3. What was Thomas Jefferson's role in American society? Why did Jefferson think that education was necessary for colonial Americans?

4. What was Jefferson's plan for education in Virginia? From a modern point of view, what was commendable and what was dubious about it?

5. Why did Jefferson, Webster, and Rush oppose educating young Americans abroad? Does their reasoning still apply today? Are there significant contributions that education abroad could make to young Americans today?

6. What was Horace Mann's major educational campaign? What arguments did he use on behalf of his views?

7. How did industrialism and immigration change the American scene? . . . change education?

8. How have the views of American educators changed in regard to a desirable education for immigrants? What are the implications of the phrases "melting pot" and "cultural pluralism" for educators?

9. Why did vocational education become necessary in late-nineteenth-century America?

10. What model for education is suggested by the experience of the settlement house workers?

11. What were the major reforms of the Progressive era?

---

[25] National Education Association, "The Seven Cardinal Principles Revisited," *Today's Education* 65 (September-October 1976), 59-60.

12. What are some of the forces in American life that accounted for the rise of the progressive education movement? What is the meaning of progressivism, according to Cremin? What are some other interpretations of progressive education you have encountered?

13. John Dewey regarded Francis W. Parker as the father of progressive education. Why? What ideas did Parker contribute to the progressive education movement?

14. Basically, what is John Dewey advocating in the quotation from *My Pedagogic Creed*?

15. What tradition in education did the Committee of Ten represent?

16. Why was the College Entrance Examination Board created?

17. Why does the report on the Seven Cardinal Principles of Secondary Education mark a milestone in the development of American education? How did the approach of the sponsoring commission differ from that of earlier committees? Do the principles still point to desirable directions for secondary education today?

18. How did the Great Depression influence secondary education?

19. What is the view of the social reconstructionist, as typified by George S. Counts?

20. Which of the issues described in *Youth Tell Their Story* are still alive today? Which issues have been resolved? If we judge by these issues, have we made substantial progress in American life and education since the time of *Youth Tell Their Story*?

21. How did the wings of the progressive movement differ from each other? What was John Dewey's viewpoint on these differences? What role did he play?

22. What was the Eight-Year Study and what were its major findings? What are the implications of these findings for contemporary education?

23. According to the Educational Policies Commission, what are the imperative needs of youth? Do these continue to be the imperative needs of youth in the later 1970s? If not, how are needs different today?

24. What are the similarities and differences between the right-wing criticism of education and the views of the academic critics? Did they differ in the criticisms they made of progressive education?

25. Why is the year the Russians sent Sputnik into space, 1957, significant in the story of American secondary education?

26. What were the projects of the 1960s? . . . their nature, their assumptions? Why did the subject matter reform movement of the 1960s decline?

27. What is meant by compensatory education? What are some examples of programs? Do you see any weaknesses and strengths in this approach?

28. How do the three contemporary groups of critics differ as to the desirable goals of education? Which of these are closest to the classical tradition? Which are closest to the socially and individually useful approach? What interpretations of

individually and socially useful goals are made by some of the contemporary critics of education?

29.   What evidence is there that American education is moving generally toward individually and socially significant learning?

INVOLVEMENT

1.   Supplement your own knowledge of Benjamin Franklin through reading his autobiography or one of the biographies of this amazing man. Look particularly for interrelationships between his life and his educational ideas. Share what you have learned in writing or through a report.

2.   Become more acquainted with Thomas Jefferson through his writings, the accounts of historians, or, if at all possible, through a visit to Monticello.

3.   Engage in argument with other class members on whether Jefferson was a supporter of education and of the democratic way of life or an elitist aristocratic educator and practitioner of slavery. In your discussion, raise such questions as the extent to which it is reasonable or unreasonable to expect historical figures living in other periods to perform in accordance with high contemporary expectations. In short, should Jefferson be blamed or condemned for what seemed today to be limitations of his views? Or should he be applauded and appraised for the forward steps he took in the climate of ideas in which he lived?

4.   Share with the class information on Horace Mann derived from history of education textbooks and library research into his reports as secretary of the state board of education in Massachusetts from 1837 to 1849. How do you appraise Mann's arguments today? Raise in connection with Mann the same type of questions raised above as to Jefferson. Were his arguments for universal tax-supported public education consistent with each other? Should he have appealed with differing arguments to different groups in American society?

5.   Through tracing the ancestries of members of the class, identify times and places of immigration by their families to America. Gather accounts of the educational experiences of these immigrants and of successive generations of their descendants. Do you find evidence of a shift from melting pot philosophy to cultural pluralism?

6.   Pursue persistently the educational history of your own family. Trace that history back as far as you can.

7.   Visit a vocational school in your vicinity. If none exists, visit the classes in your high school that are closest to vocational orientation. What seems to be the prevailing atmosphere? What are the advantages and disadvantages of vocationally oriented education as you observe it?

8.   Visit the social institutions in your own community that derive from reform movements in American life, such as settlement houses, halfway houses, and

centers for first offenders. Compare their programs and goals with those of the reformers mentioned in this chapter.

9. Determine which of the schools in your vicinity is closest to progressive education practices. Visit the school and find opportunities to converse with both teachers and students. Compare the atmosphere and program with the ideas of Francis W. Parker and John Dewey.

10. Read one of John Dewey's short books, *Experience and Education,* to gain some idea of his views of education and his advice to progressive educators. Bring to the classroom for a talk a member of the faculty who is well informed on Dewey's ideas.

11. Obtain an outline of the curriculum of your local high school. Compare and contrast it with the recommendations of the Committee of Ten.

12. On your next observation of secondary education, carry with you a list of the Seven Cardinal Principles. In a report to your class describe the extent to which the class you observed reflects these principles.

13. Summarize the issues described in *Youth Tell Their Story* without mentioning the date of the report. Ask friends and other students in class to guess the date. Do many assume that the issues are current, rather than forty years old?

14. Ask people their objections to progressive education. Inform them of the results of the Eight-Year Study. How do they react?

15. Summarize the imperative needs of youth, as described by the Educational Policies Commission. Ask friends and teachers whether they are still valid. Get their responses; then inform them that the recommendations were made thirty years ago.

FURTHER READINGS

Cremin, Lawrence A. *The Genius of American Education.* Horace Mann Lecture 1965, University of Pittsburgh Press, Pittsburgh, 1965. A lecture on popular education and its relationship to popular culture and to politics.

Cremin, Lawrence A., ed. *The Republic and the School: Horace Mann on the Education of Free Men.* Teachers College Press, New York, 1957. Mann's twelve reports as secretary of the board in Massachusetts. Includes an essay on Mann's legacy by Cremin, an outstanding American historian of education.

Davis, O. L., Jr., ed. *Perspectives on Curriculum Development 1776–1976.* Association for Supervision and Curriculum Development, Washington, D.C., 1976. An historical account of curriculum development in America during our first 200 years. An attempt to give the reader a view of the historical past, the present, and the future.

Dewey, John. *Democracy and Education.* The Free Press, New York, 1916. A classic in education that introduces the thought of the most influential twentieth-century philosopher of education.

Levit, Martin, ed. *Curriculum*. University of Illinois Press, Urbana, 1971. Philosophic approaches to curriculum problems, emphasizing aims of education, the disciplines and experience in the curriculum, and curriculum as a field of study.

Lucas, Christopher J., ed. *Challenge and Choice in Contemporary Education*. Macmillan, New York, 1976. An introductory survey of ideological forces and movements that are making a difference on today's educational scene.

Morris, Van Cleve, and Young Pai. *Philosophy and the American School*. Houghton Mifflin, Boston, 1976. An introduction to philosophy that discusses various schools of thought and ways of thinking about educational philosophy.

Park, Joe, ed. *Selected Readings in the Philosophy of Education*, 4th ed. Macmillan, New York, 1974. An excellent set of readings on philosophy of education. Includes ways of analyzing and then synthesizing philosophical considerations. Considers some fundamental issues in education.

Raubinger, Frederick M., et al., eds. *The Development of Secondary Education*. Macmillan, New York, 1969. Reproduction of significant reports in the development of secondary education such as "The Seven Cardinal Principles," Eight-Year Study of the Progressive Education Association, American Youth Commission. Also commentary on the reports.

Skinner, B. F. *Beyond Freedom and Dignity*. Alfred A. Knopf, New York, 1971. An argument by a behaviorist that calls for a revision of contemporary thought on freedom and dignity and that proposes a technology of behavior. This controversial book has been widely discussed by laypersons as well as philosophers, psychologists, and educators.

Tesconi, Charles A., Jr. *Schooling in America*. Houghton Mifflin, Boston, 1975. A book on social philosophy that deals with questions and issues. The author's viewpoint stresses existentialism and cultural pluralism.

7.

The Secondary School Program Today

If the legendary creature from Mars came to earth to learn about American secondary schools, its first reaction might be one of confusion. It would observe a wide variety of classes, activities, and student experiences. For instance, it would find students discussing fiction, cutting up frogs, solving equations, reading maps, speaking haltingly in a foreign language; students creating pottery, singing as a chorus, building sets for plays, preparing foods, running down the school track; students working with the motors of cars, typing from dictated materials, learning about packaging; students in classrooms, corridors, offices, athletic locker rooms, on trips, at work on jobs within the community. The creature from Mars would observe students in animated discussions, times of silent study, periods of fierce competition; would visit students in formal classrooms, science laboratories, art studios, auditoriums, theaters, athletic fields, small discussion circles, individual carrels, listening laboratories, libraries; would find students enrolled in a compulsory four-year program in English and also enrolled in minicourses lasting only a few hours or days; would see a substantial group of human activities tacked on to the secondary school curriculum and given the label of "extracurricular" or "cocurricular" activities. The host of possible student activities encountered would include chess, hiking, journalism, sketching, dramatics, book reviewing, sewing, collecting, photography, model building, choir, yearbook editing, newspaper production, camping, school government, and so on, ad infinitum. The visitor to earth would soon conclude that today's secondary schools have tried to accommodate many demands and respond to multiple forces.

If the Martian were a scholarly visitor, it might retire to a library to learn something of the history of secondary education and of philosophies of education that have influenced secondary schools. There it would learn, as readers have from the last two chapters, that the course offerings of contemporary secondary schools reflect the requirements of colleges for admission to higher education institutions. This would account for the occasional student still studying Latin and Greek, and for a much larger group of students meeting college requirements broadened to include English, history, mathematics, some of the sciences, and languages. From the library study, the Martian visitor would recognize a high priority placed by American secondary education on practical vocational training, and would thus understand the many business education and industrial education programs of the contemporary high school, as well as the career education observed in many nonvocational classes. The visitor would note that the social problems that America faced eventually became part of the content of the American secondary school curriculum. Whether Americans were concerned with education of a new nation for nationalism, as was Jefferson, or education of a more mature nation for an industrial society, as was Dewey, the American secondary schools reflected the social concern in the curriculum.

Perhaps, above all, the interplanetary visitor would conclude from library research on history and philosophy that the American people wanted an individually and socially useful education, defined broadly. They wanted much more than vocational education alone. They asked for useful education for mind and body, for spirit and emotions, for the American as a citizen and a creator. And they constantly quarreled among themselves as to what was really most useful.

The Martian visitor, newly confident, might emerge from the library with the feeling that today's secondary school could be described through naming all course offerings. However, it would find that if it attempted to name all the courses ever offered in American secondary schools—courses that have been responsive to a wide variety of demands and that are multioriented—it would be setting forth a truly encyclopedic list. Even if limited to all the courses offered by American middle, junior high, and high schools in the late 1970s, the list would be formidable. The broad field of the social studies alone includes, at the very least, history, geography, economics, sociology, civics, anthropology, social psychology, and problems of democracy. Furthermore, the subject of history alone includes American and world history, ancient as well as medieval history, modern history, along with the histories of specific regions, nations, states, and communities. Each of these historical subjects can, in turn, be subdivided into chronological periods.

The most manageable grouping that the visitor to earth could discover is one that classifies many secondary school subjects into a dozen broad fields. With the passage of the years, the number of fields change and even the titles of the fields are modified. As of the late 1970s, the broad fields of the secondary school curriculum are English language arts, social studies, mathematics, science, physical education and health and recreation, modern foreign languages, art, music, home economics, industrial arts, business education, and a vocational cluster emphasizing agricultural, industrial, and technical occupations. The largest number of teachers employed are in the English language arts, the social studies, mathematics, the sciences, and physical education and health and recreation. Fewer teach modern foreign languages, art, music, home economics, industrial arts, business education, and vocational education.

The balance of this chapter will describe in summary form some characteristics of and tendencies in curriculum and instruction. We will attempt to provide some guide for both you and our mythical Martian visitor to mid-1970s developments in each of these twelve fields. Obviously, such a summary can be only a brief introduction to the current broad fields in which today's secondary school teachers specialize.

SCIENCE

In his book *The Structure of Scientific Revolutions* scientist-historian Thomas Kuhn defined "normal" science as "research firmly based upon one or more past scientific achievements, achievements that a particular scientific community acknowledges for a time as supplying the foundation for its further practice."[1] For Kuhn, such achievements were labeled "paradigms" and all shared two distinguishing characteristics: "Their achievement was sufficiently unprecedented to attract an enduring group of adherents away from competing modes of scientific activity. Simultaneously, it was sufficiently open-ended to leave all sorts of problems for the redefined group of practitioners to resolve."[2]

Kuhn continued by pointing out that advancements in science occurred when competing models clashed with existing paradigms and in a sense produced a crisis. If the result of the crisis was the rejection of the time-honored paradigm for the newer one that was incompatible with it, a "scientific revolution" occurred. Following on the heels of the revolution came a quieter period when the scientific community explored the boundaries and limits of the new paradigm.

There does seem to be an analogy between revolutions in science and revolutions in science teaching and curriculum development. Curriculum reform in the late 1950s and early 1960s was characterized by the reform of

[1] Thomas S. Kuhn, *The Structure of Scientific Revolutions,* 2nd ed., University of Chicago Press, Chicago, 1970, p. 10.
[2] Ibid., p. 10.

FIGURE 7.1 *Science students*

science education. The projects in the sciences, in one sense, became the paradigms for curriculum reform in other areas of the secondary school.

The revolution in science curriculum reform was characterized by (1) enlistment and extensive use of research scholars in the field, (2) reformulation of the content of the subject based upon the concepts or generalizations that comprised the structure of the discipline, (3) instructing the student in the process used by the scholar in the discipline, and (4) less reliance on a single textbook and greater use of multimedia materials.

The archetype of the sciences curriculum projects was the Physical Sciences Study Committee (PSSC) directed by Professor Jerrold R. Zacharias of the Massachusetts Institute of Technology. Beginning formally in 1956, the PSSC triggered a massive effort in curriculum reform in both mathematics and the sciences that has continued to date.

The mode of curriculum development for the PSSC consisted of assembling some thirty or forty persons with diverse backgrounds and specialties, all interested in physics education, for a summer writing conference lasting four to six weeks. During the first summer, objectives of the course were developed and basic materials were written. During the following school year, the materials were field-tested in selected high schools and notes were taken for feedback for the second summer of work.

During the second summer another group of writers was assembled, including scientists, science educators, psychologists, and classroom science teachers. Some were members of the group from the previous summer, but many were new. More detailed material was generated and supplementary materials in the form of audio-visual aids including films, laboratory exercises, and laboratory equipment were developed. Again, the material was field-tested but with greater emphasis on the evaluation of course achievement by the students.

The third summer the PSSC began to finalize the total package. More sophisticated activities could be generated, based on the feedback from the two previous years. After the third and final year of testing, the final package was opened for bidding by commercial publishers. In the case of the PSSC physics package, D. C. Heath won the contract and produced the first commercial edition.[3]

What resulted from this project was a complete curriculum package that became a model for many other projects that followed. Included in many of the packages were basic texts, films, filmloops, filmstrips, overhead transparencies, tapes, teacher guides, and student supplementary materials. Projects that followed were the Biological Sciences Curriculum Study (BSCS), the Earth Science Curriculum Project (ESCP) the Chemical Education Materials Study (CHEM), and many others. In fact, a joint project of the Commission on Science Education of the American Association for the Advancement of Science and the Science Teaching Center of the University of Maryland reported in 1975 over 390 science and mathematics curriculum projects currently operating worldwide.[4]

As Kuhn had described, there was a period of relative calm following the adoption of the new paradigm in curriculum reform. But the period of calm was short-lived. Student achievements in the "new" projects were compared to student achievements in the traditional programs. The results were most discouraging to the supporters of the new projects. Critics began to level charges against the projects as being too structured and formal. The projects, it appeared, had failed to account for the wide variance in student aptitude and motivation. Even Jerome Bruner, an early advocate of the projects, began to modify his previous position.[5] Thus, a new paradigm began to emerge.

---

[3] For a more detailed discussion see J. David Lockard, ed., *Science and Mathematics Curricular Developments Internationally, 1956–1974*, A Joint Project of the Commission on Science Education of the American Association for the Advancement of Science and the Science Teaching Center of the University of Maryland, College Park, 1975.
[4] Ibid.
[5] Jerome Bruner, "The Process of Education Reconsidered," in *Dare to Care/Dare to Act*, ed. Robert R. Leeper, Association for Supervision and Curriculum Development, Washington, D.C., 1971.

The new model retained many of the characteristics of the earlier reform movement but placed more emphasis upon the learner. The new projects exchanged the guided discovery process, which was logically constructed by the teacher, for a more personalized model of problem solving and individualized instruction. Such projects as Individually Prescribed Instruction (IPI-Science) at the University of Pittsburgh and Individualized Science Instructional System (ISIS) at the Florida State University began to emphasize minicourses and materials designed to facilitate individualization.

The criticism, however, was not just within the field of science. Society at large began to raise basic questions regarding science and technology. Ecology and the environment became issues that science education could not ignore. America's fundamental belief in the excellence of technology began to dissolve.

Realization of the social pressures led Howard Birnie to suggest that a new science teaching revolution based on a humanistic paradigm may be emerging.[6] Some support of this position can be seen in recent curriculum projects. Science courses are becoming more interdisciplinary in their approach, particularly in environmental education. A project that may be a model for others is Man: A Course of Study (MACOS), a social studies program for upper elementary and middle school students that makes great use of science and technology in its materials.

If the humanistic paradigm of science teaching is followed, increasingly science studies will deal with affective or value-related materials. Students will be directed to consider the consequences of science and technology and the social implications of science. Interdisciplinary approaches will be adopted. Science will be taught not only in the laboratory but in the community as well.

MATHEMATICS

Undoubtedly, the broad field of mathematics has recently enjoyed a period of unprecedented favor and occupied a position of prominence in the curriculum of American secondary schools. Regarded as essential to scientific and technological advancement, mathematics shared with the sciences the highest priority in the curriculum reform movement of the 1950s and 1960s. Spurred on by the rapid growth in knowledge, the Cold War, the space race, and abundant spending by the federal government and private foundations, educators developed mathematics curriculum projects across the nation.

---

[6] Howard H. Birnie, "The Revolution in Science Teaching: Where Do You Stand?" *The Science Teacher* 42 (October 1975), 13–15.

The many projects that were developed had several common characteristics: content was drastically altered; the structure of the discipline became the basic organizing pattern; the instructional approach favored deductive thinking or Socratic dialogue; the projects were developed by teams that brought mathematics scholars together with educators specializing in methods and with psychologists; the projects were heavily endowed by the federal government and/or private foundations.

The most ambitious of the projects was the School Mathematics Study Group (SMSG), started at Yale University in 1958 and moved to Stanford University in 1960. It brought together research mathematicians, mathematics educators, teachers, and curriculum specialists for the purpose of curriculum development and improvement in mathematics for all grade levels (kindergarten through grade twelve). The approach included the development of courses, teaching materials, and instructional methods that enhanced the students' understanding and competencies in regard to basic concepts in the structure of mathematics.

A unique feature of SMSG grew out of a recognition of a possible pitfall. Compartmentalization often occurs when new courses are developed singly instead of as part of a truly unified curriculum. Aware of this danger, the SMSG attempted to take a different approach to mathematics in the curriculum,

viewing it as a whole rather than as a collection of six separate courses. The hope was expressed that this project would not be just a revision or an integration of material already in the present series, but a bold, new approach that would attempt to further break down compartmentalization, to develop a logical sequence of topics that might lead to a more efficient curriculum, and to include some topics that have arisen as major forces in current mathematical developments.[7]

Because of the scope and nature of the SMSG, it became synonymous with the "new math" model. Important projects in other universities were the University of Illinois Committee on School Mathematics (UICSM), which aimed at high school students (grades nine through twelve), and the University of Maryland Mathematics Project (UMMAP), which focused on new courses in grades seven and eight.

Following this period in which it was held in great esteem, mathematics in the secondary school in the late 1970s faces a less certain future concerning its goals. Much of the current concern grows out of widespread criticism and controversy both within and without mathematics education. The public controversy and criticism has been provoked by recent reports of continually declining mathematics test scores, particularly on the Scholastic Aptitude Test (SAT). Critics are quick to point to the new math as the cause.

---

[7] E. G. Begle, "SMSG: The First Decade," *The Mathematics Teacher* 61 (March 1968), 242.

Criticism from within mathematics itself has been directed at many of the basic characteristics of the projects. Claims have been made that the new math is excessively formal and places an overbearing emphasis on deductive logic. Morris Kline argues that the overemphasis on the logical approach makes mathematics "a sophisticated, artificial reconstruction of discoveries that are refashioned many times and then forced into a deductive system."[8] He goes on to point out that the new math has taken intuition away from mathematics: "All I can say here is that mathematics is understood intuitively and that the logic is entirely subordinate."[9]

Mounting criticism from the public and the popular press plus internal disagreements have left the mathematics community polarized on issues such as old versus new, skills versus concepts, concrete versus abstract, intuitive versus formal, inductive versus deductive.[10] The critical issue for the mathematics curriculum in the near future relates to the back-to-basics drive. Shirley Hill noted that the impact of the movement is manifested in several recent reactions:

Textbooks for elementary grades now place greater stress on arithmetic at the expense of experiences in geometry or statistics. Many teachers at all grade levels devote an increasing amount of time to drill of arithmetic and algebraic manipulative skills. State and local school systems are initiating basic proficiency testing as a special criterion for high school graduation, and the definition of basic proficiency in mathematics usually focuses on arithmetic skills.[11]

Some leaders in mathematics fear that the back-to-basics drive will force teachers of mathematics to retreat to outmoded goals and to discard the best of the current curriculum practices rather than to build upon them.

To begin to deal with new challenges facing mathematics, the Conference Board of the Mathematical Sciences formed the National Advisory Committee on Mathematics Education (NACOME) in 1974.[12] The committee's main task was to provide an overview and analysis of mathematics in the schools today; inevitably, their analysis led them to consideration of the future. Among the many emerging curricular emphases discussed was a concern for bridging the gap between the concepts of pure mathematics and the application of those concepts in problem-solving situations. Morris Kline, a major critic of the overemphasis on deductively taught pure mathematics, stated: "Mathematics is not just applied to the real world. It comes from the real world."[13] Because of this recognition, mathematics may be increasingly integrated with other subjects.

---

[8] Morris Kline, "NACOME: Implications for Curriculum Design," *The Mathematics Teacher* 69 (October 1976), 451.
[9] Ibid., p. 451.
[10] Shirley Hill, "Issues from the NACOME Report," *The Mathematics Teacher* 69 (October 1976), 442.
[11] Ibid., p. 442–443.
[12] Ibid., p. 441.
[13] Kline, "NACOME," p. 451.

Another development noted by the NACOME report was the calculator. Modern technology has made the hand-held or pocket calculator available at a nominal cost. NACOME warns that the widespread use of the calculator to do arithmetic computations may mean that the movement to place greater stress on arithmetic is the wrong direction in which to move. Rather, emphasis needs to be placed upon decimal numeration while diminishing the role of common fraction notation. Skill at arithmetic estimation needs to be stressed. NACOME recommended "that no later than the end of grade 8 all students should have access to a calculator for all mathematics work."[14] Still other emerging trends recognized by NACOME were growth in the use of the computer, the metric system, and statistics involving probability.

In the area of instruction, mathematics is moving in the late 1970s in the direction of individualized instruction. Most of the curriculum reform projects were aimed at the college-bound students, leaving to those less able the traditional general and remedial mathematics courses. In recent years, efforts at providing all students with outstanding mathematical instruction has caused an increase in the use of individualized instruction. Yet research to date has not been encouraging. Harold Schoen, after reviewing twelve studies comparing individualized instruction with more traditional forms, found no significant differences in mathematics achievement between the two approaches. In fact, he noted that if a mathematics teacher adopts an individualized program in its entirety that "(1) it will be more expensive and (2) it will be more work for the teachers. In addition, (3) mathematics achievement is not likely to increase and may very well decrease, and (4) student attitude is not likely to improve except perhaps in primary grades."[15] Richard L. Miller, after reviewing 145 studies, took a more optimistic stance with regard to individualized instruction. He reported that approximately one-third of the studies indicated an increase in mathematics achievement when individualized instruction was used.[16] Thus, the final decision on individualized instruction in mathematics has not been reached.

SOCIAL STUDIES

The social studies occupy a unique position in the secondary school. No other field of study is singled out to meet as many broad objectives of the school. The objectives of the social studies may

---

[14] Hill, "Issues," p. 443.

[15] Harold L. Schoen, "Self-Paced Mathematics Instruction: How Effective Has It Been in Secondary and Postsecondary Schools?" *The Mathematics Teacher* 69 (May 1976), 356.

[16] Richard L. Miller, "Individualized Instruction in Mathematics: A Review of Research," *The Mathematics Teacher* 69 (May 1976), 345–351.

range from transmitting the cultural heritage, to teaching children and youth how to think, to preparing children and youth to be good citizens. Still another view argues that the social studies serve as a simplified introduction to the social sciences, including political science, economics, sociology, anthropology, psychology, geography, and history.

The social studies program touches all students at some point in their secondary education. A recent analysis of students enrolled in grades seven through twelve of public schools in America revealed a heavy enrollment of students in some social studies course.[17] In addition, the same analysis indicated that over sixty separate course offerings in the social studies were available in the public secondary schools. Thus, the broad field of the social studies is an area of both high student enrollment and wide diversity.

The multipurposes of social studies, its eclectic content, and the wide variance in student population that social studies serves make this an area filled with controversy and ferment. For example, a survey conducted in 1960–61 showed no U.S. public secondary schools offering an Afro-American studies or black history course.[18] Yet in 1972–73, 1803 schools were offering such a course or courses.[19] The civil rights movement, the riots in Los Angeles, Detroit, and other cities, and the black power movement made schools aware of their shortcomings in providing for study of the cultural heritage of many minorities. Quite naturally, the social studies curriculum was called upon to provide this needed area of study.

Perhaps the most important factor that makes social studies unique in the secondary school curriculum is its particular sensitivity to all kinds of social and cultural pressures seeking to direct or remold the functions or educational purposes of the school. The current social studies curriculum in the secondary school to a large extent reflects the changing values of the society that the school serves.

To understand the current social studies curriculum a brief examination of the recent past is necessary. In 1957, when the Soviet Union launched the first space satellite and moved ahead in technology and the space race, the American government and public sought a reason for the seemingly vast gap between the Soviets and ourselves. The schools proved to be an easy prey for the critics. The federal government responded by enacting the National Defense Education Act (NDEA) of 1958. In this instance the social forces at work on the schools changed the role of education to national defense. It was reasoned that if the United States had fallen behind the Soviet Union in technology and scientific enterprise it was

---

[17] Logan Osterndorf, *Summary of Offerings and Enrollments in Public Secondary Schools, 1972–73*, U.S. Government Printing Office, Washington, D.C., 1975, p. 17.
[18] Grace S. Wright, *Subject Offerings and Enrollments in Public Secondary Schools*, U.S. Government Printing Office, Washington, D.C., 1965.
[19] Osterndorf, *Summary of Offerings*, p. 9.

because our schools were not producing people with the needed skills. Thus the thrust of the NDEA was to support research and curriculum development in the sciences, mathematics, and foreign languages. As a result, the broad field of the social studies was relegated to a minor role in curriculum research and innovation.

With the thrust for curriculum development came a new curricular model. Meeting at Woods Hole on Cape Cod in September 1959, a group of thirty-five scientists, psychologists, and educators developed the basic concept of what was later to be called the "spiral curriculum."[20] The model rested on the assumption that "intellectual activity anywhere is the same, whether at the frontier of knowledge or in a third-grade classroom."[21] The spiral curriculum came to be characterized by the structure of a discipline approach and the primary mode of learning became inquiry. Any subject, it was hypothesized, "can be taught effectively in some intellectually honest form to any child at any stage of development."[22] The mature scholar who inquires into the structure of the discipline became the model for students to follow.

Recognizing the impact of the curriculum reform movement of the late 1950s upon mathematics and the sciences, the National Council for the Social Studies and the American Council of Learned Societies embarked on a cooperative venture to better formulate the objectives and content of the social studies.[23] Their report focused upon the role the various social science disciplines should play in the social studies curriculum. However, instead of helping the social studies to reconceptualize the program it should offer, the report led to greater fragmentation. Each of the people who spoke for the social sciences represented argued that his or her subject deserved greater emphasis in the curriculum. The report helped to create more confusion and resolved few issues.

In 1962 the U.S. Office of Education established the Social Studies Program, originally labeled Project Social Studies. Through this program, many centers were established at universities and colleges throughout the nation. Edwin Fenton pointed out that the centers were established with the purposes of restating objectives in terms of specific mental and physical behaviors expected of the students; developing a variety of teaching strategies; producing new materials based upon an updating of content; studying new classroom organization; and preparing a new breed of social studies teachers.[24]

The projects modeled themselves along the same lines as the projects in

[20] Jerome S. Bruner, *The Process of Education,* Harvard University Press, Cambridge, 1960.
[21] Ibid., p. 14.
[22] Ibid., p. 33.
[23] American Council of Learned Societies and the National Council for the Social Studies, *The Social Studies and the Social Sciences,* Harcourt, Brace and World, New York, 1962.
[24] Edwin Fenton, *The New Social Studies,* Holt, Rinehart and Winston, New York, 1967.

both mathematics and the sciences; that is, they emphasized the structure of the discipline. Inquiry or problem solving became the major instructional mode. In addition, new materials, making use of the boom in instructional technology, were developed. The new math became the model for the "new social studies."

Closely integrated with inquiry skills in the new social studies was concept formation. The development of a concept, it was noted, went hand in hand with recognizing a problem, arriving at a tentative hypothesis, analyzing available information, forming a generalization, and synthesizing. Allan O. Kownslar pointed out that: "Within the framework of the New Social Studies the term 'concept' came to signify any word or phrase which evoked an appropriate image." [25]

To the proponents of the new social studies, the development of inquiry or critical thinking skills became all important. Coupling this with the work in instructional objectives simultaneously going on in education resulted in a renewed focus on goals in the cognitive domain. More particularly, cognitive goals as they relate to the separate disciplines in the social studies curriculum were stressed.

By the end of the 1960s the new social studies was widely recognized as the accepted thrust of the social studies curriculum. However, drastic changes were occurring in society at large. Students were in rebellion against the Establishment, and new value systems were emerging. Because of vulnerability of the social studies to social forces, and because of internal conflict over the new social studies, a different thrust emerged.

As social studies educators selected new content for inquiry and concept formation, they began to realize that much of what was selected had an important affective dimension. Concepts did not exist for students only as cognitive material but also contained feelings and values. Thus, with the addition of affective goals built upon the existing cognitive structure, a "new" new social studies emerged.

Empathizing and valuing became a vital part of the social studies curriculum. Students were now asked to deal with emotions, attitudes, and values. Conflict and controversy in the society became the content of many social studies classes. Purposes in the classroom shifted from memorizing certain facts to understanding different viewpoints and values. For example, traditionally students might have studied the concept "revolt," and in a relatively short time have been able to define it and even list several examples. However, with the new emphasis, they would also consider under what circumstances *they* would revolt. They might discover that not everyone would revolt for the same reason or in the same manner.

Today's secondary school social studies curriculum is a result of many

---

[25] Allan O. Kownslar, "Is History Relevant?" *Teaching American History: The Quest for Relevancy,* Forty-fourth Yearbook of the National Council for the Social Studies, National Council for the Social Studies, Washington, D.C., 1974, p. 5.

forces of the recent past. The "new" new social studies is a logical development of twenty years of curriculum reform. The proliferation of courses in the social studies is the result of the field's attempt to respond to societal pressures and problems. Minicourses or phase electives are offered in women's studies, ethnic studies, environment, consumerism, law, urban studies, and the Third World. The list is endless. Simulations and games have become major instructional strategies.

Yet in spite of all the changes the social studies curriculum has initiated, the broad field still retains a traditional, discipline-centered, specialization framework. Table 7.1 shows the sequence of courses recommended by the NEA Commission on the Reorganization of Secondary Education in 1916. Now compare Table 7.1 with Table 7.2, which was a typical recommended social studies curriculum of Indiana schools in 1976–77. Some social studies educators argue that the change is not rapid enough. Doherty and Walker have stated that "we find that even though our society has undergone

TABLE 7.1 *Proposed curriculum for the social studies by the NEA Commission on the Reorganization of Secondary Education, 1916*

	GRADE	SUBJECT
Cycle I	7	European history (one-semester geography optional)
	8	One-semester American history
		One-semester civics
	9	One-year civics, or civics and economic history
Cycle II	10	European history (through 17th century)
	11	American history and/or modern European history
	12	Problems of democracy

SOURCE: Commission on the Reorganization of Secondary Education, *The Social Studies in Secondary Education* Bulletin No. 28, Bureau of Education, Washington, D.C., 1916, p. 35.

TABLE 7.2 *Curriculum program in the social studies frequently used by school systems in Indiana, 1976–77*

GRADE	SUBJECT
7	Non-Western history[a] (full year)
8	American history[a] (full year)
9	none required
10	World history or world cultures[a] (full year)
11	American history (full year)[a]
12	Government and economics[a] (one semester each)

[a] Required by the state of Indiana.

enormous social and cultural changes over the past two decades corresponding revisions in the school's social studies program have not occurred."[26]

ENGLISH LANGUAGE ARTS

The process through which children learn a spoken language has always fascinated scholars. Although language learning is often regarded as the most complex intellectual skill, children learn languages quite early and without benefit of planned, systematic instruction. The learning of the manipulated symbols of language starts as soon as, or even before, the child reaches the school.

No other subject area of the secondary school has as high an enrollment of pupils as does English language arts. In all states English is a required offering in grades seven and eight. In most states it is required for the first three years of nine through twelve high school programs. Yet by the time the child reaches the twelfth grade, he or she may be placed in a remedial English class and given a book called *English Made Easy*.[27]

The problem is complex. Shifts in curriculum planning have contributed to it. The curriculum reform movement of the 1950s, which started with mathematics and the sciences, stressed the structure of knowledge. Each discipline was to determine its own essence or structure and create a logically sequenced set of activities that would guide the learner through the discipline. The reform movement came to English late; in 1961 the U.S. Office of Education established its English Program. Following the lead of the mathematics and sciences projects, a large number of specialized English projects were started across the nation. The problem that emerged almost immediately was definition of the discipline. Working toward definition, a report issued by the NEA's Project on Instruction in 1962 declared "the growing conviction that English as a subject consists of just three things and no more: English is literature, language, and composition. These are its subject matter."[28] Following suit, the Commission on English of the College Entrance Examination Board (CEEB) recommended "that the scope of the English program be defined as the study of language, litera-

---

[26] Joan Doherty and William L. Walker, *Current Issues in Social Studies Education*, Curriculum Research and Development Center, Indiana State University, Terre Haute, 1975, p. 1.
[27] During the school year 1972–73, 2,676 public secondary schools listed a course in remedial English. Although only 195,615 students were enrolled, accounting for 1.1 percent of the total secondary school population, it did account for 7.5 percent of the enrollment in the schools offering the course. See Osterndorf, *Summary of Offerings*.
[28] Reports of the Disciplines Seminar, *The Scholars Look at the Schools*, National Education Association, Washington, D.C., 1962, p. 12.

ture, and composition, written and oral, and that matters not clearly related to such study be excluded from it."[29]

Despite wide acceptance of the three-part breakdown of English, controversy in the profession still existed. The point of contention centered on content. With the trend toward increased separation of English from other broad fields, content and sequence became of prime importance. However, English educators could reach no commonly agreed upon body of content. In fact, Donald Smith pointed out that "the secondary school English field has survived for the last half century without discovering any commonly accepted body of knowledge about language thought clearly to be teachable and worth teaching to high school students."[30]

The debate of the early 1960s over content and the nature of the discipline was cut short by external pressures before reaching any conclusions. New emphasis was directed at the culturally disadvantaged. Many students were pressing for relevance in the curriculum. Students with widely divergent backgrounds brought to the classroom the language of their environment, and it differed significantly from standard English. Teachers offered instruction in standard English, and some students rebelled, viewing the language they were being taught as meaningless and irrelevant to their lives. Structure of knowledge lost impetus as a focus for curriculum reform.

The shift of emphasis in English is now away from structure and the three-part content to more affective values. The National Council of Teachers of English (NCTE) noted the shift: "Today . . . our subject is viewed not only as a body of knowledge and a set of skills and attitudes but also as a process, an activity—something one does (i.e., one uses and responds to language in a variety of ways in a variety of contexts)."[31] With the emphasis on affective values, more classrooms today are utilizing "dramatic" activities, such as improvisation or enactments of literary works. In many classrooms, oral language is as much of a concern as is written language.

The biggest controversies as to teaching the English language arts revolve about back to basics. Two decades ago Rudolf Flesch coined the phrase "Why Johnny can't read." On its December 8, 1975, cover, *Newsweek* emblazoned "Why Johnny Can't Write." A clear implication was that the educational system was spawning a generation of semiliterates. The National Assessment of Educational Progress (NAEP) also showed writing

---

[29] Commission on English, *Freedom and Discipline in English*, College Entrance Examination Board, New York, 1965, p. 13.
[30] Donald K. Smith, "English, Speech, and the Language Arts," in *The Changing Role of English Education*, ed. Stanley B. Kegler, National Council of Teachers of English, Champaign, Ill., 1965, p. 69.
[31] Report of the NCTE Standing Committee on Teacher Preparation and Certification, Richard Larson, Chairman, National Council of Teachers of English, Urbana, Ill., 1976, p. 1.

FIGURE 7.2 *Sample question from NAEP minimal competency test*

Below is a sample application blank. Ones like it are used to get information from people who are applying for driver's licenses, credit cards, passports and other identification cards. Fill out the application below. Do not use your own name. For this application blank, each male should call himself Adam Baker Carson, each female should call herself Alice Baker Carson. Make up the rest of the information. Be sure to fill in the entire form.

Please PRINT the information required below

1. _____
   last name   first   middle initial

2. _____
                         street address

3. _____
   city or town   county   state   zip code

4. Date of Birth _____ 5. Sex _____
                 month   day   year   M or F

5. Ht. _____ Wt. _____ Hair _____ Eyes _____

   Today's Date _____

This writing exercise was administered in 1969 to ages 9, 13, 17, and adults. To be considered acceptable, all lines had to be filled in and at least the first three had to be printed. 12% at age 9, 26% at age 13, 61% at age 17 and 50% of the adults were able to do this.
SOURCE: "Testing for Minimal Competency (Try 'em!), *NAEP Newsletter* 9 (June 1976), 5.

declines. "In 1976, the percentage of coherent paragraphs written by seventeen-year-olds declined from an average of 85 percent (in 1970) to 76 percent."[32]

The back-to-basics movement is manifesting itself in English classrooms as teachers move away from creative writing, place more emphasis on mechanics, and reinstate strict grading policies. Another manifestation is the public demand for tests of basic minimum competencies for high school graduation, which many states are investigating or adopting. Those in favor of such tests argue that before students finish their formal schooling,

---

[32] "Back to Basics? Mixed Achievements in Skills Call for 'Selective Approach,'" *NAEP Newsletter* 9 (August 1976), 7.

they should be able to handle the basics. Again the NAEP has reported data that lend support to the minimum competencies proposed. Figure 7.2 is a sample question from a minimal competency test administered by NAEP in 1969. The results, especially among adults, were not encouraging; half could not fill out correctly a simple application blank.

Related major problems confronting English language arts today are censorship and control of the curriculum. These two issues have been generated by a value clash in society and have gathered support from the back-to-basics movement. The media's coverage of the Kanawha County, West Virginia, controversy brought the interrelated problems of censorship and control to nationwide prominence. Robert F. Hogan, executive secretary of the National Council of Teachers of English, noted that the censorship movement was afoot in the schools. The movement warns a parent against a "secular humanism" or "scientific humanism" that is designed to "(1) destroy any belief in the God he believes in; (2) undermine parental authority; and (3) call to question and thus erode those moral and ethical values he has been hoping to inculcate in his children."[33] Hogan further noted that if parents contact the schools to complain they are told to complete a form that requires them to read the very book they are questioning! All this guarantees that the final confrontation will be more emotional than rational. How English educators handle these problems of censorship and control will do much to influence future curricula.

PHYSICAL EDUCATION, HEALTH, AND RECREATION

With the exception of language arts, physical education has the highest student enrollment and is the most commonly required subject in secondary school. Like language arts and social studies, which are readily accessible to a large number of students, the field of physical education, health, and recreation is vulnerable to public opinion and pressure. During World Wars I and II, physical education became the scapegoat when it was found that one third of the conscripts had to be rejected because of physical deficiencies. When the drug culture emerged, both health and recreation were singled out to provide solutions to the problem. In many communities, demands were made upon the field of physical education, health, and recreation to offer sex education. Then when sex education was offered, some citizens inevitably objected. This field is used to disputes.

In spite of public controversy, the field of physical education, health, and recreation has been noted for the many goals to which it attempts to make a

---

[33] Robert F. Hogan, "Some Thoughts on Censorship in the Schools," *Focus* 3 (Fall 1976), 2.

significant contribution. Among the intended contributions and outcomes are: "character and sportsmanship, civic responsibility, physical fitness, health knowledge and habits, self-discipline, lifelong recreational skills and interests, aesthetic development, leadership, cooperativeness, wholesome competitiveness, and so on."[34] Nevertheless, many programs suffer because of inadequate facilities, lack of time, inadequate individual or small-group instruction, or overemphasis upon interschool athletics.

Recently, a new factor has precipitated upheaval and change in the physical education programs of secondary school youth. It stems from the enactment of the Title IX of the Education Amendments of 1972, which mandated the end of sex-segregated physical education classes. Now, all secondary school physical education courses must be coeducational. As can be imagined, such a basic change is causing reevaluations of facilities, schedules, and instructional techniques.

Change and criticism, however, does not derive from external forces alone. Within the broad field, many health, physical education, and recreation educators are calling for major changes, particularly in the area of physical fitness. The popular press abounds today with books on diets and physical fitness. Schemes for weight control and gadgets and equipment for exercising have grown at astounding rates. Although educators in health and physical education claim that their field is responsible for teaching young people to become and stay physically fit, too many school programs apparently are failing in this task, for the public is turning to other sources. To combat this problem, courses in achieving physical fitness at all age levels are being developed. Their emphasis is on helping students discover what fitness is for them, how to acquire it, and how to maintain it.

Another area undergoing careful analysis is the development of life-long skills and leisure activities. Although this is not a new concern, recent evaluations have suggested that health, physical education, and recreation instructors and courses have not met with the success that was initially anticipated. To combat the problem, physical education courses have become diversified. Instruction is becoming more small group or individualized in approach. For instance, schools are offering courses in sailing, cycling, backpacking, and even yoga. The school is moving more into the community and taking advantage of the surrounding community. A class in fishing may meet at a nearby lake. A family skiing vacation may earn academic credit for the student.

A new thrust in instruction is termed personalized learning. Physical education instructors are finding new ways of teaching "large numbers of

---

[34] Daniel Tanner, *Secondary Curriculum: Theory and Development*, Macmillan, New York, 1971, p. 333.

students with reasonable economy, while at the same time meeting the particular learning needs of individual students."[35] Some schools have adopted independent study and self-directed study. All personalized programs involve students in selecting and/or devising their own programs of study. The expectation is that if students select their own activities these activities will have greater carryover and meaning to the students.

The Special Olympics program, a national out-of-school activity, has brought attention in recent years to the shortcomings of physical education for the exceptional child. Physical educators have responded by developing programs in adapted physical education. Although it is a relatively new program, adapted physical education is becoming increasingly popular and will, more than likely, remain a growing specialization within the total physical education curriculum.

Within recreation, a major thrust is developing in career education programs. Increasingly, society is calling for more recreational services. Students in the secondary schools often receive credit for working as camp counselors or in summer recreational programs.[36]

Although the field of physical education, health, and recreation has moved into a position of greater importance in the secondary school program, it still faces many problems. Paramount among them is the "five-year test." Five years after having left secondary schools will students be purchasing physical fitness books and apparatus to regain fitness? Will they be bored? Will they have no life-long leisure pursuits? These are major questions that the broad field of physical education must face.

MODERN FOREIGN LANGUAGES

Perhaps no other area of the modern secondary school curriculum has undergone so intensive an internal analysis as has modern foreign languages. During the early 1960s the field of modern foreign languages was riding the crest of a wave of interest, research, and exploration. By the beginning of the 1970s the wave had been replaced by a calm. NDEA funding had ceased. There was no longer a large trust fund to support research and to aid in development of new programs. Enrollments in foreign languages had fallen sharply. The requirement of foreign language study was no longer essential for a student to either enter or

---

[35] "Personalized Learning in Physical Education," *Journal of Physical Education and Recreation* 47 (June 1976), 32.
[36] Martin W. Johnson, "Career Education and Physical Education," *Journal of Physical Education and Recreation* 47 (May 1976), 39.

graduate from college. The press for utility or job preparation relegated the study of foreign language to the status of a nonessential yet useful leisure or cultural activity. However, the most pertinent reason for the decline in interest in foreign language study could be found in the foreign language classroom.

Increasingly, during the 1960s, the foreign language classroom became a technological dream and an instructional nightmare. The principal instructional model was labeled the "audiolingual approach." This approach embraced the best of the reinforcement theories of learning and renounced the visual forms of language instruction. The foreign language classroom became the foreign language laboratory. Tape recorders, record players, earphones, and miles of wire became the symbol of foreign language instruction. The approach tended to downplay the importance of the teacher and the student. It did not relate foreign language learning to any overriding curriculum model or purpose. Instead, foreign language teaching rested primarily upon a system of instruction that "focused on the design of materials (as approved by a consultant psychologist and linguist), which expressed a point of view, pious hope, and promised to be effective without contradiction provided the teacher faithfully adhered to the over-elaborate directions of class activities supplied by the basal text."[37] Thus, the acceptance of a mechanistic theory, which downplayed the teacher's role in the instructional process and pictured the student as a nonperson ready to push buttons and react, lead to a decrease in the popularity of the study of foreign languages.

Confronted by these and other challenges, foreign language educators are beginning what T. Bruce Fryer calls a "new era of exploration in foreign language education."[38] Exemplifying this new era is a report on a new foreign language program for the seventies prepared by a special committee of the Modern Language Association. The committee noted the need to reevaluate the foreign language program, especially the traditional curriculum. The committee acknowledged that language instruction had been primarily for the purpose of studying the literature of the language and suggested that "broader humanistic values of a particular work" be stressed.[39] Accordingly, the committee projected several suggestions appropriate for the secondary school:

1. To attract students by teaching the literature initially in English translation;

2. To place the emphasis on language and culture and not language and literature;

---

[37] Roger A. Pillet, *Foreign-Language Study: Perspective and Prospect*, University of Chicago Press, Chicago, 1974, p. 117.

[38] T. Bruce Fryer, "Free to Explore: Curricular Developments," in *Perspective: A New Freedom*, ed. Gilbert A. Jarvis, National Textbook, Skokie, Ill., 1975, p. 9.

[39] "A National Foreign Language Program for the 1970s," *ADFL Bulletin* 6 (1974), 7–17.

3. To develop courses about human language and how it functions in culture; and,

4. To provide a variety of special interest courses for secondary school youth.[40]

Essentially, the committee was calling for foreign language educators to put life back into the study of foreign language by stressing the cultural aspects of a language. This would be a step toward greater stress on social realities in language teaching.

The new era of exploration has not been limited to curricular concerns. Instructional procedures in the language classroom have recently been modified. One instructional area receiving much attention relates to time variables in instruction. Such programs as self-paced instruction and other forms of individualized instruction are being recommended.[41] Another change related to time involves intensive or immersion programs in foreign language. In this type of arrangement, students are given a full day's instruction in a foreign language for a specified period of time, such as four or six weeks. Achievement in this type of program compares favorably to that in the traditional program of one class period a day for a year. The real educational advantage of immersion is the additional activities that can be arranged. Some schools establish an authentic café for the students, show movies in the language, sponsor social events, and provide other activities. This type of arrangement allows students to experience vicariously the culture of people in foreign lands. Sometimes students are involved in actual participation with ethnic groups at home.

Another area of exploration has been the learning style of the student. Individuals have distinct learning styles. The self-pacing program may be appropriate for some, but certainly not all. Helen P. Warriner has pointed out the danger associated with individualization in foreign language instruction. She noted that often teachers do not go beyond the self-pacing program and do not attempt to individualize other aspects of instruction.[42] As Jack R. Frymier and associates have pointed out, when it comes to individualizing instruction in schools there is no single best way of doing things.[43]

To meet the needs of students with different learning styles, Papalia has described several models that can operate in a classroom concurrently: (1) group investigation, which allows students to learn from each other; (2)

[40] Ibid., pp. 11–12.

[41] Vince Bradley, "Highly Individualized German Program at Reno H.S.: A Nevada Success Story," *Tape Hiss: Nevada Foreign Language Newsletter* 9 (1975), 6–9.

[42] Helen P. Warriner, "The Teacher as Quality Control: Program Options," in *Student Motivation and the Foreign Language Teacher*, ed. Frank M. Grittner, National Textbook, Skokie, Ill., 1974, pp. 30–44.

[43] Jack R. Frymier, June Wilhour, and Alfred Rasp, "Curriculum," in *A School for Tomorrow*, ed. Jack Frymier, McCutchan, Berkeley, Calif., 1973, pp. 87–127.

information process, which makes use of inductive and deductive thinking process; (3) personal inquiry, which allows the student to generate his or her own program; and (4) operant conditioning, which rewards correct response from programmed or audiolingual materials.[44] These and other models are currently being tried.

Within today's foreign language curriculum, students are being given increasing opportunities to study new content through new instructional techniques. Cultural awareness, and with it broadened understanding of social realities, are receiving attention along with language acquisition. Trends in curricular and instructional programs include minicourses, interdisciplinary courses, intensive programs, international programs, and community-oriented programs. All the activity indicates a vital and growing awareness among foreign language educators of a new era of exploration.

MUSIC

No culture anywhere exists without music, the anthropologists point out. Music plays an important role not only in the rituals of the society but also in the personal lives of its citizens. Music is truly one experience that makes us human. It gives one a source of personal enjoyment and an opportunity to enhance the quality of life; provides an outlet for creativity and self-expression; supplies a needed avenue that allows one to develop full esthetic potential to the utmost. These characteristics of music help account for the goals and objectives of music education programs in secondary schools. However, despite its worthwhile cultural and human aspects, music may remain a virtually unknown area of study to many secondary education youth.

Part of the responsibility for the lack of interest in the study of music shown by students of secondary school age must be assumed by music educators and the traditional music curriculum they offer. The vast majority of music courses offered in the secondary school are performance-oriented—band, choir, and occasionally orchestra. The major exception seems to be at the junior high and middle school levels where general music is offered. However, general music courses (nonperformance-oriented courses) have met with little success at the high school level. Recent efforts at music reform have attempted to change this and to bring music into the curriculum as a viable area of study for the nonperformer.

Part of the reason for this change has been a renewed commitment on

[44] Anthony Papalia, "Using Different Models of Second-Language Teaching," *The Canadian Modern Language Review* 31 (1975), 212–216.

the part of music educators to provide music education for all students. Two publications by the Music Educators National Conference emphasized the need for a music program that provides every student with an opportunity to form a permanent and lasting relationship with music.[45] Malcolm E. Bessom and colleagues pointed out that the role of music in the secondary school is "to develop music understanding and appreciation through the ability to perceive and react—to experience music aesthetically."[46] To attain this goal a two-pronged approach is needed, which "(1) provides opportunities for the musical growth of *all* students as a part of the *common experiences* of general education, and (2) discovers the musically talented and furnishes them with experiences that extend *beyond* those in the core of general education."[47]

A comprehensive program of studies that reaches every student in school has been called for, and this has caused the music educator to rethink classroom procedures. For too long music educators perpetuated a form of discrimination in their classrooms. Perceiving themselves as connoisseurs of "good" music, they felt required to dispense in their classrooms only the music that had been judged by experts as being good or had withstood the test of time. This reliance upon eighteenth and nineteenth-century music of the European tradition ignored the pluralistic nature of American society and the needs of secondary school youth.

Now, however, music educators recognize the fact that American society is composed of many cultures and subcultures each of which has nurtured a form of music that possesses its own set of traditions and esthetic values. The recognition of the sociocultural differences and needs of secondary school youth was best stated by the Tanglewood Symposium participants when they declared that music programs should include

music of all periods, styles, forms, and cultures. . . . The musical repertory should be expanded to involve music of our time in its rich variety, including currently popular teenage music and avant-garde music, American folk music, and the music of other cultures.[48]

The new music classroom seeks a balance in presenting the many types of music representing a broad spectrum of cultural values.

Much of the support and research base for the comprehensive music

---

[45] Charles L. Gary and Beth Landis, *The Comprehesive Music Program*, Music Educators National Conference, Washington, D.C., 1973; Paul R. Lehman, et al., *The School Music Program: Description and Standards*, Music Educators National Conference, Washington, D.C., 1974.
[46] Malcolm E. Bessom, Alphonse M. Tatarunis, and Samuel L. Forcucci, *Teaching Music in Today's Secondary School*, Holt, Rinehart and Winston, New York, 1974, p. 41.
[47] Ibid.
[48] Allen Britton, Arnold Broido, and Charles Gary, "The Tanglewood Declaration," in *Music in American Society: Documentary Report of the Tanglewood Symposium*, ed. Robert A. Choate, Music Educators National Conference, Washington, D.C., 1968, p. 139.

curriculum now being advocated developed from the Contemporary Music Project (CMP), a highly successful and influential project jointly supported by the Ford Foundation and the Music Educators National Conference from 1959 until 1973. Above all, the project stressed an integration of the functions of performance, analysis, and teaching of contemporary music. It emphasized and developed the concept of comprehensive musicianship and the innovative instructional technique of the common elements approach. This approach organized elements common to all music (such as pitch, loudness, and timbre) into a conceptual scheme that facilitated the study of music of other cultures in widely varying contexts.[49]

Just as the scope of the type of music used in classrooms is changing and expanding, so are the techniques of teaching. Among the most influential projects aimed at improving instruction in music was the Manhattanville Music Curriculum Program (MMCP).[50] This project emphasized discovery learning, independent study, problem solving, and what became labeled as the "compositional approach." Although not a new idea in music instruction, it did seem to be mimicking the mathematics and science projects of the late 1950s and early 1960s. In fact, it led one recent writer to examine the similarities between learning science and learning music through discovery and inquiry instruction.[51] The compositional approach emphasized a hands-on approach to learning about music. Students created and wrote their own musical compositions and were thus able to learn much about musical elements as they solved their own compositional problems.

Music, like other fine arts, should not be isolated from the mainstream of the school curriculum. Music has much to contribute to the growth and development of secondary school youth. It offers outlets for artistic expression and esthetic growth; offers a natural bond with other community institutions and organizations; provides ample opportunity to gain insights, understandings, and knowledge about various cultures; correlates well with other areas of study in the school curriculum. Despite these worthwhile contributions to the growth of youth, however, music remains virtually an unknown quantity to many students. Bessom and colleagues recognized this problem and advanced its solution when they stated:

If music is to enter the mainstream of American life, if it is to become a real part of general education, then music programs in the schools must consider the social relevance of music—the role that it plays in people's lives.[52]

---

[49] "Contemporary Music Project," *Music Educators Journal* 59 (May 1973), 33–48.
[50] *MMCP Synthesis*, Media Materials, Bardonia, N.Y.
[51] Patricia J. Watson, "Discovery and Inquiry—Techniques of the New Breed of Learner," *Music Educators Journal* 61 (January 1975), 50–53.
[52] Bessom, Tatarunis, and Forcucci, *Teaching Music*, p. 41.

Unfortunately, the fine arts have fallen prey to a false dichotomy in the curriculum of contemporary secondary schools. Expanding technology and science, the economy, and other factors have been forces calling for narrow practicality and utilitarianism in the high schools. The fine arts, including art and music, have come to be viewed as luxuries or nonessential elements of the secondary school curriculum. The study of art is seen as a leisure activity with little bearing upon the daily life of the student. In actuality, the broad field of the arts is highly useful to human beings. Dewey recognized the false dichotomy between the cultural and utilitarian subjects when he noted that "only superstition makes us believe that the two are necessarily hostile so that a subject is illiberal because it is useful and cultural because it is useless."[53]

In fact, the very forces that call for limited utilitarian emphasis can also be used to justify the study of art. If you were placed in the heart of a large metropolitan city, everywhere you looked, save for the small amount of sky visible above the tall buildings, you would see an environment designed and created by human beings: buildings, automobiles, signs, streets, sidewalks, clothing. All of these creations reflect our human capacity for creativity and are our expressions of how life is to be lived. In short, our designs reflect our culture and the individuals within it.

The broadest rationales for art education are the relationships of art and the individual, art and the community, and art and the culture. Experiences in art should provide an opportunity to have feelings of self-esteem and self-accomplishment; to personally experience as well as understand art expressions of many cultures; to be involved directly in the visual qualities of art; and to develop discriminating judgment that leads to the improvement of esthetic decisions in both personal and community life.[54] From this broad based rationale, the National Art Education Association has suggested that school art programs should contain basically four aspects: "*seeing* and *feeling* visual relationships, *producing* works of art, *knowing* and *understanding* about art objects, and *evaluating* art products."[55] The objectives, then, of art courses in the secondary school evolve from perceiving, performing, appreciating, and criticizing art.

The status of art in the curriculum of secondary schools is difficult to assess. In recent years regulations have appeared in some states requiring a minimum of study in art, usually in grades seven or eight. Art is often

---

[53] John Dewey, *Democracy and Education*, Macmillan, New York, 1916, p. 279.
[54] *Art Education: Senior High School*, Angela G. Paterakis, Chairperson, National Art Education Association, Washington, D.C., 1972.
[55] *The Essentials of a Quality School Art Program: A Position Statement*, John Benz, Chairperson, National Art Education Association, Reston, Va., n.d., p. 3.

found as an elective in the high school. Current estimates are that approximately 10 percent of the secondary school population is enrolled in art.[56]

Like other areas of the curriculum, art has experienced growth in the numbers and types of courses being offered. Those courses that have "markedly grown in popularity in recent years include jewelry, ceramics, photography, printmaking, sculpture, and drawing. The 'Basic Design' or generalized Art I courses are disappearing in favor of the specificity desired by both students and teachers."[57]

As is the case with music educators, art educators are increasingly trying to make art available to all students and to include art as a vital dimension of general education. In attempting to bring art to a large school audience, art educators have moved in the direction of esthetic education. The development is a significant one. David Baker has explained:

Art education has, in reality, focused on teaching art *to* children with the artist being the primary model in curriculum building. Aesthetic education methodology places an emphasis on teaching the child through multiple arts experiences, striving to maintain a balance between cognitive and affective learning. This approach translates the artists' modes of activity into a structure for learning sometimes called the arts process.[58]

In addition to esthetic education, art educators are joining forces with other subject matter specialists to develop interdisciplinary courses in the fine arts or the humanities. One such program that offered a unified arts approach was Project IMPACT,[59] which attempted to enhance many students' understanding of the fine arts and to provide an opportunity for art-inclined students having trouble with other aspects of the school curriculum to succeed.

Another development in art education has been the use of the community as an instructional medium. Programs in art history are being offered in museums. Two examples are the programs at the Museum of Fine Arts, Boston, and the Cleveland Museum. Not only is art going out into the community, the community is coming to the schools for leisure activities. Courses in ceramics, jewelry, printmaking, and photography are only a few of the popular adult education courses being offered by secondary schools.

---

[56] Guy Hubbard, "Trends in Secondary School Art. Emphasis: Senior High," *Art Education* 29 (February 1976), 12–13.

[57] Ibid., p. 12.

[58] David W. Baker, "Trends in Secondary School Art. Emphasis: Middle and Junior High School," *Art Education* 29 (February 1976), 11.

[59] J. David Boyle, *Interim Evaluation Report, 1970–71: Interdisciplinary Model Program in the Arts for Children and Teachers (IMPACT)—Conwell Project*, Arts IMPACT Evaluation Project, University Park, Penn., 1971.

Perhaps no other broad field in the secondary school has as immediate an application for students as does home economics. This is particularly true for junior high or middle school students who are beginning to seek, reach out, and explore adult roles and models. A well-balanced home economics program in the secondary school can contribute to students' psychological and social development, as well as physiological health and development; can help the students to understand and improve their immediate environment; can improve the students' consumer competency and future use of family resources; can alert students to the availability of community services designed to enrich family life; can provide students with the needed basic concepts of parenthood; and can contribute to career and vocational development.

At one point home economics functioned to teach youth the skills of cooking and sewing, but today it deals with more than these two skills. Increasingly, emphasis has been placed on the home and family. At the same time that the home economics curriculum is focusing on the home and family, new programs in vocational home economics are being developed, directed primarily toward service-oriented occupations. Among the many programs are institutional management, of schools and hospitals, for instance; public business management, of restaurants for instance; interior decorating; and cleaning services.

In spite of the readily apparent relevance of home economics for school youth, the field is not without its critics both from within and without.

The first and most controversial issue that home economics must face today is in the area of content selection. Because it is so relevant to students, home economics is closely tied to the society at large. Changing values and family structure, technological advancement, and economic conditions all touch the curriculum of home economics. As in the social studies, the close relationship between society and home economics is accompanied by public pressure and censorship. For example, as a part of a course in family life, the home economics educator may select family planning as a topic for study. This, in turn, may produce a widespread critical reaction in the community, leaving the teacher torn between loyalty to academic honesty on the one hand and fear of public censorship on the other. Because of the public pressure, many home economics programs have retreated from controversial content. In doing so, they have greatly restricted the curriculum and the learning of the students they serve.

Another criticism of home economics deals with what has often been called the "hidden curriculum." That is, how teachers deal with students and the type of values they unconsciously transmit may be what students are learning rather than the subject matter. Hazel Spitze recognized the hidden curriculum of home economics when she asked home economists:

"Have we not: (1) spent over much time on sewing a fine seam? Overemphasized the importance of making muffins? (2) promoted standards of living that are too high and require excessive demands on our natural resources? (3) overstressed specific meal patterns so that people are prejudiced against other ways of obtaining adequate nutrition? (4) understressed the principles that help people live with each other? (5) told people what they *ought* to consider beautiful or in good taste . . . ? (6) overglorified the family and encouraged people to have too many children? (7) taught that "women's place is in the home" and led men and women to believe that *many* children are needed to keep her busy there?[60]

Too, extreme care needs to be exercised by the home economics educator to prevent students from receiving messages that their life styles or families are inferior because they may not agree with the hidden curriculum.

Much recent activity in home economics has taken place in the area of instruction. For years the primary instructional technique employed in home economics was the project method. Although this instructional procedure is appropriate for home economics, it was criticized for poor implementation. While assigning students a project, the teacher often demonstrated the "correct" process involved and then required the students to imitate the steps. This, in turn, decreased opportunities for students to think creatively or use any problem-solving techniques. It fostered in the student reliance upon the teacher and encouraged imitation. In answer to criticism of the project method, home economics educators began experimenting with different instructional techniques.

More recently, individualized instruction based upon the needs of the student has received attention. Home economics educators are increasingly using the community to meet program needs. Students are given assignments in a variety of community agencies. Volunteer work done by students in hospitals, nursing homes, or other agencies is being given credit and is replacing in-school courses. Nontraditional or nonformal education is being used.[61] Some schools are establishing child-care centers so students can have firsthand experience with children. This type of program and instruction can provide a basic experience that has long been overlooked by the secondary school.

Although overshadowed by other areas of the secondary school curriculum, home economics can continue to make a contribution to the youth the school serves if it can meet the challenges of change. Few fields of the secondary school will be as influenced by technological changes in the future as home economics. Consider the microwave oven and the changes

---

[60] Hazel Taylor Spitze, "Home Economics in the Future," *Journal of Home Economics* 68 (September 1976), 7.
[61] Arlene A. Hamilton and Gayle S. Girard, "The Community as a Classroom," *Journal of Home Economics* 68 (March 1976), 7–10; Jamie B. Yule, "Expanding Our Concept of Home Economics Education," *Journal of Home Economics* 67 (May 1975), 23–25.

it will bring, or synthetic foods and beverages, or the possibility that in the future, automated grocery and department stores may become commonplace. Already there is evidence that automated universal credit and automated banking will soon be part of our lives. Spitze suggests that home economics teachers need to be sure they "are not teaching people how to use equipment that is going to become obsolete very quickly; or how to sew on obsolete fabrics; or how to plan meals with foods that are becoming 'priced out of sight' or are less nutritionally desirable than we once thought."[62]

INDUSTRIAL ARTS

The broad field of industrial arts is frequently misunderstood by educators. Many secondary educators who do not specialize in industrial arts unfortunately regard this important field as a kind of dumping ground for nonacademic students. They view the industrial arts area of the school as the "shop" and to it they relegate students who fail to meet their high standards. It is assumed that in the shop students who cannot work with their minds will work with their hands—they will at least learn a trade and become ready for occupational life. What these misinformed teachers fail to realize is that industrial arts plays a general education role in the secondary school curriculum. The broad field of industrial arts is not intended to be a narrow vocational training program.

Perhaps the misinterpretation of the nature of industrial arts comes about because it entered the school curriculum in the nineteenth century under the title "manual training," which was a technical manipulative skill program valued primarily for its vocational preparation aspects. But industrial arts has remained in the program of the contemporary secondary school because it is an area designed for all, regardless of occupational intentions.

The program of industrial arts is needed in the contemporary secondary school because it introduces individuals of varied backgrounds to our technological culture. U.S. society has created a stupendous technology involving tools, materials, processes, and products upon which Americans are heavily dependent. Our machines and industrial processes, our cities and our mechanized farms, our elaborate networks of production, communication, and transportation, determine our levels of comfort. Some will even claim that they are necessary to the very survival of our present population.

---

[62] Spitze, "Home Economics," pp. 7–8.

Yet many Americans are ignorant of the technology that surrounds them. To cite two everyday illustrations: they have no idea why the lights go on or the motor runs. The function of industrial arts is to help young people gain a wider understanding of the physical world created by human beings. The field helps young people to know more about materials and how they are produced; to understand the place of tools, machines, materials, and people in industrial processes; and to understand the role of work in American life.

Rather than to attempt to teach about technology and industry in the abstract, industrial arts provides learners with a wide variety of experiences that are manipulative as well as informative. Learners are constantly involved in working with their hands as they discover their talents in technical and industrial fields. For instance, in the contemporary industrial arts program on the junior high school level, students work in such areas as drafting, wood, metal, and electricity. Sometimes they deal with power mechanics and the graphic arts. A unit titled "manufacturing" might provide students with an orientation to the occupations and technology of major manufacturing industries. A unit called "metal technology" might focus on metals and their use in various categories of industry. Since students are constantly using their hands as they grow acquainted with the technological environment in which we live, the false assumption is sometimes made that they are engaged in vocational training.

Some contemporary industrial arts educators, perhaps despairing of making the distinction between their field and vocational education, and perhaps in recognition of the growing strength of vocational education in secondary education, are willing to blur the distinction and conceive their field as vocationally oriented industrial arts. This has been the case especially at the upper years of the senior high school level.

Although most discussion of Title IX of the Education Amendments of 1972 deals with the termination of sex segregation in physical education classes, the provisions of the amendments apply equally to industrial arts. Most industrial arts programs have long been open to both male and female students. Now, however, any of the last closed doors are being opened. Women as well as men need to understand our technological environment. This observation would not have surprised the sponsors of industrial arts as general education. In the late 1970s an ever-increasing number of female students are enrolling voluntarily in industrial arts, partly for the opportunity it provides them to understand their surroundings, partly because of the joys of working with their hands, and partly to assert their right to occupational training. Consequently, both sexes today are sharing programs in woodworking, metalworking, ceramics, plastics, printing and graphic arts, electricity, automobile mechanics, airplane mechanics, textile working, mechanical drawing, and still other specialized courses of study.

Business education is one of the most diversified programs in the secondary school. A quick glance at the offerings under the business education rubric of a secondary school illustrates the diversity: "typing, bookkeeping, recordkeeping, business math, economics, computer science, stenography, business English, general business office machines, career education, distributive education, business law, consumer education, basic business, cooperative education."[63] Many other variations exist.

In general, most business education programs have three main thrusts: basic business education, office skills, and distributive education. The first, although often offered in combination with the other two, is less skills-oriented. It is the program most often pursued by those desiring to study business at the university level. It is also aimed at meeting many general education functions of the secondary school. The second and third thrusts are more skills-oriented; the intent is for the student to gain job-entry-level competencies.

The climate of the society exerts a tremendous pressure on school curricula. This phenomenon is well illustrated by the pressures on business education. Each day the public is alerted to its economic problems: inflation, recession, stagflation, and unemployment, especially high among youth. Thus there is pressure on business education to provide a better understanding of capitalism and business practices for all secondary school youth and not just for those pursuing specific business vocational skills. Simultaneously, there is criticism of business education for presenting an overly favorable picture of business practices.

Adding to this dilemma is another set of dichotomous demands. On the one hand, well-meaning businesspeople see business education's mission as providing a ready-made work force, one that is literate, knowledgeable, obedient and skilled for entry-level employment. Yet, on the other hand, many educators argue that business education should foster individual needs and place them far above the demands of businesspeople. Thus business education often faces an identity crisis. What should be the highest loyalty of a business educator?

Business education has responded to some pressures by adopting and adapting many programs influenced by contemporary career education. Although career education was a curriculum model originally proposed for the total school program, it has been more widely accepted by vocationally

---

[63] Stowell Symmes, "The Contribution of Secondary Schools to Education for Business," in *Foundations of Education for Business*, Thirteenth Yearbook of the National Business Education Association, ed. Gladys Bahr and F. Kendrick Bangs, National Business Education Association, Reston, Va., 1975, p. 280.

oriented subject areas. Within business education, two of the four career education models developed by the U.S. Office of Education have been used. These are the school-based model developed at the Center for Vocational and Technical Education at the Ohio State University and the employer-based model developed jointly by the Far West Laboratory for Educational Research for Better Schools in Philadelphia.

In the school-based model, "eight areas of educational experience were identified as the basic conceptual elements of career education: career awareness, self-awareness, appreciations/attitudes, decision-making skills, economic awareness, beginning competency, employability skills, and educational awareness."[64] These eight elements were then translated

FIGURE 7.3 *School-based Career Education Model*

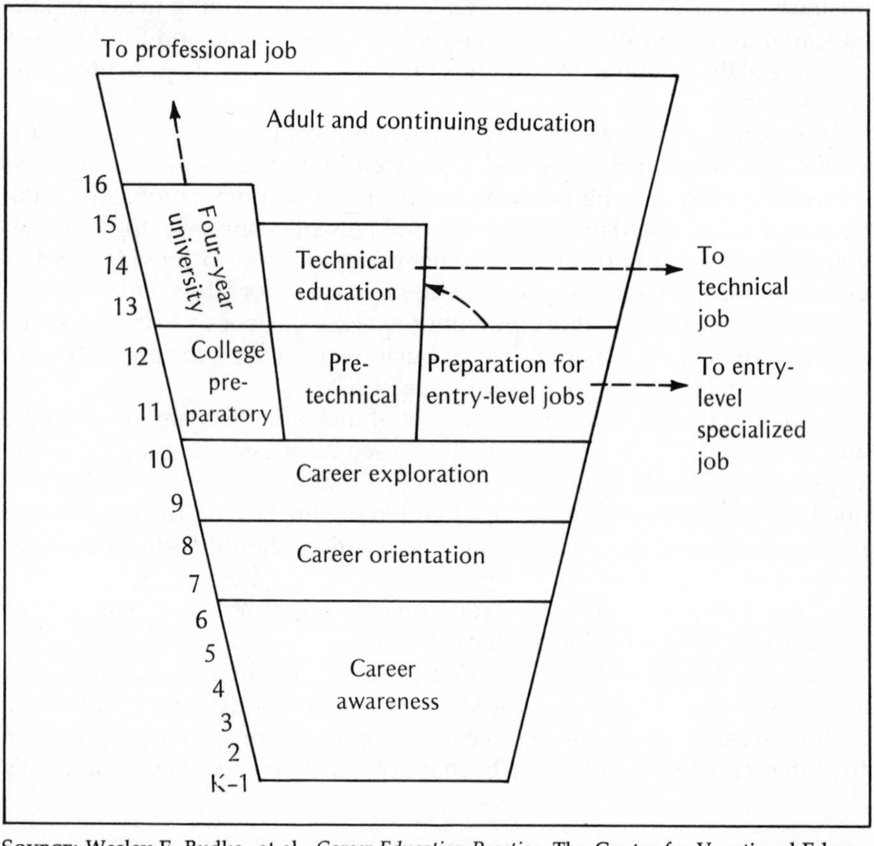

SOURCE: Wesley E. Budke, et al., *Career Education Practice*. The Center for Vocational Education, The Ohio State University, Columbus, Ohio, 1972, p. 19.

---

[64] Calfrey C. Calhoun and Alton V. Finch, *Vocational and Career Education: Concepts and Operations*, Wadsworth, Belmont, Calif., 1976, p. 126.

to eight educational outcomes. Primary among these were career identity, self-identity, employment skills, and career placement. Figure 7.3 represents graphically the school-based curriculum model. Business educators have used this model in their attempt to blend together student pressures for self-fulfillment and business's demand for a skilled work force. The model lends itself to both the general education function and to preparing students for postsecondary schooling.

The second model frequently used is the employer-based model, which emphasizes year-round operation and open entrance and exit by students. In this model, a student may learn job entry skills for a secretarial position, then exit to work as a secretary. For instance, assume the new secretary goes to work with a local lawyer who is participating in the program. After a period of time, the student decides that being a law clerk would be more rewarding. He or she reenters the program to gain those skills, and then rejoins the lawyer as a law clerk. As can be seen, this model offers endless opportunity for training, exploration, and retraining. To some extent, this is the model often used for distributive education programs.

In either model, it should be noted that the student is given opportunities for horizontal or vertical mobility. This is an attempt on the part of business education to combat the possibility that specific training received today may well be outdated a few years from now.

VOCATIONAL EDUCATION

The major difficulty in discussing vocational education at the secondary school level is the difficulty of defining it. Suppose, for instance, we believe that the term *vocational* includes "all education and preparation for occupations, professions, and careers in the sphere of work."[65] As George L. Brandon points out, this is an all-embracing and generous definition; it would interpret language arts as vocational for would-be writers, the sciences as vocational for would-be scientists, and so on.

Consequently, another approach to a definition of vocational education at the secondary school level is one that helps to limit its scope to three broad fields. For instance, *The Educator's Encyclopedia* by Edward W. Smith, Stanley W. Krouse, Jr., and Mark M. Atkinson, limited the areas of vocational education to homemaking education, business education, and industrial arts education.[66] Although each of these broad fields serves a general education function, their major impact is to contribute to the

---

[65] George L. Brandon, "Vocational and Technical Education," in *Encyclopedia of Educational Research*, ed. Robert L. Ebel, Macmillan, Collier-Macmillan Canada, Toronto, 1969, p. 1506.
[66] Edward W. Smith, Stanley W. Krouse, Mark M. Alkinson, eds., *The Educator's Encyclopedia*, Prentice-Hall, Englewood Cliffs, N.J., 1961, pp. 359–363.

vocational training for homemakers, employees in business, and industrial workers and technicians. This definition becomes increasingly accepted, particularly as Americans recognize in the mid-1970s that homemaking is indeed a vocation and an honorable one, a fit competitor to paid professional, business, or industrial employment. Indeed, there are even indications that Americans may begin to consider payment for homemaking.

To some educators and students of American society, however, not enough stress is placed upon vocational education at the secondary school level. This has been caused by the decision to limit vocational education to the comprehensive school and to the jurisdiction of three of the smaller of the broad fields: home economics, business education, and industrial arts. One of the most pungent and recurring criticisms of American secondary education comes from dedicated vocationalists. Urgently, they point out that stronger emphasis on vocational education is needed, including separate vocational schools. That their voices to a degree are heeded is evidenced by the existence of 545 vocational-technical high schools in the United States at the close of 1975. Agricultural courses also exist.

Supporters of greatly increased vocational offerings, to the extent of separate schools, defend their position by pointing out that, as they see it, the American high school has failed to serve all Americans, for secondary education clings to aristocratic ideas of learning, defends irrelevant general education, and provides programs that ensure that many will drop out. Their conception of vocational education goes beyond bare training of people for employment. They feel that it should meet the needs of young people through an enriched curriculum that is aware of supply and demand in the occupations, that recognizes that individuals have special requirements or disadvantages, and that is willing to experiment with realistic new patterns of learning built about vocational goals. Finally, they point to what they regard as the tragic lack of preparation for any kind of gainful work on the part of the average graduate (see Figure 7.4).

Proponents of more vocational education are given attentive hearing by the U.S. Congress, particularly in periods of specific laborpower shortages, such as the dearth of technicians during the Sputnik era or strong demands for employment by minorities during the 1960s. Now the legislators are listening with special care to the demands of women for employment opportunities. For instance, a 1975 article in the *American Vocational Journal* comments:

Strong challenges to the ways in which states have traditionally chosen to expend their vocational funds and recurring accusations that vocational education is reinforcing society's restraints on women's attempts to secure high-status, well-paying jobs have been the two most controversial issues to surface during Congress' year-long review of vocational education. . . .

The fight for the Equal Rights Amendment and the enactment of Title IX of the Education Amendments of 1972 forbidding sex discrimination in educational programs have served to galvanize women's groups throughout the country. It should

FIGURE 7.4 *Use of Specialized Training in Employment.* *Females used specialized high school training more often in employment than did males.*

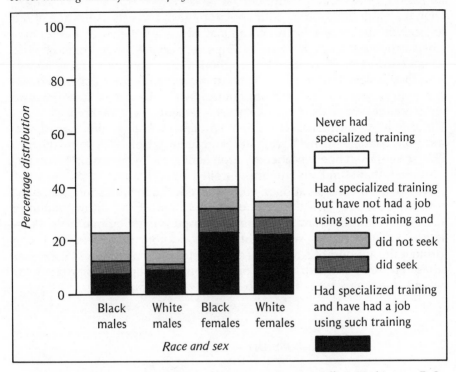

SOURCE: *The Condition of Education,* U.S. Government Printing Office, Washington, D.C., 1976, p. 111.

be of little surprise, therefore, that women's voices were heard during hearings on vocational education this year as never before. And these voices were saying that vocational education is perpetuating the inferior position of women in the job market and has to undergo change in order to meet modern needs. . . .

Testimony presented by various women's organizations to the House Sub-committee on Elementary, Secondary, and Vocational Education showed that 44 percent of all women work, but earn on an average only 60 percent of a man's salary.[67]

Supporters of marked expansion of vocational education at the secondary school level have three substantial allies, one old and two recent. The old ally is federal aid to vocational education, which has been in existence since 1917. The recent allies include supporters of alternative schools who call for schools with varying specializations, and mid-1970s educational

---

[67] John F. Jennings, "Emerging Issues in Vocational Education," *American Vocational Journal* 50 (September 1975), 29–31.

reformers who want more work experience and alternative transitions to adulthood for American youth.

On the other hand, some critics point to the overvocationalization of the curriculum and note that the vocational educators themselves recognize "costs estimated as high as 50 to 75 percent above other forms of high school education."[68] Although they think vocational education is important, they believe that it would be a sad day for America if general education with respect to the needs of young people, to values, and pressing social realities other than vocational requirements were slighted.

Meanwhile, vocational education enrollment has grown remarkably since the passage of the Vocational Education Act of 1963. From 1965 to 1974 secondary school vocational enrollment grew by almost 200 percent, with more than 8 million students enrolled in 1974.[69]

We leave our consideration of vocational education with some yet unanswered questions. Will the secondary education of the future minimize vocational education and delegate this responsibility primarily to post-secondary education? Will vocational education flourish and thrive through the support of Americans oriented toward practicality? Will career education, implying a structured orientation and preparation program for every student as a part of his or her every course, prevail?

DISCUSSION

1. Try your own hand at naming some of the various classes, activities, and student experiences within a contemporary secondary school.

2. In what way did the Physical Sciences Study Committee establish a pattern that influenced curriculum reform of the 1960s?

3. What are some of the new trends in science education that depart from the earlier reform movements of the 1950s and 1960s?

4. How did the School Mathematics Study Group differ from other projects in the curriculum reform movement of the 1950s and 1960s?

5. What is the nature of today's controversy over the new math?

6. How did the field of the social studies respond to the new emphasis on study of the structure of disciplines?

7. What is meant by the "new" new social studies?

8. To what extent has major change taken place in the structure of the social studies curriculum since 1916? Is the change a deep one or a superficial one?

---

[68] Angelo C. Gilli, Sr., "A Personalized System of Vocational Education," *American Vocational Journal* 50 (November 1975), 37.
[69] Jennings, "Emerging Issues," p. 30.

9.   What is the three-part function of English as seen by specialists in the field?

10.   Why is the challenge of back-to-basics advocates particularly felt in the area of English language arts?

11.   How has the question of sex discrimination affected physical education programs?

12.   What are some of the new thrusts in the broad field of physical education?

13.   How did the audiolingual approach change the teaching of modern foreign languages? What were the weaknesses in the approach?

14.   In what ways are teachers of modern foreign languages attempting to acquaint students with the cultures and societies that use the language being taught?

15.   What is the justification for inclusion of music in the secondary school curriculum?

16.   Cite some of the evidence indicating that music taught in secondary schools differs widely from the music enjoyed by contemporary youth.

17.   In what way is art useful in the lives of human beings?

18.   What evidence is there that art educators are attempting to make art available to all students rather than to artists alone?

19.   What are some of the characteristics of home economics that make this field important to both male and female students?

20.   Illustrate some of the dangers of obsolescence of content encountered by teachers of home economics.

21.   Can you illustrate the tendency to use industrial arts as a "dumping ground"?

22.   Why have industrial arts educators yielded ground on their earlier insistence on industrial arts as general education?

23.   What are some of the dilemmas faced by business educators in relationship to the demands of businesspeople and the contemporary emphasis in education upon meeting the needs of the individual?

24.   What advantages or disadvantages do you see in the school-based model and the employer-based model of business education?

25.   What is the case for a markedly increased vocational education made by advocates of vocational-technical high schools?

26.   In what ways does vocational education reinforce restraints on women's progress toward better-paying jobs?

INVOLVEMENT

1.   Concentrate your observation upon the field of the secondary school curriculum in which you are specializing. Visit and then compare and contrast several secondary school classes in your broad field. To what extent are fundamental,

long-established purposes apparent to you from these observations? To what extent do you see evidence of the emphasis on curriculum reform projects in the separate disciplines that characterized the 1960s? To what extent do you see evidence of movement in newer directions more characteristic of the 1970s?

2. Try to list as many as possible course offerings in secondary education within the broad field of the curriculum you know best. Compare your list with those of students who specialize in other broad fields.

3. Talk to teachers in the broad field in which you specialize about changes in content and instruction during their lifetimes. Identify for yourself those who have had the most varied experiences. As a class, invite those teachers to share their experiences through a panel made up of representatives of several broad fields.

4. Carry on your own survey of the newest developments in your own broad field through reading the most recent issues of the major magazine in your field.

5. Build a list of purposes and objectives in the broad field of the curriculum in which you specialize. How does your list contribute to the needs of students? . . . to illuminating the social realities of their times? . . . to helping them clarify their values? . . . to acquiring knowledge that is generally relevant? Which of the goals and objectives that you have listed do you regard as most important in the education of secondary school youth?

6. Identify the elements in the broad field in which you specialize that seem to you to be most individually and socially useful to high school age young people. Join in a panel with students specializing in other broad fields to specify this content. Then, as a panel, ask yourselves what individually and socially useful content important to young people has been minimized or left out.

FURTHER READINGS

Bailey, Larry J., and Ronald Stadt. *Career Education: New Approaches to Human Development.* McKnight, Bloomington, Ill., 1974. Describes career development theory and research; develops a curriculum model for its implementation.

Bessom, Malcolm E., Alphonse M. Tatarunis, and Samuel L. Forcucci. *Teaching Music in Today's Secondary School.* Holt, Rinehart and Winston, New York, 1974. The esthetic experience of music education as a basis for curriculum development in secondary schools.

Brown, Thomas, Mary Gallagher, and Rosemary Turner. *Teaching Secondary English: Alternative Approaches.* Charles E. Merrill, Columbus, Ohio, 1975. Presents three major alternatives for the teaching of English in the secondary schools, including the revised traditional approach, the new English approach, and the experience approach.

Doherty, Joan, and William L. Walker. *Current Issues in Social Studies Education.* Curriculum Research and Development Center, Indiana State University,

Terre Haute, 1975. A report of the current status of the social studies curriculum.

Kenneth B. Hoyt, et al. *Career Education in the Middle/Junior High School.* Olympus, Salt Lake City, 1973. Application of education for careers to a particular level of secondary education.

Kline, Morris. *Why Johnny Can't Add: The Failure of the New Math.* St. Martin's Press, New York, 1973. A serious criticism of the new math by a mathematician who points out what he regards as its excesses.

Kownslar, Allan O., ed. *Teaching American History: The Quest for Relevancy.* Forty-fourth Yearbook of the National Council for the Social Studies, National Council for the Social Studies, Washington, D.C., 1974. A discussion by proponents of the new social studies of the development of inquiry and critical thinking skills.

Law, Gordon F., ed. *Contemporary Concepts in Vocational Education: The First Yearbook of the American Vocational Association.* American Vocational Association, Washington, D.C., 1971. A useful review of current thought on vocational education.

Lockard, J. David, ed. *Science and Mathematics Curricular Developments Internationally, 1956–1974.* Commission on Science Education of the American Association for the Advancement of Science and the Science Teaching Center of the University of Maryland, College Park, 1975. A report on over 390 science and mathematics curriculum projects currently operating worldwide.

Lowenfeld, Viktor, and W. Lambert Brittan. *Creative and Mental Growth,* 6th ed. Macmillan, New York, 1975. A text that explores art and creativity, and reports on cognitive and social growth through twelfth grade.

Marland, Sidney P. *Career Education.* McGraw-Hill, New York, 1975. The first book on the subject for general readers. Marland presents the impact of career education today within a historical setting and points out its potential for revitalizing the school.

Piercey, Dorothy. *Reading Activities in Content Areas: An Ideabook for Middle and Secondary Schools.* Allyn and Bacon, Boston, 1976. Classroom techniques that can be used in a variety of subject areas in the middle and secondary schools.

Pillet, Roger A. *Foreign-Language Study: Perspective and Prospect.* University of Chicago Press, Chicago, 1974. The audiolingual approach to language instruction and the results of this technique.

Schafer, R. Murray. *Creative Music Education.* Schirmer, New York, 1976. A handbook for the modern music teacher stressing instruction and the study of music.

Schultz, David A., and Stanley F. Rodgers. *Marriage, the Family and Personal Fulfillment.* Prentice-Hall, Englewood Cliffs, N.J., 1975. Perspective on the process of change in marriage and family life taking place today.

Symmes, Stowell. *Foundations of Education for Business,* ed. Gladys Bahr and F. Kendrick Bangs. Thirteenth Yearbook of the National Business Education Association, Reston, Va., 1975. An introduction to business education with a chapter dealing with the contributions of secondary schools to education for business.

Taylor, Harold, ed. *The Humanities in the Schools.* Citation Press, New York, 1968. Noneducators discuss the role of arts and humanistic studies in high schools. Plea for educators to become active participants in cultural-artistic exposures for students and to be brave enough to confront students with genuine moral, intellectual, and esthetic options.

Thomas, Ellen Lamar, and H. Alan Robinson. *Improving Reading in Every Class,* 2nd ed. Allyn and Bacon, Boston, 1977. A range of material for improving reading in middle and secondary schools.

Troelstrup, Arch W., and Jack R. Crutchfield. *The Consumer in American Society.* McGraw-Hill, New York, 1974. Basic fundamentals of consumerism plus up-to-date information about changes in marketing scene.

Warriner, Helen P. *Student Motivation and the Foreign Language Teacher*, ed. Frank M. Grittner. National Textbook, Skokie, Ill., 1974. Individualized learning styles are spotlighted and alternative teaching methods suggested.

Part 3.
The Quest for Better Secondary Education

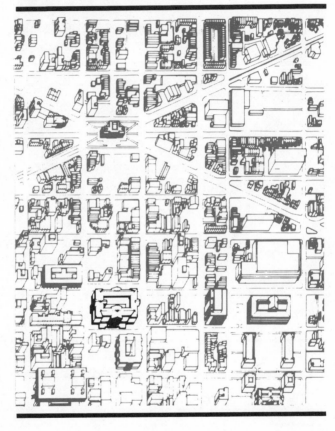

8.

Searching
for Better
Content

In a vigorous nation like the United States, we take pride in changing, developing, and growing. We do not regard ourselves as old, static, and finished; we are proud of being a vital, evolving, and unfinished country. We like to think of ourselves as the country of a permanent American Revolution.

We look at our secondary education similarly. In secondary education, as in American life, the quest for better content, setting, organization, and staff goes on. This chapter deals with the quest for content. It proposes problem areas that are highly important to the secondary school curriculum.

At one time in our nation's history, only the privileged few went to secondary schools. In an uncomplicated agrarian society, a little knowledge sufficed. Rudiments of reading and calculation took care of our communication needs. What to teach and learn was a less complex matter than it is today.

Three social forces clearly apparent in American life today are having a marked influence on the question of what should be taught and learned through secondary education. These powerful social forces are secondary school attendance by all American youth, an explosion of knowledge, and the pervasive new media of communication.

The problem of content, of what should be taught and learned, becomes much more difficult when the target audience is all young people in the United States rather than an elite slated for leadership. What may have been appropriate for the few is not necessarily appropriate for everybody. Instead of a secondary education reserved for a limited number of future leaders in business and professions, we now have a secondary education open to all and attended by all. Regardless of social class, ethnic background, degree of intelligence, or occupational destiny, all young people, with only rare exceptions, attend secondary schools during the early years of secondary education, such as the seventh and eighth grades. A high proportion of American youth graduate from high school and this figure rises annually. In 1900, 6.3 percent of persons eighteen years old graduated from high school. In 1920, 16.4 percent graduated from high school. In 1950, 60 percent graduated from high school. In 1976, 74.3 percent graduated from high school. You may speculate for yourself as to what the percentage will be in the year 2000 if the curve continues to climb throughout the rest of the twentieth century.[1] Still, the Bureau of the Census projects a flattening out of the curve.

While universal secondary schooling for American young people was coming close to achievement, the volume of potentially available knowledge was growing by leaps and bounds. Books in the libraries multiplied. New disciplines emerged. Interdisciplinary studies were created. Specialists were hard put to keep up with the growth of knowledge even in fields of narrow specialization. There would never be another Leonardo da Vinci, renowned for his grasp on all the knowledge available in his era. Today, choice as to knowledge to be taught and learned is inescapable.

Meanwhile, the ways in which humankind could communicate changed. The first communications revolution had come about when Gutenberg invented the movable printing press in 1437. Primitive communication with those within the sound of one's voice and with those who could obtain handwritten manuscripts was supplemented by printed communication in the form of books, newspapers, and magazines. About 500 years later came the second revolution in communications. In the past century humankind invented the phonograph, telephone, movies, radio, and television. In America the new media of communication became available to all, whether prosperous or poor. Devices for communication grew more sophisticated. Phonographs became stereos; bulky recorders became portable cassettes; silent films became sound movies; primitive radio signals became AM and FM and drivers communicating via CB; black and white television expanded onto wide screens, used color, and developed private and public channels. The typical young American of secondary school age spent a high proportion of his or her waking time with the new media, listening and looking. The new media flooded the young with information and bombarded their attitudes. The new media taught and young Americans learned.

---

[1] U.S. Bureau of Census, *Statistical Abstract of the United States,* 1976, 97th ed., U.S. Government Printing Office, Washington, D.C., 1976, p. 140.

WHAT SHOULD SECONDARY SCHOOLS
TEACH?

Any one of these three social forces would have confronted secondary education with a problem of selecting from among the great variety of possible learning experiences. But, when these three social forces developed simultaneously during the past century, the problem of content selection became inescapable and crucial. What did everybody, rather than the few, really need to be taught in secondary schools? In the great explosion of knowledge, what knowledge was of most worth to the secondary school age population? In a world of pervasive and insistent media of communication, what could be taught and learned through the new media and what could schooling best provide? In summary, what should be the content of secondary education for all American young people in the face of knowledge that was exploding and mass media of communication that were at one's fingertips? What was the needed new curriculum for secondary education?

REVISING SEPARATE SUBJECT MATTER DISCIPLINES

In the quest for a better content, necessitated by the three social forces described above, one approach proposed was to improve the content of the separate subject matter disciplines. Customarily, university scholars in the separate disciplines gave little of their attention to counterpart secondary school courses in their specializations. But after the Soviet Union sent Sputnik into space in 1957, and after the National Defense Education Act of 1958, scholars of the disciplines in institutions of higher learning began to look hard at these counterparts. They became involved in secondary school projects in their specialties that were supported by funds from foundations and the federal government.

The specialists soon recognized that much that was being taught in such fields as mathematics and the sciences was obsolete. With the swift growth of new knowledge, updating the disciplines was necessary. Courses were often crammed with facts about a particular subject but lacked broad concepts and generalizations. Students were often required to memorize but not to inquire.

With the support of NDEA funds from the federal government, projects in the separate subject matter disciplines developed. The first wave of projects followed the national legislation supporting programs in the sciences, mathematics, foreign languages, and guidance. A few years later, with the inclusion of more disciplines in national legislation, projects increased in the social studies, the language arts, and physical education. The arts, including fine arts, industrial arts, home economics, and music, received substantially less attention in the post-Sputnik world.

More than a hundred important curriculum projects developed during the 1960s. A characteristic project dealt with a single subject matter field, not with a broad area such as the sciences or social sciences as a whole, or with problems that cut across subject matter fields such as international affairs, consumer problems, or race relations. Such a project might deal with a particular year or level of schooling or cover elementary school through high school.

The projects usually were developed by scholars specializing in a particular discipline and teachers of the subject in public and private schools who were familiar with methodology. Seldom involved were curriculum workers, supervisors, administrators, or professors of education. The projects usually produced materials for use in schools. Project activities often included programs of teacher education through summer institutes and in-service sessions. But, in general, the sponsors of projects gave more attention to the production of programs than to the strategic questions of making sure that their products were used in schools.

The Physical Sciences Study Committee reconstructed instruction in physics under the leadership of Jerrold R. Zacharias of Massachusetts Institute of Technology. They followed procedures designed to determine the precise boundaries of a unit, identify the appropriate subject matter, embody the subject matter in material form, and prepare teachers to use the new materials. The work of the Biological Sciences Curriculum Study under Arnold Grobman at Boulder, Colorado, was more diversified in that three alternative versions of biology textbooks and materials were developed. The acronyms multiplied in the sciences: chemistry projects initialed CHEM Study and CBA, an earth science project initialed ESCP. Major universities, such as Illinois, Yale, and Maryland, sponsored projects in mathematics. Many language teaching laboratories were installed in schools to increase students' abilities to understand and speak foreign languages.

During their heyday in the 1960s, the projects in the separate subject matter disciplines made substantial contributions to the improvement of content in the specialized fields. They did eliminate much of the obsolete matter and update the content. Increasingly, they fostered inquiry and understanding of the major concepts of the specialized subjects.

However, in the 1970s increasing disillusionment with the projects in the separate subject areas became evident. The social situation that had given original impetus to the projects, the Cold War with the Soviet Union and the competition to reach outer space, no longer seemed so important. Americans had been forcibly reminded of domestic problems by racial disturbances, youth revolt, and environmental deterioration. The need for dealing with problems of American young people and of American society that cut across the tight boundaries of the separate subjects became increasingly apparent. With the reduction of availability of government funds for projects during the Nixon administration, university specialists in the disciplines became less involved in secondary school reform.

Difficult questions as to curriculum were asked in the 1970s. Among the multiplicity of disciplines available for study, which ones should be singled out? Were the projects designed primarily for bright students, already motivated, and were they inappropriate for less able students, less motivated? Were the projects designed for students who brought to them upper- and middle-class experiences? Criticisms were heard in the early 1970s not only from those who supported greater focus on problems but also from thoughtful educators who were originally attracted to the disciplines proposal. For instance, Arthur W. Foshay wrote:

> What are the limitations of the disciplines idea? . . . First, the disciplines proposal begs the question of the integration of knowledge. We must recognize that the integrity of the fields of inquiry—the disciplines—must be preserved if they are to be learned. But this immediately makes it impossible in theory to combine disciplines into multidisciplines for instruction. . . . But to teach subjects separately leaves the problem of integration of knowledge to the student himself to carry out, more or less unaided.
>
> Second, the disciplines proposal does not deal directly with the relationship between education and life—what we call "relevance." One of the oldest questions in education is how education is to be related to real life. The disciplines proposal deals with the question only in terms of the application of separate fields of knowledge. It does not deal, of itself, with the kinds of life problems . . . which do not come packaged in disciplines. . . . To the degree that we allow the school curriculum to be dominated by the disciplines proposal, we fail to offer students the opportunity to become more than superficially acquainted with great public problems. . . .
>
> The questions of the integration of knowledge and the relevance of knowledge to the real world will not be denied. They demand a response from the school curriculum, one way or another.[2]

Perhaps the most telling criticism of the separate subject matter approach came from Jerome S. Bruner, whose book *The Process of Education* was the intellectual manifesto of the separate subject approach. In 1960 Bruner, a Harvard psychologist, had urged in *The Process of Education* that the curriculum of a subject should be determined by the understanding of underlying principles giving structure to that subject. He had called for an end to the teaching of a mass of unrelated facts. Bruner had advocated that educators should work for student understanding of major ideas, relationships, principles, and major concepts within each separate discipline. He had also urged that a major reason for studying each discipline was to learn the ways of inquiry that scholars in that field used. But a decade later

---

[2] Arthur W. Foshay, "How Fare the Disciplines?" *Phi Delta Kappan*, March 1970, pp. 351–352.

Bruner "revisited" *The Process of Education.* He had come to the conclusion that the study of the separate disciplines, while desirable, was not a total answer. Now he also called for study of "immediate and compelling concerns." In an article, Bruner wrote:

The movement of which *The Process of Education* was a part was based on a formula of faith: that learning was what students wanted to do, that they wanted to achieve an expertise in some particular subject matter. Their motivation was taken for granted. It also accepted the tacit assumption that everybody who came to these curricula in the schools already had been the beneficiary of the middle-class hidden curricula that taught them analytic skills and launched them in the traditionally intellectual use of mind. . . . Failure to question these assumptions has, of course, caused much grief to all of us. . . .

In a recent article . . . I proposed that it is possible to conceive of a Monday-Wednesday-Friday curriculum covering the standard topics, and a Tuesday-Thursday and Saturday way of doing things in which immediate and compelling concerns are given the central place—activism? Let them on Tuesdays and Thursdays prepare "briefs" in behalf of their views, make a case for things they care about. Let them prepare plans of action, whether they be on issues in the school, on the local scene, or whatever.

I believe I would be quite satisfied to declare, if not a moratorium, then something of a de-emphasis on matters that have to do with the structure of history, the structure of physics, the nature of mathematical consistency, and deal with it rather in the context of the problems that face us. [3]

The dominant secondary school curriculum thrust of the 1960s, the reform of separate subject matters, answered in part the question of how to deal with the explosion of knowledge by emphasizing processes of inquiry, generalization, and principles rather than amassing unrelated facts. But the question of dealing with knowledge that cut across subject matter lines, as human problems have a way of doing, remained unanswered. The separate subject approach answered the question of what should be learned in a world of new media of communication by stressing cognition as the province of secondary education. But it did not deal with affective education, social education, and community understanding, or whether education in these important realms was to be the province of schooling or left to the powerful educational forces exerted by the mass media of communication. The separate subject approach provided exciting materials of instruction for the academically talented, but it did not resolve the question of what educational content was most appropriate for all American young people of secondary school age. As the quest for content went on in the 1970s, many educators opted to explore another road toward improved content for secondary education, an emphasis on life problems of young people in American society.

---

[3] Jerome A. Bruner, "The Process of Education Revisited," *Phil Delta Kappan,* September 1971, pp. 19–21.

An alternative to a curriculum based on separate subject matters has long existed and has influenced the secondary school program, yet it has not prevailed. In this alternative, the curriculum focuses on the life problems of young people in American society. Such a curriculum involves identifying major problem areas, using varied methods and materials to foster understanding of a significant aspect of a problem area, sharing with others and acting upon what has been learned, and reconstructing the experience through evaluation and appraisal.

The progressive educators of the early twentieth century were among those who struggled toward a problem-oriented curriculum characterized by use of the method of intelligence. The early progressives, however, were largely needs-oriented; they stressed a variety of experiences to meet needs during their experimentation and seldom tried to identify the most common clusters of content for the secondary school curriculum.

One wing of educators of the early twentieth century, influenced by progressive education experimentation, proposed centering upon social functions and social demands. They argued that there were major centers about which the activities of individuals and groups tended to cluster, and that these were the appropriate centers for education. For instance, Hollis L. Caswell and Doak S. Campbell specified several social functions:

Protection and Conservation of Life, Property and Natural Resources

Production of Goods and Services and Distribution of the Returns of Production

Consumption of Goods and Services

Communication and Transportation of Goods and People

Recreation

Expression of Aesthetic Impulses

Expression of Religious Impulses

Education

Extension of Freedom

Integration of the Individual

Exploration[4]

Another curriculum specialist, Henry Harap, proposed a similar list:

Living in the Home

Leisure

Citizenship

---

[4] Hollis L. Caswell and Doak S. Campbell, *Curriculum Development*, American Book, New York, 1935, p. 178.

Organized Group Life

Consumption

Production

Communication

Transportation[5]

This structure is espoused today by community educators Edward G. Olsen and Phillip A. Clark who list the following basic life concerns activities and enduring experiences of living:

Securing Food and Shelter

Protecting Life and Health

Communicating Ideas and Feelings

Adjusting to Other People

Satisfying Sexual Desires

Enriching Family Living

Bearing Children

Securing Education

Sharing in Citizenship

Controlling the Environment

Utilizing Leisure Time

Enjoying Beauty

Appreciating the Past

Meeting Religious Needs

Finding Personal Identity

Adjusting to Change

Growing Old, Facing Death.[6]

Both men think that dealing with such clusters of content is the most effective way of approaching the personal and social problems of young people in American society.

The contemporary quest for curriculum based on the personal and social problems of young people in modern society must take into account the three social forces mentioned earlier in this chapter: secondary school attendance by all American young people, the explosion of knowledge, and the existence of mass media of communication. It must be also based solidly on the foundations for decision making in education.

What are the sources to which we must turn to find a satisfactory

---

[5] Joint Committee on Curriculum, Henry Harap, ed., *The Changing Curriculum*, D. Appleton-Century, New York, 1937, p. 96.
[6] Edward G. Olsen and Phillip A. Clark, *Life-Centering Education*, Pendell, Midland, Mich., 1977, p. 107.

basis? Today, as yesterday, there are three major foundations for such decision making. One clue to the answer comes from the sociological foundations of education. The social realities that characterize the culture and the times, and that influence the past, present, and future of young people, give us insights into what should be taught, experienced, and learned. A second clue derives from the philosophical foundations of education. Humane values must be a guiding force in the education of young people; the philosophical values that we prize help educators in making judgments on desirable curricula. A third clue is provided by the psychological foundations of education. Since adolescence coincides with the period of secondary education in America, the characteristic needs, concerns, and interests of adolescents must play a significant role in determining their educational experiences, what we should teach, and how they can best learn.

Only after we have taken into account the best we can learn from contemporary sociological, philosophical, and psychological foundations of education can we make reasonable judgments and decisions as to what content of secondary education to draw from the knowledge base. These three foundations are inextricably linked. All bear on what must be selected from the mass of knowledge humankind has acquired and is continuing to acquire. Only after we have considered what social realities, humane values, and the needs of adolescents say to us with respect to what should be taught, learned, and experienced can we select from the vast knowledge explosion of our own times those disciplines and inter-disciplinary studies that will be of most worth in contemporary secondary education.

To answer the question, What should be taught and learned through secondary education? we will draw upon earlier chapters of this book. Data interrelating social foundations to the social concerns of secondary school students are contained in Chapter 2, The Social Crisis and Secondary Education. Alternatives as to life styles that are emerging in the lives of secondary school youth have philosophical implications; some possible allegiances of youth are discussed in Chapter 3, Value Options of Youth. The most common characteristics of young people during adolescence, their sex roles, special characteristics of social class and ethnic group members, and deviations from the norm contribute to understanding of psychological foundations; Chapter 4 deals with Characteristics of Young People. The knowledge base, currently classified into twelve broad fields and their constituent subjects, is the topic of Chapter 7, The Secondary School Program Today. All these sources of the curriculum must be drawn upon in the quest for a better content.

If useful secondary education today, derived from sociological, philosophical, and psychological foundations of education and drawing upon the knowledge base, is to illuminate social realities, foster humane values, meet the needs of young people, and use relevant knowledge, what should it teach? What are the central concerns on which the learning experiences of young people should center? What clusters of problems are most worth study today?

The remainder of this chapter will propose sixteen such problem-oriented centers of experience that are important in secondary education. The relationship of each to social realities, to humane values, and to needs of adolescents will be summarized. Disciplinary and interdisciplinary studies that can help students to encounter these centers of experience will be suggested. The descriptions of sixteen centers of experience that follow are quoted with few modifications from this author's chapter, "What Should Be Taught and Learned Through Secondary Education?" in *Issues in Secondary Education*, the 1976 Yearbook of the National Society for the Study of Education.[7]

MAJOR CLUSTERS OF CONTENT

The sixteen centers of experience discussed below are suggested by the author as highly important in a balanced and significant program of secondary education today: (1) war, peace, and international relations; (2) overpopulation, pollution, and energy; (3) economic options and problems; (4) governmental processes; (5) consumer problems; (6) intercultural relations; (7) world views; (8) recreation and leisure; (9) the arts and esthetics; (10) self-understanding and personal development; (11) family, peer group, and school; (12) health; (13) community living; (14) vocations; (15) communication; (16) alternative futures.

Obviously, these clusters of content are not proposed for eternity; as new developments within the interacting sources require new adaptations, the clusters of content will change. The suggested list of centers of experience represents no particular rank order of priority. Each center will be discussed in four paragraphs that will relate each cluster of content to social realities, values, needs, and ways of organizing knowledge.

WAR, PEACE, AND INTERNATIONAL RELATIONS

International problems of war and peace are crucial to the survival of the human race. Overkill is no longer the monopoly of a few great powers; steadily, the new capacity to destroy through nuclear

---

[7] William Van Til, "What Should Be Taught and Learned Through Secondary Education?" in *Issues in Secondary Education*, The Seventy-fifth Yearbook of the National Society for the Study of Education, University of Chicago Press, Chicago, 1976, pp. 178–213.

weapons moves into the hands of smaller nations, too. Military expenditures expand, though the world seeks understanding, détente, and peaceful relations through the United Nations and the negotiations by world powers.

Ways of living of the varied nations of the world must be studied if international understanding is to prevail. Long gone are the days when international studies could be limited to Western Europe. Now the values of such powers as the Soviet Union, China, and the bloc of Arab states must be understood. The nationalistic ambitions of countries in Africa, Asia, and South America must be reckoned with.

In the late 1960s American (and world) youth graphically demonstrated how important to them were the world's problems of war and peace. The war in Vietnam and throughout Southeast Asia contributed to youth dissent and anger on an unprecedented scale. Wars are fought by the young and no one knows this better than the young people themselves. Problems of military service and establishing a lasting peace are high among the genuine concerns of young people.

In such a setting, secondary education in America must deal with war, peace, weaponry, nationalism, imperialism, gaps between developed and underdeveloped nations, blocs, alliances, conflicting world views on the international scene, and the like. The social studies, language arts, and foreign languages can make contributions to international understanding. Cross-disciplinary studies of world areas and dilemmas offer another desirable opportunity to teach about war, peace, and international relations.

OVERPOPULATION, POLLUTION, AND ENERGY

In the 1970s people and their leaders began to sense that the interrelated problems of overpopulation, pollution, and energy depletion were creating a crisis for human survival comparable to global war. On the world scene there appeared grim manifestations of famine and hunger, poisoning of land and air and oceans, and oil shortages. Population soared, especially in underdeveloped lands. The headlong rush to industrialism gouged the earth, fouled the air, and killed life in rivers, seas, and oceans. Meanwhile, the limits to growth grew nearer as the developed nations used up much of the earth's resources even before the underdeveloped nations had their opportunity to exploit nature's bounty.

One such problem as overpopulation, pollution, or energy depletion is deadly enough, but taken together the problems are deadlier still. The value choices involved are delicate and complex; policies adopted today can haunt tomorrow's generations.

The concern of American young people for this cluster of problems is apparent. They enlist in campaigns to save and improve the environment. Many demonstrate their support for population controls in their own family planning. They are aware of the necessity for conserving energy and often more willing to forego material goods than their elders are. Youth is keenly aware that they are the inheritors of decisions with respect to the three interrelated problems.

Potential contributors to the study of these problems in the secondary schools include disciplines within the sciences, mathematics, physical education, home economics, the social studies, and the language arts. The three interrelated problem areas and the attendant growth dilemmas might also be attacked through interdisciplinary approaches.

ECONOMIC OPTIONS AND PROBLEMS

The U.S. economy soured in the early 1970s. Inflation combined with stagnation and produced a hybrid, stagflation. The classical economic assumptions did not work automatically in an economy made rigid by oligarchic price maintenance, closely protected profits, collective wage demands, and fixed governmental budgets.

In an inflationary setting, those who lived by the work ethic were penalized and those who followed the philosophy of the grasshopper which played all summer were rewarded. In a recession-depression situation, inequalities in income distribution became increasingly apparent as unemployment grew. The possible alternative systems of production and distribution within a democracy ranged from free enterprise to socialism and involved different assumptions as to the good life, the nature of humanity, and human behavior. Analysis of choices had to extend beyond economic factors alone and into philosophical, social, and psychological realms. Questions of values became inescapable.

Economic trouble hits youth particularly hard. In economically depressed times the proportion of young people unemployed exceeds that of the general population; the problem is particularly acute for black and Hispanic-American youth, whose rate of unemployment is greater than that of the rest of the youth population. Young people are necessarily caught up in the work and distribution dilemmas.

The need for studying economic relationships through the discipline of economics and through interdisciplinary social education approaches becomes increasingly apparent in the economically troubled 1970s.

GOVERNMENTAL PROCESSES

Although civic education has long been a major objective of American education, political and governmental developments in the 1970s demonstrated that the nation had far to go to achieve the informed and active citizenry envisaged by Thomas Jefferson and Horace Mann. In the post-Watergate atmosphere, cynicism was widespread; whether personally involved or not, all politicians had been tarred by the

Watergate brush. Apathy followed disillusionment; in the elections of 1974, with the entire House of Representatives and one-third of the Senate up for election, only 38 percent of the electorate bothered to vote.

Survival of the fittest, a value that rationalized exploitation by predatory vested interests, challenged the values inherent in the American dream of a free, self-governing citizenry. Ends-justify-means philosophies were blandly accepted in high places in American life. The hope of using governmental institutions for social welfare and human enhancement was threatened by a cumbersome, lethargic bureaucracy. Were venality and indifference so entrenched that Americans could no longer depend on their political and governmental processes to help create a better society? Study and action in politics and government offered many opportunities for value analysis.

Opportunities for the young to participate in the political and governmental process had been increased through lowering the voting age to eighteen, but it remained an open question in the late 1970s whether youth would take advantage of its potential to make a difference. Although there was evidence that youthful idealism persisted, there was evidence, too, of apathy and escape into privatism within an apolitical youth culture. Perhaps a new emphasis on action learning might teach the young how they could make a difference in their communities.

The challenge involved not only the social studies but also such broad fields as the sciences, the language arts, business-vocational education, and the various art areas. At issue were questions of the potentiality of the common people to govern themselves democratically and to achieve their potential through individual and group action.

CONSUMER PROBLEMS

Choosing, buying, and using goods and services has become increasingly complex in the United States. Not only has the variety of goods and services available increased and not only does the problem of shoddiness and even harmfulness of products persist. There is an added element in consumer education. As Harman puts it, there is "the 'new scarcity' of energy, materials, natural fresh water, arable land, habitable surface area, capacity of the natural environment, and resilience of life-supporting ecological systems."

Consuming always involves value choices; each time a person buys, he or she is casting an economic vote. Now that vote represents more than an expression of personal idiosyncratic preference. That decision can now preempt goods and services that will be needed by the immediate descendants of the consumer. We have come grudgingly to recognize that resources are finite and that reliance on the ingenuity of technology to solve all our energy problems is a great gamble. Consumer education must today involve value decisions about life styles. Thoreau once advised other

Americans to simplify their lives; now the advice may be mandatory if human survival is to be assured.

The new issues are of major concern to contemporary young people. Behind many of the youth challenges of the later 1960s was a criticism of the overly materialistic patterns of their elders. Youth responses in the form of communes and simplified "greenings of America" may have had their ludicrous overtones, yet the gropings reflected the recognition by young people that happiness could not simply be measured quantitatively by one's volume of possessions.

The field of consumer education embraces many broad areas of the secondary school curriculum, notably home economics (not for females only), industrial arts (not for males only), business education, mathematics, the social studies, and the choices inherent in reading and viewing in the language arts. Consumer education also affords an opportunity for interdisciplinary studies.

INTERCULTURAL RELATIONS

That human beings worldwide and in our nation have different racial, religious, national, and socioeconomic backgrounds suggests the desirability of including human relations education in the school curriculum. The additional fact that relationships among people of such varied backgrounds have been characterized by discrimination, prejudice, hostility, and outright violence makes intercultural education imperative. Individuals receive highly differential treatment. Being black or white, Spanish-speaking or English-speaking; of Native American or of varied European stocks; Catholic, Jew, Protestant, or unchurched; of one or another of the social classes—all the factors initially, and sometimes permanently, beyond the young person's control make a difference in the life Americans lead.

One great test of a nation's values is how it treats its varied group members. The historic values of democracy simply cannot be reconciled with discrimination. Nor can Judeo-Christian religious ethics be reconciled with racism. Nor can equal justice under the law be reconciled with preferential treatment based on ethnic differences. Nor does the objective quest for truth by science validate master race theories.

Young people of minority group backgrounds find their daily experience permeated with problems of human relationships; strategies as to human relations, such as desegregation-integration and identity-separatism, involve difficult decisions. Majority group white youth also encounter intercultural relationships; actual or vicarious encounters with people of diverse backgrounds are inescapable.

There is no field of the secondary school curriculum that is unrelated to human relations education. The need for a massive renaissance of intercultural education in a multiethnic society is urgent. Interdisciplinary approaches drawing upon such fields as language arts, the social studies, and the biological sciences hold promise.

WORLD VIEWS

The world view of the democratic way of life relying upon the use of the method of intelligence by the common people competes with the world view of authoritarianism relying upon fixed answers determined by elite groups. This fundamental cleavage carries over into the affairs of nations, religions, philosophies, and institutions.

A variety of value orientations persist and new world views develop. Nations ally themselves into blocs based on ideologies and interests, such as the Western democracies, the two major communist blocs, the Arab oil bloc, and the Third World nations. Long-established religions such as multidenominational Christianity, Judaism, Buddhism, Hinduism, and Islam attempt to maintain and extend their spheres of influence. Schools of philosophic thought set forth their assumptions and principles and attempt to refute each other's claims. Newer industrial institutions replace older agrarian-based ways of organization.

Individual young people grow up surrounded by world views that are dominant in their particular culture. As they mature, they become increasingly curious about the basis for the assumptions, principles, and beliefs about society that they have inherited; their curiosity extends to those who hold world views different from their own. Thus opportunities to teach about divergent ways of conceiving the life of humankind emerge.

Secondary education provides many opportunities to study world views; for instance, through the study of national and world literature in the language arts, the study of a variety of civilizations in the social studies, the study of knowledge accumulated in the sciences, the recognition of varied art expressions in the humanities, the world study of foreign languages. Cross-disciplinary studies of comparative cultures, religions, philosophies, and institutions provide opportunities for high school youth to understand and improve world views they have inherited and to understand and respect the world views of others.

RECREATION AND LEISURE

The Bible reminds us that we shall not live by bread alone. Nor should humankind live by the bread of social problems alone, however necessary these may be for human survival. A vital area in the social experience of modern Americans is the use of recreation and leisure time. In a developed nation like ours, people have substantial free time, mandated by the nature of our industrial system. Even the most work-oriented moonlighters in the United States have more free time than their ancestors had.

Contemporary recreational and leisure opportunities necessitate value choices. For instance, being a spectator vies with participating. Participation is frequently praised for gains such as mental and physical health that accompany taking part in games and sports, tours and travel, and the like. Being a spectator is often maligned as simply an obsessive fixation on the omnipresent television set. Yet a spectator can watch and appreciate the best performances the contemporary world can provide. A reader of books is a spectator, yet at the same time can be a mentally active participant. A viewer of a movie is a spectator, yet simultaneously can be a participant whose experience is being expanded. Perhaps more important than whether one's recreational time is characterized by the supposed passivity of being a spectator or the supposed action of participation may be the extent to which the potential capacities of the person are stretched by the leisure experience.

That youth is actively expanding experiences in leisure and recreation is so apparent that the point need not be amplified here.

In secondary education, recreation and leisure have frequently been regarded as the province of the physical education specialists. Their contribution is not to be deprecated, yet we might well maximize the additional contributions of a variety of fields of the secondary school curriculum. To cite one among many, consider the potential contribution of the language arts with its long-established emphasis on reading and its newly established emphasis on communications media.

THE ARTS AND ESTHETICS

For civilized people the use of one's time reaches its apogee in the arts. It is no accident that civilizations throughout history have developed music, fine arts, drama, poetry, and prose. Through the arts, humankind expresses creativity and moves beyond a pedestrian life.

The arts encourage the humane values of self-expression and creativity. Admittedly, the arts are most significant when an individual participates by shaping clay, playing a dramatic role, evoking music, or mobilizing words. Yet not to be deprecated is the art experience of the art consumer who looks or listens and enters into the mood and the spirit of the art product. To be prized are the communication with the painter and sculptor in the gallery, the hush as the curtain goes up, the mood created by the music, the recognition of similar experiences expressed on a printed page.

The fascination of the young with the arts has been repeatedly demonstrated. Even our too frequently dull and routine approaches to the arts often fail to turn off youthful eagerness to create or to react to the creations of others. Young people are frequently most alive when encountering art experiences.

Much of the high school curriculum exists for the cultivation of art experiences in such aspects as music, fine arts, home economics, and industrial arts. The field of language arts, at its best, goes far beyond teaching the mechanics of communication; language arts instruction can foster creative participation and absorption. If in high school education we could learn to blend art experiences into cognitive intellectualized studies, we might make the arts even more integral in the lives of the young. We might teach young people that there are other ways of expressing ideas than through speech and writing alone. We might encourage them to communicate their insights through painting, dramatization, dance, composition, and a host of creative activities in various fields and in interdisciplinary studies.

SELF-UNDERSTANDING AND PERSONAL DEVELOPMENT

There is abundant social justification for including self-understanding and personal development in the secondary school curriculum. After all, the social order is no stronger than the units that comprise it—individual persons. The struggle for a better society must begin in the hearts and minds of individual human beings.

Fundamental in a democratic philosophy of education is respect for the worth and dignity of each individual. If respect is to prevail, the individual must have faith in his or her own personal worth and dignity. To attain a desirable self-concept the individual must struggle for self-understanding and must cope with the inevitable problems that impede personal development. Therefore, if schools are to foster a democratic philosophy that values the individual, the secondary school must help young people to come to terms with themselves.

Concern for self-understanding and personal development is conspicuous among the needs of young people. Early and late adolescence are times when the young seek to know who they are and who they might become. Adolescence is a period when the young try to come to terms with a bewildering rapid physical development, accompanied by emotional, intellectual, and social perplexities. Consequently, a variety of personal problems arise, typified by the area of human sexuality. If the schools ignore personal needs, these become a hidden agenda for the young person, to the detriment of learning whatever the school blandly assumes that individuals are learning. Meeting the personal needs of the learner is a prerequisite to an individual's learning much else.

Guidance staffs have rightly staked out a major claim to dealing with the personal problems of youth, but this area of content is too important to be left to a supporting service alone and unaided. All broad fields of the secondary school curriculum are potentially strong contributors to youth's quests to know themselves. For instance, the language arts field can draw on vast resources by way of literature and creative writing; the social studies can interrelate social and personal problems and dilemmas; the sciences can include psychology. Highly helpful can be what Kimball Wiles called "analysis groups," sessions not bound to particular subjects or fields, in which students talk through their personal problems and decisions with their peers and with a sensitive adult.

FAMILY, PEER GROUP, AND SCHOOL

One of the paradoxes of secondary education is that much more instruction is provided concerning such institutions as government and industry than concerning family, peer group, or school. Yet the immediate environment in which the high school student lives pervades his or her life. Surely, social understanding of students' surrounding milieu—home and the family, peer-group members with whom individuals must closely relate, and present and prospective schooling—is essential if students are to become acquainted with social realities that they recognize as actual.

Since the student must daily make decisions within the home-friends-school environment, opportunities for value education are abundant. How should one live in these immediate environments? What makes for good relationships with the many people encountered? What are the possible consequences of plans contemplated for the future?

Since the home-friend-school complex of relationships is immediate and inescapable, this cluster of content ranks high among the expressed needs of youth. Students of highly varied backgrounds and of a wide range of intellectual abilities are apt to recognize the relevance of such discussions and inquiry.

In the usual high school program, home economics often plays a significant role with respect to family and peer groups. Other broad fields occasionally touch on family and friends but seldom extensively explore these topics. Learning about education is frequently neglected. Core and orientation programs in junior high schools sometimes deal with home, school, and friends. However, still more focus on the immediate environment in which youth lives is needed if secondary schools are to be realistic.

HEALTH

Despite its famed technology, the United States lags far behind other developed nations in its health program. Once again it is a case of having the know-how and potentiality but failing with respect to social arrangements. Despite elaborate equipment, Americans fail to provide sufficient medical care for all people at a reasonable cost. It is not only the lower-income groups and the minorities who are shortchanged; the cost of private medical care pinches the middle classes too. Inadequacy of health care is a perennial problem that looms large in any appraisal of social deficits in America.

A nation's health has sometimes been accorded high priority because of the relationship between good health and defense against foreign enemies. Draft rejections statistics have led to crusades for better health programs. But surely civilized people can recognize a higher social justification for good health than the presence or threat of war. Simply put, does not a society where good health is prized have a higher quality of life than one in which poor health is prevalent? Disease, physical handicaps, malnutrition, and poor health care wear no uniforms yet are life's deadly enemies.

That young people often behave as though they assume they could never be ill, injured, or dead is a reason to include, not neglect, health education in the curriculum. True, the problem of motivation is more difficult when one does not attribute a need to oneself. However, young people can often be reached through appeals to their feelings for other human beings.

Two broad fields have a special responsibility for fostering good health: physical education and the sciences. Physical educators rightly recognize the challenge in the very name of their organization: physical education, health, and recreation. The sciences include biology, which, rightly taught, can foster understanding and improvement of health. Yet, too often health appears to be an afterthought in secondary school programs. A greater impact on the personal and social aspects of health could be achieved if the study of health as a total pervasive problem were a fundamental part of a general education that crossed disciplinary lines.

COMMUNITY LIVING

Save for hermits, humanity, whether primitive or cosmopolitan, lives in communities. People must produce, distribute, and consume goods and services. They must communicate their messages. They must work out the organization of their group life; for instance, they must protect lives and property. They must agree on ways of governing themselves or else be subject to the governance of others. They must control their environment and conserve their resources. They must develop institutions to facilitate exchange of ideas, to educate their young, to meet their religious needs, to foster their artistic expression, and to use their leisure time.

Their interrelationships are fraught with value choices. What version of the good life should we strive for? What image of humankind should guide us? The abstractions become translated into practical decisions in respect to the aspects of life just named. The choices become real in business and industrial organizations, in labor and agricultural groups, in governing bodies.

Steadily, the interest of adolescents in the community expands. They see that many of the home, peer group, and family relationships that have absorbed them because of their immediacy are community-influenced. The world out there with its procedures and taboos, its customs and expectancies, becomes increasingly recognized as important to the individual. To understand community life, and in time to change it in desirable directions, becomes a concern of youth.

In the usual high school curriculum, the social studies area has the primary responsibility for helping youth to understand and participate in social living. However, in a school that seeks relationships to the community, social education cannot stop at an area boundary. Consequently, fields such as the sciences, language arts, business education, and home economics use the community to apply the insights they have developed. Yet the characteristic separate-subject structure secondary school curriculum is such that comprehensive study of the community and its functions is difficult and participation in the life of the community through action-learning becomes well nigh impossible. Thus support grows for community education programs that cross subject boundaries and involve experiences in the community marked by action-learning. As community problems, such as those of the inner city or the rural slum, grow more vexing, the need for tapping the reservoir of youth energies grows more imperative.

VOCATIONS

Among all social realities, the field of vocational orientation and preparation has achieved highest recognition in the secondary school curriculum. Today high school educators are bombarded by those who advocate career education, vocational education, and making the occupational transition to adulthood. If anything, secondary educators may need to guard against a possible overvocationalizing of the curriculum.

Value considerations are prominent in instruction related to vocations. Not only are there long-established problems, such as reasonable vocational choices based on dependable data, today the rationale of the work ethic itself is being questioned. The relative importance of work in a person's total life is being reexamined by social critics in an age that suspects that materialism is a dead end. Meanwhile, one segment of the population, youth from families living on welfare, finds little opportunity to experience the prevalent work ethic; to such young people any debate about the work ethic is academic.

Despite challenges to or inexperience with the work ethic, so strong is the prevalent emphasis on work in the United States that the vocational area continues to be of great importance to the large majority of young (and older) people. Preparation for a job is often perceived as the basic reason for attendance at school. School, as youth frequently views it, is to train you for a job, help you to do better than your family, provide you with a higher income than if you lacked a diploma or a degree. *Practical* is often a good word in youth's lexicon, whereas *theoretical* and *abstract* are bad words.

In recognition of the importance of vocations in contemporary American life, secondary education sets aside a substantial proportion of time for the "third environment," namely work. Part of the curriculum is identified by its title as vocational, such as business education, industrial education, distributive education, agricultural education, and homemaking. Separate schools exist, whether broadly labeled vocational or called by the names of particular trades and occupations. Even the curriculum areas less identified as vocational by their titles are currently urged by U.S. Office of Education proposals to gear their offerings to career education. The high school reform proposals of the mid-1970s, typified by Coleman's *Youth: Transition to Adulthood,* call for still more emphasis on the world of work, whether within or beyond the aegis of secondary schools.

COMMUNICATION

Despite the deprecation of the three R's by those who contend that modern technology, such as television and electronic calculators, has rendered them obsolete, the ability to read, write, and handle mathematics remains important in communicating with people in today's pattern of social realities. To be a competent member of society today one must possess not only rudimentary skills but also a degree of mastery. Much of our knowledge is still set down in the form of words and symbols. Rather than minimize the relative importance of the three R's, we would be more sensibly employed in teaching them well while also recognizing the value of using the newer communications media. We would be foolish indeed if we ignored either the force of the tide of the new technology or the enduring power of earlier skills and media. Of course, we need skills beyond the original three R's, but teaching the new basics need not imply discarding the old basics.

Whether the communication skills are old or new, they frequently communicate concerning matters of right and wrong, good and bad. This is as true in today's secular society as when the Puritans interpreted the function of reading as that of enabling people to read and interpret the Bible.

Value analysis is still essential. That today's communications media advance conflicting messages through commercials, propaganda, manipulated statistics, and attempts to shape public opinion heightens the need for the development of reflective thought applied to all communication.

Youth is sometimes caricatured as resisting learning the three R's by celebrating the end of the school term or an unanticipated "snow day." The criticism inherent in this caricature might be better directed to unimaginative routine methods of instruction by teachers. In a classroom that relates both the skills and the new media to the young person's living experience, rather than simply teaching skills as something apart from reality, the process of communication via mathematics and language arts can become integral to meeting the needs of youth. In the hands of the creative teacher, communication processes can become vital to the solution of problems and perplexities faced by youth in modern society.

The curriculum area that has the major responsibility for teaching two of the original three R's and the uses of new media is the language arts. Still, the truism that every teacher should be a teacher of oral and written communication is sound. Team relationships between language arts teachers and teachers of other curricular areas hold promise and do not threaten the additional responsibilities of language arts teachers.

ALTERNATIVE FUTURES

Consider a twelve-year-old who is about to enter a secondary school in 1978. About half this youngster's life will be lived in the twenty-first century! By the end of the twentieth century he or she will be only thirty-four years old. Some hardy specimens will still be alive into the second half of the twenty-first century. To confine study of social realities to the past or even to restrict such study to the present would be to shortchange today's twelve-year-old by depriving him or her of the opportunity to learn about the alternatives that lie ahead.

Contemporary futurists do not predict that any single, fixed future pattern will inevitably emerge. Instead, they emphasize that alternative futures must be projected and examined. Some alternative futures are preferable to others; some are highly desirable, whereas others are repugnant. Consequently, study of alternative futures forces secondary school students to examine their values. They can no longer conceive their value choices simply as abstract preferences; they come to recognize the power of daily operational decisions in shaping alternative futures.

The twenty-first century can no longer be conceptualized as an era inhabited by people whom we vaguely term our "posterity." It is, instead, that segment of time in which the individual will live most of his or her life. Today's value-related decisions on energy, pollution, population, the economy, and the like take on real significance when an individual recognizes that what people do today will shape a highly personal tomorrow in which the individual will live, sharing its triumphs, dilemmas, or disasters. Whether academically inclined or not, young people can see the relationship of alternative futures to their own lives, and thus contemporary problems take on greater meaning.

Teachers of all subjects in the secondary school curriculum might profitably relate their instruction to alternative futures. Their potential gains would include more meaningful subject matter and a more motivated student group as students consider, for instance, alternative futures in the arts, in the sciences, in literature, and in society. But the most exciting approach to alternative futures is interdisciplinary study through which youth, with no holds barred, can envision the full sweep and range of the possible futures in which they may live.

POSSIBLE CURRICULAR ORGANIZATION

Although each of the above clusters of content is desirable in a well-rounded secondary education, schools will probably continue to differ in the relative emphasis they will place on each center of experience. For instance, while specialized vocational schools exist it is realistic to expect that such schools will place heavier emphasis on the vocational component of the above list. One might realistically expect that an alternative school that focuses heavily on the environment might especially stress the overpopulation-pollution-energy cluster of content. Similarly, a comprehensive high school in an inner-city area might understandably judge communication to be an aspect of the curriculum deserving highest priority. While such differences are to be anticipated, a broad coverage of the centers of experience is desirable if a secondary school is to provide education based on needs, social realities, values, and knowledge. The total omission of one or more of the components of the list would serve neither the individual student nor American society.

We might well anticipate, too, that the forms of curricular organization adopted for implementation of these clusters of content will continue to be varied. No doubt the traditionally organized high school program will continue to implement these clusters of content through incorporating them in whole or in part in the separate curriculum areas and in disciplines within these areas. Thus we might expect to find certain clusters of content incorporated within disciplines in the areas of the social studies, the sciences, the language arts, mathematics, the several arts, the business-vocational subjects, physical education, and foreign languages. Other schools might emphasize certain centers of experience in more integrated teaching through, for instance, social studies instruction that interrelates social studies disciplines or subjects. Still more experimental forms of organization will use and extend core, team, humanities, and similar inter-disciplinary and cross-disciplinary approaches to some of the clusters of content.

However the curriculum is organized, it is reasonable to anticipate that recognition of the importance of the centers of experience cited will grow in a relevant late-twentieth-century secondary education based on the interaction of social realities, needs, values, and meaningful bodies of knowledge. Reconsideration of the content of secondary education seems inescapable in the years ahead. Let us welcome reconsiderations rather than resist them.

DISCUSSION

1. What social forces in American life are markedly influencing what should be taught in secondary schools?

2. How has the situation with respect to secondary school attendance changed in the past century?

3. Illustrate the explosion of knowledge through examples from the subjects or broad field you know best.

4. How did Sputnik and the National Defense Education Act of 1958 contribute to the revision of separate subject matter disciplines? What was the role of subject matter specialists in the revision process?

5. Generalize on the nature of the major curriculum reform projects of the 1960s. Illustrate with specific programs.

6. Why did the drive to reconstruct the curriculum through the revision of separate subject matters decline in the 1970s? What hard questions were raised about the value of the disciplines approach?

7. What did Arthur W. Foshay see as the limitations of the disciplines idea?

8. In what ways did Jerome S. Bruner change his viewpoint after "revisiting" *The Process of Education?* What was the nature of the dual approach he proposed after his "revisiting"?

9. What fundamental curriculum problems are not dealt with by the disciplines approach?

10. What is the meaning of problem centering the curriculum? What are some twentieth-century illustrations?

11. Does the Olsen-Clark list of fundamental life concerns and problems of living differ from earlier formulations?

12. What are the foundations to which educators turn to make decisions about teaching and learning? Illustrate how human problems are based on interrelated foundations of education.

13. Must the curriculum maker take into account social realities? . . . human values? . . . the needs of young people? . . . relevant knowledge? Is one of the sources of curriculum most important? Are all interrelated and necessary?

14. Why is the problem of war, peace, and international relations crucial to American youth?

15. In what ways are the problems of overpopulation, pollution, and energy interrelated?

16. What is the nature of America's economic options and problems?

17. How have developments like Watergate, lethargy, and corruption affected the attitudes of young Americans toward government?

18. What kinds of consumer choices are made by young people of secondary school age?

19. Why is the problem of intercultural education a test of the values of Americans?

20. What are the major world views in competition today?

21. What social forces have resulted in an increase in recreation and leisure time on the part of all Americans, including students?

22. Why are the arts and esthetics an essential part of an individually and socially useful education? What are the defects in the claim that cultural manifestations such as art and esthetics are useless to human beings?

23. Why should the secondary school program stress self-understanding and personal development?

24. Illustrate the importance of family, peer group, and school in the life experiences of people of secondary school age.

25. What is the justification for including health in the curriculum?

26. What are some illustrations of the broad problem of community living? Can you name some aspects that are more important than others?

27. Why is vocational education regarded as a highly important aspect of secondary school program? Name and describe some of the varied ways in which vocational preparation enters into the school program. Is there a danger that schools may become overvocationalized?

28. Are the three R's still important today? Why or why not? Are new media of communication making the three R's less necessary? How strong an emphasis should be put on the basic skills and tools of communication?

29. Why is study of the future usually welcomed by high school students?

30. What are some possible forms of curricular organization for a problem-centered program?

31. Which forms of curricular organization lend themselves most readily to problem centering? Which forms present more difficulties to those who would center the curriculum on problem areas?

INVOLVEMENT

1. Obtain from your local high school available material on dropouts and the extent of secondary school attendance by youth of the community. Prepare charts or other illustrative materials that dramatize the holding power of your local high school.

2. Select a subject or topic that interests you and check the volume of related entries in the card catalogue of the major library available to you. Talk with a librarian about the problem of storage and retrieval of materials. Learn about such techniques as microfilming.

3. Visit a television or radio station for a behind-the-scenes look at new media of communication. Gather information at the station as to number of hours on the air, volume of nationally originated and locally originated programming, and conceptions of station personnel as to their social responsibilities as communicators.

4. Conduct a self-study of your own usage of various media of communications over the past week. Summarize your time investment in each. Compare with other class members.

5. Develop a questionnaire for secondary school students on use of media of communication. Compare and contrast their time investments at various age levels.

6. Discuss with high school students what they believe they learned from the various media of communication during out-of-school hours.

7. Devote one of your visits to secondary schools to attempting to identify the use of classroom materials and approaches originally provided by the subject matter projects of the 1960s. Discuss with teachers whether the use of materials and approaches developed by the projects is increasing or decreasing in the broad area you know best.

8. Think back over your own background as a student. To what extent was your own education influenced or untouched by reforms of the separate subject matters?

9. Invite to class for talks and discussions professors specializing in science and mathematics. Ask them to describe the evolution of the projects in their fields. Inquire about the current status of projects in their fields.

10. Read Jerome Bruner's *The Process of Education.* Compare the views in the book with views expressed in the article, "The Process of Education Revisited."

11. Invite a member of your faculty who is sympathetic to problem centering the curriculum to talk to your group.

12. Build your own list of fundamental life concerns and problems of living. Compare it with lists developed by others and cited in this chapter.

13. Read current magazines and newspapers and listen to radio and television to determine whether parallels to the right-wing criticism and the views of the academic critics exist today in new forms. Are the contemporary criticisms well founded? How should they be met by educators?

14. Recall your own secondary school experiences to determine whether or not they were influenced by the projects that followed Sputnik. Did your education include study of any of the life problems stressed by the progressive education movement?

15. Visit school programs especially intended for compensatory education in the interest of low-income students. What approaches are being used? Are these similar as to goals to any of the trends and movements described in this chapter?

16. What is your own conception of an individually and socially useful secondary education? Can we combine in such education both cultural and vocational aspects? Attempt to sum up in writing your beliefs about educational goals.

17. Plan ways in which some or all of the sixteen centers of experience might be taught through the broad field, such as the sciences, the social studies, or language arts, which you know best. Develop one or more units focusing on one of the centers of experience that you could use in your future teaching. Based upon the units developed by class members, make a collection of possible approaches to incorporating the sixteen centers of experience in the program of secondary schools. When engaged in student teaching or employed as a teacher, draw upon this collection with the cooperation of the teacher of the course in which you are currently enrolled.

FURTHER READINGS

Bruner, Jerome S. *The Process of Education*. Harvard University Press, Cambridge, 1960. Development of the concept of the "spiral curriculum" using the inquiry method of learning.

Bruner, Jerome S. "The Process of Education Reconsidered." In *Dare to Care/Dare to Act*, ed. Robert R. Leeper. Association for Supervision and Curriculum Development, Washington, D.C., 1971. Advocates using both a problem-centered curriculum and a structure of the disciplines curriculum. A marked revision of the position taken by the author in *The Process of Education*.

Foshay, Arthur W. *Essays on Curriculum*. Columbia University Press, New York, 1975. A collection of papers on curriculum, including Foshay's "A Modest Proposal" and "How Fare the Disciplines?" which throw light on the structure of the disciplines approach to curriculum making.

Frymier, Jack R., June Wilhour, and Alfred Rasp, eds. *A School for Tomorrow*. McCutchan, Berkeley, Calif., 1973. Projected curricular thrusts for education and society.

Goodlad, John I. *The Dynamics of Educational Change*. Charles Kettering Foundation Program, McGraw-Hill, New York, 1975. A description of recent educational reform and an advocacy of focusing change efforts on the individual school.

Hass, Glen, Joseph Bondi, and Jon Wiles, eds. *Curriculum Planning: A New Approach*. Allyn and Bacon, Boston, 1974. A highly readable anthology on trends and innovations in curriculum planning.

Hollaway, Otto. *Problem Solving: Toward a More Humanizing Curriculum.* Franklin, Philadelphia, 1975. A guide to a more humanized curriculum that identifies weaknesses of present-day schools and suggests philosophic commitments, social emphasis, sound psychology, and humane consideration of the learner as an individual. The problem-solving approach suggested takes into account the individuality of the student and his or her cultural environment.

Mason, Edwin. *Collaborative Learning.* Schocken, New York, 1973. Confirming the idea that kids need help growing up, Mason envisions a high school that collaborates with the student and fosters his or her growth in the process.

McClure, Robert M., ed. *The Curriculum: Retrospect and Prospect.* Seventieth Yearbook of the National Society for the Study of Education, University of Chicago Press, Chicago, 1971. An anthology that treats basic curricular issues and provides a large number of options for change, together with a call for reform of the schools.

Oliva, Peter F. *The Secondary School Today,* 2nd ed. Crowell, New York, 1972. A textbook on secondary education that ranges widely over the total field and includes illustrative examples. History, foundations, curriculum, instruction, guidance, discipline, and evaluation are covered.

Olsen, Edward G., and Phillip A. Clark. *Life-Centering the Curriculum.* Pendell, Midland, Mich., 1977. Specialists in community education make the case for education for life and tell the story of the development of community education. They advocate a curriculum focused on enduring life concerns and related problems of living.

Tanner, Daniel. *Secondary Curriculum: Theory and Development.* Macmillan, New York, 1971. Curriculum areas for secondary education discussed and outlined.

———, and Laurel N. Tanner. *Curriculum Development.* Macmillan, New York, 1975. A comprehensive and authoritative book on curriculum development, although it may prove difficult for undergraduate readers.

Trump, J. Lloyd, and Delmas F. Miller. *Secondary School Curriculum Improvement: Challenges, Humanism, Accountability,* 2nd ed. Allyn and Bacon, Boston, 1973. A highly practical book suggesting specific curriculum improvement and techniques. Deals specifically with individual subject areas as well as such developments as team teaching and humanizing the curriculum.

Van Til, William, Gordon F. Vars, and John H. Lounsbury. *Modern Education for the Junior High School Years,* 2nd ed. Bobbs-Merrill, Indianapolis, 1967. A comprehensive textbook that deals with all aspects of the junior high school.

Weinstein, Gerald, and Mario D. Fantini, eds. *Toward Humanistic Education, a Curriculum of Affect.* Praeger, New York, 1970. A curriculum alternative based on affective education. Relevant to what makes children want to learn and grow.

9.

Widening the Environment

The school building in America began as a one-room school, the little red schoolhouse of fond nostalgic memory. To sentimentalists, the rural one-room school of the early nineteenth century still represents an idyllic vision of education in an ideal setting. According to the romantic, woe that the Golden Age of the little red schoolhouse is gone!

Shocking as the facts may be to the romanticist, early American schoolhouses were dark, dirty, and unhealthy places.[1] The little red schoolhouse was poorly suited to educational accomplishment. Pupils of different ages were crowded onto uncomfortable benches fixed to the floor. Ventilation was bad and the walls were drab. Rural schools were often located in wasteland or wild areas where agriculture could not survive. Contrary to the stereotype that such schools were charming and comfortable, they were in fact ugly and cheerless buildings. Even in the industrializing East, schools were in poor condition:

"The great majority of the schools" of New York state in 1844 were officially described as naked and deformed, in comfortless and dilapidated buildings with "unhung doors, broken sashes, absent panes, stilted benches, yawning roofs, and muddy mouldering floors." . . . Only one third of the schoolhouses were reported in good repair, another third "in only comfortable circumstances," while more than 3,300 "were unfit for the reception of either man or beast."[2]

---

[1] Donald J. Leu, *Planning Educational Facilities*, Center for Applied Research in Education, New York, 1965, p. 2.
[2] Edgar W. Knight, *Education in the United States*, 3rd ed., Greenwood Press, New York, 1951, p. 416.

EXPANSION OF SECONDARY SCHOOL PLANTS

As Americans moved from the country to the city, the school buildings grew larger. A characteristic nineteenth-century urban elementary school was a square building of two to four stories that also had a basement and an attic. Each floor held four classrooms and a large central corridor, save for one floor, which contained an assembly hall. The toilet rooms and the heating plant were in the basement; the principal occupied an office on the first floor.

NINETEENTH-CENTURY HIGH SCHOOLS

Many of the American public high schools that grew up in the late nineteenth century cities looked like large boxes. The floors were subdivided into smaller boxes, each identical and called classrooms. The architects of the day demonstrated their ingenuity not through classroom design but through elaborate entrances, wide corridors, large lobbies, overornamented stairways, high ceilings, many columns, cupolas, parapets, and other architectural elements. The exteriors of some of the boxlike schools resembled castles or palaces characterized by Gothic, Renaissance, or Baroque styles or some hybrid of these.

In his 1888 book on school buildings, architect E. C. Gardner proudly titled one chapter, "Nothing to Grow Old." "This building is for a school having one higher grade, and four of nearly uniform rank and size. It would be suitable for a high school in a village or small city."[3] The floor plan of the "suitable" late-nineteenth-century high school for a village or small city is reproduced in Figure 9.1.

Architect Gardner was proud both of the comparative simplicity of the exterior and the durability of the high school he designed. He wrote:

The exterior design is intended to illustrate one of the many simple effects to be produced by the use of common bricks and terra cotta. The style is Italian renaissance, which adapts itself perfectly to the practical requirements of the school as regards lighting, heating, entrances, and exits, and the ordinary needs of a school. There is nothing about it to crumble or fall away; nothing to go out of fashion or to require the outlay of a single dollar for repairs in a hundred years.[4]

Reproduced in Figure 9.2 are his drawings of the village or small city high school.

---

[3] Eugene Clarence Gardner, *Town and Country School Buildings*, E. L. Kellogg, New York, 1888, p. 59.
[4] Ibid., p. 63.

PLAN OF BASEMENT

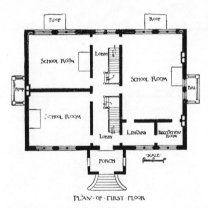

PLAN OF FIRST FLOOR

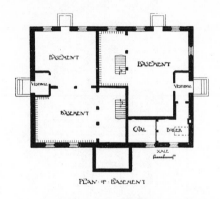

PLAN OF SECOND FLOOR

FIGURE 9.1 *A Floor Plan for a Nineteenth-Century High School.*

Source: Eugene Clarence Gardner, *Town and Country School Buildings*, E. L. Kellogg, New York, 1888, pp. 60, 61.

TWENTIETH-CENTURY SECONDARY SCHOOLS

Although Gardner optimistically predicted that his building might not need repairs till 1988, then a hundred years in the future, his simple design did not long endure. High schools grew larger and much more complex. Twentieth-century high schools included industrial arts shops, rooms for home economics, business education rooms, physical education facilities, science laboratories, and rooms devoted to instrumental and vocal music. Some designers housed such facilities in separate buildings or in additions to schools, whereas others simply expanded the usual high school structure upward or outward.

A drive for economy in school buildings during and after the Great Depression of the 1930s brought about a reduction in ornamentation in and on secondary school buildings; however, the conventional box structure was maintained. With school consolidation and the growing popularity of

FIGURE 9.2 *Exterior of a Nineteenth-Century High School for a Village or a Small City.*

Front Elevation

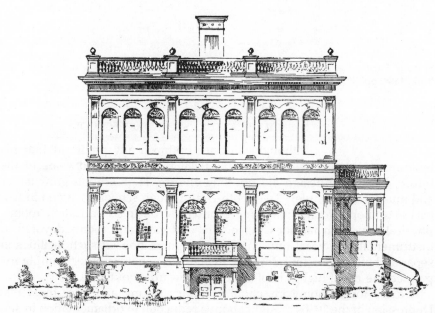

Side Elevation

SOURCE: Eugene Clarence Gardner, *Town and Country School Buildings*, E. L. Kellogg, New York, 1888, pp. 60, 62.

the comprehensive high school, secondary schools grew larger, higher, and more massive. Only the use of wide areas of glass kept them from looking like fortresses.

Architectural creativity with respect to schools dates from the close of World War II, except for earlier experimentation by such pioneers as Frank Lloyd Wright, Richard Joseph Neutra, Eliel Saarinen, and the firm of Perkins and Will. In recent decades, secondary school plants are being planned increasingly in relation to school programs. Schools are being planned for people and being related to the curriculum.

Perhaps the simplest way of describing what has happened to the design of the contemporary secondary school is to recognize that it has broken out of the traditional box. Modern secondary school design has freed itself from a layout of rooms that made the typical high school floor plan resemble an egg carton or an ice cube tray.

Designs Contemporary secondary school planners avoid problems of sameness and large size that characterize institutional-looking school buildings. To do so, they often use "clusters," "fingers," and "campus-type" designs in secondary school planning.[5]

A cluster is a grouping of related spaces that adjoin each other or are in the same general area of a building. For instance, an administrative cluster may include the general secondary school office, the health suite, and the guidance rooms. A commercial cluster may include rooms for typewriting, stenography, office machines, and bookkeeping. A library cluster may include a central reading room, conference rooms, carrels for self-instruction, and work space for the development of audio-visual materials. A shop cluster may include shops for power mechanics, metals, work with wood, mechanical drawing, graphic arts, and so on. A fine arts cluster may be included in such a shop center or exist separately. The music cluster, including band, choral, and stage activities, is often located near the school auditorium. Similarly, the gymnasium is usually located in close proximity to the swimming pool and the varied play fields in a physical education cluster. The service cluster has emerged from the basement and includes storage, custodial workshops, and power plant. Clusters characterized by necessarily noisy activities are often grouped together, separate from clusters requiring a quieter atmosphere more congenial to listening, reading, and discussion.

Fingers are relatively small buildings separated from each other by lawns and greenery, or by patios with benches and sculpture. Frequently, each of these fingerlike buildings is interconnected by walkways to the other fingers and sometimes to a main building, gymnasium, or central library. Thus massive units are broken down into smaller units marked by less

---

[5] Basil Castaldi, *Creative Planning of Educational Facilities*, Rand McNally, Chicago, 1969, pp. 250–267.

congestion and noise and by outdoor light. If the site is sufficiently large, a finger-plan school can be readily expanded through sprouting new wings of classrooms.

Campus-type buildings resemble the usual university campus in that they are made up of separate buildings scattered over a site. These buildings may contain clusters of classrooms, or each building may be a "little school" complete in itself. Each little school, or "house," has its own identity and its own student body. Some campus buildings, such as cafeterias or gymnasiums, may serve all the students of the school. A large site is needed for a campus-type school, but in an era of rising real estate costs and an increasingly urbanized society, such space is hard to come by.

The contemporary secondary school classroom also differs markedly from its conventional predecessor that had seats that were screwed down to the floor and faced the teacher's desk on the dais. Home economics living rooms, band rooms, and shops in particular differ from such conventional rooms. Today even the more academic offerings require flexible furniture for regrouping, shelves for books and magazines, work tables, bulletin boards, equipment to facilitate audio-visual instruction, spaces for displays, and so on.

Key words in the vocabulary of planners of today's secondary school plants are *flexibility, adaptability, simplicity,* and *openness.* Indeed, such promising organizational developments as the core curriculum, team teaching, open classrooms, and individualized instruction, which will be discussed in the next chapter, call for a high degree of versatility in the contemporary secondary school plant.

To visualize contemporary school design, consider two illustrative proposals by Educational Facilities Laboratories for a middle school and a comprehensive high school.[6] Educational Facilities Laboratories was established by the Ford Foundation to help educators "with their physical problems by the encouragement of research and experimentation and the dissemination of knowledge regarding educational facilities."[7]

The middle school sketched in Figure 9.3 clusters together related curriculum fields in large, open, barnlike areas. To the left is an arts barn, which includes the creative arts, industrial arts, and domestic arts. There are few dividing walls between these fields, for the emphasis is on the unity of the creative and practical arts. Below the arts barn is the science/

---

[6] Ronald Gross and Judith Murphy, *Educational Change and Architectural Consequences,* Educational Facilities Laboratory, New York, 1968, pp. 56–84. EFL cautions that the drawings are not intended as plans for schools; they were meant to bring together some of the best current ideas on environments for learning. "The reader should not be put off because he finds no indication of fire exits, or toilets, or boiler rooms, nor should he wonder at the absence of gym or cafeteria, nor try to adapt the sketches to the constraints of particular structural systems, of downtown urban real estate, or a particular school regulation or budget," p. 40.
[7] Ibid., inside cover.

math barn, which includes space for three laboratories. The communications area groups English, foreign languages, reading, and speech, and includes small rooms for listening, conferring, testing, seminars, and recordings. Just above the communications area is a typing center. At the upper right of the middle school plan are forums for languages and humanities. The language forum includes both student stations for language instruction and central space for group instruction. The humanities forum is a theater-in-the-round with a suspended projection unit; the seats can be regrouped for discussions in each quarter-section after a presentation. At the center of this middle school is the library-resource center, which includes a wide variety of books, magazines, and audio-visual and electronic resources, along with carrels for independent study.[8]

A comprehensive high school visualized by Educational Facilities Laboratories is designed for 2,000 students but is subdivided into four 500-student houses so that students and faculty members may have a sense of belonging (Figure 9.4). The four houses in this plan, along with the library, science/math cluster, and career skills cluster, could be spread out in the open country or the suburbs, but they could also be stacked on top of each other on the separate floors of a city building. Each house contains three subject matter suites: social studies, English, and foreign languages, along with a space for administration and guidance and a house commons. The house commons serves many purposes: auditorium, theater, dining space, setting for a social event or for four large-group lecture-demonstration areas. The math/science cluster includes separate laboratories and lecture rooms as well as combined laboratory and lecture rooms. The careers skills department includes space for shorthand and typing, business education, design laboratory, production laboratory, home management laboratory, along with a teacher planning center and an assembly area. Again, a library is central in the design; it includes electronic and reading resources with a display terrace and a special studies forum.[9]

Obviously, school design has come a long way since architect Gardner's 1888 building with "nothing to grow old." School designers today anticipate change and emphasize expansible, convertible, versatile, and malleable space.

In the late 1970s a major block to expansion of new and creative school buildings has appeared. Enrollments in some secondary schools have diminished because the age group formerly in elementary schools now moving into secondary schools has been dwindling in number. High school enrollment has also been reduced by the current trend toward early graduation and early college admission for many young people. Unless

[8] Ibid., pp. 58–59.
[9] Ibid., pp. 70–71.

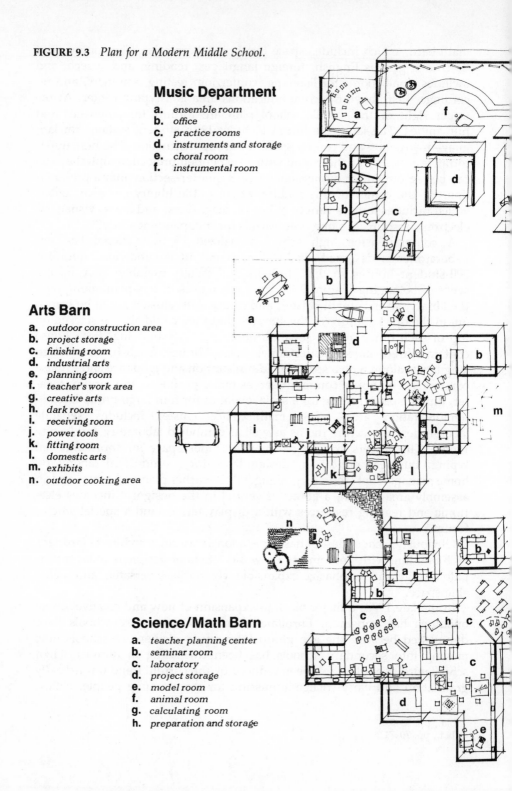

FIGURE 9.3 *Plan for a Modern Middle School.*

Music Department

a. ensemble room
b. office
c. practice rooms
d. instruments and storage
e. choral room
f. instrumental room

Arts Barn

a. outdoor construction area
b. project storage
c. finishing room
d. industrial arts
e. planning room
f. teacher's work area
g. creative arts
h. dark room
i. receiving room
j. power tools
k. fitting room
l. domestic arts
m. exhibits
n. outdoor cooking area

Science/Math Barn

a. teacher planning center
b. seminar room
c. laboratory
d. project storage
e. model room
f. animal room
g. calculating room
h. preparation and storage

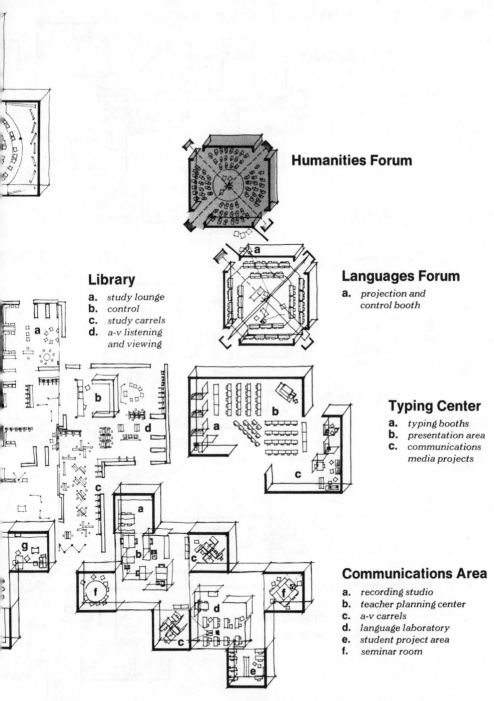

Humanities Forum

Library

a. *study lounge*
b. *control*
c. *study carrels*
d. *a-v listening and viewing*

Languages Forum

a. *projection and control booth*

Typing Center

a. *typing booths*
b. *presentation area*
c. *communications media projects*

Communications Area

a. *recording studio*
b. *teacher planning center*
c. *a-v carrels*
d. *language laboratory*
e. *student project area*
f. *seminar room*

SOURCE: Ronald Gross and Judith Murphy, *Educational Change and Architectural Consequences*, Educational Facilities Laboratories, New York, 1968, pp. 58–59.

FIGURE 9.4 *Plan for a Modern Comprehensive High School.*

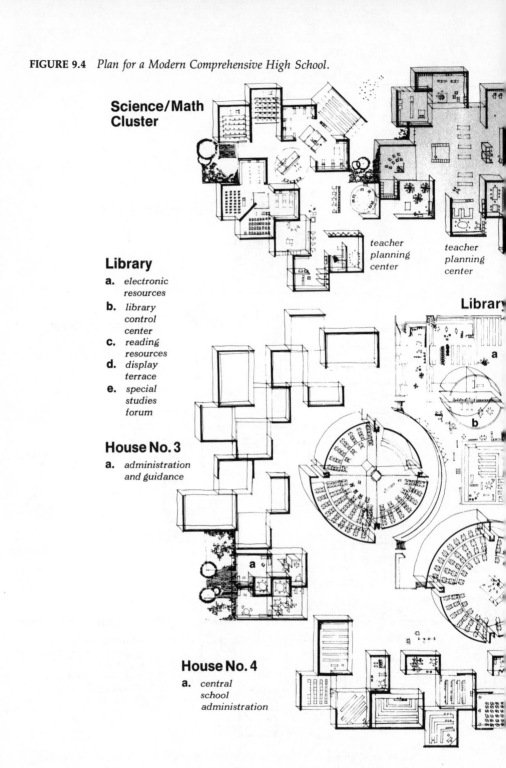

Science/Math Cluster

Library
a. *electronic resources*
b. *library control center*
c. *reading resources*
d. *display terrace*
e. *special studies forum*

House No. 3
a. *administration and guidance*

teacher planning center

teacher planning center

Library

House No. 4
a. *central school administration*

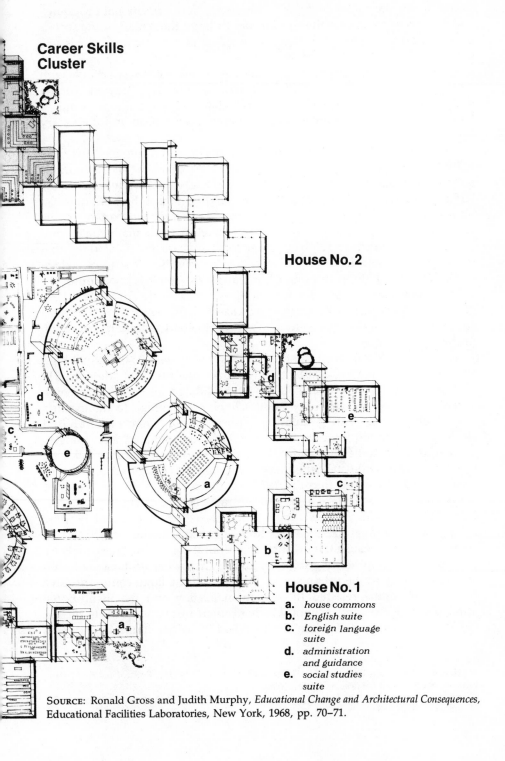

Career Skills Cluster

House No. 2

House No. 1

a. *house commons*
b. *English suite*
c. *foreign language suite*
d. *administration and guidance*
e. *social studies suite*

SOURCE: Ronald Gross and Judith Murphy, *Educational Change and Architectural Consequences,* Educational Facilities Laboratories, New York, 1968, pp. 70–71.

communities support reductions in class size, new educational programs, and new ways of serving the community through the school, some secondary schools will close in the later seventies and some school boards will file away for future reference their plans for new buildings.

Another problem hampering the building of new secondary schools with creative designs is the perennial question of financial support. In the middle and later seventies school districts have felt the economic crunch. New money has been scarce and educational costs rise in an inflationary era.[10]

Size Though all factions agree on the need for flexibility in plant planning, wide disagreement exists on the most desirable size for secondary schools. James B. Conant, a staunch advocate of the large comprehensive high school, was "convinced small high schools can be satisfactory only at exorbitant expense."[11] Conant supported opportunities for talented young people to study twelfth-grade mathematics and physics and to study a foreign language for four years. He pointed out that such classes would have low enrollments in most small schools, which could not afford these offerings. Similarly, the small school could not afford equipment and salaries for vocational education. Therefore he regarded high schools with graduating classes of fewer than a hundred students as one of the most serious obstacles to good secondary education in the United States.

At the time Conant wrote, the late 1950s, there were 17,000 small high schools with graduating classes of fewer than one hundred students. He calculated that these schools could be consolidated into 5,000 large high schools.[12] If these 5,000 consolidated schools were added to the existing 4,000 high schools with graduating classes of more than one hundred students, the United States would have 9,000 high schools. According to Conant, this would be enough for the nation. Many communities followed Conant's advice and established large comprehensive high schools.

In the late 1960s and into the 1970s, a sharp reversal in the views of many educators took place as to the desirable size of secondary schools. Critics of the comprehensive high school believed that it had become increasingly standardized and homogenized. Some objected to standardization because they wanted more local control of the schools by poor people and minority group members. They were disillusioned with the bureaucracy of the urban school system and the large comprehensive high school. Some resisted the depersonalization and the institutional atmosphere of the large school which resulted in many students feeling "lost" or even alienated. Many critics called for wider choice by students

---

[10] Educational Facilities Laboratories, *The Secondary School: Reduction, Renewal and Real Estate*, Educational Facilities Laboratories, New York, 1976.
[11] James B. Conant, *The American High School Today*, McGraw-Hill, New York, 1959, p. 37.
[12] Ibid., pp. 80–81.

and families as to the schools young persons might attend, rather than arbitrary assignment to the nearest comprehensive secondary school. Some critics of the comprehensive high schools contended that these schools overemphasized academic and cognitive development and failed to provide sufficient opportunities for the affective realm and for the development of social understandings and moral values.

ALTERNATIVE SCHOOLS

As we have already learned from Chapter 1, private alternative schools grew up across the country, and some school systems took the cue and provided public alternative schools. These provided options for students, parents, and teachers. Their proponents urged that each school should reflect the ethnic, racial, and socioeconomic makeup of the entire community. Supporters of alternative schools wanted educational programs that would have broader and more comprehensive goals and objectives than those of the usual academically oriented school.

The alternative schools that developed in the 1970s usually were smaller than the comprehensive secondary schools; the median enrollment of alternative schools was under 200. Since they were small, they were less bureaucratic. They provided more opportunities for all involved to take part in decision making.

If alternative schools were available, said their supporters, then students, parents, and teachers would have choices among learning environments and learning experiences. Since different people learn in different ways, alternative schools would facilitate learning. Few predicted that the small alternative school would replace the large comprehensive school. But as Smith and Barr have pointed out:

American secondary schools have entered a period of transition—from the large monolithic comprehensive school to a total educational structure that will include the comprehensive school along with a pluralistic realm of different and usually smaller optional alternative schools, each designed to be responsive to the learning and living needs of youth.[13]

The alternative private school movement in America, which began in the turbulent 1960s, is young. The alternative public school movement is even younger, dating from Philadelphia's school-without-walls, described in Chapter 1, which began in 1969. In the Parkway Program, students learn in museums, service stations, banks, shops—everywhere in the city. They work in tutorial groups, learn skills, and select electives in addition.[14] The schools-without-walls type of alternative schools spread.

---

[13] Vernon H. Smith and Robert D. Barr, "Where Should Learning Take Place?" in *Issues in Secondary Education*, Seventy-fifth Yearbook of the National Society for the Study of Education, University of Chicago Press, Chicago, 1976, p. 177.
[14] John Bremer, *The Parkway Program*, Philadelphia Public Schools, 1970.

St. Paul, Minnesota, has contributed significantly to the development of public alternative schools. For instance, the St. Paul Open School emphasizes individual learning through resource centers located in a former warehouse. St. Paul has also established city learning centers; students may attend these centers for one quarter of the school year and spend the balance of their time in their home schools. St. Paul students may find themselves in desegregated centers with students of varied racial and ethnic backgrounds, all of whom are interested in the performing arts or automotive transportation or other fields.

Berkeley, California, sponsored a variety of alternative schools. As pointed out in Chapter 1, their names often indicate their goals: School of the Arts, College Prep, West Campus Work Study, Casa De La Raza, Black House. Less readily identifiable by name are Lincoln, stressing environmental studies; Model A, emphasizing basic skills; On Target, job related; New Ark, intended for students of Asian background; Agora, emphasizing multicultural education.

Some alternative schools deviate radically from conventional education; conversely, some have been set up especially to emphasize teaching of the skills and conventional instruction in accordance with the views of back-to-basics proponents. Most alternative schools are small. Yet some alternative schools are gigantic educational parks, such as Dallas's Skyline Center, which offers a wide range of experiences provided by its Career Development Center, Center for Community Services, and Skyline High School.

Although alternative public secondary schools are new and very much in the experimental stage, they are spreading. Particularly promising for their future development is the finding by the Gallup Poll that American parents are favorably inclined to the idea of having choices available as to schools for their families.

For students who are not interested in, or are bored with, the usual kind of education, it has been proposed that new kinds of local schools be established. They usually place more responsibility upon the student for what he learns and how he learns it. Some use the community as their laboratory and do not use the usual kind of classrooms. Do you think this is a good idea or a poor idea?[15]

	National Totals N = 1,627	No Children in Schools 928	Public School Parents 620	Private School Parents 124	Profes- sional Educators 306
Good Idea	62%	62%	62%	61%	80%
Poor Idea	26	24	28	27	15
No Opinion	12	14	10	12	5
	100	100	100	100	100

[15] Reprinted with permission from George Gallup, "Fifth Annual Gallup Poll of Public Attitudes Toward Education," *Phi Delta Kappan*, 55, 1973, 42–43.

Secondary schools in America grew from a few classrooms into massive buildings, from excessively decorated box-like structures into complex structures with dramatic lines; from buildings on cramped sites to plants that sprawled over many well-planned acres; from single buildings into broad campuses of buildings with specialized functions. Too big, warned the advocates of alternative schools. Yet most Americans seemed to think that expansion of the physical plant afforded young people more and more opportunities for relevant learning experiences within the widened setting of the school.

Note the last words—"within the widened setting of the school"—for they carry with them the implication that education is something that goes on only within schools. An allied implication is that what goes on in the community is not educative. Such implications were challenged by thinkers who advocated education in both school and wider community settings.

Advocacy of learning experiences outside the physical boundaries of the school go back at least to a Swiss educator, Johann Pestalozzi (1746–1827), who recognized that young people could learn much from nature. He urged teachers to lead children into nature, teaching them on the hilltops and in the valley. Pestalozzi himself taught geography through walking with the children in the Swiss countryside; they drew maps and constructed models concerning their observations.

In the United States, Ralph Waldo Emerson and Henry Thoreau, eminent New England authors, recognized that much could be learned from nature, though they never deprecated the importance of books. Their friend, Bronson Alcott, stressed learning from nature in his own teaching, in the education of his children (including his daughter Louisa May, who wrote *Little Women*), and in his work as superintendent of the Concord, Massachusetts, public schools. Francis W. Parker, mentioned earlier in the discussion of the rise of progressive education, conceived the Cook County Normal School, for which he served as principal, as a small community in which children and adults would come together to share ideas and to express themselves. Assemblies brought together parents, teachers, administrators, and children. Parker conceived his school as a home, a community, and a small-scale version of democracy in action.

THE COMMUNITY SCHOOL MOVEMENT

In the early twentieth century, a pioneer in recognition of the role of the community in education was Joseph K. Hart. While an assistant professor at the University of Washington, he compiled an anthology of readings, *Educational Resources of Village and Rural Communities.* In his introduction, Hart pointed out that education originally went on through the life and work of the community itself.

There was no school in the formal sense of the word; and because there was none, all education was practical, thorough, and moral: practical because wrought out of the very life of the community; thorough because the tests were those of life itself; . . . and moral because, both in purpose and in content, it was the community's own life and purpose wrought into the life and purpose of the maturing child.[16]

Hart believed that in American society the school is too much with us, claims too much credit for educational results, and stands in the way of education through use of the community. He called for more use by schools of the educational resources of the community.

Should not the school and the teacher look deeply into the life of the community, surveying with thoughtful care all the resources, activities, interests, and elements that, within the community and its organic relationships, are making educational impression upon the growing children? Should they not determine wherein the common life and activity of the community are already sufficiently educative, and should they not be wise enough to let such phases of life alone, giving to the immediate life of the people such share in the education of the children as that immediate life can do best? And should they not find wherein the educative direction of the children is being imperfectly, or badly, done, and should they not, at those places, bravely set to work, so supplementing, where help is needed, the power of the community that created the school?[17]

To Hart, the community was "the true educational institution":

Let us become aware of our community resources, physical, social, moral. Let us recognize the part they play and will always play in the actual education of our boys and girls. Let us consciously extend their powers within legitimate bounds.[18]

Hart wrote in an era when John Dewey was urging educators "to make the school a social center"[19] and when educators were reporting upon their experimentation. The National Society for the Study of Education published in 1911 its tenth yearbook, Part I, *The City School as a Community Center*, and Part II, *The Rural School as a Community Center*.[20] City experimentation reported in the yearbook included Cleveland's public lectures; Newark's vacation playgrounds; Rochester's civic and social centers; and New York City's organized athletics, evening recreation centers, and adult education (dating back to 1888 when public school buildings in New York City were first opened for adult education lectures during evening hours). The yearbook advocated home and school associations and a

---

[16] Joseph K. Hart, *Educational Resources of Village and Rural Communities*, Macmillan, New York, 1914, p. 2.
[17] Ibid., p. 8.
[18] Ibid., p. 9.
[19] Proceedings of the National Education Association Meeting, 1902, p. 373.
[20] National Society for the Study of Education; Part I, *The City School as a Community Center*; Part II, *The Rural School as a Community Center*, Tenth Yearbook of the National Society for the Study of Education, Bloomington, Ill., 1911.

"community-used school." Experimentation in the rural school as a community center included extension work, libraries, art appreciation, and recreation, as well as the school as a general educational and social center. The yearbook recorded that rural communities appreciated helpful work by schools that were steadily in touch with the community.

Experimentation with community-related schools sometimes resulted in descriptive books such as Ellsworth Collings's *An Experiment With a Project Curriculum* (1923), based on the project method of William Heard Kilpatrick.[21] Collings, then a county superintendent, developed an experimental curriculum in a rural school in MacDonald County, Missouri, and compared the learning outcomes with those of two control schools in the county. "Excursion projects" dealt with gardening ("Mrs. Murphy's sunflowers"), a study of diseases (including "how Mr. Smith can best combat the fly in his home"), a governmental study in the local community and the state capital (including "how Mr. Tate's trial will be conducted at Pineville" and "what Mr. Tate will do in the state penitentiary"). The students traveled to a Missouri city to hear a presidential candidate talk about the League of Nations and followed up the program with study, debate, and a community meeting. "Hand projects" included such activities as participating in a community fair.

Some educators were even more venturesome in interrelating school and community. Elsie Ripley Clapp, in *Community Schools in Action*, described communities in which she lived and worked in Kentucky and in West Virginia during the 1930s. First as a principal and then as a director of school and community activities, she rejected distinctions between the life of the school and the life of the community. Both the people in the community and the students in the schools organized to meet their work, health, and recreation needs. Both the community people and the students used the schools for living and learning. Where did the school end and life outside begin? There were no boundaries, no distinctions between school and community. As Clapp pointed out, everything that affected the welfare of the children and their families was the proper concern of the schools. The focus for study and participation by the young was the urgent needs of the people of the community as a whole (see Figure 9.5). She wrote of Arthurdale, West Virginia, and its high school:

This matter of bringing the community into the work of the School was of as much importance as the directing of the work of the School into the life of the community. The two at times were interacting, but in few cases did we find that we could deal only with young people to reach the community. Just such a matter as testing milk needed the interest of the owner of the cow even more than that of his children. And the interest was such that a few men came in or sent in samples of

[21] Ellsworth Collings, *An Experiment with a Project Curriculum*, Macmillan, New York, 1923, pp. 50–87.

FIGURE 9.5 *Learning through a Community Activity.*

milk before we could get the equipment assembled. The study of the community with the children could turn rapidly into study with the adults. And since the sciences and the whole physical and cultural development of community life were at stake, it would be a long time before we would find research boring.[22]

By 1936 so many instances existed of service by American secondary school youth to the community that a collection of contributions was published. Paul R. Hanna's *Youth Serves the Community* describes youth projects contributing to public safety, civic beauty, community health, agricultural and industrial improvement, civic arts, local history, surveys and inventories, and protection of resources. Hanna suggested a way of judging the quality of the numerous projects gathered by his research staff. Projects of high quality met two criteria: educational value to the individual and significant value to the community. As to educational value to the individual:

1. The youth who participate in a project must sense its social significance. . . .

2. Youth must have a part in planning the project. . . .

---

[22] Elsie Ripley Clapp, *Community Schools in Action,* Viking Press, New York, 1939, p. 331.

3. Youth must have some sporting chance of carrying the project proposed through to more or less successful conclusion. . . .

4. Youth must accept the responsibility for success or failure of a project. . . .

5. Youth must actually grow in total personality as a result of the work undertaken. . . .

As to significant value to the community:

1. Any project must culminate in the actual improvement of living in the community. . . .

2. Projects must clearly be an obligation of youth as well as adulthood. . . .

3. In so far as possible, projects must get at the basic problems of improving social welfare.[23]

Hanna called for an American youth movement quite different from fanatical fascist and communist youth movements of his day. He saw the public school as the institution best suited to coordinate an American version of a youth movement.

But if the American school should desire to provide the leadership for socially-useful work of children and youth, school people must vastly *increase* their vision and their techniques. The school program must shift its emphasis from the classical and academic approach to an emphasis on the solution of problems facing children and youth here and now, and it must foresee the problems of the future. The typical curriculum of the traditional elementary and secondary school and higher institution has lacked a vitality and meaning for children and youth. School tasks have been almost exclusively unrelated to the life going on about the young in home and community. These young people have accomplished their appointed tasks with as little pain and effort as possible and have cheered the approaching vacation.[24]

To Hanna, the supreme challenge to educational and social statesmanship was harnessing the energy of youth to the task of progressively improving conditions of community life.

A similar book was published by the Educational Policies Commission in 1940, *Learning the Ways of Democracy*. A description of a classic community school, Holtville High School, Deatsville, Alabama, was included. The school had one objective, to improve the living conditions of the rural community. Holtville High School students operated a cannery, a meat refrigeration plant, and a chick hatchery unit on a cost-of-operation basis. Students worked closely with teachers of vocational agriculture in serving farm families. They sprayed peach orchards, did contour plowing, assisted farmers in terracing, planted cover crops, planted and pruned fruit trees, and killed peach tree borers. In the school shops they repaired farm

---

[23] Paul R. Hanna, Research Staff, *Youth Serves the Community*, © 1936, Renewed 1964, pp. 35–40. Reprinted by permission of Prentice-Hall, Inc., Englewood Cliffs, New Jersey.
[24] Ibid., pp. 269–270.

implements and built playground equipment for elementary school children. Home economics students redecorated one home each year, aided by students from agricultural classes, who planted gardens. Home economics students also sewed clothing for children in the primary grades and conducted a nursery school for small children. Holtville students published a weekly newspaper for the community and managed a cooperative store. Films were rented and shown in the school and each of four neighborhood centers. The school maintained a game loan library. Students built an archery range, a barbecue pit, and a four-acre arboretum. Students even operated a barber shop and a beauty parlor. All the money and accounts for the school's activities were handled by students through the school bank.[25]

Learning the Ways of Democracy recognized that city schools were also becoming active in community participation. For instance, at Benjamin Franklin High School in East Harlem, an area in New York City, then largely populated by Italian- and Spanish-speaking groups, the students established a Friends and Neighbors Club that helped build better understanding between the ethnic groups of the community; two abandoned stores were taken over for club rooms for meetings and neighborhood committees. Another club, set up in a store, kept dropouts in a continuing friendly contact with the school and their former classmates. The Benjamin Franklin students helped develop a Housing Committee that included representatives of the student body as well as community people. The committee campaigned for a housing project in the area and a new school building. The achievement of a low-cost housing project was celebrated with a neighborhood victory parade.[26]

Another publication of the period described the programs of nine community schools broadly similar to Holtville and Benjamin Franklin in their approaches. In *The Community School*, editor Samuel Everett described some of the differences between community schools and traditional schools:

1. All life is education *versus* education is gained only in formal institutions of learning. . . .

2. Education requires participation *versus* education is adequately gained through studying about life. . . .

3. Adults and children have fundamental common purposes in both work and play *versus* adults are primarily concerned with work and children with play. . . .

4. Public school systems should be primarily concerned with the improvement of community living and the improvement of the social order *versus* school systems should be primarily concerned with passing on the cultural heritage. . . .

---

[25] Educational Policies Commission, *Learning the Ways of Democracy*, National Education Association, Washington, D.C., 1940, pp. 192, 322–325.
[26] Ibid., pp. 262–270.

5.   The curriculum should receive its social orientation from major problems and areas of community living, *versus* the curriculum should be oriented in relation to the specialized aims of academic subjects. . . .

6.   Public education should be founded upon democratic processes and ideals *versus* the belief that most children and most adults are incapable of intelligently either running their own lives or participating in common group efforts. . . .

7.   Progress in education and in community living best comes through the development of common concerns among individuals and social groups *versus* progress best comes through the development of clear-cut social classes and vested interest groups which struggle for survival and dominance.

8.   Public schools should be responsible for education of both children and adults *versus* public schools should only be responsible for the education of children.

9.   Teacher-preparatory institutions should prepare youth and adults to carry on a community type of public education *versus* such institutions should prepare youth and adults to perpetuate academic traditions and practices.[27]

The community school movement attracted the attention of government agencies and philanthropic organizations. For instance, when during the New Deal the federal government created the Tennessee Valley Authority to plan and develop the Tennessee River region, the new town of Norris, Tennessee, was built. Rather than employing a superintendent of *schools*, Norris appointed a superintendent of *education*, committed to the use of the community for firsthand studies and experiences by students.

Charles Stuart Mott, an automobile executive, decided to make Flint, Michigan, a "laboratory and proving grounds" for dealing with urban problems, and the Mott Foundation demonstrated the community school concept through making the local schools community-centered for the young and the old. In the darkness of the night, the schools of Flint were ablaze with lights as people of all ages played, created, and studied. Under director Frank J. Manley, the foundation later developed a program for the training of community education leaders through Michigan colleges and universities. Begun in 1963, the program was expanded in 1974 to become a national training program through which still more colleges and universities trained community education leaders.

State universities in Florida, Kentucky, and Vermont cooperated with state departments of education to produce learning materials for use by community schools. A typical product of the Sloan Project in Applied Economics was a pamphlet for mountain children on how to raise goats; such simple and direct learning materials simultaneously taught children to read and to engage in an economically useful activity.

State departments of education became concerned about community

---

[27] Samuel Everett, ed., *The Community School*, D. Appleton-Century, New York, 1938, pp. 435–457.

education. In 1945 the State of Washington State Office of Public Instruction developed a Division of School and Community Relations to provide consultant services to all interested in interrelating education and community life. The director of the office was Edward G. Olsen, who wrote *School and Community* and gathered materials for *School and Community Programs*. Olsen wrote in *School and Community*:

> School people everywhere are coming to see that all life is educative; that the democratic school must become definitely concerned with the improvement of community and social living; that functional education requires active participation in constructive community activities; that the community can be utilized as a living laboratory for learning; that the school plant should be a center for community activity; that the major areas and problems of life should give direction to the curriculum; that lay participation in school policy-planning builds public support as well as better school programs; that the school must lead in coordinating community effort for better education and must practice and promote democracy; and that in the Nuclear Air Age the community must be defined in local, regional, national, and even world-wide terms.[28]

To help implement such goals, he developed a casebook of successful practices, *School and Community Programs*, which specified documentary sources, audio-visual materials, resources and interviews, field trips, surveys, extended field studies, school camping, service projects, work experiences, public relations, community coordination, and teacher education.[29]

Ernest O. Melby, a distinguished university dean, aided community education in his work, *Administering Community Education*. To Melby there were three major weaknesses in education:

> First, we have depended upon a verbal conception of education. . . . Second, we have assumed within the four walls of the schoolhouse we could carry on education which would so influence the character of boys and girls and men and women that they, in turn, would change and improve the community when they became active adult citizens. . . . A third weakness of our educational effort is a failure to understand the kind of knowledges and skills which are required for successful citizenship in the age in which we are now living. . . . Too many American teachers and school administrators were unaware of the changes that had taken place in American society and in the world outside. They were so busy teaching the three R's and the traditional knowledges and skills that they forgot to look up from their tasks and to look out the window.[30]

---

[28] Edward G. Olsen, *School and Community*, Prentice-Hall, Englewood Cliffs, N.J., 1954, p. v.
[29] Edward G. Olsen, *School and Community Programs*, Prentice-Hall, Englewood Cliffs, N.J., 1949, table of contents.
[30] Ernest O. Melby, *Administering Community Education*, Prentice-Hall, Englewood Cliffs, N.J., 1955, p. 7.

By the 1970s thoughtful educators recognized that the proper setting for secondary education was wider than the school building, however elaborate and expanded the school building might be. Educators realized that the community inevitably played a significant role in the education of youth and that education through the schools must be interrelated with education through the community.

But an important issue persists. Should community education be under the auspices and control of the community-oriented school? Or should educational functions be assumed by agencies in the community and developed quite independently of the school? There are indications that agencies other than the school—if the school only reluctantly assumed community responsibilities—might well take on a major role in the education of young people.

The very phrase *community school* was succeeded by the phrase *community education*. Significantly, the National Community School Education Association, founded in 1966, changed its name in 1973 to the National Community Education Association. The change was intended to emphasize a broad community orientation rather than a more limited conception of community education in schools during late afternoon and evening hours. The international organization in the community field is called International Association for Community Educators. This group organized in 1975, and in the same year an Office for Community Education was established in the U.S. Office of Education and advised by the National Advisory Committee for Community Education. When a journal in the community field was founded in 1971 it was entitled *Community Education Journal*. When the Mott-fostered training program outgrew its Michigan focus and became nationwide, the resultant center was named the National Center for Community Education. When the first endowed professorship in the community field was established at Florida Atlantic University in 1972 it was called the Charles Stuart Mott Chair for Community Education.

However, the word *schools* was maintained in the Community Schools Act of 1974. The act states:

The school as the prime educational institution of the community is most effective when the school involves the people of that community in a program designed to fulfill their education needs.[31]

Many educators have argued, as did Paul Hanna in *Youth Serves the Community*, that the public school is the institution best suited to coordinate community education.

[31] Community Schools Act, August 1974, *United States Statutes at Large*, Vol. 88, Statute 549, pp. 93–380, Title IV Section 405, U.S. Government Printing Office, Washington, D.C., 1976.

The school is the one universal, continuing, well-equipped and locally-controlled institution in every community. Commissions created for a specific purpose are seldom long-lived and never have the personnel or equipment needed. Where the machinery and personnel are at hand and the social cost is already cared for in the tax budget, it would seem unwise to set up a duplicate institution. The school with its trained leadership of youth, its physical plant and equipment, its libraries and laboratories, could, with some addition to staff and plant and with reorganization of some of its program, conduct such a national project better than any group existing today or likely to be created in the near future.[32]

Melby, in writing of administration, also indicated his confidence that the school should take and keep the lead in programs of community education.

From the standpoint of the total welfare of education and the growth of schools, nothing has as great a developmental effect as a widespread feeling in the community that the community needs the schools to carry out its total program of education and community development. It is much easier for us in schools to be effective when we know that we are wanted and needed. Here is the real answer to those who feel that a fully mobilized community will take over professional functions or that the schools will somehow be lost in the multiplicity of community functions. Instead of de-emphasizing education and the schools, a new vitality and emphasis results.[33]

COMMUNITY-ORIENTED REFORM MOVEMENT OF
THE 1970s

During the 1970s interest in the relationship of secondary education to the community has exploded. To say that this has been the outstanding development in contemporary thinking about secondary education is not to overstate the case. As in many educational movements, the descriptive words used by educators have changed but the central concerns endure. Today educators and citizens talk about "transitions to adulthood": these transitions are an integral part of the concept termed "community education." Today educators and citizens talk about "action learning"; this type of learning is integral to yesterday's favorite phrase, "the community school."

In Chapter I we overviewed some of the current reports on reform of the high school, thus we will supplement them only briefly here. The report of the Panel on Youth of the President's Science Advisory Committee, chaired by James S. Coleman and frequently referred to as Coleman II, called for expansion of youth participation within secondary schools. For instance, the report encouraged tutoring of younger students by older

---

[32] Hanna, *Youth Serves the Community*, p. 269.
[33] Melby, *Administering Community Education*, pp. 218–219.

students. It called for expanded work-study programs and for school programs that involved community action by students.

However, there was an underlying conviction in the Coleman II report that the present bureaucratic structure of the secondary schools did not lend itself to sufficient community orientation. The panel largely conceived the secondary school as cognitive-oriented, concerned basically with the acquisition of knowledge and with intellectually oriented functions, a place for the learning of skills.

Youth: Transition to Adulthood, the panel's report, proposed many experiences for youth under the aegis of community agencies rather than the school. For instance, the report endorsed pilot studies of alternating school and work. The report envisioned work organizations within the community, such as industries or offices, taking on educational functions as they included youth in their programs. The report recommended experimentation with the development of youth communities that would be involved in community service or social action and that might possibly even engage in the production of goods and services. It anticipated youth organizations similar to communes that would produce goods and services that might be purchased by the government.

Coleman II conceived community participation by young people as essentially the function of a variety of business, labor, and governmental agencies, rather than as forays by students into the community under the leadership, direction, and coordination of the secondary schools themselves. However, educators doubted that community people would take on such responsibilities for educating youth.

The report of the National Commission on the Reform of Secondary Education envisioned schools as providing community-related experiences for their students. Yet this report, *The Reform of Secondary Education*, asserted that schooling alone would not supply sufficient work opportunities for the young. Nor would the interdisciplinary studies, recommended by the report in such fields as career education and international education, sufficiently relate young people to the community. For this reason the report endorsed the reduction of compulsory education to age fourteen so that many students could have experiences, largely in the form of work, in the wider community prior to the customary age for high school graduation. Naturally, educators critical of the report responded that such experiences would not be as educative as induction into the community through work-study and community action programs under the leadership of secondary schools.

A panel on High Schools and Adolescent Education of the U.S. Office of Education suggested that youth obtain guidance in community activities through school sponsorship of work experience and via education in the operations of government through youth participation in the programs of government agencies. Rather than turning young people loose in the community to work at early ages, the panel recommended the establishment of community centers for youth, including community arts centers, community career education centers, and community centers for citizenship education.[34] Critics pointed out that few such centers currently existed and that communities might be reluctant to set up totally new institutions when they already had schools with the potentiality of serving as community centers.

ACTION-LEARNING PROGRAMS

One outcome of the spate of reform reports was renewed interest by schoolpeople in developing action-learning programs through the schools. Reports and conferences sponsored by the National Association of Secondary School Principals throughout the 1970s encouraged and disseminated such approaches. University centers assembled descriptions of promising action-learning projects.

One highly useful compilation of such reports of actual experiences in action-learning by secondary school students is that of Vernon H. Smith and Robert D. Barr in *Issues in Secondary Education*. In the section "Where Should Learning Take Place?" Smith and Barr group possible action-learning under the headings of learning in the great outdoors, learning in unfamiliar cultures, in service agencies, in the professional community, from the past, in construction and urban renewal projects, on the road, in the political arena, and in the world of work.[35]

In the Great Outdoors Some school districts sponsor "hiking, back-packing, bicycling, canoeing, spelunking, and camping experiences." Learning about nature and the environment while developing strength and healthy attitudes is the usual goal of outdoor action-learning. Outward Bound in Denver, Colorado, is a center designed to help educators devising outdoor programs for promoting ruggedness, endurance, and appreciation of the natural environment.

In some outdoor programs a subsidiary purpose is fostered; racial antagonisms are encountered and diminished. For instance, a wilderness program at Northwestern Junior High School in Battle Creek, Michigan, reduced racial and class conflicts. The Brown School in Louisville, Kentucky, developed a weekend outdoor camping program to place black and white students in new situations that could lead to better racial understanding.

Some outdoors action-learning also aims at improved academic growth.

---

[34] National Panel on High Schools and Adolescent Education, *The Education of Adolescents,* U.S. Department of Health, Education, and Welfare, Washington, D.C., 1976.
[35] Vernon H. Smith and Robert D. Barr, "Action-Learning," in *Issues in Secondary Education,* pp. 168–175.

For instance, the Cambridge Pilot School, Massachusetts, taught techniques of outdoor education to inner-city youths who were lacking in academic skills. In turn, these inner-city students, weak in the academic subjects, taught more academically competent inner-city students these same techniques of outdoor education. The result was improvement in the self-concepts of the students who lacked academic skills. In Grand Rapids, Michigan, after weekend camping experiences students who have worked on learning academic skills are rewarded by a week-long camp-out.

In Unfamiliar Cultures   East High School in Denver has long been known for its community participation programs. Students "have harvested beets with migrant workers, worked in welfare agencies, served food in soup lines, spent weekends on a Navajo reservation, lived with Mexican families, and collected garbage with city sanitation workers."[36] Lincoln-Sudbury Regional High School students in the Boston area have worked in social agencies and lived in the inner city with local black families. They also went to rural areas in Connecticut and Nova Scotia for an additional five weeks; here they lived with rural families while they worked on farms, in dairies, and in cooperatives.

In Service Agencies   Many schools and service agencies use secondary school students as volunteers. Among many possible illustrations are the following three drawn by Smith and Barr from the East, Middle West, and West. The Yorkville Youth Council of New York City recruits high school students as volunteer teachers. In Marion, Indiana, students volunteer to work in hospitals. Adams City High School, Colorado, students tutor and teach elementary school children.

Some drug programs use volunteer high school students. The National Commission on Resources for Youth commends such drug centers utilizing student volunteers as Project Community in Berkeley, California; "Number Nine" in New Haven, Connecticut; "Encounter" and "Compass" in New York City.

Smith and Barr provide a description of an effective use of volunteers:

Perhaps one of the most dramatic examples of the potentiality of youth volunteers was provided by the Community Medical Corps, organized in the Bronx of New York City. In the early 1970s, a group of medical students recruited 110 high school students from 14 to 17 years of age to assist in screening children in local tenements for traces of lead poisoning. The students were put through a rigorous orientation session, given white medical jackets, and put to work canvassing neighborhoods and conducting blood tests. By the end of a summer program, the students had seen over 3,000 children and taken over 2,000 blood samples. Over 2 percent of the

---

[36] Ibid., p. 170.

children tested were found to have dangerously high levels of poisoning. The following was written about the program:

> High school age youngsters had proven that they could be depended upon to do difficult work. Many of them had come into the program originally with an awe of doctors and what they did. By the end of the summer, the directors reported, "We had kids telling the doctors what to do. They had assisted with blood taking hundreds of times and knew the job as well or better than any doctor." The kids who worked here, all of the 110 kids, know more about lead poisoning than most doctors.

As a result of the program, many students are now determined to become nurses, teachers, social workers, and doctors. The program exemplifies the fact that adolescents thrive on significant, meaningful work.[37]

In the Professional Community Through internship, students work with professional people, businesspeople, government workers, social agency staffs, museum personnel, and so on. Some internships are for a semester during the junior or senior year of high school. Some even extend to a full school year. So popular are internships that national programs have been organized to help local schools to launch them. They include the Executive High School Internship Program, which works with school districts in six states from its base in New York City, and Dynamy, Inc., centered in Worcester, Massachusetts.

Learning from the Past Students in the Atlanta public schools' Independent Study Program excavated remnants of an ancient Indian culture. Brooklyn, New York, students turned up tangible traces of a nineteenth-century black community, Weeksville, in the debris of some demolition. The people of Weeksville had been reported to be shiftless folks, living in shacks, but the young archaeologists uncovered evidences of middle-class living patterns and set the record straight. High school students wrote a book about Grand Rapids, Michigan, which was used as a textbook in local schools.

Best known of the folklore projects is the Foxfire program at Rabum Gap, Georgia. Students gathered information from old-timers on how to build log cabins, weave baskets, make traps, and carry on crafts. They wrote about what they found and the public bought their books. The creator of the project, an unassuming English teacher, found to his surprise that he was invited to appear on national television programs and that he had become the custodian of substantial funds!

In Construction and Urban Renewal Projects Some action-learning projects are financially rewarding to students as well as useful to

---

[37] Ibid., p. 171.

communities. In Denver, Colorado, Creative Urban Living built and repaired houses, replaced sidewalks, and constructed miniparks. The students handled banking, payrolls, bills, loans, and insurance in connection with their enterprises. In Canton, Ohio, Candlelight Youth Corps renovated houses for the handicapped, the elderly, and the blind, and built and sold a house and two duplexes.

Some construction and renewal projects stress volunteer aid. A Minnesota Teen Corps organized 350 teenagers to build summer camps for mentally retarded youth, a home for juvenile delinquents, a social center for a migrant worker camp, and an inner-city park. In Sacramento, California, volunteers have assisted people on welfare in refurnishing and repairing their homes.

On the Road Community-conscious educators have long used social travel that combines visits to places with study of problems. Now social travel extends still further afield. St. Paul, Minnesota, Open School students have traveled to the Dakota Badlands and to the Gettysburg battlefield; they have combined study of science with study of the social sciences on such trips. In Lake Geneva, Wisconsin, the American Essence Traveling School provides personal participation in the past for high school seniors and postgraduates. The travel groups invest nine months in journeying through the United States by rail, highway, footpath, inland waterways, and wagon trails.

In the Political Arena Smith and Barr reported that:

The Connecticut Citizens Action Group, the first state affiliate of Ralph Nader's Center for the Study of Responsive Law, provided a model for youth participation in communities all across the United States. The students in Connecticut have conducted a statewide survey of food prices, developed an Earth Platform for election campaigns, and lobbied state legislators for a disposable bottle tax. And all this has been done after school and on weekends, without school credit.[38]

The Washington, D.C., Street Law Program provides high school courses in street law that use discussion groups and special projects. At the conclusion of each course students conduct a simulated trial at which a federal judge presides. Law students from Georgetown University teach the courses. The high school students and the law students receive credit for their participation.

In the World of Work For many years business education has provided youth with chances for action-learning. Business and

---

[38] Ibid., p. 174.

industry have cooperated through the National Junior Achievement Program. In communities throughout the nation the media have reported on how students, with the advice of businesspeople, have organized and run business enterprises.

Now the federal government is supporting career education.

The Office of Education has developed an Experimental Based Career Education that is much more than a terminal program for noncollege bound students and that is a far cry from on-the-job training. Experimental Based Career Education defines careers broadly to mean "one's progress through life" or "life paths"—not a restricted nine-to-five segment of life. The program enables students to complete the last two years of high school by participating in extensive experiences, independent and group study, and many activities.[39]

Smith and Barr illustrate with Tigard, Oregon, where students during the last two years of high school attend no classes but instead demonstrate their "survival competencies" in life.

THE CHANGING SETTING

The modern secondary school has come a long way from the simple designs of architect Gardner. The comprehensive high school has been created and has grown large. Today this Goliath is being challenged by David, the small alternative school.

The setting of secondary education has expanded to reach out into the community, as recommended first by the community school movement and now by the community education movement. New transitions to adulthood that stress work experience and community participation are recommended by influential national committees and commissions. The proposed transitions to adulthood contemplate more assumption of responsibility for education by the citizenry. Some educators call for the schools to take the lead in community education through action-learning.

Action-learning is the outgrowth of earlier efforts to widen the setting in which secondary education takes place. Action-learning is the contemporary version of the community school and community education movements. Today the number of secondary schools offering action-learning opportunities steadily grows. Although such schools are still a minority of all secondary schools, they point the way toward a future in which walls of separation between secondary schools and communities are broken down and in which secondary education takes place both in schools and communities.

---

[39] Ibid., p. 175.

DISCUSSION

1. What is the romantic notion and the reality of the little red schoolhouse?

2. Describe in broad terms the secondary school plant of the nineteenth-century high school. Fundamentally, how does it differ from the high school you attended? . . . the better high schools of today? . . . the high school of the future?

3. What do we mean by the contemporary secondary school "breaking out of the traditional box"? Why is this a gain?

4. What is the difference between "clusters" and "fingers" in the school design?

5. What are the advantages and disadvantages of a campus-type secondary school?

6. What are the key concepts of contemporary planners of schools?

7. What are your criticisms of the middle school illustrated in Figure 9.3? What are your criticisms of the comprehensive high school illustrated in Figure 9.4?

8. What are the various opinions in the current debate about the most desirable size of a secondary school? What is your own view of a desirable size? Why?

9. Do you believe that the alternative school will replace the comprehensive high school? What is the case for the small alternative secondary school?

10. What are some illustrations of contemporary alternative schools? Can you categorize them into types?

11. What was Joseph K. Hart's justification for education through the community? Do you agree or do you regard the view as overstated? What were some earlier illustrations of the programs of community schools?

12. According to Paul R. Hanna, what are some of the characteristics of community school projects of high quality?

13. What is your appraisal of the programs of Holtville and Benjamin Franklin high schools?

14. How do community schools and traditional schools differ?

15. Illustrate how the community school idea influenced foundations, state universities, and state departments of education.

16. Why was the label "community school" succeeded by the label " community education"? Is there a useful purpose served by the change?

17. For good community education, should we depend upon adaptations by schools or create new community institutions with educational functions?

18. What reports of committees and commissions in the mid-1970s accelerated further the development of community education? How were the reports similar or different?

19. What is the meaning of action-learning? How does the concept differ from or resemble earlier community school and community education concepts?

20. Illustrate programs of action-learning in the outdoors, in unfamiliar cultures, in service agencies, in the professional community, from the past, in construction and urban renewal projects, on the road, in the political arena, and in the world of work. Do you think of other classifications? Can you find illustrations locally?

21. In broad terms, how has the modern secondary school changed from earlier simple designs? Has the change in design improved the quality of education? In broad terms, how has the setting of secondary education changed from the patterns used in the nineteenth century?

22. How valuable do you think action-learning is? What contribution can it make to the lives of contemporary students? Could this have been helpful to you? Is it overrated?

INVOLVEMENT

1. In your previous visits to schools, you have looked primarily at program. Now visit schools to observe the school plant. Begin by visits to both the oldest and the newest secondary schools in your locality. Take notes on the setting and environment. Compare and contrast.

2. On visits to schools look particularly carefully at the design of rooms. Is there evidence of the continuation of the boxlike design? Is there evidence of flexibility, adaptability, simplicity, and openness in design?

3. Does the most modern secondary school available to you for observation include "clusters" or "fingers"? Is there a "campus-type" school? How does it resemble and differ from the middle school and comprehensive high school illustrated in this chapter?

4. Interview an administrator of a comprehensive high school. Learn from the administrator what he or she considers to be the advantages and disadvantages of this type of school.

5. Interview a teacher in an alternative school, if one exists in your area. Ask how the school differs from the comprehensive secondary school. Obtain the teacher's reactions to the size of the alternative school. If no alternative school exists, interview a teacher within the smallest of the secondary schools of your area. Inquire particularly as to the advantages and disadvantages of a smaller school.

6. Attempt to envision the kinds of community activities in which students might engage if the secondary school you know best became heavily oriented to community realities and thus became a community school.

7. Determine what classes in secondary schools in which you observed are most closely related to the community. Study their programs. If possible, accompany the students in their community responsibilities and relationships. Include observation of both community work experience and community service by students.

8.   Build upon the illustrations of action-learning at the close of the chapter. Plan several action-learning possibilities that relate to your own interests and employ your own abilities.

FURTHER READINGS

Arms, Myron, and David Denman. *Touching the World: Adolescents, Adults, and Action Learning*. Charles Scribner's, New York, 1975. A vigorous argument that people should encounter the world of experience through action and learning. A readable and exciting advocacy of interrelating knowledge with action.

Bremer, John, and Michael von Moschzisker. *The School Without Walls*. Holt, Rinehart and Winston, New York, 1971. A provocative book on Philadelphia's school-without-walls program by the director of the program and a teacher of journalism.

Conant, James B. *The American High School Today*. McGraw-Hill, New York, 1959. A report on the American high school that advocates the comprehensive high school and sets forth twenty-one recommendations for improving secondary education. This book was highly influential in the late 1950s and early 1960s.

Educational Facilities Laboratories. *Educational Change and Architectural Consequences*. Educational Facilities Laboratories, New York, 1968. A handsome primer on school design emphasizing simple, open, and flexible patterns. Contains detailed and useful drawings of possible schools.

Fantini, Mario. *Public Schools of Choice*. Simon and Schuster, New York, 1973. The case for developing within the public school system a variety of alternative schools.

Glatthorn, Allan. *Alternatives in Education: Schools and Programs*. Harper & Row, New York, 1975. A consideration of the growing number of alternatives that are developing in American schools.

Hanna, Paul R. *Youth Serves the Community*. D. Appleton-Century, New York, 1936. A classic collection of specific projects through which youth has participated in American communities. Many projects now more than forty years old provide useful implications for today's practioner of action-learning.

Irwin, Martha, and Wilma Russell. *The Community Is the Classroom*. Pendell, Midland, Mich., 1971. A contemporary version of the ideas of sponsors of the community school movement.

Olsen, Edward G., ed. *School and Community Programs*. Prentice-Hall, Englewood Cliffs, N.J., 1949. A wide-ranging and comprehensive collection of significant practices in relating school and community. A useful source for today's educators who are attempting to develop action-learning.

Robischon, Thomas G., Jerome Rabow, and Janet Schmidt, eds. *Cracks in the Classroom Wall*. Goodyear, Pacific Palisades, Calif., 1975. Advocates alternatives to today's schools. The authors believe that alternatives will not be successful unless they are grounded in historical, sociological, and philosophical analyses of schools and education.

Scribner, Harvey B., and Leonard B. Stevens. *Make Your Schools Work.* Simon and Schuster, New York, 1975. Ten plans for reform of schools that parents might campaign for without unduly increasing educational costs.

Smith, Vernon, Robert Barr, and Daniel Burke. *Alternatives in Education: Freedom to Choose.* Phi Delta Kappa, Bloomington, Ind., 1976. An optimistic book on the growing alternatives available to schools and communities. Includes chapters on pluralism, the right to learn, and current developments.

10.

Improving
the
Organization

The customary pattern of organization in conventional programs of secondary education is based on several sets of assumptions. The assumptions deal with place and time, subjects for study, school day, school classes, and roles of teachers and students.

As to place, it is assumed that secondary education should take place within a school (not through community life). As to time, it is assumed that the schools should be open for regular classes from about 8:30 A.M. to about 3:30 P.M. Mondays through Fridays (not during late afternoon, evening, or night, on weekdays, and not during the approximately sixty-two hours that constitute the weekend). As to calendar, it is assumed that students should attend school from about Labor Day to some time in June (not during late June, July, or August).

Assumptions are also made as to what subjects should be studied (and why) within the secondary school during the limited hours and months for student attendance. It is assumed that students are to study certain distinct and separate subjects (not life problems, interdisciplinary fields, or centers of experience). Usually, they are to study these subjects to acquire knowledge of them (not to apply or act upon knowledge; not to meet needs, illuminate social realities, clarify values; not for affective education or participation in the common life).

Assumptions are made about organization of the school day. Each subject is to be taught in a class that meets for forty-five or fifty minutes (not for longer or shorter periods of time or through individualized instruction with flexible time periods). At the end of a class period, a bell is to ring and all students are to proceed to another class in a different room (not to move to new studies or activities at varying times).

Assumptions are made about organization of the classes that constitute the school day. Each class is to be taught by one teacher who specializes in knowledge of the subject matter taught to that particular class (not by a teacher equally well informed in other fields, or by several teachers, or by a person from the community not certified to teach). Each teacher is responsible for teaching that subject matter to the class (not for sharing in counseling and advising students). Each class is to be made up of approximately thirty students (not large listening groups or small discussion groups or people studying individually). Each class is to function as a group (not each person learning through individualized instruction).

Assumptions are made about the proper roles of teachers and students. The teacher is supposed to talk most of the time (not the students). Between classes, the students are to read textbooks and prepare homework (not use a variety of sources, prepare individual projects, or learn from the community and the communications media). At the end of the school year in June, the students are to be examined and graded by the teacher, and notified by school authorities whether they have passed or failed (not evaluated by other procedures or on their demonstrated competencies).

These are a few of the standard assumptions about the organization of secondary education that evolved in America in the eighteenth and nineteenth centuries and continue into the twentieth century. Yet, as each of the parenthetical phrases imply, each one of these assumptions is questioned today.

Why should secondary education be offered exclusively through schools, rather than through the community in addition? Why keep the school open only weekdays for a few hours each day? Why should not secondary education take place year round?

Why should separate subjects be studied, rather than life problems, interdisciplinary studies, centers of experience? Why should secondary schools be almost exclusively devoted to cognitive (knowledge-oriented) learning?

Why should all classes run forty-five to fifty minutes? Why should bells control movement to new studies and activities?

Why should a class be taught by one specialist teacher at a time? Why should the teacher have no responsibility for guidance and advising? Why thirty students? Why should students be instructed in groups rather than individually?

Why should the teacher rather than the students talk most of the time? Why should textbooks be the sole sources of learning in a world of varied materials? Why should one teacher examine, grade, pass, or fail members of a class rather than students be judged on competencies to perform?

The past fifty years have been a time of experimentation with better ways of organizing the secondary education curriculum.

Some secondary schools began to use blocks of time made up of two or more class periods. A block-time program replaces two or more completely separate class periods. Such block-time classes usually combine English and social studies. Sometimes science is added to block-time classes. Occasionally, a school uses two blocks of time, one of which combines English and social studies and the other science and mathematics. A block-time class may be taught by a single teacher or a team of teachers.

CORRELATION AND UNIFIED STUDIES

An early block-time program of the 1920s was the subject area block. In a subject area block each of the areas that had been taught completely separately was correlated (co-related) to the other subject.

For instance, in a subject area block class, a particular era in U.S. history might be studied during a history class. During the English class, American literature written during that particular period in the development of the United States might be the subject matter content. The two correlated classes were scheduled together within a two-hour block of time.

In the 1930s some schools took a step beyond the subject area block class and instituted a time block for unified studies. In unified studies the subject matter was not simply co-related; it was fused and merged. Rather than two separate though correlated classes in history and English, a unified course was developed.

As in the illustration of the subject area block, a unified studies class might center upon a particular era in American history. But no bell would arbitrarily separate the study of history from the study of literature. To help the student understand the era, other related material necessary to understand historical and literary developments might be tied in, such as musical compositions, the arts, and scientific developments. Aside from the central unit, the teacher gave attention to the development of creative writing and recreational reading. The teacher also dealt with the development of skills that students needed to work successfully on the subject matter taught through the unit.

CORE PROGRAMS

Out of such experimentation grew the core curriculum form of organization. The core program was more frequently used in middle and junior high schools than in senior high schools. Like its predecessors, the core curriculum took place in a block of time. This block of time replaced certain subject matter areas, sometimes English and social studies and sometimes science and mathematics. On college transcripts, students received credit for the subject fields that were replaced. But the core curriculum did not simply correlate (like the subject area block) or unify (like unified studies) the conventional content of English and social studies or science and mathematics. It focused on problems of young people and on problems of society.

The problems of young people and of society—often interdisciplinary problems—cut across the boundaries of the separate subjects taught in the conventional secondary school program. Content drawn from several subjects is usually necessary if an individual or social problem is to be understood and dealt with effectively. A core curriculum usually deals with problem areas or centers of experience such as those suggested in Chapter 8. Some problem areas emphasize strongly the personal problems, interests, and needs of individuals. Other problem areas emphasize strongly problems of society. However, most problem areas involve both the needs of individual young people and the social issues in the culture, which are usually interrelated and always involve questions of values.

To visualize the kinds of learning units taught at the junior high school level to deal with problem areas, consider these suggested by Jean V. Marani for a core program replacing English and social studies in the public schools of Sarasota, Florida:

SUGGESTED PROBLEM AREAS FOR A JUNIOR HIGH SCHOOL CORE PROGRAM THAT REPLACES ENGLISH AND SOCIAL STUDIES

PROBLEM AREA	ILLUSTRATIVE LEARNING UNITS
Grade Seven	
1. Education and School Living	Orientation to Junior High School What Are My Talents?
2. Self-understanding	Growing Up How to Make Wise Decisions
3. Living in the Community	The Outlook for Teenagers in Sarasota How Florida Meets the Problems of a Growing State
4. Economic Understanding	How Our Natural Resources Are Utilized Business Around the World
5. Intercultural Understanding	Teenagers Around the World Understanding Our Asian Neighbors

1. Education and School Living	Orientation
	How to Study
2. Personal-Social Relations	Achieving Maturity
	Boy Meets Girl
3. Democratic Government	Documents of Democracy
	Our Old World Heritage
	The Beliefs of a Democratic People
4. Vocational Preparation	Planning for High School
	Vocational Orientation
5. Relationships with Minority Groups	The Negro's Role in Our Society
	Religions of the World
6. Intercultural Understanding	Men and Achievements of the 20th Century
	The U.S.'s Rise to World Leadership

Grade Nine

1. Education and School Living	Assessing My Potential
	Our Educational Future
2. Personal-Social Relations	How to Deal with Juvenile Delinquency
	Youth's Status
3. Healthful Living	The Community Health Program
	Healthful Products
4. Economic Understanding	My Role as a Consumer-Producer
	Money Management
	World Economic Systems
5. Democratic Government	Comparative Governments
	The Citizen's Role in Policy Making
6. Intercultural Understanding	The World's Resources
	Ways of Achieving Peace[1]

Not all core programs are as systematic as the one above in specifying problem areas and illustrative learning units. Some are unstructured and depend upon whatever a particular group of students, with their teachers, decide is worth studying. However, even these unstructured core programs usually deal with a problem area or a combination of problem areas.

Within the block of time allotted to the core program, a particular unit is usually central and occupies most of the learners' time. In addition to work

---

[1] Gordon F. Vars, ed., *Common Learnings: Core and Interdisciplinary Team Approaches*, International Textbook, Scranton, Pa., 1969, pp. 8–9.

on the central unit, students within core classes engage in other activities during the core block of time. Sometimes their program focuses on reading chosen by individuals in accordance with their interests. Sometimes creative writing unrelated to the unit is undertaken. Sometimes students carry on class business through homeroom-style activities. Though they learn communication skills as they read, write, and speak in connection with the central unit, they may take additional time during a core class to develop these skills of communication.

The teachers and learners within a core class often make use of the aid of school and community specialists. For instance, within a school the problem area to be dealt with may use the contributions of any of a number of other teachers, such as those who specialize in home economics, fine arts, industrial arts, music, science, and mathematics. Though the selected unit will usually include substantial content from the language arts and the social studies (when the core program replaces these two subject areas in the total program), contributions from other subject areas are often necessary for a full consideration of the selected learning unit. After all, the purpose of the core program is not to systematically teach the subjects that make up the language arts or social studies subject areas. Instead, it is to help students understand and cope with selected problem areas or centers of experience through study units (see Figure 10.1).

Similarly, a core program will often draw heavily upon community resources through social travel, participation in community programs, the development of community-oriented projects, action-learning, and so on. Therefore, during the block of time allotted to core, members of a core class often may not be found within the rooms assigned for the program. They may be hard at work in the community on activities related to the selected unit as they learn about a center of experience.

In a core program the block of time replacing the language arts and social studies subject areas does not constitute the entire school day of a student. Even two blocks of time, language arts–social studies and science–mathematics, do not constitute their entire school day. Outside of the core block of time, opportunities exist for physical education and for specialized study in such areas as foreign languages, and the various arts, or in such subjects as science and mathematics, if these are not included within the core block. Some of these subjects, for instance, physical education, may be required common experiences. Others, such as foreign language, may be electives.

Most educators employing core programs believe that common learnings through problem areas should be supplemented by opportunities for specialized learnings. Specialized learning is necessary because of the wide diversity of interests and career plans of the individuals who attend secondary schools. Thus the common learnings program through the core class or core classes is only part of the total learning experience offered by an experimental secondary school program.

FIGURE 10.1 *Interdisciplinary Approach to Problem-solving.*

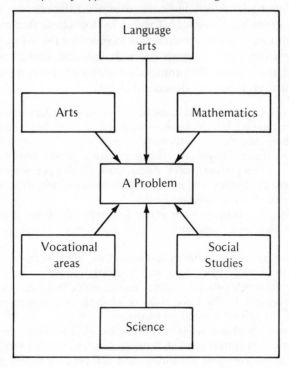

EXPERIMENTATION WITH CORE PROGRAMS

Acceptance of the core curriculum as a way of reorganizing secondary education has risen and fallen along with high tides of experimentation and low tides of conformity in American education. Many of the schools in the Eight-Year Study used the core curriculum. Since the results of this study showed clearly that students from the progressive schools did as well with subject matter content in college as did students from the conservative schools with whom they were paired, the study demonstrated that academic-minded parents and teachers need not fear that students from progressive programs would fail in college. When one took into account that the students from the progressive schools made a markedly better showing than their pairs on many desirable education outcomes quite aside from academic success, the potentiality for good education through core programs became apparent to experimental-minded educators.

Consequently, when the Educational Policies Commission publicized ten imperative needs of youth in 1944, a recommendation to use common learnings at both the junior and senior high school levels accompanied the list of new significant content in *Education for All American Youth*.[2] A summary, *Planning for American Youth*, described the content of a common learnings program for American City, a hypothetical American community. The common learnings course was to meet for the equivalent of three periods daily from grades seven through ten and two periods daily in grades eleven and twelve. Recommended content for common learnings in grades ten through twelve is described below:

In grade ten, pupils learn to feel at home in the senior secondary school. They study the use of their time effectively; take tests on speed of reading, understanding of what is read, basic abilities in mathematics, English, and study habits, and study ways to improve these. They study American City at work—how people live—by visits, reading, motion pictures, talks, discussions; check upon their own qualifications for different occupations: fit together these learnings into an economic system and then try to see how the system works.

Later, certain other problems are studied—family life, labor unions and management, sanitation and community health, consumer spending, and personal problems.

Certain studies are made of life in American City, such as the voluntary service organizations and what they do for youth, recreation in American City, and planning in residential neighborhoods. All of these combine instruction in understanding and improvement in the basic skills of analysis, study expression, and the scientific method applied to social problems.

In grade eleven, emphasis is placed upon education for civic competence, civic leadership, community improvement, housing projects, welfare services, problems of group living, employment situations, and the process of city planning. The connections between these problems in the city and the nation are examined.

The roots of these problems in our national history are studied. Interdependence between city and rural communities and between city, state, and the nation are stressed. Literature and history provide sources for these ideas, supplemented by a continuation of visits and the use of much visual material. Teachers try to make certain that all youth reach an understanding of the development of our nation as a democracy and as a country with a definite culture.

In grade twelve, youth study the problems of the nation in a world setting. Usually about three domestic and three international problems are singled out for study. Such problems as the maintenance of our domestic economy on a high level of production and employment (our domestic problem number one) and the problem of international organization for peaceful living (our international problem number one) are examples. In both of these problems, international interdependence is stressed. American foreign policy and its background, and the problems and lives of other peoples which affect our foreign policy are examined. Literature and art of our own and other nations are studied.

In grade twelve, personal problems again arise, and the teachers return to them, especially those involving family living in which the responsibilities of homemakers

---

[2] Educational Policies Commission, *Education for All American Youth*, National Education Association, 1944.

are stressed. In this grade comes the very popular unit on *Friendship, Courtship, and Marriage.*

In all these unified courses, study and work experience are combined; skills are taught as needed; and guidance is carried on by the teachers of Common Learnings classes, acting as counselors to the youth in their classes.

Each unified class is in charge of one teacher who is assisted by other teachers as needed. All teachers meet together weekly to plan their work.

The unified class is the local unit of the school government, electing representatives to the school council.[3]

Despite the rejection of core by right-wing critics and by academic critics of secondary education, block-time programs including core blocks grew rapidly throughout the 1950s, especially at the junior high level. In a U.S. Office of Education publication, *The Junior High School: A Survey of Grades 7-8-9 in Junior and Junior-Senior High Schools, 1959–60,* the researchers point out that while only 16 percent of junior high schools had block time classes in 1948–49, the number of junior high schools with such programs rose to 40 percent by 1959–60.[4]

SOCIETAL DEVELOPMENTS INFLUENCING CORE

With the arching of the Soviet Union's Sputnik across the skies in 1957, interest revived in updating and improving the teaching of the separate subjects. Concern for common learnings declined in the period of the Cold War, of the subject matter projects and of the structure of the disciplines.

However, educational concerns have a way of continuing to shift with societal developments. The later 1960s saw a growing concern for compensatory education. With compensatory education came a recognition that the separate subject matter approach had less meaning for disadvantaged young people than did a realistic problems orientation. So secondary schools attended by lower-income young people often initiated core-like experimentation, though schools usually did not apply the name "core" to their "Higher Horizons," "Upward Bound," and "Schools Without Walls" programs. The late sixties also strongly reaffirmed that America had persistent problems of race, war, environment, and political processes that could scarcely be dealt with by an education adhering to rigid subject matter boundaries.

Two other developments, one early in the 1960s and the other early in the

---

[3] National Association of Secondary School Principals, *Planning for American Youth,* Washington, D.C., 1951, pp. 45–46.
[4] Grace S. Wright and Edith S. Greer, U.S. Office of Education, *The Junior High School: A Survey of Grades 7-8-9 in Junior and Junior-Senior High Schools, 1959–60,* Bulletin 1963, No. 32, U.S. Government Printing Office, Washington, D.C., 1963, p. 20.

1970s, have contributed to renewed interest in the reorganization of secondary education along interdisciplinary lines. The first development was team teaching; the second the fruition of the community education movement in the form of today's campaign for action-learning.

TEAM TEACHING

Team teaching made its first impact on the American educational scene through a commission of the National Association of Secondary School Principals. Under the leadership of J. Lloyd Trump, the Commission on the Experimental Study of the Utilization of the Staff in the Secondary Schools fostered team-teaching arrangements.[5] Trump has pointed out that team teaching requires two or more teachers and their assistants to work with a group of students equivalent in size to two or more conventional classes. With the students, the teachers plan, instruct, and evaluate in one or more subject areas. Team teaching employs large-group instruction, small-group discussion, and independent study. Thus students may sometimes hear lectures or watch films with hundreds of other students, sometimes meet in discussion groups of twelve to eighteen members, or sometimes work alone in independent study.

Team teaching is not synonymous with core teaching. Core programs have sometimes been staffed by a single teacher and sometimes by two or more as in team teaching. Team teaching may take place in a single subject area; a core program by definition cuts across two or more subject areas. Team teaching is always characterized by a combination of large-group instruction, small-group discussion, and independent study; historically, core teaching has experimented with various sized groups but is not necessarily committed to the trio outlined in the Trump plan.

Team teaching often cuts across subject matter lines and emphasizes interrelated subject fields. As he looked back one decade later upon his work with the NAASP's commission, Trump wrote with his collaborator, Delmas F. Miller:

Although present research does not favor one kind of team over the other, we prefer teams that cut across subject lines. Such teams tend to plan instruction that recognizes better the interrelatedness of subject content. (In this regard, teaming has some of the same objectives as the core or common learnings curricular approach.) Teachers still work primarily in their specialties, even with special interests

---

[5] J. Lloyd Trump, *Images of the Future—A New Approach to the Secondary School*, National Association of Secondary School Principals, Washington, D.C., 1959, pp. 19–22; J. Lloyd Trump, *And No Bells Ring*, black and white sound film with narration by Hugh Downs, National Education Association, distributor, Washington, D.C., 1960; J. Lloyd Trump and Dorsey Baynham, *Focus on Change—Guide to Better Schools*, Rand McNally, Chicago, 1961, pp. 24–33.

within their subject fields, but they benefit from working in group activities with colleagues in other subject fields.[6]

Trump's comment about benefits to teachers from team-teaching arrangements seems to be supported by current research. Martin and Pavan, in a summary of research on innovations, comment about team teaching:

Research in this area is not very comprehensive, nor are the results definitive. It would appear, however, that planning, understanding the program goals, and cooperation are essential to the successful implementation of team teaching. While specific advantages in achievement have not been demonstrated, students and teachers alike have expressed positive attitudes toward the innovation.[7]

Team teaching contributed to the changing form of secondary school buildings. Obviously, the ice cube tray design could not suffice if students were to meet in the large groups, small discussion groups, and individual study arrangements inherent in team teaching. As Trump and Vars wrote recently:

A school needs a variety of spaces for independent study with an equally wide variety of supplies and equipment if individual needs are to be served. Schools also need a variety of places for students to meet in small groups. Also needed is a teaching auditorium quite different from the theater-like auditoriums that many schools provide. A teaching auditorium provides close contact between the listeners and the presentation.[8]

A chart illustrating space arrangements suitable for team teaching appears in Figure 10.2.

COMMUNITY PARTICIPATION MOVEMENT

The community participation movement that characterized secondary education reform proposals of the 1970s also contributed to interdisciplinary teaching within substantial time blocks. Though the term *core* was seldom used, action-learning obviously required large blocks of times for implementation.

Not only is time needed for learning outside the walls of the school building; time for planning, reading, reporting, and appraisal with teachers and fellow participants within the school building is also required. If action-learning is to be educationally sound, substantial time must be

---

[6] J. Lloyd Trump and Delmas F. Miller, *Secondary School Curriculum Improvement: Proposals and Procedures,* Allyn and Bacon, Boston, 1968, pp. 318–319.
[7] Lyn S. Martin and Barbara N. Pavan, "Current Research on Open Space, Nongrading, Vertical Grouping, and Team Teaching," *Phi Delta Kappan,* January 1976, pp. 310–315.
[8] J. Lloyd Trump and Gordon F. Vars, "How Should Learning Be Organized," *Issues in Secondary Education,* Seventy-fifth Yearbook of the National Society for the Study of Education, University of Chicago Press, Chicago, 1976, p. 231.

FIGURE 10.2 *School Building for 1,200 Students. Team teaching facilities and space arrangements.*

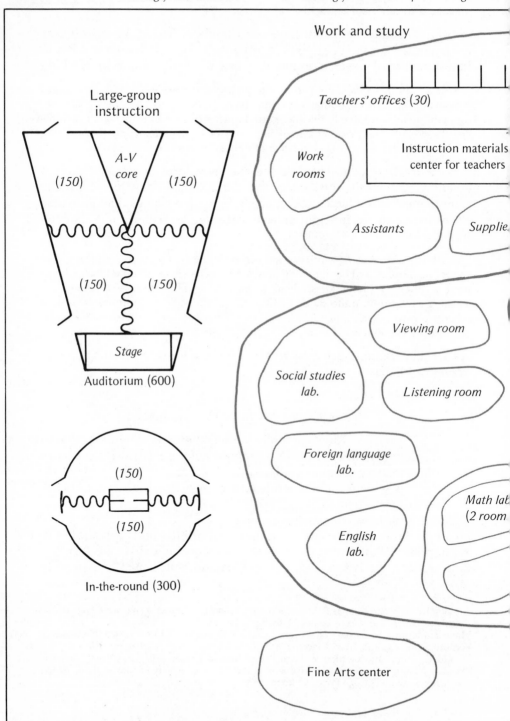

Large-group instruction

A-V core

(150)   (150)

(150)   (150)

Stage

Auditorium (600)

(150)

(150)

In-the-round (300)

Work and study

Teachers' offices (30)

Work rooms

Instruction materials center for teachers

Assistants

Supplies

Viewing room

Social studies lab.

Listening room

Foreign language lab.

Math lab (2 rooms

English lab.

Fine Arts center

SOURCE: Trump, J. Lloyd, and Baynham, Dorsey, *Focus on Change—Guide to Better Schools,* © 1961 by Rand McNally and Company, Chicago, pages 36–37.

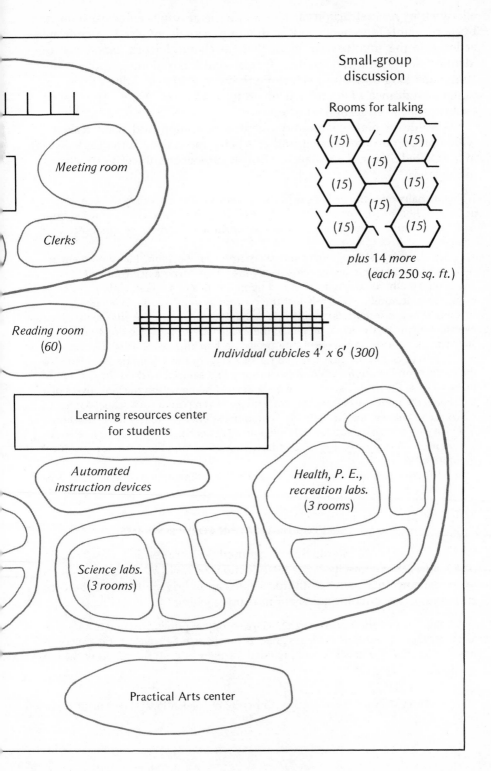

Small-group
discussion

Rooms for talking

(15) (15)
(15)
(15) (15)
(15)
(15) (15)

plus 14 more
(each 250 sq. ft.)

Meeting room

Clerks

Reading room
(60)

Individual cubicles 4' x 6' (300)

Learning resources center
for students

Automated
instruction devices

Health, P. E.,
recreation labs.
(3 rooms)

Science labs.
(3 rooms)

Practical Arts center

allocated for reconstruction of the experiences through reflective thought by participants, teachers, and community people involved. Significant action-learning involves far more than mechanical work experience or identification with a civic project. It necessitates envisioning a total problem, embarking on many steps along the way, and evaluating the educational significance of individual or group endeavors. Core organization facilitates these educational processes.

The value of both community-oriented education and team teaching within programs of integrated studies is being recognized abroad as well as in the United States. For instance, a British author recently wrote of schools in England:

> Traditionally our schools have held themselves aloof from society at large. A part of the neighborhood, yet essentially apart from it, they have been regarded both from within and without as oases of culture in a wilderness of ignorance and anarchy.
>
> Today there is a strong movement away from this position. Many teachers are seeking to make their appeal less vicarious, more experience-centered. . . . Traditional methods, though, are based upon the idea of a school within, yet apart from, the community—which is just the concept currently being challenged.
>
> A whole new approach is coming into being. It entails complete afternoons given over to realistic fieldwork of all kinds; the availability of two or more members of staff simultaneously involved in one project; a breaking away from the conventional form of classroom divisions; and a 'blocking' of the school timetable to give the facilities and space required. It is a process that seeks to cast off the concept of the teacher as the "2-4-7 man"—someone most at home within the two covers of a text-book, the four walls of a classroom, and the seven periods of a school day. . . .
>
> Are we to believe, for example, that children experience life in subject divisions? Is a visit to the parish church a rich religious experience, or even *chiefly* a religious experience? And the Tower of London—does this provide food for historical thought only? . . .
>
> In all these considerations "team teaching" and "integrated studies" are very closely linked. [9]

TEAM TEACHING WITHIN CORE PROGRAMS

Harold Spears, formerly superintendent of schools in San Francisco, comments in the introduction to David W. Beggs's book on team teaching that many of the principles and early patterns of the core curriculum "are bobbing up again in team teaching."

Among the common features are (1) a large group of pupils assigned to a team of teachers, (2) a curriculum block assigned as the area to be covered, (3) a block of time longer than the usual period provided for the work, (4) the provision within

---

[9] David William Warwick, *Team Teaching*, University of London Press, London, 1971, pp. 26–29.

the program of class groups varying in size from exceedingly large to exceedingly small, (5) freedom for the teachers to plan among themselves the flexible scheduling within the program that meets the instructional objectives of the moment and (6) the correlation of curriculum content naturally related.[10]

Writing of team teaching in America, Edward G. Buffie stresses the promise of integration of subject matter on the junior high school level.

Team teaching has taken many forms, of which one of the most promising is the type of organization whereby two or more teachers work together to integrate more effectively their respective subject matter areas. Is it not reasonable, therefore, to expect junior high teachers to be very much concerned about this type of working arrangement, since typically their students have come from elementary school programs where self-contained classrooms lend themselves extremely well to the integration of learning activities?[11]

Advocates of interdisciplinary programs, such as the core curriculum, believe that students should work together on problems that are of importance to students and society. They use team teaching and community participation as students study and act on life problems. They include individualized work in programs but usually do not depend on individualized instruction exclusively. They believe that in a democracy individuals must also learn to interact with and work together with others. Thus common learnings and experiences are stressed in interdisciplinary core programs.

INDIVIDUALIZED INSTRUCTION

The aspiration to teach through individualized programs is as old as the profession of education itself. The impetus toward individualization stems from the recognition that each person is unique, different. People learn at different speeds, and in different ways. Ideally, each student should experience his or her own individualized curriculum and instruction.

In pursuit of the elusive goal of individualized instruction, educators have long attempted to teach individuals. For instance, teachers have often directed questions and made comments designed particularly for individuals in a class. Teachers have made differentiated assignments based on the varied levels of competence and accomplishment of individual students. They have assigned students to develop individual projects and term papers. However, such attempts at individualization have usually been

---

[10] Harold Spears, "Introduction," in *Team Teaching: Bold New Venture*, ed. David W. Beggs, Unified College Press, Indianapolis, 1964, pp. 8–9.
[11] Edward G. Buffie, "Potentials for Team Teaching in the Junior High School," in *Team Teaching: Bold New Venture*, p. 72.

compromises that have had little effect upon the predominantly mass instruction of groups or subgroups. Only in recent years have methodological and technological developments increased the possibility of achieving a higher degree of individualized instruction. Currently, attempts are under way to provide what is sometimes called personalized instruction, independent study, self-paced instruction, or individually guided education. The term that embraces these approaches is *individualized instruction*.

A curriculum is made up of all the learning experience under the control of the school. An individualized curriculum plan describes what *individual* students are to learn, the possible ways of learning, and the procedures for assessing learning. Individualized instruction provides content and processes at the appropriate times for each individual student. As a consequence, if educators are to achieve individualized instruction, they must begin with broad general goals of education and become increasingly more specific. Decisions have to be made as to problems, topics, subjects, or skills to be taught; some curriculum plan has to be adopted. The plan may come from outside the individual school in the form of curriculum guides, published curriculum materials, textbooks, programmed instruction, or, more recently, computerized instruction. The curriculum plan may be derived from student-teacher planning within a school, such as teacher-student planning of curriculum and instruction, or student planning without teacher participation.

To individualize the plan, still more specifics are needed. Instructional objectives must be developed. Some are long range, as are the objectives of units. Others are short term; they deal with briefer periods and specify what is to be done within relatively limited time spans.

After instructional objectives are decided upon, educators must supply students with learning alternatives and resources. These consist of a variety of educational activities and materials from which the students select as they attempt to reach the selected instructional objectives. Possible learning alternatives use many ways of learning—reading, writing, and discussing; building and experimenting; creating films, plays, and artistic productions. Among the possible learning resources are books, pamphlets, magazines; radio, television, and newspapers; social travel and community participation; the wide variety of human beings in the local and more distant environment.

At the heart of individualized instruction is thoughtful and effective prescription of learning alternatives. To prescribe well, the teacher must know the individual learner intimately. A preliminary diagnosis or preassessment is required so that the person presuming to prescribe learns the student's interests, experiences, and background; recognizes the student's characteristic learning style; is familiar with what the student already knows. Helpful in such assessment are tests, observations, anecdotal records, and sociograms, as well as any previous student products such as writing, experiments, art products, dramatic performances, and recreational activities. After such preassessment, the teacher is in a better position to prescribe.

Obviously, determination of general goals, adoption of a curriculum plan, and statement of specific objectives, followed by the development of learning alternatives and the gathering of learning resources, are formidable tasks—so formidable that earlier generations of aspiring individualized educators have despaired. However, today's educators have methodological and technological advantages that their predecessors lacked. Contracts, learning packages, learning centers, and programmed or computerized instruction are helpful in development of learning alternatives.

CONTRACTS

Among the methodological devices that make individualized instruction more feasible today than formerly are contracts. A contract specifies learnings to be pursued through alternative learning activities. Both the teacher and the student understand and agree upon procedures to be used in determining whether the student accomplishes the objective. The student works at his or her own rate, determining how to spend the time, and makes choices as to specific activities. In a highly structured contract the student has few or no choices; in a less structured contract the student has a high degree of choice, even as to objectives. In carrying out the contract the student uses a wide variety of resources in the course of writing, reading, listening, and thinking. He or she may report on his or her study through essays, tapes, art productions, teaching others, etc. The teacher monitors the student's progress as the student proceeds.

LEARNING PACKAGES

Many possible contracts can be entered into through the suggestions included in the typical learning package. Learning packages deal with some specific problem, topic, or aspect of subject matter. A package, usually in printed form, contains an introduction, some instructions, a list of objectives, suggestions for alternative learning activities that will help the student to reach each objective, and ways of testing. Through a learning package, a student proceeds at his or her own pace to learn prescribed concepts and skills related to the problem, topic, or aspect of subject matter.

A package can be used by one student or by many students. Since the package contains many alternatives, students will differ in their choices of textbooks or audio-visual materials or community resources. The learning alternatives tell the student what to learn, what media to use, and what to do with anything the student produces. In the process, the student may find that he or she is engaged in reading or writing or listening or viewing, or drawing or painting or building or dramatizing; or working in the library or the classroom or the community.

Blackburn and Powell supply an illustration of a learning package on black-white problems in America. The objectives include developing both black and white responses on the place the black person has in society, deciding whether slavery was harsh or kind, describing what happened in a ghetto day, and setting forth a position on race relations. Activities to determine possible white responses include making lists and answering questions on *The Clansman* by Thomas Dixon or viewing the film *Birth of a Nation*, viewing television's "All in the Family," reading Faulkner's *Intruder in the Dust*, comparing contemporary with earlier newspaper articles for and against segregation, interviewing white people, reading *Black Like Me*, viewing *Guess Who's Coming to Dinner?* To determine black responses, students respond to questions based on interviews in the community or reading of Booker T. Washington, W. E. B. Du Bois, Martin Luther King, Marcus Garvey, the Black Panthers, Malcolm X, Ralph Ellison, and others. Responses to the remaining objectives are similarly based on books, films, newspaper accounts, tapes, dramatizations, and preparation of essays.[12]

LEARNING CENTERS

Another methodological development facilitating individualized instruction has been widely used in elementary schools, is increasingly being used in middle and junior high schools, and is occasionally introduced into senior high school classes. This is the inclusion of learning centers in classrooms (and sometimes even in corridors). A classroom learning center is a special space in the classroom that contains learning alternatives such as learning utensils and related resources to follow through on these alternatives. Open classrooms use centers.

Learning centers may be set up by the teacher alone, or with students, or by the students independently. Some are for the development of specific skills. Others are intended to enrich the teaching of a unit on which an entire class is engaged. Some are intended to encourage the further exploration of individual interests by students. The learning alternatives and materials in centers are frequently changed as the school year goes on; sometimes old learning centers are replaced by new ones.

A learning center might be as simple as a corner of a senior high school classroom devoted to books, magazines, and materials related to the sepa-

---

[12] Jack E. Blackburn and W. Conrad Powell, *One at a Time All at Once*, Goodyear, Pacific Palisades, Calif., 1976, pp. 103–105.

rate subject matter taught in that particular class. Or a learning center environment might be as complex as a middle school classroom in which a teacher or a team is responsible for several curricular areas. In such a room one might find centers devoted to arts and crafts, music, mathematics, science, social studies, writing, and reading. There might be centers for typing, for plants and animals, for cooking, for group meetings. The customary grouping used in a conventional class, whether desks in rows or chairs grouped around tables, might be completely missing. There might not even be a teacher's desk.

The possible variety of learning resources in classroom learning centers defies description. They include a wide variety of books, magazines, newspapers, realia, games, tools, maps, equipment, varieties of paper, recordings, and tapes. They also contain charts or cards or files or journals in which students keep records of their accomplishments.

By now, it should be apparent to the reader that the role of the teacher in individualized instruction is quite different from the conventional role of the teacher as lecturer, conductor of recitations, or discussion leader. Instead, the teacher in fully individualized instruction specifies objectives, designs contract packages and learning centers, secures equipment and materials, develops specific learning alternatives, and manages a classroom in which all the students are at work either completely alone or in small groups on activities that contribute to defined objectives.

Obviously, this is a formidable assignment for any individual teacher. However, modern educational technology and communication help make greater individualized instruction more feasible. Organizations supply and disseminate individualized materials. For instance, the Education Development Center at Newton, Massachusetts, provides bibliographies, curriculum materials, and films primarily in science, mathematics, and social sciences. Research for Better Schools in Philadelphia provides individualized programs and materials in science, reading, literature, mathematics, and spelling. Westinghouse Learning Corporation in Sunnyvale, California, provides lists of behavioral objectives, learning directories that describe many educational materials, procedures for developing learning packages, and individualized materials beginning with objectives and culminating in tests. The IDEA Materials Center in Anaheim, California, has developed UNIPACS, self-contained sets of teacher-learning materials designed to teach single concepts.

TEACHING MACHINES AND COMPUTERS

Still another approach to individualizing instruction depends heavily on the use of educational technology. An early step in this direction was programmed instruction through teaching machines. Here the student is presented with a series of multiple-choice questions or statements. To answer, the student pushes keys. If the answer is right, the machine proceeds to the next question. If the answer is wrong, the machine records the error, then requires the student to try again to arrive at the right answer before he or she can go on to the next question. Some machines can "branch" the student into a remedial program.

Computer-assisted instruction is a sophisticated technological extension of the earlier teaching machines. The student, in a cubicle, can receive visual and auditory instruction from a film projector, tape recorder, or television. The student responds through a switchboard. The computer then records, analyzes, and decides what instructional materials to present next. Thus the computer analyzes difficulties and presents sequences to remedy the learner's problem.

To date, the computer has been most useful in situations requiring the repetition of drill. A limitation of computers is that they can provide only specific predetermined programs. Despite science fiction, the computer cannot "think"—as yet.

Indeed, some proponents of individualized instruction believe that educational technology, such as computer-assisted instruction, contributes only to differentiated rates of learning and provides only pacing. They believe that the only factor that is actually individualized in programmed learning is the rate of speed and they think that the approach is better described as individual pacing than as individualized instruction.[13] Individual instruction, they say, cannot be prepackaged or preprogrammed and prescribed for every child at an academic or age level. Individualized instruction instead requires knowing the individual student, prescribing a program related to the individual's motivations and involvement, and providing a variety of alternatives.

A 1975 survey on computers and secondary schools conducted by the American Institutes for Research found that since 1970 computing in secondary education has steadily increased. Of the schools that responded to the survey, 58.2 percent indicated current use of a computer for administrative and/or instructional purposes. In schools that used computers, computer-assisted instruction has increased from 8.4 percent in 1970 to 13.8 percent in 1975. The most frequently used instructional application of the computer to secondary education was "as a problem-solving tool" and as the subject of "computer science" courses. The broad field of the curriculum that made the greatest use of computers in 1975 was mathematics. In administration of schools, the computers were most frequently used for student accounting and resource management.[14]

---

[13] Rita Dunn and Kenneth Dunn, *Practical Approaches to Individualizing Instruction*, Parker, Nyack, N.Y., 1972, p. 45.
[14] "Computers in Secondary Schools—1975," *Creative Computing*, September-October 1976, p. 51.

INDEPENDENT STUDY

If the complexities of contracts, packages, learning centers, and technology deter readers, they might fall back on a simple approach to individualization—independent study. Independent study simply involves allowing a student some unscheduled out-of-class time. During this "free" time, the student is expected to carry on study activities of his or her choice alone or with others. The student might even legitimately relax! The major requirement in a program of independent study is faith in the student. The major environmental change is the establishment of teaching resource centers and laboratories in which the student might work. For independent learning is not best fostered by simply assigning students to the quiet isolation of the typical austere school library.

GOAL OF INDIVIDUALIZED INSTRUCTION

Whether the individualized instruction adopted is simple or complex, the educator must bear in mind what individualized instruction is fundamentally for—adapting learning to each individual. This fable, which has often been mimeographed by educators and seldom credited to its author, George H. Reavis, might be a useful reminder of the goal of individualized instruction.

Once upon a time the animals decided they must do something heroic to meet the problems of a new world. So they organized a school. They adopted an activity curriculum consisting of running, climbing, swimming, and flying. To make it easier to administer, all the animals took all the subjects.

The duck was excellent in swimming, better in fact than his instructor, and made passing grades in flying, but he was very poor in running. Since he was slow in running, he had to stay after school and also drop swimming to practice running. This was kept up until his web feet were badly worn and he was only average in swimming.

The rabbit started at the top of the class in running but had a nervous breakdown because of so much overwork trying to compete in the swimming area.

The squirrel was excellent in climbing until he developed frustration in the flying class where his teacher made him start from the ground up instead of from the tree-top down.

The eagle was a problem child and was disciplined severely. In the climbing class he beat all the others to the top of the tree but insisted on using his own way to get there.

At the end of the year, an abnormal eel that could swim exceedingly well and also run, climb, and fly a little had the highest average and was valedictorian.

The prairie dogs stayed out of school and fought the tax levy because the administration would not add digging and burrowing to the curriculum. They apprenticed their child to a badger and later joined the ground hogs and gophers to start a successful private school.[15]

And after having laughed at the fable, we might ask, as do the sponsors of the core curriculum, whether there are not some common experiences that even the animals of the fable should have together. Significant as individualized instruction is, is there not a need for common activities or experiences for secondary education school age young people in today's interrelated, complex society?

GUIDANCE

Good teachers have always tried to provide guidance to students. But systematic provision of guidance services as part of the organization of American secondary education dates only from early in the twentieth century. Among the several services guidance programs can provide, vocational guidance emerged first.

FROM VOCATIONAL TOWARD BROADER GUIDANCE SERVICES

Concern for vocational education in an increasingly urban and industrial America increased as the nineteenth century yielded to the twentieth. New vocations developed and the number of vocational schools and vocationally oriented students increased. Newcomers to the complex cities, including immigrants from abroad, did not have the know-how to guide their children into increasingly specialized occupations or into the early occupational decisions that vocational education required. Thus vocational guidance developed under the impetus of vocational education.[16] In the years prior to World War I, such groups as the National Society for the Promotion of Industrial Education recognized that vocational education had to be supplemented by vocational guidance if young people were to be trained effectively for the world of work.

During World War I technicians and specialists in industry and the armed forces were required. Psychologists responded by developing tests in order to screen personnel. After the war, the tests were used in schools to aid vocational choices and to place students on the educational ladder.

Many advocates of vocational guidance were also advocates of guidance for human development so that people might lead lives that were fulfilling

---

[15] Phi Delta Kappa, *George H. Reavis, Educator—Editor—Philanthropist*, Phi Delta Kappa, Bloomington, Ind., 1971, unpaged.

[16] W. Richard Stephens, *Social Reform and the Origins of Vocational Guidance*, National Vocational Guidance Association, Washington, D.C., 1970.

as well as vocationally useful. Progressive educators reaffirmed the importance of guidance as they stressed an education based on the needs of learners and in the interest of the fullest development of individuals. The new science of psychology supported the development of guidance as a way of fostering mental health. Humanistic psychologists such as A. H. Maslow, Earl Kelley, and Arthur W. Combs increasingly expressed their opposition to authoritarian guidance that assumed that guidance counselors had all the answers and that placed too much dependence on rigidly interpreted tests. Humanistic counselors, such as Carl R. Rogers, stressed decision making by clients.

New guidance skills derivative from World War II emergencies were drawn upon by the guidance movement. Screening individuals for difficult war-time assignments and helping people who were encountering war-created mental illness were needed. When veterans came home from the war and reentered schools and colleges, they required realistic counseling.

In the late 1950s, during the period of the Cold War, the National Defense Education Act aided the development of guidance services. Mathematics, sciences, foreign languages, and guidance were stressed in the 1958 NDEA. Although the hope of the legislators may have been that more students would be guided into science, mathematics, and foreign languages, the three fields of the secondary school curriculum favored by Cold Warriors, the guidance movement used the federal financial aid for the broad development of improved guidance services for all youth.

In this way, the field of guidance grew beyond its original limitation to vocational choice-making. By the mid-1970s, guidance services were being "designed to help students to recognize, accept, and develop their potential, to adjust to school, and to develop the skills they needed to cope with the problems they meet."[17] Though the word *adjust* persisted in the guidance vocabulary, it was no longer interpreted as unquestioning acceptance. Adjustment was now interpreted as people learning to face their own problems, set their own goals, and change their own behavior.

GUIDANCE SERVICES TODAY

Guidance services became part of the organization of secondary schools. One form of guidance service is *counseling*. Young people need counseling when they meet problems that they cannot solve by themselves or with the people they normally encounter, such as their parents, friends, and teachers.

Another type of guidance service is *student assessment*, an effort to determine the student's present level of performance, readiness for new learning, and degree of continuing progress. Student assessment helps the

---

[17] Merle M. Ohlsen, *Guidance Services in the Modern School*, Harcourt Brace Jovanovich, New York, 1974, p. 1.

teacher to be helpful and the student to make decisions based on realistic information about himself or herself. Testing is often used in assessment programs.

Vocational guidance is not neglected in contemporary guidance services. It has broadened beyond its early focus on industry to become *career development*. It is supplemented by *job placement* service so that young people can learn what jobs are available, exercise some degree of choice, and obtain work.

Still another guidance service is *orientation* service so that the young person may move from one section of the educational ladder to another with greater ease and less personal perplexities. All such guidance services call upon *information* services that supply materials contributing to educational, vocational, and personal development.

The good secondary school provides still another service, *follow-up* of students to help them and to improve the program of the school.[18]

To provide such services, secondary schools often employ guidance counselors as a part of the school's total organization. Conscious of the range of their responsibilities, guidance counselors frequently struggle against becoming pigeonholed. Sometimes guidance counselors are pigeonholed as simply disciplinarians, or vocational advisers, or test givers, and so on. Although guidance counselors often recognize the necessity to fill these roles, they often aspire to more opportunities for *counseling* service in which they can develop an accepting and trusting relationship between themselves and their clients. They recognize the great need of youth for someone upon whom they can call confidently, someone who will not constantly sit in judgment but will be, instead, a dependable confidant.

As guidance services developed within the organization of secondary schools, a question naturally arose: What are the proper responsibilities of the guidance staff and what are the proper responsibilities of the teaching staff? One possible answer is that guidance counselors should be assigned and should accept full responsibility for helping students to develop their potential, adjust to school, and cope skillfully with their problems. Given this interpretation, the teacher would have nothing to do with such matters and should concentrate simply on conveying subject matter. But no teacher who takes seriously the relationship of teaching to the needs of learners, the social realities of our times, the development of humane values, or even to the relevance of knowledge can accept such an interpretation.

Another answer to the question of the relationship between guidance staff and teaching staff holds that teachers are fully and exclusively responsible for developing the student's potential, adjustment, and skills for

---

[18] Ibid., pp. 32–34.

dealing with problems. Given this interpretation, there is no room whatsoever for a guidance staff on the secondary school level. Obviously, this too is an unsatisfactory solution, for teachers need the knowledge and skills that guidance counselors are especially qualified to offer. Guidance experts believe that good counselors can develop a special relationship with students that even a very good teacher has difficulty in achieving. They point out that counseling is often a one-to-one, time-consuming relationship. Trust and acceptance is built slowly. It takes time for students to learn to face their problems, to talk out difficulties, to consider alternatives and consequences, to act, and to learn to live differently.

Consequently, a reasonable resolution of the question of the respective role of the guidance staff and the teaching staff is to recognize both overlap and specialization. Both guidance staff and teaching staff must be concerned about achieving the goals of counseling. Thus the good teacher is also a counselor. Yet there should be recognition that specialized services, such as those mentioned above, require specialized knowledge and skills. The good counselor has these skills and puts them into action, at the same time working cooperatively with the teaching staff. The appropriate relationship is one of cooperation, not competition.

Both parties need help from each other. Both fight the limitations that go with their roles. For instance, the typical secondary school teacher finds individual counseling difficult, if not impossible, to achieve with thirty students for a fifty-minute period, followed by another thirty students for another fifty-minute period, and so on. The counselor encounters difficulty in that his or her responsibilities sometimes focus on selected groups, perhaps low achievers, perhaps students confronted with choices of colleges. The counselor has no time to develop the helping relationships with others who need and want assistance. A reasonable conclusion is that counselors and teachers, and indeed students, need all the help that can be made available. There is no need for jurisdictional disputes in secondary education concerning counselors and teachers.

Secondary educators should constantly be on the alert for new forms of organization that maximally use the abilities of teachers and counselors with respect to guidance. One such proposal was suggested by Trump and Vars in 1976, a counseling program staffed by teacher-advisers who are supervised by counselors:

The differentiated counseling staff includes teacher-advisors with roles markedly different from teacher roles in conventional homeroom or advisory groups. These advisors are supervised by professional counselors who are freed from routine work related to attendance, discipline, making out student programs, and the like—tasks that others perform. Each professional counselor supervises the work of approximately twelve teacher-advisors who, in turn, are responsible for monitoring the progress of 300 to 350 students. Thus, a school of 1,000 or so pupils would have three professional counselors who supervise three clusters of twelve teachers each and the 300 to 350 students that each cluster of twelve teachers advises. . . .

The students assigned to a given teacher-advisor should represent two or more of the grades or age levels in the school and the teacher-student relationship should extend over several years. It is always possible for the guidance counselor or the administrator in charge to make changes when it is in the best interests of either a given student or of a given teacher. . . .

Incidentally, this assignment changes the role of the teacher. The teacher-advisor no longer is interested only in the subject or broad field he or she teaches, but now becomes interested in all of the educational opportunities that the school affords, because advisees are involved with all of them. The advisor receives reports and has contacts with all aspects of the students' educational program in the school, in the community, and in the home. This development is wholesome for teachers. It does not detract from their specialized interests in the subjects or broad fields they teach; in fact it improves their teaching because they now see what they teach in relation to all of the other learning opportunities that the school provides.[19]

Whoever is involved with advisement should recognize that guidance is fundamentally *helping*. The teacher-adviser helps students to know themselves, to get new information, to open up new opportunities, to learn to decide, and to act and reassess. There should be many occasions on which teacher-advisers and counselors discuss students in the interest of being helpful to individual young people. Both teachers and counselors will grow in such a relationship and, even more important, students will benefit. One result should be that students become more able to use their abilities and interests fully, know how to participate more completely in and out of class, become more independent, relate better to the school, and increasingly achieve more self-actualizing personalities.

TOWARD BETTER ORGANIZATION

The quest for better organization of the secondary school program goes on. Sometimes it takes the form of core or common learnings programs, team taught or community-oriented. Through such programs, students can work together on interdisciplinary problems encountered by young people in our society. Sometimes it assumes the form of individualized instruction through contracts, learning packages, learning centers, technology, and independent study. Sometimes it takes the form of guidance services to supplement instructional organization. A good case can be made for each of these approaches to a better organization of secondary education.

---

[19] J. Lloyd Trump and Gordon F. Vars, "How Should Learning Be Organized?" *Issues in Secondary Education,* Seventy-fifth Yearbook of the National Society for the Study of Education, University of Chicago Press, Chicago, 1976, pp. 227-228, 234-235.

DISCUSSION

1.   Review the assumptions about the organization of secondary education with which the chapter begins. Can you supplement with some additional assumptions?

2.   A list of questions follow the assumptions. What are your own answers to these questions? Do you find your own answers to these questions persuasive?

3.   What is the meaning of block-time program?

4.   How does correlation differ from unified studies? Develop an illustration different from the one used in the chapter.

5.   What is a core program?

6.   Discuss the Sarasota proposal. Are there problem areas or illustrative learning units that you would add?

7.   In addition to the central unit, what activities are included in the core block of time?

8.   What subject areas or broad fields are not included in the usual core?

9.   How did the results of the Eight-Year Study influence the development of the core curriculum?

10.   Appraise the common learnings program proposed by the Educational Policies Commission for American City. Though proposed more than thirty years ago, would the program be appropriate for a contemporary school? If modifications are needed, specify these. How was concern for common learnings affected by emphasis on teaching of the separate subjects in the early 1960s and compensatory education in the late 1960s?

11.   What is team teaching? What are the differences between team teaching and core teaching? What are the similarities?

12.   What type of school design is preferable for team teaching? Could a conventional building be used for team teaching? What adaptations could be made in a conventional secondary school building to make team teaching feasible?

13.   How are community participation and interdisciplinary teaching interrelated?

14.   What is Harold Spears's perception of common features of team teaching and the core curriculum?

15.   Why is there a greater possibility of achieving individualized instruction today than in earlier periods of time?

16.   In individualized instruction, why is the development of instructional objectives essential? What are some possible learning alternatives and resources that might be used in individualized instruction?

17.   What knowledge is helpful to the teacher who is attempting to prescribe learning alternatives?

18.   What is a contract? . . . a learning package? After reviewing the illustration of a learning package contained in the chapter, develop your own illustration of a desirable learning package.

19. What is a learning center? Supply both a simple and a complex illustration of a learning center.

20. What is the role of the teacher in individualized instruction?

21. What is the nature of a teaching machine?

22. How does computer-assisted instruction differ from earlier teaching machines?

23. Discuss the possible contributions and limitations of the computer as a form of individualized instruction.

24. What is independent study? Do you think that secondary school students can be depended upon to carry on independent study?

25. What is the moral of George H. Reavis's fable?

26. Should schools depend completely upon individualized instruction? . . . upon common activities for experiences? Should there be some combination of both?

27. Why did vocational education become necessary in late-nineteenth- and early-twentieth-century America? Why was it necessary that vocational guidance accompany the development of vocational education?

28. What social developments of the twentieth century encourage the growth of the guidance movement?

29. In what way is the modern guidance movement different from the original vocational guidance movement?

30. Review the several types of guidance services described in the chapter. Attempt to supply an illustration of each.

31. What are the roles of guidance counselors? . . . of teachers? How are they alike? How do they differ?

32. What are the difficulties and limitations that the guidance counselor often encounters? What are the difficulties and limitations encountered by teachers when they assume the role of counselors and advisers?

33. What role does Trump and Vars's proposal assign to the professional counselor? . . . to the classroom teacher? According to Trump and Vars, what are the advantages of their proposal?

34. Which of the new approaches to better organization—interdisciplinary organizations, individualized instruction, guidance—seems the better possibility? Would use of all three be desirable?

INVOLVEMENT

1. On a visit to a secondary school, set down as many of the basic assumptions about the organization of the school day and of classes as you can. Ask yourself whether all the assumptions can be justified.

2. Bring back to class the assumptions as to organization that you have noted in your observation. Examine with class members the justification or lack of justification for the practices you have observed.

3. After reviewing the proposed core program for Sarasota, Florida, set forth your own proposal for problem areas and illustrative learning units for a junior high school. Adapt your proposal to the special characteristics of the community you know best.

4. Take one illustrative learning unit from your own proposal and suggest learning activities that might be carried within this unit. Share your proposed activities with others in the class and, in turn, read theirs. As a class, develop a file of units.

5. If there is a school utilizing the core curriculum or team teaching in your vicinity, visit classes and talk with teachers.

6. Develop a learning package. In so doing, sketch the broad general goals of your field of specialization. Decide upon specific instructional objectives for a unit. Set forth learning alternatives for inclusion in your learning package. Describe materials useful in carrying out the alternative learning activities.

7. Observe a conventional classroom. Then sketch what this classroom might look like if the learning center idea were applied.

8. Visit a computer installation, whether in a school, university, or business enterprise. Talk to the individuals responsible for programming in order to acquire some preliminary acquaintance with this technological development.

9. Invite to class both a guidance counselor and a guidance-oriented teacher to get their views on the provision of guidance to students.

10. Visit the office responsible for vocational guidance within the local high school; become acquainted with some of the instruments and questionnaires used in vocational counseling.

FURTHER READINGS

Blackburn, Jack E., and W. Conrad Powell. *One at a Time All at Once: The Creative Teacher's Guide to Individualized Instruction Without Anarchy.* Goodyear, Pacific Palisades, Calif., 1976. "An educator's catalogue": theory, process and projects for individualized instruction within a classroom setting. Includes reproducible worksheets for classes K–12 and bibliography of additional resources.

Dunn, Rita, and Kenneth Dunn. *Practical Approaches to Individualizing Instruction: Contracts and Other Effective Teaching Strategies.* Parker, West Nyack, N.Y., 1972. A practical guide to using contracts and other individualized programs.

Dyer, Charles A. *Preparing for Computer-Assisted Instruction.* Educational Technology Publications, Englewood Cliffs, N.J., 1972. A primer on the general principles of operation of computers and the concepts and methods used in programming.

Education for All American Youth. Educational Policies Commission, Washington,

D.C., 1944. A classic in American educational history on the imperative needs of youth in two fictitious communities: Farmville and American City. An outstanding statement of the need for common learnings programs.

Georgiades, William, and Donald C. Clark, eds. *Models for Individualized Instruction.* MSS Information Corporation, New York, 1974. Source materials and examples to assist teachers and administrators in implementing individualized instruction. Descriptions of new patterns for staff utilization, ways of organizing individualized curriculum, service programs, and evaluation.

Lewis, James, Jr. *Administering the Individualized Instruction Program.* Parker, West Nyack, N.Y., 1971. Preparing and developing individual study units based on personal experiences with individualized learning.

Ohlsen, Merle M. *Guidance Services in the Modern School,* 2nd ed. Harcourt Brace Jovanovich, New York, 1974. A comprehensive and useful description of various services in the field of guidance, including a chapter on secondary school guidance.

Perrone, Philip A., Antoinette Ryan and Franklin R. Zeran. *Guidance and the Emerging Adolescent.* International Textbook, Scranton, Penn., 1970. Focusing on early adolescence, this text presents an organized program of guidance services. A synthesis of theory and research in the social sciences with practical know-how.

Roberts, Arthur D., ed. *Educational Innovation: Alternatives in Curriculum and Instruction.* Allyn and Bacon, Boston, 1975. Examines alternative ideas, programs, techniques, and schema in curriculum and instruction that have potential for improvement of schools. Many of the authors are University of Connecticut staff members.

Shertzer, Bruce, and Shelley C. Stone. *Fundamentals of Guidance,* 3rd ed. Houghton Mifflin, Boston, 1976. Designed for use in introductory guidance courses, this book presents a broad overview of the field of guidance. It provides a perspective on existing issues and emerging trends.

Trump, J. Lloyd and Dorsey Baynham. *Focus on Change.* Rand McNally, Chicago, 1961. A proposal by the Commission on the Experimental Study of the Utilization of the Staff in the Secondary School for team teaching using large-group instruction, small-group discussion, and individual study.

Vars, Gordon F. ed. *Common Learnings: Core and Interdisciplinary Team Approaches.* International Textbook, Scranton, Pa., 1969. A definitive book on common learnings through core or interdisciplinary approaches and their relation to innovations such as team teaching, the nongraded curriculum, independent study, and humanities programs. A useful guide for experimental-minded educators.

Warwick, David William. *Team Teaching.* University of London Press, London, 1971. A British educator describes the theoretical basis and practical procedures in developing team teaching.

11.

Using
Varied
Personnel

A common-sense observation about education is that
the quality of an educational program depends upon
the people who conduct it and upon their interrelationships. However wide and realistic the setting,
however relevant and meaningful the content, and
however effective and adaptable the organization, the
caliber of a secondary school program depends, in the
final analysis, upon the men and women who teach,
make policy, administer, and supply community
help. So in this chapter we will emphasize the quest
for better personnel—better teachers, board members, principals, and community helpers. We will
take into consideration the respective power of these
groups within the total personnel providing secondary education programs for young Americans.

TEACHERS

EVOLUTION OF SECONDARY SCHOOL TEACHERS

The early American secondary school teachers were
employed by the academies after 1749 and by the new
public high schools after 1821. The first American
high school teachers were poorly paid, when judged
by contemporary standards. Their communities did
not rank them high in status. They were almost always males who often taught for a few years and then
moved on to other jobs that might prove more rewarding, both financially and socially. Communities
were sometimes reduced to employing whatever itin-
erant scholars might happen to appear. Some
academy and high school teachers had few more
years of education than their students. Some had no
degrees.

From the point of view of the influential people of the town, the idea candidate for high school teaching was a graduate of the classical curriculum of a liberal arts college. Although such a graduate had no teacher training, this did not trouble many Americans of the colonial and early national periods prior to the Civil War. Staffs of higher education institutions assumed that the liberal arts prepared for life and were relevant to any vocation. Although college professors did not completely ignore the relationship of liberal to professional education, they gave strictly limited attention to this problem.[1]

A major shift in the evolution of the American high school teacher came in the latter part of the nineteenth century. Two factors contributed to the change. The number of high schools accelerated sharply. Higher education programs changed markedly; the professional education of teachers became part of the higher education curriculum in some colleges and in the new universities.

The last half of the nineteenth century was a remarkable growth period for the public high school. The academies reached their peak about 1850. "By 1850 there were some 6,085 academies, although the count is not certain, enrolling approximately 263,000 students taught by a staff that numbered more than 12,000."[2] In the same year, there were only sixty high schools in the United States.[3] In 1874, a quarter of a century later, the Kalamazoo decision established the right of school districts to levy taxes upon the public for the support of high schools. The public high school boom began. By 1890 there were 2,526 high schools;[4] by 1905, 7,230 high schools.[5] (For statistics on the number of twentieth-century public secondary schools, see Table 11.1.) In the decade after 1889 the population (age fourteen to seventeen) in school almost doubled, from 359,949 to 699,403. In the decade after 1899 it almost doubled again, then more than doubled in the decade following 1909. By the school year 1919–20 there were more than 2.5 million young people fourteen to seventeen years of age in schools. (See Table 11.2 for further information.) High school teachers wanted!

Simultaneously, higher education changed. Many more subjects were included in the curriculum of the liberal arts college. Electives increased. Practical and useful knowledge related to a variety of vocations became part of the program. Some colleges included teacher education courses in their expanded offerings.

---

[1] Merle L. Borrowman, *Teacher Education in America,* Teachers College Press, New York, 1965, p. 4.
[2] Robert H. Beck, "A History of Issues in Secondary Education," *Issues in Secondary Education,* Seventy-fifth Yearbook of the National Society for the Study of Education, University of Chicago Press, Chicago, 1976, p. 38.
[3] Ibid., p. 48.
[4] Ibid.
[5] William M. Alexander, J. Galen Saylor, and Emmett L. Williams, *The High School: Today and Tomorrow,* Holt, Rinehart, and Winston, New York, 1971, p. 28.

TABLE 11.1 *Number and percentage of public secondary schools, by type of school, selected years, 1919–20 to 1970–71*

SCHOOL YEAR	TOTAL	TYPE OF SCHOOL			
		Traditional[a]	Junior[b]	Senior[c]	Junior-senior[d]
1	2	3	4	5	6
1919–20:					
Number	14,326	13,421	55	22	828
Percent	100.0	93.7	0.4	0.2	5.8
1929–30:					
Number	22,237	16,460	1,842	648	3,287
Percent	100.0	74.0	8.3	2.9	14.8
1937–38:					
Number	25,057	15,523	2,372	959	6,203
Percent	100.0	62.0	9.5	3.8	24.8
1945–46:					
Number	24,122	13,797	2,653	1,312	6,360
Percent	100.0	57.2	11.0	5.4	26.4
1951–52:					
Number	23,746	10,168	3,227	1,760	8,591
Percent	100.0	42.8	13.6	7.4	36.2
1958–59:					
Number	24,190	6,024	4,996	3,040	10,130
Percent	100.0	24.9	20.7	12.6	41.9
1967–68:					
Number	26,531[e]	6,433	7,437	4,318	8,343
Percent	100.0	24.2	28.0	16.3	31.4
1970–71:					
Number	24,682[e]	6,618	7,750	4,647	5,667
Percent	100.0	26.8	31.4	18.8	23.0

[a] Includes regular four-year high schools preceded by eight-year elementary schools; no reorganization has taken place.
[b] Includes two- and three-year junior high schools.
[c] Includes three- and four-year high schools preceded by junior high schools.
[d] Includes five- and six-year high schools. Beginning in 1967–68, also includes combined elementary-secondary schools.
[e] Excludes incomplete high schools and vocational or trade high schools (480 in 1967–68 and 670 in 1970–71).
NOTE: Data through 1958–59 are for forty-eight states and the District of Columbia. Because of rounding, percents may not add to 100.0.
SOURCES: U.S. Department of Health, Education, and Welfare, Office of Education, *Statistics of Education in the United States*, 1958–59 Series, Number 1, *Public Secondary Schools*; *Statistics of State School Systems*, 1967-68; and *Statistics of Public Elementary and Secondary Day Schools, Fall 1971.*
From W. Vance Grant and C. George Lind, *Digest of Educational Statistics*, 1975 ed., National Center for Education Statistics, U.S. Department of Health, Education, and Welfare, U.S. Government Printing Office, Washington, D.C., 1976, p. 59.

TABLE 11.2 *Enrollment in grades 9–12 in public and nonpublic schools compared with population 14–17 years of age, 1889–90 to fall 1974*

SCHOOL YEAR	ENROLLMENT, GRADES 9-12[a] All schools	Public schools	Nonpublic schools	POPULATION 14-17 YEARS OF AGE[b]	TOTAL NUMBER ENROLLED PER 100 PERSONS 14-17 YEARS OF AGE
1	2	3	4	5	6
1889–90	359,949	202,963[c]	94,931[c]	5,354,653	6.7
1899–1900	699,403	519,251[c]	110,797[c]	6,152,231	11.4
1909–10	1,115,398	915,061[c]	117,400[c]	7,220,298	15.4
1919–20	2,500,176	2,200,389[c]	213,920[c]	7,735,841	32.3
1929–30	4,804,255	4,399,422[c]	341,158[cd]	9,341,221	51.4
1939–40	7,123,009	6,635,337	487,672	9,720,419	73.3
1941–42	6,933,265	6,420,544	512,721	9,749,000	71.1
1943–44	6,030,617	5,584,656	445,961	9,449,000	63.8
1945–46	6,237,133	5,664,528	572,605	9,056,000	68.9
1947–48	6,305,168	5,675,937	629,231	8,841,000	71.3
1949–50	6,453,009	5,757,810	695,199	8,404,768	76.8
1951–52	6,596,351	5,917,384	678,967	8,516,000	77.5
1953–54	7,108,973	6,330,565	778,408	8,861,000	80.2
1955–56	7,774,975	6,917,790	857,185	9,207,000	84.4
1957–58	8,869,186	7,905,469	963,717	10,139,000	87.5
1959–60	9,599,810	8,531,454	1,068,356	11,154,879	86.1
1961–62	10,768,972	9,616,755	1,152,217	12,046,000	89.4
Fall 1963	12,255,496	10,935,536	1,319,960	13,492,000	90.8
Fall 1965	13,020,823	11,657,808	1,363,015	14,145,000	92.1
Fall 1969	14,418,301	13,084,301	1,334,000[e]	15,550,000	92.7
Fall 1971	15,226,000	13,886,000	1,340,000[e]	16,279,000	93.5
Fall 1973	15,427,000	14,142,000	1,285,000[e]	16,743,000	92.1
Fall 1974[f]	15,447,000	14,207,000	1,240,000[e]	16,876,000	91.5

[a] Unless otherwise indicated, includes enrollment in subcollegiate departments of institutions of higher education and in residential schools for exceptional children. Beginning in 1949–50, also includes federal schools.

[b] Includes all persons residing in the United States, but excludes armed forces overseas. Data from the decennial censuses have been used when appropriate. Other figures are Bureau of the Census estimates as of July 1 preceding the opening of the school year.

[c] Excludes enrollment in subcollegiate departments of institutions of higher education and in residential schools for exceptional children.

[d] Data for 1927–28.

[e] Estimated.

[f] Preliminary data.

NOTE: Beginning in 1959–60, includes Alaska and Hawaii.

SOURCES: U.S. Department of Health, Education, and Welfare, National Center for Education Statistics, *Statistics of State School Systems; Statistics of Public Elementary and Secondary Day Schools; Statistics of Nonpublic Elementary and Secondary Schools;* and unpublished data.

From W. Vance Grant and C. George Lind, *Digest of Educational Statistics,* 1975 ed., National Center for Education Statistics, U.S. Department of Health, Education, and Welfare, U.S. Government Printing Office, Washington, D.C., 1976, p. 37.

Normal schools widened their focus. Earlier in the nineteenth century, normal schools were created to develop the craft of management of *elementary* school classrooms. The first private normal school opened in 1823; the first state-supported normal school opened in Massachusetts in 1839. Normal schools grew rapidly, with the support of such educational leaders as Henry Barnard and Horace Mann. They replaced the former dependence on academies for elementary school teacher training. At the close of the nineteenth century, normal schools embraced within their programs the training of secondary school teachers.

As Borrowman has pointed out: "By 1900 the normal school and liberal arts traditions were coming together in the university."[6] The American university stressed research and professional education. Teacher education also became a part of university education. In the new twentieth century the education of secondary school teachers was carried on through the programs of liberal arts colleges, normal schools, and universities.

The growth of the high school and the new hospitality in higher education to the professional education of teachers heralded the end of the century of the secondary school teacher without professional preparation for his or her post. The new developments marked the beginning of a century in which the secondary school teacher was to be educated both through liberal arts programs and through professional studies.

THE RESPONSIBILITIES OF SECONDARY SCHOOL TEACHERS

Many twentieth-century secondary school teachers aspired to be professionals and to be regarded by their communities as such. But there were blocks in their way. For a vocation to be a profession, it must demonstrate several characteristics:

1. A profession must provide a unique and essential social service. Most people agree that the education of the young is an essential service, but some do not regard it as unique. They believe that many people, in addition to licensed teachers, can teach effectively.

2. A profession uses and emphasizes intellectual techniques in doing its work. But programs of some of the normal schools attempted to reduce education to methodology and management and to minimize the use of intellectual techniques. Some teachers saw themselves simply as classroom "mechanics" who had no need for theory.

3. A profession requires a long period of specialized training. But liberal arts colleges often crammed education courses into a senior year in which teacher education vied for a place with ongoing liberal arts programs. In periods of scarcity of teachers (unlike the late 1970s), teachers were often employed with emergency, substandard, conditional accreditation.

---

[6] Borrowman, *Teacher Education*, p. 25.

4. A profession requires professional autonomy. But many teachers are not participants in the basic decisions about the content and methodology of their teaching. Teachers often do not have freedom to exercise their own judgment in the classroom or with respect to the regulation of the profession.

5. Practitioners of a profession accept broad personal responsibility for their judgments and performances within the perimeters of professional autonomy. But some educators think that the social forces of the family, society in general, and the complex administration of schools are so overpowering that teachers cannot be held responsible for the outcome of their work.

6. A profession emphasizes service rather than economic gain. But teachers sometimes comment critically that some teachers seem to work simply for pay rather than for service.

7. A profession has its own self-governing organization. Teaching does have increasingly powerful organizations: the National Education Association (NEA) and the American Federation of Teachers (AFT). But competition between the two organizations continues and a unified professional impact by teachers is thereby reduced.

8. A profession has a code of ethics. The NEA has a code of ethics of the education profession and the AFT has a bill of rights. But some teachers are not familiar with them and few violators are called to account.[7]

Despite the blocks, some argue that education has achieved or is approaching the status of a profession. Look again at the eight characteristics of a profession. The following persuasive arguments can be made: (1) Laypersons are not qualified to teach the complex subjects of the contemporary high school curriculum. (2) The normal schools have vanished; the colleges and universities now emphasize intellectual techniques in programs of teacher education. (3) Contemporary colleges and universities are offering long periods of specialized training. State certification agencies are requiring longer periods of specialized training. (4) Many teachers are highly autonomous within their classrooms. Many work through their organizations for more autonomy for the profession as a whole. (5) Many teachers accept personal responsibility for their judgments and acts. They are willing to accept accountability for their teaching, if accountability proponents will recognize that out-of-school experience also heavily influences student learning. (6) The lengths to which many educators go in providing help to students is a point of pride in the profession. (7) Teacher organizations are becoming increasingly active in fostering teacher participation in the governance process. Teachers are increasingly participating in

---

[7] The eight characteristics are adapted from Myron Lieberman, *Education as a Profession,* Prentice-Hall, Englewood Cliffs, N.J., 1956, pp. 2–6.

matters of curriculum, certification, and innovation, in addition to improvement of salaries and working conditions. Progress toward an NEA-AFT merger waxes and wanes. (8) Codes of ethics are being publicized and there have been applications of the codes to concrete cases.

Americans will continue to debate the extent to which secondary school teaching is a profession. That the secondary school educator is struggling toward a greater degree of professionalism is apparent. That the secondary school teacher has achieved professionalism to a substantial degree but not completely seems a reasonable conclusion as of today.

To be an effective professional teacher is especially difficult in some urban areas of the United States today. Through press and television, the problems of our big cities are reported—inadequate finances, unemployment, decaying housing, overcrowding, drug abuse, and rampant crime. Such problems necessarily spill over into schools and heavily influence the quality of secondary education. It is one thing to teach in an environment in which a school is well financed, in which parents are employed and young people have a promising prospect of employment, in which families live in adequate housing, in which there is space for recreation and the exercise of privacy, in which drug abuse is only occasionally encountered, and in which crime is under control. It is quite another thing to teach in an environment in which many of these factors are not present.

In many urban areas, threats of municipal bankruptcy have drastically reduced necessary school services. The mayors of many large U.S. cities are urgently asking President Carter's administration for federal government help with financial crises.

Unemployment hits the young people of inner-city areas especially hard. Low-income families in general and disadvantaged members of minority groups in particular have a disproportionate share of the burden of unemployment. Nationally, unemployment was 7.9 percent when President Jimmy Carter assumed office in 1977. However, unemployment among blacks was 15.5 percent in August 1977. Unemployment among Mexican-Americans was 11.5 percent in 1976.[8] Unemployment among black and Mexican-American inner-city young people was still higher. In August 1977 the unemployment rate for black teen-agers was over 40 percent.

Home conditions are not conducive to productive study by secondary school students of the inner cities. Housing is often bad; privacy is wanting; recreation takes the form of hanging out in the streets. Escape through drugs is too readily available; economic success seems to be reserved for drug pushers and pimps. Crime moves readily from the streets into the schools in the form of extortion, robbery, and vandalism (see Figure 11.1).

---

[8] "Hispanics' Wages Trail Whites', Pass Blacks', Study Says," *Washington Post*, December 10, 1976, p. A10.

FIGURE 11.1 *Student Violence as Viewed by Teachers. Top: Teachers reported an increase in personal attack and property damage since 1973 in their replies to the question: "Have you as a teacher been physically attacked or have you had your personal property maliciously damaged by a student this school year?" Bottom: A growing percentage of teachers believe that student violence is a problem in schools, as is shown in their answers to the question: "Generally is student violence a problem in your school?"*

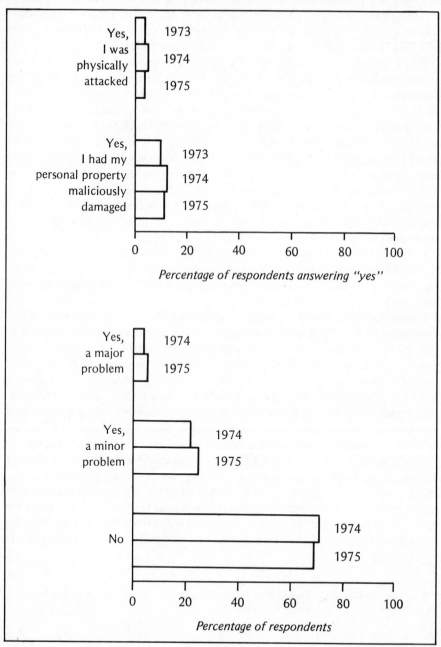

SOURCE: *The Condition of Education*, U.S. Government Printing Office, Washington, D.C., 1976, p. 56.

A Senate subcommittee has reported graphically on how these problems affect the schools. An Associated Press dispatch reports:

The primary task for a growing number of students and teachers is self-preservation rather than education, a Senate subcommittee report on school violence said Friday.

Sen Birch Bayh (D-Ind.), said in releasing the report that an estimated $600 million is spent each year as a result of vandalism in the schools. This is more money than was spent for textbooks in 1972, he said, and is enough to hire 50,000 more teachers.

"Even more shocking, however, is the 70,000 serious physical assaults on teachers and the literally hundreds of thousands of assaults on students perpetrated in our schools annually," he said.[9]

Under such adverse conditions, it is remarkable that in inner-city schools so many teachers have persisted and achieved some degree of success. Inner-city schools have launched programs on behalf of disadvantaged young people. They have developed vocational education programs. Sometimes they have departed from the traditional curriculum and have focused their programs on the real problems of young people in their current surroundings.

SECONDARY SCHOOL TEACHERS AND POWER

While aspiring to professional status and coping with the teaching problems that have accompanied America's transition from a rural to an essentially urban nation, secondary school teachers have simultaneously been engaged in economic struggles to gain better salaries, fringe benefits, and working conditions. The oldest and largest of the teacher organizations, the National Education Association, was organized in 1857. By 1976 it had 1.3 million members. The NEA has long been devoted to fostering teaching as a profession, as well as to advancing the economic welfare of teachers. The newer and smaller organization is the American Federation of Teachers, organized in 1916. By 1976 it had over 420,000 members, up 100 percent from 1970.[10] From the beginning, the AFT, a part of the labor movement, put its emphasis upon the economic welfare of teachers.

As their organizations grew, the power of teachers increased. Today the NEA, by virtue of its size, can make its voice heard on behalf of teachers in the halls of state legislatures and Congress. For the first time in its history, the NEA in 1976 endorsed a presidential candidate, Jimmy Carter. The

---

[9] "Unsafe—Violence Reports Are an Education," *The Commercial Appeal*, Memphis, February 26, 1977, p. 12.
[10] James Browne, "Power Politics for Teachers, Modern Style," *Phi Delta Kappan*, October 1976, p. 163.

AFT, by virtue of its affiliation with organized labor, speaks for teachers as an integral component of organized labor's advocacy. State and federal legislators take into careful account the proposals of labor. The AFT also endorsed the Democratic party candidate, Jimmy Carter, in the 1976 presidential campaign. Leaders of teacher organizations attributed President Carter's election at least in part to teacher support. Critics of political endorsements by educational organizations claimed that the NEA and AFT cannot "deliver" teacher votes since the well educated are influenced by a wider range of campaign issues than economic welfare alone.

Yet the long-run potential power inherent in the millions of teachers in the United States is tremendous. Myron Lieberman has dramatized this power in a *Saturday Review* article in which he envisioned a future Democratic party convention in which the delegates who were teachers played a strategic part in bringing about the election of an education-oriented candidate. In Lieberman's scenario the nominee went on to achieve the presidency of the United States with the help of a political education fund raised by teacher organizations.[11]

Contemporary secondary school teachers are much more vigorous and aggressive in working for higher salaries and improvements in working conditions than their predecessors were. Whether they are members of the NEA or the AFT, they often engage in bargaining through representatives who sit at the conference table with governing bodies of school districts. According to a 1976 National School Boards Association member survey, two thirds of the nation's school boards engage in collective bargaining with teacher unions. Agreements are reached as to salary schedules and working conditions. In extreme cases, when agreement cannot be achieved, today's teachers, whether AFT or NEA members, sometimes strike (see Figure 11.2).

There is a continuing controversy over the right of teachers as public employees to strike. The conflict over collective bargaining legislation rages at the state level in the late 1970s. However, a new dimension in the controversy is the expansion of negotiation into areas formerly thought to be the province of school boards and administrators. Representatives of teacher organizations argue that under poor working conditions teachers cannot discharge their responsibilities effectively. Therefore, they contend, teachers should have a substantial voice through negotiation in determining reasonable sizes for their classes, the number and duration of teacher meetings held after regular classroom hours, the committees to which they may be legitimately assigned, and other matters. Furthermore, teachers as trained professionals should have an effective voice in determining the content and methods used in the school curriculum.

Some opponents of teachers having a substantial say on such matters

---

[11] Myron Lieberman, "The Union Merger Movement: Will 3,500,000 Teachers Put It All Together?" *Saturday Review*, June 24, 1972, pp. 50-51.

FIGURE 11.2 *Teacher Involvement in Work Stoppage.* *Teacher involvement in work stoppages reached a high of 145,000 teachers in 1968.*

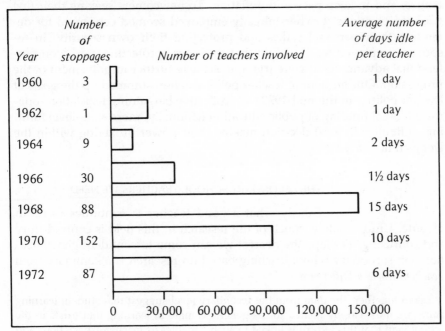

Year	Number of stoppages	Number of teachers involved	Average number of days idle per teacher
1960	3		1 day
1962	1		1 day
1964	9		2 days
1966	30		1½ days
1968	88		15 days
1970	152		10 days
1972	87		6 days

0   30,000   60,000   90,000   120,000   150,000

SOURCE: *The Condition of Education,* U.S. Government Printing Office, Washington, D.C., 1976, p. 131.

take the position that such decisions properly belong exclusively to administrators. They reduce the problem to the question of who should properly exercise the power of decision.

However, a more reasonable objection is advanced by those who hold that administrators and teachers, instead of engaging in a power struggle, should be engaged in a cooperative effort on behalf of the education of students. This viewpoint recognizes that administrators once had arbitrary powers and does not recommend transferring comparable arbitrary power to teachers. Too many rules and regulations as to time of meetings, committee assignments, and other matters would, in this view, destroy needed teamwork and militate against good education. Although teachers should have a voice in curriculum decisions, giving total power to teachers might result in the defense of vested interests in obsolete subject matter or methodology. In such circumstances, it is argued, teaching would not be a profession but would resemble a trade marked by excessive rules and regulations.

The combination in the early 1970s of economic recession and decline in enrollment in educational institutions put teachers on the defensive with respect to the exercise of teacher power. Many struggles of the mid-1970s were attempts to hold what teachers had already gained, to maintain tenure, and to keep pace with inflation. To newcomers seeking their first teaching positions, teachers already employed seemed concerned for defending their personal stakes and protecting their own security. In response, employed teachers said that they were protecting hard-won professional advances and were trying to achieve further improvement of the profession. One student of teacher political action summed up the goals of teacher politics in the mid-1970s as "collective bargaining legislation, one-third federal funding of public education nationally, more state-level funding, influence in local decision making, and power brokering within the Democratic party."[12]

THE SECONDARY SCHOOL TEACHERS WE NEED

Exactly what a good teacher is continues to be in dispute. Unfortunately, much of the research in this field is contradictory and confusing. Perhaps the nearest we can come to confident generalizations on secondary school teaching based on research is a summary from *Teachers Make a Difference:*

> Taken together, the data from the secondary level suggest that student learning gains are most closely related to the general climate of learning that exists in the school, and that this in turn is linked to such variables as teacher expectations and teacher relationships with students. Affective teacher variables such as gaining student respect and forming good relationships with students appear to be particularly important.[13]

The following specifications as to good secondary school teachers should be regarded as the author's opinion rather than demonstrated fact.

In our opinion, good secondary school teachers are sensitive to the needs, problems, and aspirations of the young people they teach. They try to relate their teaching to the lives of the students. They try to motivate them. They work toward the encouragment of self-actualizing personalities. They have faith in the potential of students.

Good secondary school teachers are aware of social issues and problems. They are particularly alert to their effect upon the reactions and responses of students. They try to help students understand the broad social situation.

As to values, good secondary school teachers are committed to the democratic values of respect for individual personalities and working together for common purposes commonly arrived at. They believe in the

---

[12] Browne, "Power Politics for Teachers," p. 159.
[13] Thomas L. Good, Bruce J. Biddle, and Jere E. Brophy, *Teachers Make a Difference,* Holt, Rinehart and Winston, New York, 1975, p. 80.

exercise of intelligence and struggle to develop teaching situations in which students are required to think.

Good secondary school teachers are knowledgeable persons, so comfortable in their grasp of subject matter that they can adapt it to the understanding of the students. They can relate the areas that they know well as teachers to the necessarily more limited experiences of the learners.

Thus, the quest for a better personnel includes a quest for teachers who can combine sensitivity to the needs of individuals, social understanding, democratic value commitment, and mastery of knowledge.

If the teaching profession could achieve consensus on some such formulation, and if research could demonstrate that these qualities do have a significant impact on learning by the student, we would be in a better position than we are now to develop relevant teacher education and to hold teachers to a reasonable degree of accountability.

SOME FACTS ABOUT SECONDARY SCHOOL TEACHERS

If we assembled a composite picture of the American secondary school teacher, who would be the representative or "average" person? In 1977 the National Education Association, which reports on the status of the American public school teachers every five years, released its most recent survey updating data to 1975–76. In that year, 52.2 percent of secondary school teachers were male and 47.8 percent were female. The secondary school teacher was only slightly younger than the characteristic elementary school teacher; the average age of secondary school teachers was 36 and the average age of elementary school teachers was 37. The reported median years of teaching experience for high school teachers was eight years. Secondary school teachers worked a 36-hour week and the average hours a week devoted to teaching duties was 48. Our representative teacher averaged 180 days of classroom teaching.

As in the early 1970–71 survey 99 percent of secondary school teachers held a degree. For slightly more than half (53.8 percent) it was a bachelor's. However, the percentage of secondary school teachers who held a master's degree or a six-year diploma rose to 44.5 percent. As in the earlier survey, less than 1 percent held a doctoral degree.[14]

The salary of our representative secondary school teacher reached $12,800 in 1976. Even after taking inflation into account our representative teacher is substantially better off than his or her counterpart of twenty years earlier. Yet the fight against inflation is interminable and the struggle to achieve a salary comparable to the average American professional is apparently an endless one. (See Figure 11.3 and Table 11.3.)

---

[14] National Education Association Research, *Status of the American Public School Teacher, 1975–76*, National Education Association, Washington, D.C., 1977.

FIGURE 11.3 *Average Salaries of Instructional Staff. The average salaries of public elementary and secondary school teachers have declined in constant dollars recently.*

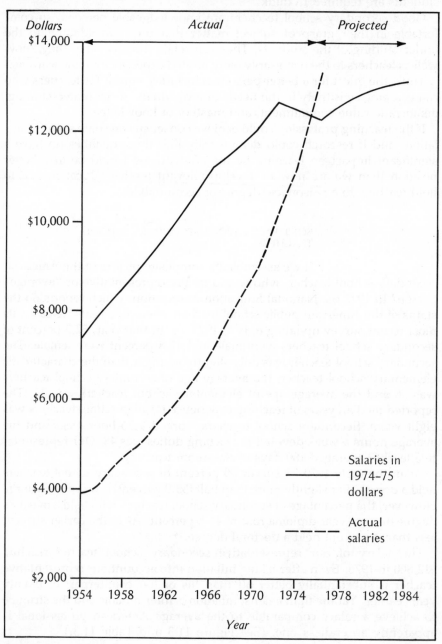

Source: *The Condition of Education,* U.S. Government Printing Office, Washington, D.C., 1976, p. 132.

TABLE 11.3 *Public elementary and secondary schools—average salary of classroom teachers, 1960 to 1976*

Schools classified by type of organization, rather than by grade-group; elementary includes kindergarten and secondary includes junior high schools

ITEM		1960	1965	1969	1970	1971	1972	1973	1974	1975	1976
Average salary, all teachers	$1,000	5.0	6.2	8.0	8.6	9.3	9.7	10.2	10.8	11.7	12.5
Elementary	$1,000	4.8	6.0	7.7	8.4	9.0	9.4	9.9	10.5	11.3	12.1
Index (1967 = 100)		72.7	90.4	116.6	127.0	136.2	142.3	149.1	158.7	170.6	183.2
Secondary	$1,000	5.3	6.5	8.2	8.9	9.6	10.0	10.5	11.1	12.0	12.8
Index (1967 = 100)		74.2	90.7	115.5	125.1	134.6	141.1	147.7	155.8	168.2	180.7
Percentage of teachers—											
Under $7,500		88.1[a]	81.8	49.5	36.6	24.7	20.3	14.9	8.9	(NA)[b]	(NA)
$7,500–$8,499			10.1	18.1	19.7	18.8	17.5	16.8	14.6	(NA)	(NA)
$8,500–$9,499		11.9[b]	5.5	13.4	14.4	15.6	16.5	16.0	15.6	(NA)	(NA)
$9,500–$11,499			2.6	14.6	19.1	21.9	22.6	24.7	28.1	(NA)	(NA)
$11,500 and over			—[d]	4.3	10.3	19.0	23.1	24.7	27.7	32.7	(NA)	(NA)

[a] Percentage under $6,500.
[b] Not available.
[c] Percentage $6,500 and over.
[d] Represents zero.

SOURCES: National Education Association, Research Division, Washington, D.C., *Estimates of School Statistics, 1975–76.* (Copyright © 1976 by the National Education Association. All rights reserved.)

From U.S. Bureau of the Census, *Statistical Abstract of the United States, 1976*, 97th ed., U.S. Government Printing Office, Washington, D.C., 1976, p. 134.

EVOLUTION OF SCHOOL BOARDS

From the very beginning of American history, communities in the New World delegated authority over education to selected community members. Small though the Massachusetts Bay Colony may have been by modern standards, the people of the settlement decided early that they had to delegate major responsibilities to "chosen men." The first law concerning education made in the New World in 1642 reads, in part:

This court, taking into consideration the great neglect of many parents and masters in training up their children in learning, and labor, and other employments that may be profitable to the Commonwealth, do hereupon order and decree, that in every town the chosen men appointed for managing the prudential affairs of the same shall henceforth stand charge with the care of the redress of this evil.[15]

The people of the colony meant literally that selected people whose respectability and responsibility the community recognized were to manage educational affairs. (The word *selectman* passed into the language and even now is used to describe "one of a board of town officers chosen annually in New England communities to manage local affairs.")

The early selectmen of New England often found themselves heavily burdened. Consequently, committees on school visitation were appointed. Such committees represented the selectmen. But the roles and responsibilities of the school committees grew larger. So Massachusetts in 1826 decided that school committees should be a separate governing body. Out of such a beginning in Massachusetts evolved the school board, sometimes called the school committee.

RESPONSIBILITIES OF SCHOOL BOARD MEMBERS

School boards usually consist of five or more members, most often elected directly by the people. School boards are occasionally appointed by public officers, such as the mayors of communities.

The school board works within the state laws on education and the regulations of the state education authority, usually a department of public instruction or of education. A school board determines policy rather than administers the schools. This means that the responsibility of a board is to determine educational goals and develop policies to carry them out. It appoints a superintendent of schools to administer the program and works with him or her to improve education.

A local school board plans plant facilities and obtains financial support,

---

[15] Laws of 1642, reprinted in *Records of the Governor and Company of the Massachusetts Bay,* William White, Boston, 1853, vol. 2, p. 6.

evaluates the program of the school district, attempts to keep the people of the district informed about the school, and cooperates with statewide efforts to improve education. In recent years, local school boards have negotiated agreements with teachers directly or through representatives of the board.

In the past century, as large cities emerged in America and the apparatus of education grew more complex, much responsibility for professional leadership moved to educators. Consequently, school boards made fewer professional decisions as to curricular policies. Instead, they concentrated more heavily on matters related to purchasing, acquisition of sites, and the building of schools. Unfortunately, corruption sometimes entered into contracts in the form of favoritism toward relatives or a readiness to perform special favors for friends. Municipal reform campaigns early in the twentieth century included crusades against school corruption and favoritism.

With the increase of the size of educational establishments, board members became more remote and less accessible to those who elected or appointed them. The distance between the people and their supposed representatives increased.

Large cities in particular encountered problems of imbalance in representation on school boards. Minority groups were underrepresented. In 1968 there were only twenty-five black school board members in the United States. In the 1960s and 1970s, ethnic groups have grown increasingly aware of the relationship between education and the economic position of ethnic group members. So demands for participation in educational policy making have steadily increased. In the period of civil rights ferment, school boards were often targets of criticism and their offices were the sites of sit-ins and sometimes of violence. The number of minority group members on boards of education increased in the 1970s. Currently, attempts to increase the number of women on school boards are underway; women have long been markedly underrepresented on school boards.

One response to the demand for greater participation was decentralization of schools in some of the larger cities. Decentralization involves the shifting of all or some responsibility for the work of a city board of education to smaller units, whether at the borough, district, or neighborhood level. A decentralized unit operates like a central board of education, but its proponents regard it as closer to the wants and wishes of the local citizenry. They regard decentralization as an extension of democracy in school affairs. They see the decentralized approach as another opportunity for ethnic group members to participate in board of education activities. Opponents believe that ethnic considerations too often outweigh professional considerations. They argue, for instance, that blacks may appoint blacks and whites may appoint whites without regard to seniority or professional skills. Opponents fear a return to the favoritism and corruption that reform movements fought in the early twentieth century.

Despite increased participation in policy making by citizens through decentralization and an increase in representation of minorities, women, and educators, school boards are still barely visible governing bodies. A Gallup poll found that 63 percent of adults could not mention one thing their local school board had done in the past year. Only 38 percent thought that school boards acted as representatives of the public. Only 42 percent thought that when disputes arose in school systems the school boards worked in the interest of students. Only half the adults polled knew that there was a difference between a school board and a school administration.[16]

A major responsibility of a school board is to see that money is available to finance the educational program. For many school boards of the middle and later 1970s, financing the schools has become their greatest problem. As large cities plunge deeper into debt, their school systems suffer. New York City's widely publicized financial problems of 1975 and 1976 resulted in substantial cutbacks in both school and library services. In December 1976 the Toledo schools temporarily closed for lack of funds. Some smaller school systems in Ohio, Connecticut, and Oregon also closed in late 1976. Many school systems are particularly vulnerable to financial stringency because they depend on favorable votes by their communities on proposed tax levies and bond issues. When members of the public feel financial pinches on their own personal budgets, they often vote "no" on support for schools.

Almost one half the total revenue receipts for public schools come from local sources (see Figure 11.4). Consequently, local boards of education often turn urgently to state and federal governments for additional funds. Experts in school finance usually recommend an increase in school funding through taxes raised by state and federal governments and a decrease in reliance on local property taxes. They point out that reliance on property taxes results in rich communities supporting their schools handsomely while poor communities find it hard to maintain minimum services. Consequently, equality of educational opportunity is denied many young people. Increasingly, the courts are lending a sympathetic ear to this argument.

SCHOOL BOARDS AND POWER

Most members of local school boards serve because of a genuine desire to foster good education in their communities; those motivated by selfishness or profit seeking are a minority. Yet serving on a school board is no way to achieve popularity. School board members often find that they are the targets of community members dedicated to their

---

[16] *Education USA,* March 31, 1975, p. 178.

FIGURE 11.4 *Expenditures of Elementary and Secondary Schools by Source. Total expenditures of elementary and secondary schools were projected to reach an estimated $81.9 billion in 1976–77. Of this total, about 8 percent was to come from federal sources, 38 percent from state sources, 42 percent from local sources, and 11 percent from other sources.*

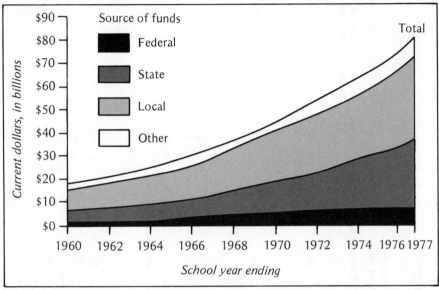

SOURCE: Mary A. Golladay, ed., *The Condition of Education*, U.S. Government Printing Office, Washington, D.C., 1977, p. 42 (public and nonpublic schools included in Figure 11.4).

own conceptions of good education, teachers active in the struggle for better salaries and working conditions, and students charging infringement on student rights. The eternal search by school boards for financial support for schools alienates many community members—obviously, no one enjoys paying taxes.

Despite their unpopularity, school boards have traditionally exercised considerable power because of their role and responsibilities. Now, however, some of that power is ebbing. Though the legal responsibilities of boards remain the same, limitations on their use of powers has increased. Militant community groups express their views through the mass media or in person in school board meetings. They may campaign for back to basics or for greater humanism in education. They may claim discrimination against minorities or the majority. They may represent taxpayers concerned for economies or support-the-schools groups. They may be opponents of busing to desegregate schools or advocates of broader programs of integration. Sometimes groups form to protest a specific decision, such as the location of the school or inclusion of a swimming pool in school facilities; once the fight is over, such groups often dissolve with equal abruptness. In many communities, school boards can no longer decide

TABLE 11.4 *How board members and administrators see things (in percent)*

PROPOSITION	SCHOOL PEOPLE (BOARD MEMBERS AND ADMINISTRATORS)		SCHOOL BOARD MEMBERS		SCHOOL ADMINISTRATORS		IT'S AN ISSUE IN MY DISTRICT		
	Support	Oppose	Support	Oppose	Support	Oppose	School people	Board members	Superintendents
1. Merit pay for teachers and administrators	83	17	85	15	75	25	12	13	4
2. A public education for all handicapped children, regardless of expense	80	20	80	20	82	18	9	10	7
3. More emphasis on teaching traditional subjects, reading and math	93	7	93	7	87	13	9	9	2
4. Student's right to practice individual freedoms in school setting	39	61	50	50	43	57	6	7	5.5
5. A staff for school boards (other than superintendent and his staff)	32	68	34	66	10	90	2	2	0
6. Reducing class size	66	34	68	32	73	27	10	10	7
7. Citizen committees to advise boards	69	31	71	29	63	37	8	8	4
8. Compulsory schooling ending at age 14 rather than 16 or 18	24	76	23	77	50	50	0.3	1	0

9	Tighter discipline in the schools even if expression of students rights must be curtailed	67	33	69	31	76	24	7	7	4
10	More emphasis on open education, schools without walls	47	53	48	52	47	53	7	7	4
11	Year-round schooling	61	39	60	40	56	44	5	5	0
12	Making principals a more integral part of the district's management team	94	6	95	5	96	4	8	8	0
13	More school board involvement in curriculum matters	83	17	84	16	77	23	8	9	2
14	Streaking	19	81	25	75	8	92	5	4	7
15	Use of outside educational consultants by local districts	71	29	69	31	85	15	4	4	2
16	Giving "special consideration" to minority applicants for administrative and teaching jobs	28	72	31	69	22	78	7	5.5	9
17	Spending whatever money necessary to ensure safe school buses	81	19	79	21	88	12	2	1	2
18	President Nixon	56	44	50	50	64	36	3	2	4
19	Teaching metrics in the schools	88	12	90	10	85	15	2	2	5.5

Table 11.4 continued

TABLE 11.4 *continued*

PROPOSITION	SCHOOL PEOPLE (BOARD MEMBERS AND ADMINISTRATORS)		SCHOOL BOARD MEMBERS		SCHOOL ADMINISTRATORS		IT'S AN ISSUE IN MY DISTRICT		
	Support	Oppose	Support	Oppose	Support	Oppose	School people	Board members	Superintendents
20. More efficient methods for conducting board meetings	93	7	95	5	98	2	4	3	2
21. Neutral party's evaluation in board-superintendent relationships	53	47	55	45	54	46	3	4	0
22. Seek pupil opinion in board policy areas such as curriculum, discipline, etc.	74	26	76	24	69	31	5	5	4

SOURCE: *American School Board Journal* 161 (August 1974), 32. Copyright © National School Boards Association. Reprinted with permission.

unilaterally, without negotiation, upon the salaries and working conditions of teachers. Even supervisory staff members, who formerly accepted board designation of their salaries, are considering following the example set by some of their colleagues by entering into collective bargaining. Some illustrations of the way that school board members see things are detailed in Table 11.4.

THE SCHOOL BOARD MEMBERS WE NEED

School board members should be widely representative of the community. Not only should they reflect the diversity of ethnic groups, they should also reflect income distributions and social-class levels. Historically, school board membership has been the province of well-educated business and professional people of the community who were understandably concerned for the development of education. But the result was overrepresentation of lawyers, doctors, businesspeople, and similar affluent influentials. Underrepresented were labor union members, unpropertied farm workers, and other low- or middle-income Americans. However, a 1976 survey of fifty-one of the nation's largest school districts by the National School Boards Association shows that there are half as many attorneys and five times as many professional educators on boards in 1976 than there were one decade ago. With more balanced representation of all social-class groups, school boards would be inclined to view educational needs in a broader perspective. Members would be more inclined to see education as an investment in people and less inclined to conceive their mission as holding down taxes, regardless of demonstrated school problems or documented school needs.

Above all, the school board member we need is the person who works on behalf of the children and youth of the community. The standard by which a school board member should be appraised is whether his or her highest priority is the welfare of young people. Their age and inexperience make it hard for young people, even senior high school students, to plead their case for a high-quality education or to act effectively on their own behalf. The school board member has the opportunity to represent these most important clients. The simple fact is that elementary and secondary education exists to help the young.

This does not mean that the school board member has no responsibility or role in relation to the community as a whole, or to administrators or teachers. A board member has many such relationships and roles as he or she develops policies taking into account community needs, encouraging program development by administrators, and recognizing the legitimate economic needs of teachers. But all board activities should be undertaken with the goal in mind of improved education of young people.

EVOLUTION OF SECONDARY SCHOOL PRINCIPALS

The role of the administration of a school system is to carry out the policies established by the board. The chief executive officer of the board, the superintendent of schools, has the responsibility of preparing regulations and instructing employees directly or through delegated subordinates. The superintendent and staff prepare a budget, spend within the appropriations approved by the board, and recommend candidates for employment. They develop and administer a program of supervision and provide professional leadership for the program. Both superintendent and staff must depend heavily upon the administrators of the individual schools in the school system.

The key administrator in an American secondary school is the principal. He or she (although usually it is *he*) is, of course, responsible to the superintendent of schools of the entire system. However, the superintendent is not a completely free agent, though skeptical teachers may charge some superintendents with behaving as though they were. All who are employed within a public school system are expected to work within a framework of policy established by the board of education. Beyond the board, the state legislature is the controlling authority.

The first secondary school principals in America were called headmasters. In their Latin grammar schools and their academies, they were influential men. Before becoming headmasters they were schoolmasters and after their appointments most of them continued to teach. Their schools were small, and elaborate administrative procedures were not needed. If the headmaster taught effectively and maintained discipline in his school, he was regarded as a success. The early headmaster was expected to practice model behavior and not engage in "wanton dalliances and unseemly behavior with women, [nor to be] a follower of vain, gaudy fashions of apparel, a papist, a wearer of long curled hair, a puffer of tobacco, or addicted to dicing, carding, or other unlawful games." [17] Save for the requirement that he not be a "papist," a derogatory term for a Roman Catholic, the same expectations are not uncommon today!

The headmaster influenced education. Historically, this figure appeared on the American scene before the elementary school principal and even before the superintendent of schools. In many nineteenth-century American communities the headmaster (and later the nonteaching principal) ran the show independently. The early superintendents of schools had no authority over secondary schools. Sometimes the secondary school principal reported directly to the board of education. As might be expected,

---

[17] Forest C. Ensign, "Evolution of the High School Principalship," *The School Review* 31 (March 1923), 184.

under such conditions superintendents and high school principals some-times clashed. Operating on the headmaster model, the high school prin-cipal often regarded the high school as a personal domain. But, in time, the scope of the emerging high school made the headmaster model obsolete. Yet even today you may encounter a high school principal behaving like a headmaster.

The growth of the high school in size and number, with attendant widened scope and increased complexity, has resulted in administrative teams in both the central office of the school system and in the individual secondary school. The central office staff came to include not only assistant superintendents and various directors but supervisors as well. The respon-sibility of the supervisor is to exercise educational leadership so that teachers will grow in effectiveness, productivity, and general competency. Supervisors necessarily have to work closely with teachers within the schools. Consequently, the responsibilities of the principal and those of the supervisors, who often specialize in a subject or broad field, overlap and sometimes result in conflict.

Teams were also required within individual secondary schools. Team members include the principal's chief aide, usually called an assistant principal, dean, vice-principal, or administrative assistant. Large schools also necessitated department heads. Clerical help supported the team.

RESPONSIBILITIES OF SECONDARY SCHOOL PRINCIPALS

Contemporary secondary school principals are pulled in many directions. They are responsible for discipline, are expected to know and counsel students, have the responsibility for organizing the school schedule, must supervise the instructional program, must appraise the work of teachers, must manage the building, should supervise the development of the program of instruction. Their supervisory respon-sibilities include not only teachers but members of the custodial and food service staff. They stand between the teachers and the central offices of the superintendent. They are expected to be professional leaders. Obviously, this is no easy task. It is a jack-of-all-trades role, and few people are capable of filling it. And, in an age of specialization, the jack-of-all-trades concept of the principalship should yield to a better utilization of the individual's training and experience.

Yet these multiple responsibilities must be carried out by the numerous principals and assistant principals that staff our schools. So contemporary secondary school principals must assume new roles as executives, mana-gers, and coordinators of the educational enterprise. They must learn to delegate responsibility rather than vainly attempting to attend to all details themselves. Communities, in turn, must learn that a variety of personnel are necessary in the contemporary high school (see Table 11.5). J. Lloyd

TABLE 11.5 *Instructional staff: Estimated number and percentage distributions of full-time public school professional employees, by sex, 1972–73*

POSITION	NUMBER OF PERSONS			PERCENTAGE DISTRIBUTION		
	Total	Men	Women	Total	Men	Women
1	2	3	4	5	6	7
Instructional staff						
Teachers	2,110,368	709,084	1,401,284	100.0	33.6	66.4
Principals:						
Elementary (including teaching principals)	48,196	38,750	9,446	100.0	80.4	19.6
Junior high	9,374	9,102	272	100.0	97.1	2.9
Senior high	15,827	15,605	222	100.0	98.6	1.4
Total principals	73,397	63,457	9,940	100.0	86.5	13.5
Assistant principals:						
Elementary	6,483	4,486	1,997	100.0	69.2	30.8
Junior high	7,817	7,223	594	100.0	92.4	7.6
Senior high	13,289	12,439	850	100.0	93.6	6.4
Total assistant principals	27,589	24,148	3,441	100.0	87.5	12.5

Other instructional staff:					
School librarians	40,540	3,324	37,216	100.0	8.2	91.8
Counselors	49,770	26,378	23,392	100.0	53.0	47.0
School nurses	17,074	239	16,835	100.0	1.4	98.6
Other[a]	33,691	16,812	16,879	100.0	49.9	50.1
Total other instructional staff	141,075	46,753	94,322	100.0	33.1	66.9
Total instructional staff	2,352,429	843,442	1,508,987	100.0	35.9	64.1
Central-office administrators					
Superintendents	13,037	12,972	65	100.0	99.9	0.1
Deputy and associate superintendents	853	800	53	100.0	93.8	6.2
Assistant superintendents	5,337	5,054	283	100.0	94.7	5.3
Other central-office administrators[b]	48,488	31,614	16,874	100.0	65.0	35.0
Total central-office administrators	67,715	50,440	17,275	100.0	74.4	25.6
Total full-time professional employees	2,420,144	893,882	1,526,262	100.0	37.2	62.8

[a] Includes heads of departments, social workers, visiting teachers, psychologists, and psychometrists.
[b] Includes central-office administrator for General Administration, Finance and School Plant, Pupil Personnel Services, Instruction Administration, and Special Subject areas.

SOURCES: National Education Association, Research Division, *26th Biennial Salary and Staff Survey of Public-School Professional Personnel, 1972–73* (Washington, D.C.: NEA, 1973). Copyright © 1973 by the National Education Association. All rights reserved. Reprinted with permission.

Trump and Gordon F. Vars believe that large high schools in particular should move toward a reallocation of responsibilities:

The principal needs to spend three-fourths of his or her time on instruction and one-fourth in general supervision of other staff persons. Assistant principals should spend all of their time working with teachers and students on the improvement of instruction. There should be one such assistant principal for each 1,000 students in a school or major fraction of that figure.

Other functions are performed by four persons: the building administrator, the external relations director, the personnel administrator, and the activities director. These positions would be full-time in a school of 2,000 pupils; in a school one-half that size two full-time persons would perform the tasks indicated here. The *building administrator* greets visitors, sees salesmen, looks after the condition of the building, and the like. The *external relations director* handles school finances and public relations, working with various individuals and groups in the community as well as with the central office, the state education department, regional accrediting agencies, and other external bodies. The *personnel administrator* works with juvenile and welfare agencies in the community, supervises the general program for dealing with the students and staff, and performs related functions. The *activities director* is responsible for all of the entertainment and athletic programs of the school as well as the varied program of extracurricular activities.[18]

SECONDARY SCHOOL PRINCIPALS AND POWER

Despite their multiple responsibilities, secondary school principals find themselves caught in a power squeeze among contending forces: students, teachers, community members, superintendents, and school boards. They are expected to live by the policies of the school board and to carry through the implementation of policies planned by the superintendent and the central staff. They are also expected to represent the best interest of students, teachers, and immediate neighborhood. As Goldhammer and Becker describe it, the principal is a

man caught in the middle. His position is uncertain and ambiguous. On the one hand he is supposed to speak for his school, his teachers, pupils, and neighborhood, hoping to achieve for them the resources essential for providing the best possible . . . education. On the other hand, he is supposed to represent the school board and the central office and enforce their policies.[19]

Moreover, principals' relationships with these groups are changing. Although principals may want to regard themselves as allied with their teachers, teachers may regard principals as adversaries who are part of the

---

[18] J. Lloyd Trump and Gordon F. Vars, "How Should Learning Be Organized?" *Issues in Secondary Education*, pp. 228–229.

[19] Ray Bass, Jr., "The Case for Keeping Your Principal Out of the Collective Bargaining Brawl," *American School Board Journal*, June 1973, p. 36, quoting Goldhammer and Becker.

administrative team. Although principals may regard themselves as administrators dedicated to implementing boards' policies and the superintendents' programs, boards and the superintendents may regard them as overly solicitous for the welfare of their particular secondary school and overly identified with their particular students, teachers, and parents. However, the newest and most significant shift in relationships is the one that has occurred in principals' relationships with students.

Until recently, a principal's role in relationship to students was similar to that of the captain of a ship. The principal was in unquestioned command. However, captains have been known to become tyrants and this sometimes happened in the case of officious principals.

Even excesses by principals have been regarded by the courts as an exercise of the parental function by schools in the absence of a young person's parents. When cases reached the courts, judges often ruled that principals and teachers were within their right in acting *in loco parentis* when they disciplined students, searched lockers, enforced dress codes, or suspended students without a hearing. Student protests against such practices grew in the unruly 1960s.

A turning point in court interpretation came with the Gault case of 1967. This case challenged legal procedures in Arizona whereby a child could be declared delinquent. The Supreme Court ruled that the procedures used deprived the child of his liberty and that constitutional guarantees of due process applied in this case. However, the major decision came in a case involving five Des Moines, Iowa, students who wore black armbands to school as part of a Vietnam War protest and thus violated a district administrative policy. In *Tinker v. Des Moines Independent Community School District,* the Supreme Court said:

First Amendment rights, applied in light of this special characteristic of the school environment, are available to teachers and students. It can hardly be argued that either students or teachers shed their constitutional rights to freedom of speech or expression at the schoolhouse gate.[20]

In effect, the legal concept of due process of law prevailed over *in loco parentis.*

A further series of cases extended the precedent set by *Tinker* v. *Des Moines.* The end result was that principals found themselves unable to establish arbitrary dress codes or to search lockers or to suspend at will. Legal safeguards, such as the necessity for hearings, circumscribe the principal's power. As students gained power, principals tended to lose it.

Simultaneously, teachers gained power through the development of collective negotiations. A balanced portrayal of the pro and con of this development is contributed by David C. Smith, who says that

---

[20] U.S. Supreme Court, United States Reports, October Term, 1968, *Tinker* v. *Des Moines Independent Community School District,* 393, p. 503.

collective negotiations contribute to an increasing erosion of the human judgment that a principal must exercise in the administration of the school. On the one hand, no one mourns the passing of the building tyrant. On the other hand, it makes sensitive and more effective administration nearly impossible, while it makes bureaucratic administration more comfortable.[21]

Morris L. Cogan sums up the forces that today's principal must face. He says that principals

must work within an unparelleled array of imperative demands: militant and often irreconcilable parent groups, rioting students, merciless budget cuts, unionized teachers, local control, rapid shifts in the socioeconomic character of school neighborhoods, to name a few. Many principals could readily extend this list *ad infinitum*.[22]

One response by some principals has been to join the unionization movement. By 1975 there were 1,276 administrator/supervisory unions in twenty-four states. Only a small percentage of them were affiliated with a national organization of supervisory unions. Fifty-two of these unions created the American Federation of School Administrators (AFSA) of the AFL-CIO.[23] Although the unionization movement among middle-management school personnel is young, it is growing. Almost half the respondents to a 1976 National Association of Secondary School Principals membership survey favor collective bargaining by principals with the school boards for salaries and working conditions. Three principals in ten directly oppose it, and the other quarter are still undecided. So new teachers may find that not only are their teaching colleagues unionized, their principal may also have taken this course as a way of increasing salary and power.

THE SECONDARY SCHOOL PRINCIPALS WE NEED

What is the major responsibility of the secondary school principal? The constant effort of the contemporary principal should be to improve the teaching and learning in the school.

An effective modern principal does this by helping to make various resources available to teachers who need them in the teaching-learning process. In an age of multiple media, this involves not simply a distribution of textbooks and paper at the opening of the school year; it means making available to teachers, and thus to learners, films, television cassettes, buses

---

[21] David C. Smith, "Professional Negotiations—the Impact of Negotiations on Instruction," *National Elementary Principal*, May 1974, p. 68.
[22] Morris L. Cogan, "The Principal and Supervision," *National Elementary Principal*, May 1974, p. 21.
[23] Bruce S. Cooper, "Collective Bargaining Comes to School Middle Management," *Phi Delta Kappan*, October 1976, pp. 202–204.

for trips, and other resources. It involves administrative readiness to develop and dip into a contingency fund for material that is crucial to learning activity but the need for which was impossible to predict long in advance. It involves helping a faculty to learn about education in a wider world than the teacher's own classroom through visits to other schools, conferences, and meetings.

The modern secondary school principal should not be content to be a swift respondent to teacher-student needs alone. The principal we need in American schools is, in addition, a leader. Principals should be sources of ideas, encouraging—indeed, daring—teachers to adopt needed new content, to vary their methodologies, to be creative and innovative in instruction. Through reading, visiting, conferring, and attending meetings, principals should acquaint the faculty with the best of old and new approaches to teaching and learning that are currently being discussed.

A good principal is infectious. He or she can, indeed, infect the total school environment with the educational diseases of passivity, pessimism, and indifference, or with the willingness to try new things, a cordial climate of human relations, a reasoned hopefulness, a welcoming of the new day. But to be infectious in the interest of improved teaching and learning, the principal must be relieved of the burden of routine, the expectation that he or she will be a jack-of-all trades, and the possessive attitude that marked a headmaster. He or she must move effectively into the classes and meeting rooms of the building, into the work and lives of the teachers, and into the organizations and structure of the community.

COMMUNITY MEMBERS

EVOLUTION OF COMMUNITY PARTICIPATION

Too often when we think of the staff of a school we take into account teachers, administrators, a variety of custodial, clerical, and food staff workers—and we stop there. If we do, we leave out of consideration an important ingredient in educational staffing that is currently expanding steadily. Men and women from the community are this forgotten element in staffing.

Community members play a dual role in education. Their primary role is that they are the owners of the public schools! The right to build, alter, or even abolish schools and to shape their policies is held by the citizenry of the nation. In a democracy the schools belong to the people as a whole. A National Conference on Parent Involvement held in California in 1976 pointed out that parent participation and teacher power were on a collision course triggered by the teacher collective bargaining movement that is now reaching beyond wages and working conditions and into territory that many parents believe is at least partially theirs. The conference stressed that parents should have a say in student discipline, curriculum, and general educational policies. Conference participants thought that parents should be involved in collective bargaining.[24]

In a second role, many community members help by participating in the day-by-day programs of the schools; such participation will in all likelihood increase further. Participation by community members in the education of young people is increasing. A combination of circumstances accounts for this development. For one thing, as education grows more complex and specialized it follows the model of other professions, such as medicine, in employing a variety of helpers and facilitators. Too, as community members play a wider role in policy making, some of them see opportunities for actual participation in the daily work of the schools. In addition, the growth of action-learning creates new relationships between students and adult members of the community who have formerly been uninvolved in the education of young people (see Figure 11.5).

FIGURE 11.5   *Teachers, Community Participants, and Students Plan Together.*

[24] "Parents vs. Teachers: Something's Got to Give," *Education USA*, December 6, 1976, p. 108.

Some community helpers work for pay. In the contemporary secondary school there are many duties other than teaching which community helpers can readily assume. They include supervision of the lunch room, study halls, corridors, and recreation areas; secretarial assistance, help in grading objective examinations, and aid with miscellaneous paperwork; preparing instructional resources and helping to create an attractive classroom environment. Sometimes the work of paid helpers includes offering remedial instruction to small groups or individuals. And, sadly enough, in an era of school vandalism and violence still other paid school workers must stand guard to police schools in the inner city.

Paid workers are often neighborhood people who bring a variety of backgrounds to their new work. They range in educational background from dropouts to highly educated individuals, from youth through old age, from part-timers active in another occupation to retirees. They are often called aides, assistants, or liaison people. But the most popular title for most of the paid community helpers is paraprofessional.

Because of their varied backgrounds and personalities, they make a genuine contribution to the education of high school students. A student may sometimes build a relationship with a paraprofessional from the neighborhood that cannot be achieved with a teacher. Some paraprofessionals, having grown up in a neighborhood, can identify with the needs, anxieties, perplexities, and feelings of local young people. To the student, a school in which paraprofessionals work often becomes a more real-life environment. When they are successful, paraprofessionals become active participants in the learning team.

The role of the paraprofessional is to provide services needed by the teacher for the improvement of the learning situation. However, the paraprofessional is not a trained teacher and should not be cast in this role. Although the pool of paraprofessionals provides a promising source of future teachers, distinctions between paraprofessional and teacher roles should be agreed upon and respected. Nor should unpaid community helpers attempt formal instruction. Their focus should be upon the knowledge and skills in which they specialize. They should be friends and advisers but should not aspire to be counselors, much less psychologists. With clearer definitions of role and responsibilities, potential conflicts should be reduced, although they will never disappear completely.

THE VARIED COMMUNITY PEOPLE HELPING WITH ACTION-LEARNING

New as the paraprofessionals are to secondary school education, the community helpers called for by action-learning are newer still. These community members are usually fully employed people and their incomes derive from their occupational specialty rather than from the school. Indeed, these new community helpers are seldom seen within the school building, for the locus of their work is elsewhere in the community. As secondary education increasingly calls upon community people in an expanded version of education, these community helpers who have specialized knowledge become a growing resource in the education of youth. Young people are assigned to them as observers, helpers, assistants, apprentices, and in other roles.

The new action-learning may take students anywhere in a community. As Smith and Barr say:

Where should learning take place? On an airstrip? At an aquarium? In an artist's studio? In a computer center? At a drug crisis center? In a hospital? In a hotel? At a medical center? In a museum? In a national monument? In an office building? At a Playboy Club? In a railroad station? On a showboat? In a storefront? In a TV studio? At a theater? In a Victorian mansion? In a warehouse? On wheels? At a zoo? These are a few of the settings for alternative schools and action-learning programs currently in operation.[25]

Not only are the settings varied, so are the community people who cooperate. They include "workers and supervisors in business, industry, medical facilities, churches, museums, social agencies, and other governmental and nongovernmental organizations; . . . instructors in formal and informal training programs outside the schools; . . . legislators and bureaucrats."[26]

Some of the settings are related to commercial activities, such as "business and industry, service companies," and the people are "apartment house owners and managers, large and small manufacturers, repair men, environmental leaders, school custodians, professional men and women, secretaries, and office supervisors." Some action-learning takes place in noncommercial settings: "social service agencies, political parties, local, regional, state and national governments, schools, colleges, universities, nurseries and day-care centers, law enforcement agencies, drug and crisis intervention groups, environmental groups, product evaluation groups, and hospitals."[27]

Action-learning may begin small through occasional instances of voluntary student action. It may grow into accredited school programs. Principal Gerald E. Kusler illustrates:

If we can get starter programs in a variety of areas, we'll have less trouble showing that action-learning is valuable for everybody. Some areas are naturals: from volunteer "candy-stripers" to a credit program in pre-nursing; from "mayor for a day" to a credit program in service in local governments; from school-ignored

---

[25] Vernon H. Smith and Robert D. Barr, "Where Should Learning Take Place?" *Issues in Secondary Education*, p. 153.
[26] Ronald C. Doll, "How Can Learning Be Fostered?" *Issues in Secondary Education*, p. 272.
[27] Gerald E. Kusler, *NASSP Bulletin*, November 1974, p. 50.

"private" instruction in music and language to school accredited independent study; from "student view" reporters in the local newspaper to newswriting for credit.[28]

COMMUNITY PARTICIPANTS AND POWER

If we are going to successfully link school and community and foster learning in an environment that is broader and more complex than that of the school, administrators and teachers will have to become skillful in working with community people. Questions of roles and relationships arise in the interrelationship of school and community. The new roles and responsibilities inevitably bring with them possibilities of conflict. To reduce potential conflicts, community helpers must be carefully chosen. Not everyone is equipped to share in the serious responsibility for the education of youth. Community participants should be competent in their specialized fields.

Our new partners in education must be granted sufficient authority. Action-learning cooperators may especially require motivation, since their own work may understandably have precedence over the education of the student. They must have some understanding of what educational goals might be reached through student activity.

Community helpers, when selected, will need encouragement to fully realize their potential for fostering learning. They may underrate their importance in the education of their young partners.

Action-learning participants may need advice on the kinds of tasks which students are equipped to undertake. They may also profit from warnings on too large or too little allocations of responsibility to high school students.

Working with community helpers will test the human relations skills and knowledge of representatives of the schools. After all, the cooperating community member is not some subservient menial. He or she is a peer of the school person. Fairness, friendliness, consistency, and dependability will be required of the school person. The representatives of the schools will need to listen as well as to talk.

Community workers who work with students must recognize their responsibilities. They must simultaneously be held accountable and yet not feel threatened by their new responsibilities. They must be willing to attempt to evaluate the outcomes of action-learning with students and with representatives of the school.

The new relationships will not come easy. Despite the above cautions, conflicts, disillusionments, and even terminations of relationships will occur. But the achievement of participation by laypersons, whether paraprofessionals or action-learning participants, in the educational process is a

---

[28] Ibid., p. 52.

worthy goal. With broader participation by the citizenry should come greater understanding and support for education, wider experiences for students, a breaking down of the barriers that have long separated schools from the real world. The results should be increased learning, decreased problems, improved relationships, and, for all involved, a higher quality of life.

THE COMMUNITY PARTICIPANTS WE NEED

We need in our secondary schools community participants who are competent in their fields of specialization and who enjoy working with students. They should not self-consciously conceive themselves as formal teachers. They need only be themselves and share as best they can what they know. As to personal characteristics, community participants should be honest and direct in their dealings with both students and school representatives. They should keep their objectivity. But, above all, they should enjoy the experience of working with young people and communicate that enjoyment to those with whom they work.

DISCUSSION

1. Why does the quality of educational program depend not only upon the people who conduct the program but upon their interrelationships? Illustrate.

2. What was the nature of teacher training in the colonial and early national periods?

3. Generalize on the growth of high schools and the forces that account for the growth.

4. How did the professional education of teachers change in the late nineteenth century? . . . throughout the twentieth century?

5. What seem to you the advantages or disadvantages of being educated for teaching in a normal school, a liberal arts college, or a university?

6. What are several characteristics of a profession? In what way does teaching fall short of being a profession?

7. Can you think of additional characteristics of a profession in addition to the eight listed?

8. What are the major problems of teachers working in inner-city areas?

9. Do you have any theories as to why violence and vandalism in connection with schools is on the increase?

10. When were the NEA and the AFT organized? What is their present membership?

11.   What role have the NEA and AFT usually played in national elections? What role did they play in the election of 1976?

12.   What roles do the NEA and AFT play in influencing state legislatures? . . . Congress?

13.   What is the conflict over collective bargaining legislation concerning teachers that takes place in state legislatures? What is the nature of the controversy over teachers having a voice in size of classes, meetings attended, committee work, and so on?

14.   What social forces of the mid-1970s slowed down the pace of the movement toward greater teacher power?

15.   It appears to be difficult to define what a good teacher is. Why is this so?

16.   What is your own conception of the secondary school teachers we need?

17.   Speculate on how education in secondary schools might be different if teachers were much younger than they are now? . . . much older?

18.   From the tables and the text, generalize on the economic position of the teacher.

19.   What was the role of the "chosen" person or selectman in the early colonies? Discuss how this tradition contributed to the early establishment of school committees and eventually school boards.

20.   How many people constitute a school board? How are they elected?

21.   What is the difference between determining policy and administering an enterprise? Which of these responsibilities belongs to a school board with respect to education?

22.   What are some of the more specific responsibilities of school board members?

23.   What accounts for the frequent unpopularity of school boards?

24.   What is the nature of the controversy over decentralization of schools in large cities?

25.   The nature and work of school boards is frequently misunderstood. Why?

26.   What is the controversy over local funding of education through property taxes versus state and federal funding?

27.   Why does the power of school boards appear to be ebbing?

28.   What are the characteristics of the school board members we need, as you see it?

29.   What is the role of the secondary school principal in relationship to the superintendent and central staff?

30.   What were the expectations of a headmaster in early America? To what extent have these expectations changed, as you see it? What were the powers of the headmaster?

31.   What are the responsibilities of today's secondary school principals? Is too much expected of the principal?

32. What delegations of authority are suggested by Trump and Vars? What new posts would be called for? Do you agree? Do you think schools are already overadministered?

33. In what way is the secondary school principal the person caught in the middle?

34. What was the principal's former role with respect to young people attending the school he or she administered? Translate *in loco parentis*.

35. What was the *Tinker* v. *Des Moines Independent Community School District* decision of the Supreme Court? What legal concept was involved? What adaptation by secondary school principals (along with teachers and school boards) became necessary?

36. How did a gain in power by teachers affect the power of the secondary school principal?

37. What is your opinion of unionization for principals? Why?

38. What is your conception of the secondary school principal we need?

39. Who owns the public schools?

40. Why is participation by community members in the education of young people increasing?

41. What are the responsibilities of paid community participants in education? What are their characteristics and backgrounds? What new word has been coined to describe this type of paid community helper?

42. How do the community helpers involved in action-learning differ from paraprofessionals? Where does action-learning take place?

43. What is the nature of desirable interrelationships between community participants, teachers, and administrators? What are some dangers in the new relationships? How much power should community participants have as contrasted to the power people collectively possess in a society in which the citizens own the public schools?

44. What is your own conception of the community participants we need?

INVOLVEMENT

1. With the help of local historians, attempt to trace the development of secondary schools in your own community. Can you determine the periods of fastest growth?

2. Invite to class a teacher, an administrator, and a college professor to talk about the extent to which education seems to them a profession. Or organize a debate among class members on the topic of whether or not education is a profession.

3. Plan a trip to a school in an inner-city area. Make careful arrangements so that this will be a significant experience for the class.

4. Invite to class a teacher or administrator to comment on any violence and vandalism in the local schools.

5. Invite to class a spokesperson for the NEA and AFT if these groups have local branches. Ask them questions concerning the desirability of collective negotiations and a wider voice by teachers as to class size, meetings, and committees. Attempt to get a picture of the current status of teacher bargaining in your community.

6. Investigate research that has been carried on as to the nature of good teachers. Attempt to account for the lack of confidence the researchers have in broad generalizations on this complex matter.

7. Through the cooperation of teacher organizations or local administration, determine precisely the salary scale of teachers in communities in which you hope to teach.

8. Visit one or more school board meetings. Talk to school board members, before or after the meetings. If this is inconvenient, invite school board members to class. Ask them to describe their major problems and the work of the board.

9. Make an informal study of the number of school board members who are of minority origin. Can you generalize on their social-class status? . . . their occupations?

10. Determine the actual situation in your community regarding financial support for the schools.

11. Talk to leaders of groups that have been campaigning for certain educational goals in your community.

12. Invite a secondary school principal to class to discuss his or her responsibilities and how they have changed over the years. Inquire particularly as to changes in school law and attendant modifications of school procedures as to students. Encourage him or her to talk about teacher organizations and about the relationships of teachers to the principal.

13. If the schools of your community use paraprofessionals, observe their work and roles. Talk with some individually.

14. If the schools of your community utilize action-learning with unpaid community helpers, observe some of the situations in which these helpers work. Talk to the students who are involved and the community people who supervise them. Ask both groups the same questions and compare their responses.

FURTHER READINGS

Doll, Ronald C. *Leadership to Improve Schools*. Charles A. Jones, Worthington, Ohio, 1972. Acquaints the reader with the roles of principals and supervisors and their major leadership tasks.

Education U.S.A., Special Report. *Differentiated Staffing in Schools*. National School Public Relations Association, Arlington, Va., 1970. An informal and readable survey of differentiated staffing that includes profiles of three schools, a selected list of differentiated staffing schools, and a bibliography.

Fantini, Mario D. *What's Best for the Children?* Anchor Press/Doubleday, New York, 1974. The struggle between teachers and parents for power and its effect on the education of children.

Fantini, Mario D., and Marilyn Gittell. *Decentralization: Achieving Reform.* Praeger, New York, 1973. The case for decentralization by writers who see promise in this approach to reform.

Good, Thomas L., Bruce J. Biddle, and Jere E. Brophy. *Teachers Make a Difference.* Holt, Rinehart and Winston, New York, 1975. An examination of the difference that schools can and do make in the progress of students. It illustrates both the contributions and the limitations of current research in helping to document the desirable results of education.

Hostrop, R. W., J. A. Mecklenburger, and J. A. Wilson, eds. *Accountability for Educational Results.* Linnet, Hamden, Conn., 1973. Fifty selections on methods of developing accountability, including both endorsements and criticisms.

Knezevich, Stephen J. *Administration of Public Education,* 3rd ed. Harper & Row, New York, 1975. A basic textbook on administration for persons who aspire to the principalship, superintendency, or central office roles and responsibilities.

Lipham, James M., and James A. Hoeh, Jr. *The Principalship: Foundations and Functions.* Harper & Row, New York, 1974. An interpretation of the principalship as a potentially powerful force for effecting change in schools. Relates the principalship to theory.

National School Boards Association, Educational Policies Service. *School Board Policy Development for the '70s.* National School Boards Association, Evanston, Ill., 1970. A handbook of policy development for school boards; basically a system of developing written school board policies and administrative rules.

Ornstein, Allan C., ed. *Accountability for Teachers and School Administrators.* Fearon, Belmont, Calif., 1973. A collection of articles on the controversy surrounding accountability.

Proefriedt, William A. *The Teacher You Choose to Be.* Holt, Rinehart and Winston, New York, 1975. Stresses teachers helping students to develop critical capacities and to make value choices.

Ryan, Charlotte. *The Open Partnership—Equality in Running the Schools.* McGraw-Hill, New York, 1976. Focuses on school-community relationship from the viewpoint of administrators, teachers, parents, students, school board members, and the general community. Offers plans and suggestions for improving school-community relationships.

Saxe, Richard. *School Community Interaction.* McCutchan, Berkeley, Calif., 1975. Discusses how the educator can understand and deal more effectively with decentralization and the cultural pluralism that makes effective school-community relations a vital necessity.

Taft, Philip. *United They Teach.* Nash, Los Angeles, 1974. A study of the character and nature of the teachers' union in New York City.

Welty, Don A., and Dorothy R. Welty. *The Teacher Aide in the Instructional Team*. McGraw-Hill, New York, 1976. A useful discussion of a new position in education, the teacher aide. Includes chapter on several broad curricular fields as well as general information concerning aides.

Winecoff, Larry, and Conrad Powell. *Focus: Seven Steps to Community Involvement in Educational Problem Solving*. Pendell, Midland, Mich., 1975. Describes a model educators may use to develop problem-solving skills and to involve diverse groups of people in seeking solutions to real problems of concern to them through a community involvement process.

Part 4.
The Future of Secondary Education

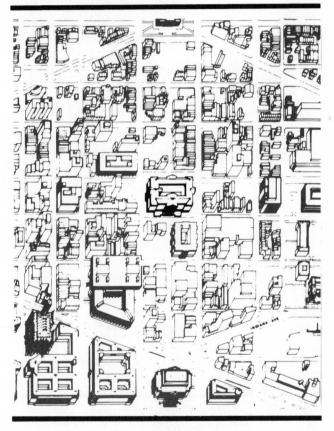

12.

The Year 2000: Secondary Education Through the Schools and the Community

FUTURISM

What will secondary education be like in the year 2000? Obviously, no one knows for sure. As educational philosopher Boyd H. Bode often said, "The gods give no guarantee." However, that should not keep us from speculating on the future.

Although it may sound paradoxical, speculation on the future is an especially useful approach to improving the present! In speculating on the future, a person usually encounters some current trends that, if continued, would markedly affect the future. Some of these trends the individual rejects, some the individual supports. Supporting certain present trends of which one approves and opposing certain present trends of which one disapproves can contribute to shaping the future in those directions that the person values. Thus, through concern about the future the individual may improve present conditions. As Alvin Toffler said:

> The ultimate purpose of futurism in education is not to create elegantly complex, well-ordered, accurate images of the future, but to help learners cope with real-life crises, opportunities and perils. It is to strengthen the individual's practical ability to anticipate and adapt to change, whether through invention, informed acquiescence, or through intelligent resistance.[1]

---

[1] Alvin Toffler, "The Psychology of the Future," *Learning for Tomorrow: The Role of the Future in Education*, Vintage, New York, 1974, p. 13.

FUTURISM AND UTOPIANISM

In the past, those who speculated on the future were often utopians. They envisioned an ideal society and assumed that if they described it graphically it just might come about! In their projections they criticized things as they were and often described a fundamentally reformed social order. However, they seldom specified how their utopias were to be reached, how one was to travel from here to there. In the *Republic*, Plato described a utopia that was ruled by an intellectual elite through philosopher-kings. In *The City of God*, St. Augustine described a theocratic ideal that attracted religionists in the Middle Ages. Sir Thomas More described a society where poverty and misery had been eliminated; the word *utopia* comes from the title of his 1516 book. A socialist utopia was described in *Looking Backward* by Edward Bellamy. Contemporary authors have also written satires of utopias and have described horrifying future societies, for instance, Aldous Huxley in *Brave New World* and George Orwell in *Nineteen Eighty-Four*. Whether the futures they portrayed were utopias or infernos, such creators did not present alternative futures; each developed a single prediction.

Contemporary futurists who speculate on what's ahead for humankind differ markedly from utopians. For one thing, today's futurists project alternative futures. They are highly conscious of change. Repeatedly, they point out that *if* certain trends and tendencies continue or emerge, *then* the future is likely to be marked by certain characteristics.

Unlike the utopians, contemporary futurists recognize and respect the likelihood of "system breaks." This phrase describes the discontinuities, turning points, and surprises that repeatedly occur in modern society. System breaks in our own century have included the invention of the automobile, the development and use of the atomic bomb, World War I, the rise of both communism and fascism, and U.S. involvement for years in the war in Vietnam. Such system breaks markedly influence trends, sending some shooting skyward and others plummeting downward, causing unanticipated ones to emerge. Consequently, contemporary futurists are well aware that they cannot accurately predict the future by simply extending, or extrapolating, present trends into the future. They must always take into account the possibility of system breaks.

For instance, Kenneth Boulding reminds us that system breaks have occurred in the past and will probably occur in the future. Among the system breaks that are possibilities are nuclear world war, worldwide famine, major technological developments (for instance, electronics, automation, cybernation, computer development), biological developments (for instance, advances in genetics, pharmacology, artificial organs), global developments (for instance, international sharing of wealth, Third World revolutions).

Contemporary futurism originated in Europe. In the United States, it was given impetus by the American Academy of Arts and Sciences through the academy's magazine *Daedalus*. An issue titled "Toward the Year 2000" brought together the contributions of outstanding scholars on alternative futures. The academy's Commission on the Year 2000 gave the movement increased reputability. Futurism was widely publicized through Alvin Toffler's 1970 book *Future Shock*, which described the disorientation brought about by the premature arrival of the future. Books by Herman Kahn and collaborators pulled together actual data useful in speculation and provided a variety of scenarios concerning the future. Kahn and Anthony J. Wiener's *The Year 2000* appeared in 1967; Kahn and B. Bruce-Briggs's *Things to Come: Thinking About the Seventies and Eighties* was published in 1972.

In *The Year 2000*, Kahn and Wiener speculated that almost half the American people will live in three megalopolitan clusters by the year 2000. One will stretch from Washington to Boston; the authors label this megalopolis Boswash. Another will concentrate around the Great Lakes, stretching from Chicago to Pittsburgh and extending north to Canada; they call it Chipitts. A third cluster will be Sansan, stretching from Santa Barbara to San Diego.

Contemporary futurists try to avoid confusing what they *hope* will or will not happen with what they *think* will or will not happen, based on descriptions of possibilities that are well reasoned and rely on facts. Kahn and Bruce-Briggs make this important distinction between what *should* happen and what *will* happen in *Things to Come*:

It may be impossible to completely separate descriptive from normative futurology; nevertheless, we feel it is extremely important and rewarding to make a serious attempt. Unfortunately, the field of future studies is thick with normative forecasting masquerading as descriptive. Many prognostications of many distinguished American thinkers are statements of what the author wants to happen, not necessarily what he thinks will happen, and frequently they are a bald pitch for some express policy or program. If done openly and honestly this is a perfectly valid method of political advocacy, with many honorable precedents (such as Bellamy's *Looking Backward*), but it tells us very little about what the future *will* be, except insofar as it is influenced by the ideas and desires of important men today.[2]

To summarize the varied projections and scenarios of contemporary futurists is obviously not possible in limited space. However, one of the most widely known projections of the future is Kahn and Bruce-Briggs's

---

[2] Herman Kahn and B. Bruce-Briggs, *Things to Come*, Macmillan, New York, 1972, pp. 245–246.

projection of a long-term, multifold trend of Western culture. The trend might whet the reader's appetite for learning more about the views of futurists.

1. Increasingly sensate (empirical, this-worldly, secular, humanistic, pragmatic, manipulative, explicitly rational, utilitarian, contractual, epicurean, hedonistic, etcetera) cultures.

2. Bourgeois, bureaucratic, and meritocratic elites

3. Centralization and concentration of economic and political power

4. Accumulation of scientific and technical knowledge

5. Institutionalization of technological change, especially research, development, innovation, and diffusion

6. Increasing military capability

7. Westernization, modernization, and industrialization

8. Increasing affluence and (recently) leisure

9. Population growth

10. Urbanization, recently suburbanization and "urban sprawl"—soon the growth of megalopoli

11. Decreasing importance of primary and (recently) secondary and tertiary occupations; increasing importance of tertiary and (recently) quaternary occupations

12. Increasing literacy and education and (recently) the "knowledge industry" and increasing role of intellectuals [see Figure 12.1]

13. Innovative and manipulative social engineering—i.e., rationality increasingly applied to social, political, cultural and economic worlds as well as to shaping and exploiting the material world—increasing problem of ritualistic, incomplete, or pseudo rationality.

14. Increasingly universality of the multifold trend

15. Increasing tempo of change in all the above[3]

Today, study of the future is taken seriously. Research is being carried on by large corporations, university policy research centers, and independent institutions. Universities teach courses on the future; a magazine, *The Futurist,* is published by the World Future Society.

In general, futurist thinkers today project as most likely developments a growing gross national product, increasing technological developments, and a continuation of the knowledge explosion. They foresee both a national society bound together through mass media, modern transportation, and contemporary government, and a creative federalism employing increased sharing among local, state, and national governments. An increase in leisure for average Americans, though not necessarily for their leaders,

---

[3] Ibid., pp. 8-9.

FIGURE 12.1 *Educational Attainment of the Labor Force.* *The educational attainment of the labor force is expected to continue to increase.*

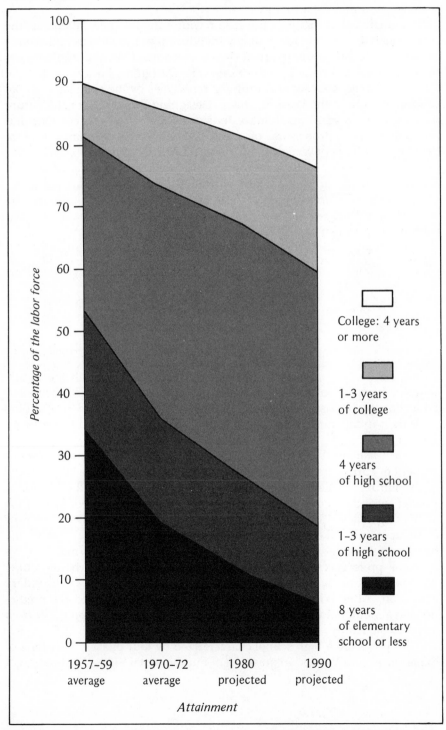

Source: *The Condition of Education*, U.S. Government Printing Office, Washington, D.C., 1976, p. 120.

is anticipated. Problems will persist, as the scholars see it, including organized crime, environmental difficulties, housing deterioration, and obsolescent governmental structures.

Recognizing that many of the major wide-ranging speculations on the future dealt lightly or inadequately with education, individuals and groups active in education prepared their own projections. One of the better early ventures into futurism by educators was Designing Education for the Future, a project sponsored during the mid-1960s by the chief state school officers of eight of the Western states. Designing Education for the Future was a group program involving extensive collaboration by scientists and humanists with professors of education and school administrators. Scholars in a variety of fields contributed to the leadoff book, *Prospective Changes in Society by 1980. Implications for Education of Prospective Changes in Society* was made up of essays by educators on future educational directions. *Preparing Educators to Meet Emerging Needs* was written primarily by teacher educators. School and college administrators were the major contributors to *Planning and Effecting Needed Changes in Education.*

SPECULATION ON FUTURE SECONDARY EDUCATION

KIMBALL WILES'S HIGH SCHOOL OF THE FUTURE

One still provocative 1963 projection dealt specifically with the high school. Later a group of contemporary leaders in secondary education reappraised the book through an anthology and contributed their own independent speculations on the high school of the late twentieth century.

In *The Changing Curriculum of the American High School* Kimball Wiles, a student of curriculum and supervision, wrote a chapter, "The High School of the Future." This chapter was an attempt by an informed educator to predict secondary education developments that he anticipated. Wiles took as his target date 1985, then almost a quarter of a century away but now close upon us. Like the work of the utopians, and unlike that of the futurists whom he preceded, Wiles's projection contained many of his personal preferences, an approach against which Kahn warns us today. Yet the Wiles model is a pioneer speculation on the future of secondary education. After Wiles's death, his contemporaries reviewed his predictions in a memorial volume with the same title as his last chapter, *The High School of the Future.*

Wiles projected a high school characterized by four phases: "Analysis of Experiences and Values, Acquisition of Fundamental Skills, Exploration of the Cultural Heritage, and Specialization and Creativity."[4] For analysis of experiences and values, Wiles anticipated discussion groups of eleven students of the same age with a teacher-counselor. These analysis groups were to meet six hours weekly. The dozen group members would discuss anything relating to ethics, social concerns, experiences of group members, out-of-school events, and implications of knowledge encountered in school classes. The attempt would be to help each student to discover meanings, grow in commitment to values, and examine conflicts in values and viewpoints among members of society. Basically, Wiles's analysis group was aimed at fostering the development of values.

Prophetically, Wiles commented, "In the late sixties, it will begin to be recognized that unless citizens have values that they accept, understand, and can apply, the social structure will disintegrate until authoritarian controls are applied."[5] A generation that has known the Vietnam War, the youth rebellion of the late 1960s, and the Watergate horrors of the early 1970s can only agree with the insight.

As to acquisition of fundamental skills, Wiles, writing in a period that preceded computerized education, projected the increased use of "teaching machines." He projected that each student would be told the skills that he or she *must* master and anticipated that students would work at their own paces through the needed programs.

A third ingredient in Wiles's model was exploration of the cultural heritage. He proposed devoting approximately one third of the program of each high school student to acquisition of basic knowledge of the culture. He anticipated large classes, even sections of as many as 500 or 1,000 students. He saw the teaching as conducted through television, films, or a highly competent lecturer. Knowledge would be drawn from the humanities, social sciences, and the physical and biological sciences. Discussion of emergent ideas would be delegated to the many analysis groups.

Finally, Wiles predicted and prescribed programs for the development of specialization and creativity. Specialization would be developed for all in shops, studios, and work laboratories in the school, and for noncollege-bound students through work experience in various industries and businesses in the communities. A variety of creative activities would be offered, including writing laboratories in which school newspapers, magazines, and telecasts might be prepared. Seminars in various disciplines and inter-disciplinary fields would be offered.

Wiles added that rooms would be of many different sizes in the school plant, ranging from small work cubicles to large halls for mass media

---

[4] Kimball Wiles, "The High School of the Future," in *The High School of the Future: A Memorial to Kimball Wiles*, ed. William M. Alexander, Charles Merrill, Columbus, Ohio, 1969, p. 5.
[5] Ibid., p. 6.

programs. This is a direction in which school architecture continues to develop today.

REACTIONS TO THE HIGH SCHOOL OF THE
FUTURE

William M. Alexander assembled commentaries in 1969 on Wiles's projections. Understandably, the authors provided their own predictions and preferences as to education in the closing years of the twentieth century. For instance, through raising questions, Alexander suggested that work experience should be provided for all students rather than simply those not planning to attend college. He suggested that physical education and some type of organized student government would be needed. He indicated skepticism of fundamental skills divorced from the other curriculum areas and taught only through technology.

Trafford P. Maher, S.J., contended that "the new curriculum will have to be implemented in a human school environment that is characterized by non-judgmental acceptance, non-selfconsciousness, sincerity, integrity, relevance, and participatory democracy."[6] He called for a curriculum which would place strong emphasis on what is to come and "introduce students to a sense of personal purpose, . . . capable of producing people who are unafraid of love (whether to give or to receive), who know that aloneness is necessary and that loneliness starves and leads to death."[7]

In her chapter in *The High School of the Future*, Alice Miel urged that the cultural heritage not be made synonymous with knowledge, leaving out values and skills. She criticized viewing the cultural heritage as knowledge alone; instead of passivity, she called for more social action on the part of youth.[8]

Franklin Patterson saw the emergence of a society characterized by "the immense and accelerating growth of the technical-scientific nature of industry."[9] To Patterson, such a postindustrial society "gives us that chance, as Norbert Wiener said, to discover and enlarge the human uses of human beings, or to fail at this."[10] Our ultimate future need in education, as Patterson saw it, is "education for all our people that is diverse, flexible, and sane enough to meet all the needs of a diverse society—not one big system for the middle class and a number of disparate programs for the dispossessed."[11]

---

[6] Trafford P. Maher, S.J., "Education for Survival," *High School of the Future*, p. 43.
[7] Ibid., p. 49.
[8] Alice Miel, "Rationale for a Curriculum Design: A Critique," *High School of the Future*, pp. 56–57.
[9] Franklin Patterson, "Human Issues in Post-Industrial Society: The Context of Education Tomorrow," *High School of the Future*, p. 63.
[10] Ibid., p. 64.
[11] Ibid., p. 69.

Two internationally oriented educators, Theodore Rice and Chandos Rice, "would place a strong emphasis on the importance of actual involvement and participation of students in all of the communities of which they are part."[12] They state that "in our vision of the school of the future, youth would have direct contact with youth of other countries, through an extension of current exchange programs, through such organizations as the Peace Corps, and through use of modern technology, such as the communication satellites."[13] They also anticipated much greater emphasis on the arts. "In our school of the future, training in the arts would become part of the general education program for all, rather than specialization for the talented only."[14] They add that "It is also apparent that we would add community service and experience as a fifth area, and a laboratory-studio-shop experience as yet another part of the total program."[15] Thus while the Rices support individualization of education, they are careful not to remove the individual from social contacts and social contributions.

Psychologist Arthur W. Combs understandably reacted in terms of the psychology needed in the future.

A mechanistic psychology is totally inadequate to deal with the humane kind of high school Wiles predicted. What is needed for such a high school is a concept of the nature of man and his behavior which helps to see young people more clearly as human beings. We need a psychology capable of dealing with man's experience—a psychology interpretive of students' feelings, values, beliefs, understandings, and personal meanings.[16]

Robert S. Fleming indicated that "the high school of the future should place greater priority on the concerns of youth. This means the particular youth in a particular school."[17] To Fleming,

Current efforts to describe the educational program of the future give much attention to uses of technology, to organizational changes, and to updating the content of the curriculum. Perhaps the most important factor which is missed is enunciated by the adolescents themselves when they say that "something more" includes "being respected," "becoming involved," and "learning things of value."[18]

In his chapter, Earl C. Kelley indicated agreement with Fleming. To Kelley, "No matter how many courses have been added, there is one basic

---

[12] Theodore Rice and Chandos Rice, "The School of the Future—A Commentary," *High School of the Future,* p. 90.
[13] Ibid., p. 91.
[14] Ibid.
[15] Ibid., p. 95.
[16] Arthur W. Combs, "A Curriculum for Learners," *High School of the Future,* p. 127.
[17] Robert S. Fleming, "Needed: Greater Student Involvement," *High School of the Future,* p. 133.
[18] Ibid., pp. 138–139.

ingredient lacking in our present educational system. That is the involvement of the learner in the planning of what is to be done."[19] Kelley believed that "the whole secondary school system has failed the American society almost completely."[20] He commented, "I cannot say what the high school of the future will be like. I can only say that no operation, business or public, can go on forever while losing thirty or forty per cent of its product without either changing or going out of business."[21]

Robert H. Anderson believed that the high school that Wiles envisioned was essentially a nongraded school; thus he was critical of analysis groups consisting of pupils of the same age. Anderson envisioned the future high school as made up of multiaged classes taught through cooperative planning and cooperative evaluation by high school staff members.[22]

To Hollis A. Moore, Jr., out-of-school laboratory situations were important. "It may be possible in the years ahead for our students to spend significant amounts of time in laboratory situations in which solutions to social problems and personal identity can be incentives."[23]

To Galen Saylor, "the most serious problem facing the educational agencies of this country in the decades ahead is the development of programs that will serve effectively, meaningfully, and significantly the educational, economic, social, physical, and emotional needs of young people who are frustrated and disillusioned."[24] He called for a program ensuring acquisition of basic skills, a more meaningful and significant instructional program, and extensive vocational and prevocational education with a coordinated work-experience program.[25] The projected shift in employment toward white-collar jobs (Figure 12.2) and the occupational expectations of young adults (Figure 12.3) show how important such data is and the educators' responsibility to be aware of, and to make their students aware of such trends.

CURRENT PROJECTIONS BY INDIVIDUALS

Marien Michael Marien is an able student of alternative futures who is interested in education. He was formerly with Syracuse University's futures study program and is now with the World Institute. In one of his articles for *The Futurist*, a publication of the World Future

---

[19] Earl C. Kelley, "Humanizing the High School of the Future," *High School of the Future,* p. 143.
[20] Ibid., p. 142.
[21] Ibid., p. 140.
[22] Robert H. Anderson, "Is the Wiles 1963 Model Still Futuristic?" *High School of the Future,* pp. 164–165.
[23] Hollis A. Moore, Jr., "In Search of Self," *High School of the Future,* p. 174.
[24] Galen Saylor, "A Complete Education for Adolescents," *High School of the Future,* p. 187.
[25] Ibid., pp. 189–190.

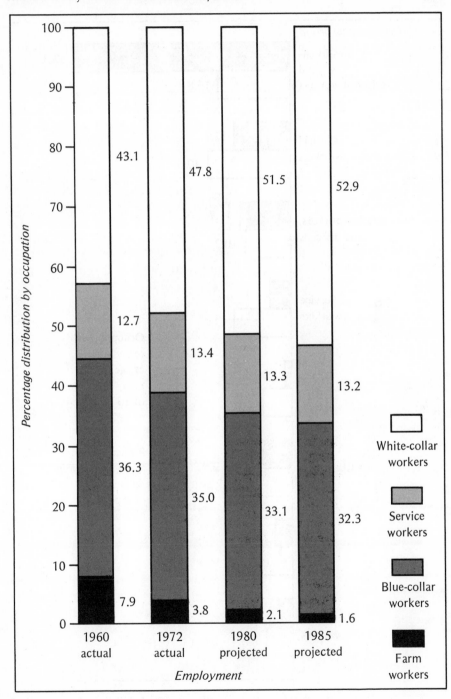

FIGURE 12.2 *Employment by Major Occupational Group. Employment is expected to continue to shift toward white-collar occupations.*

SOURCE: *The Condition of Education*, U.S. Government Printing Office, Washington, D.C., 1976, p. 121.

FIGURE 12.3 *Occupational Expectations of Young Adults.* *Job aspirations at age 30 of the high school class of 1972 are different from the projected composition of the labor force in 1985.*

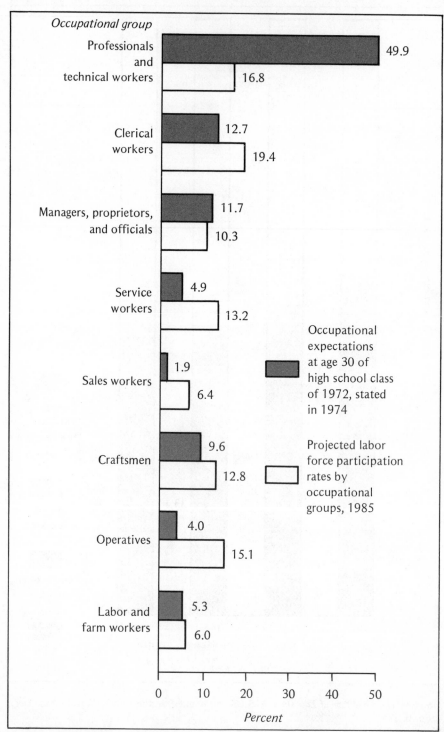

SOURCE: *The Condition of Education*, U.S. Government Printing Office, Washington, D.C., 1976, p. 123.

Society, Marien looks at the implications of what Kahn called the basic, long-term multifold trend. Marien summarized that trend as:

Increasingly sensate cultures (empirical, secular, humanistic, hedonistic).

Bourgeois, meritocratic elites; literacy and education.

Institutionalization of change and increasing tempo of change.

Population growth, urbanization, and megalopolitanization.

Worldwide industrialization and modernization.[26]

With this trend providing a general sense of societal direction, Marien devised his version of the basic, long-term multifold trend for education. As he saw it, the movement was from yesterday's "closed teaching systems" to tomorrow's "open learning systems." His chart is reproduced here as Table 12.1.

TABLE 12.1 *From yesterday to tomorrow: The basic long-term multifold trend in education*

CLOSED TEACHING SYSTEMS	OPEN LEARNING SYSTEMS
Alternate titles	
Teacher and/or institution centered	Student and/or child centered
Tight system; Rational mechanics; Cause-effect paradigm	Loose system
Control-centered	Learning-centered; Inquiry approach; Developmental; Discovery education
Societal context	
Agricultural; Industrial	Postindustrial; Knowledge-based, service society
Autocratic; Plutocratic; Gerontocratic	Democratic; Meritocratic; Self-renewing
Static and simple	Dynamic and complex
Beliefs about learning	
Teaching results in learning	Good teaching aids learning, bad teaching inhibits it
Learning requires discipline, work, drill, memorization, pain control	Learning is enjoyable, follows from pursuit of interests
Teacher as source of knowledge, student as passive absorber	Learning from many sources, including peers; student as active participant
Capability confined to a few; the genius, the gifted	Extensive latent potential in all

Table 12.1 continued

---

[26] Michael Marien, "The Basic Long-Term Multifold Trend in Education," *The Futurist*, December 1970, pp. 220–223.

TABLE 12.1 *continued*

CLOSED TEACHING SYSTEMS	OPEN LEARNING SYSTEMS
Administration	
Input oriented	Input-service-benefit oriented, PPBS
Hierarchical leadership	Pluralistic, participatory
Curriculum	
Narrow, fixed, retrospective	Broad, changing present and future-oriented
Classics, principles, truth, facts, deduction, maxims	Methods, principles, induction, creativity, intuition, randomness
Determined by teacher and/or extra-classroom authority	Determined by teacher and/or student
Programmatic, sequential; Lesson plans strictly followed	Interchangeable programmettes, modular learning; Lesson plan as guide to options
Group study prescribed for all students	Independent study designed to fit individual needs and interests
Western culture as superior to primitives, heathens, Noble Savages, and the underdeveloped; Us-Them: emphasis on differences	Humanistic, pan-cultural; Us: emphasis on similarities
Student-teacher relations	
Students are a collectivity	Compensatory education for exceptional children, the physically and linguistically handicapped, the underprivileged
Teacher as Authority, student as follower; control as instrumental technique	Professional as learning facilitator or senior learners; student as junior colleague
Feeling withheld; I-It	Feelings exposed and respected, student evaluation of teachers; I-Thou
Single Teacher	Multi-adult exposure, team teaching, guests, differentiated staffing
Student conduct	
Compulsory attendance: no choice of institution	Optional participation: alternatives offered
Physical punishment for "misbehavior"	Counseling for personal difficulties
No student recourse for injustice	Ombudsman, legal measures
Dropping out is fault of student; shaming for ignorance	Many possible sources of failure: environmental, institutional and individual
Established rules and routines	Democratic development of rules and routines as necessary

Feedback

Formal, mechanistic, "Right" answers	Multi-faceted, formal and informal, open-ended
Strong reliance on quantitative measures	Use of quantitative measures as necessary

Rewards

Grades, fixed proportion of failures, class rankings, honors, medals, degrees	Pass-fail, non-grading
Recognition through competition in a few areas of excellence	Deemphasis of competition, promotion of diversity and many areas of excellence; a taste of success for all
Learning has vocational and social utility	Rewards of learning are inherent

Goals

Socialization, training, moral education, passing on civilization, knowing; education of intellect only	Development of whole individual, investigation of cultural heritage, questioning
Getting an education, being educated, terminal education	Learning how to learn, lifelong learning, education as a beginning

Extra-classroom environment

Restrictive, "In Loco Parentis"	Permissive, largely peer controlled
Physical and intellectual separation from world	Interlinkage of school and life, "School Without Walls"

Space

"Grid" architecture, stationary furniture	Omnidirectional space and flexible furnishings, choice of environments
Arbitrarily assigned seats	Student freedom to choose seats
Teaching in classrooms	Learning in classrooms, learning resource center, home, dormitory, community, world
Specially designated learning institutions, outside learning ignored	Recognition and encouragement of formal and informal learning opportunities throughout society, equivalent credit for outside learning

Time

Collective pace	Individual pace
Ordered structure of class hours and course credits	Flexible scheduling
Uninterrupted schooling, followed by interrupted work	Learning and work interspersed throughout lifetime; learning a living

SOURCE: Reprinted from: *The Futurist,* A Journal of Forecasts, Trends and Ideas About the Future. Published by: World Future Society, An Association for the Study of Alternative Futures, 4916 St. Elmo Avenue, Washington, D.C. 20014, U.S.A., 301-656-8274.

Faithful to the insight that alternative futures are likely rather than some fixed, static, utopian future, Marien suggested three scenarios for the rate of transition in education to open learning systems. The first scenario assumed that open learning systems would not be widespread but would instead be short-lived, largely because of severe financial stringency. In that case, Marien foresaw the growth of alternatives outside the public school system. His second scenario anticipated differential adaptation, led by affluent suburban school districts in the Northeast and the West. But young people from poorer areas, whether city, rural, or small town, might be denied opportunities for more open learning systems. A third scenario assumed extensive adaptation of open learning systems. On the assumption that students learn more in open than in closed systems, he foresaw an increased generation gap between the old, brought up in closed systems, and the young, brought up in open systems.

Shane An outstanding scholar in futuristics among contemporary university educators is Harold G. Shane. Shane is a versatile curriculum generalist who has recently written widely in yearbooks and magazines about the need for educators to face the implications of futures studies. Through Alvin Toffler's publications, which preceded his best-selling book, Shane early became aware of Toffler's concept described in *Future Shock* as "the dizzying disorientation brought on by the premature arrival of the future."[27] Shane saw the same dizzying disorientation in contemporary education. Shane pointed out that since only 1950, education had been faced by the knowledge explosion, implementation of civil rights legislation, expansion of higher education, power structure changes, shifts in education funding, inequality in educational opportunities in inner-city schools, educational technology with its accompanying "learning businesses," the effects of television on the young, cybernetics, and new approaches to many disciplines.[28] To cope with future shock in education, Shane proposed creative in-service education programs including teacher exchanges, leaves, and residencies; giving higher priority to early childhood education; a model of a lifetime curriculum using an organization for individual instruction; and using media and machines fully.

In his recent writing on futures, Shane has given much attention to the "big questions" as to content. In analyzing a study of issues in education identified by the membership of Phi Delta Kappa, he urged schools to focus on the dangers of ruthless exploitation of resources, pollution, warfare, and waste; called for a study of population increases and the distribution of the world's economic goods; asked for a study of the mass media;

---

[27] Alvin Toffler, *Future Shock*, Random House, New York, 1970, p. 11.
[28] Harold G. Shane, "Future Shock and the Curriculum," *Phi Delta Kappan,* October 1967, pp. 67–70.

urged school experiences that would build personal inner strength, discipline, and self-control; suggested more emphasis on study of the future. He summarized, in a mock resolution:

That, while the basic issue of what our children and youth shall learn actually has been partly obscured by most curriculum reform in substantive fields such as mathematics and linguistics, which are indispensable means to improved education, the ends of education—future-oriented knowledge and survival skills needed to cope with technology, mass media, pollution, the peace deficit, inflation, and a myriad of similar problems—now be given "compensatory attention." Further resolved: That the curriculum be more fully anchored to the lifelong "human needs" concept of womb-to-tomb educational experience provided under the sponsorship of the schools.[29]

In the 1976 Yearbook of the National Society for the Study of Education, Shane, with collaborator Virgil A. Clift, described the social decisions that the United States must face in order to give new directions to the nation and its secondary schools.

1. What policies shall govern our future use of technology?

2. At a global level, what shall our goals be, and how can we reach them?

3. What shall we identify as the "good life"?

4. How shall we deploy our limited resources in meeting the needs of our human subsets?

5. Shall we seek to modify the wide range in income that characterizes the so-called "haves" and "have-nots," and, if so, how?

6. How can we, without censorship or other imposed controls, maximize the value of the mass media—particularly television—and minimize their shortcomings?

7. What use shall be made of psychological, chemical, and electronic approaches to the modification of behavior?

8. What steps shall we take to insure the future integrity of our political-military-economic-industrial systems?

9. What, if anything, are we willing to relinquish—and in what order?

10. Since perfection presumably is unattainable, what honorable compromises shall we make as we contemplate the nine previous questions?[30]

There was a high note of urgency in the conclusion of the chapter:

---

[29] Harold G. Shane, "Looking to the Future: Reassessment of Educational Issues of the 1970's," *Phi Delta Kappan*, January 1973, p. 333.

[30] Virgil A. Clift and Harold G. Shane, "The Future, Social Decisions, and Educational Change in Secondary Schools," *Issues in Secondary Education*, Seventy-fifth Yearbook of the National Society for the Study of Education, ed. William Van Til, University of Chicago Press, Chicago, 1976, pp. 301–304.

We should bear in mind that as of 1976 time is short and increasingly precious. Decisions in society and in education should be undergoing critical study between 1976 and 1980. Also, *there should be substantial and prompt implementation of our planning, since many scholars in futures research see no more than twenty years and perhaps only ten before irreversible harm is done to the biosphere and to our long-range prospects for a viable life for humankind.* Let us not use the enormity of our problems as a pretext for expressing fatalism and the deadly dangerous inactivity that it encourages.[31]

Cremin Lawrence A. Cremin, currently president of Teachers College, Columbia University, is an outstanding historian of education rather than a futurist. However, he contributed significantly to thought about the future of education in *Public Education*. Cremin's thesis is that educators focus so heavily on the potentialities of the school that they ignore the potentialities of other educative institutions. He called attention particularly to

the educational transformation brought by mass television. In 1950, fewer than 10 percent of American homes had television sets. Today, the figure has leveled off at around 96 percent. Moreover, so far as can be determined, at least one member of the average American household is looking at a television set more than six hours out of every twenty-four, with the greatest amount of viewing being done by the very young, the very old, and the very poor. Once one recognizes that television teaches—and not only via channels specifically labeled educational but across the entire spectrum of public and commercial programming—the fact of television in 96 percent of American homes being looked at six hours a day is in itself a revolution.[32]

In addition to the teaching inevitably done for better or for worse by television, Cremin points out that family life, religious life, and organized work each educate. In effect, every family, every church and synagogue, and every employer has a curriculum that is taught deliberately and systematically. So does every library, museum, Boy Scout troop, and day-care center. Thus there are a "multiplicity of individuals and institutions that educate—parents, peers, siblings, and friends, as well as families, churches, synagogues, libraries, museums, summer camps, benevolent societies, agricultural fairs, settlement houses, factories, radio stations, and television networks."[33]

We know secondary education already takes place through schools. We are urged by reform reports of the mid-1970s to develop and encourage additional transitions to adulthood—work experience and community participation. Still another expansion of secondary education is envisioned in Cremin's suggestion that the secondary education of the future must take place not only in the school and in the community but through many of the

---

[31] Ibid., p. 315.
[32] Lawrence A. Cremin, *Public Education*, Basic Books, New York, 1976, pp. ix-x.
[33] Ibid., p. 29.

institutions of society that are educative. If our conception of secondary education is comprehensive, we will in the future include this third dimension and consider policies with respect to a variety of institutions that educate. Secondary educators will try to relate to and influence the instruction of educators in institutions other than the school alone. They will try to make students especially aware of the additional educative forces so that students may consciously use these agencies in their education. They will try to get educators in the varied educational institutions involved in the debates and discussions that continuously go on concerning desirable education.

If, during the years ahead, secondary educators take seriously this broad conception of learning, educators will become concerned with the occupations and professions that supplement school and community education. Indeed, some educators would find new employment in that broad range of educational institutions beyond the walls of the school. For instance, educators might be associated with commercial as well as public television enterprises, might be employed by religious institutions in nonclerical roles, might be employed by business and industry as educators.

Toffler   Following publication of *Future Shock*, Toffler increased his attention to the role of education in the world of the future. He served as a consultant to Melbourne High School in Melbourne, Florida, in designing a Twenty-First-Century Course. He designed simulation games such as the population game in which students occupy increasingly limited segments of the classroom in order to feel the effects of a population crisis. In 1974 he edited a book in which were assembled many ways in which the future is being studied in schools and colleges. *Learning for Tomorrow* is especially valuable to teachers in quest of suggested methodologies for studying the future with their students.[34] Toffler explains that the materials were assembled for use in schools because "despite efforts at radical reform, the vast majority of young people in the technological societies will continue, for at least the next half-decade, to receive their experience of formal education inside, not outside, the system."[35]

However, from a long-range futurist point of view, Toffler believes in the community as educator. In an interview in the *National Elementary School Principal* in 1973, Toffler said:

We have enormous problems in every community that are not being met by government or by the private sector. Whenever we ask why a problem—air pollution, noise, traffic congestion, or crime—is not being resolved, we are usually told we don't have the budget or the resources to solve it. And yet there are more than

---

[34] Alvin Toffler, ed., *Learning for Tomorrow: The Role of the Future in Education*, Vintage, New York, 1974.
[35] Ibid., p. xxiii.

fifty million young people in our society, representing an enormous pool of imaginative, energetic, enthusiastic, but as yet relatively unskilled resources for helping us deal with some of these problems. I would like to move much of education into the community, with teams of young people working with community adults, as well as with faculty, on the whole range of neighborhood problems that are presently neglected due to "lack of resources."[36]

Asked about whether the schoolhouse as we now know it is going to be effective in housing the new education, Toffler responded:

There is no single answer to what the school of the future ought to look like. Maybe it ought to look like a local office, a local store, a world's fair, an automated factory, or a sports arena. There are different purposes to be served, and therefore different environments required for learning to take place.[37]

Toffler implies here one aspect of desirable education for the future that is curiously neglected by contemporary futurists—learning through travel. Though seldom mentioned, social travel has high potentiality for future education in a society such as ours that can transport people swiftly and economically. Current school trips consist largely of larks to Washington, D.C., to observe the cherry blossoms or to visit the galleries of the U.S. Congress. They can be replaced by social travel, which involves intensive preliminary study of a problem, a sustained visit to a new locale for field study, and follow-up conclusions on return home. Schools could sponsor youth hostel trips in the region in which the school is located. They could develop sustained trips to study the life of cities for noncity students and to study life in rural and small-town America for city young people.

Secondary schools could take cues from such groups as Experiment in International Living, student exchange programs, or collegiate years abroad, and develop international travel programs for secondary school youth. Perhaps in a better tomorrow, ships and planes originally designed for war might be used to transport young American ambassadors of good will abroad on expeditions to foster international understanding. The idea is not new. At the close of World War II, a practical American businessman, Beardsley Ruml of Macys, crusaded unsuccessfully for allocation of merchant ships and naval vessels to transport American youth abroad to help reconstruct Europe and to bring a message of peace. But false notions of economy resulted in merchant ships rusting in mothball fleets and fighting ships deteriorating into obsolescence in harbors.

CONTEMPORARY PROJECTIONS BY GROUPS

Research for Better Schools, a regional educational laboratory supported by funds from the National Institute of Education,

---

[36] James J. Morisseau, "A Conversation with Alvin Toffler," *National Elementary School Principal*, January 1973, p. 13.
[37] Ibid., p. 14.

Department of Health, Education, and Welfare, sponsored during the mid-1970s a national conference on alternative futures of education. Essays presented by social scientists and educators at the conference were gathered together in *The Future of Education: Perspectives on Tomorrow's Schooling.*

Harold D. Lasswell, a distinguished political scientist, opened this book with a projection on the future of government and politics in the United States. In a world of global interdependence he saw the future of the United States as heavily conditioned by the world environment, and the future of other nations as deeply affected by developments in the United States. He pointed out that, as matters stand today, we live in a divided and militant world marked by conflicts. Should this situation continue, the nuclear arms race and "little wars" will extend into the foreseeable future. A new element in a world of large armies and destructive weapons is individual and small-group terrorism. The growth of terrorism will result in more public support for political surveillance; the scope of the political police will expand.

Lasswell thought it likely that ethnic violence will continue. He antici-pated that political corruption will continue, although money used to influence candidates for office might be somewhat reduced in future elec-tions. He saw the Congress as focusing greater attention on a variety of policy structures related to power, enlightenment, well-being, affection, respect, rectitude, and resources.

Lasswell hoped for the strengthening of participatory democracy, de-spite his fears that elite elements might persist. He anticipated that com-munications technology would make knowledge widely available to of-ficials, voters, and organizations.[38]

Daniel Bell, professor of sociology at Harvard University and chairman of the Commission on the Year 2000, identified three major social frameworks in his forecast. In Bell's first framework, he described the United States as a "national society" in that the shock in one part of society has swift repercussions everywhere else in the society. He attributed our becoming a national society to revolutions in technology and communica-tions, such as transportation, direct telephone dialing from coast to coast, and television. Bell's second framework is the "communal society" marked by a shift away from decision making by the market to public decision making. More and more decisions are public decisions and more and more claims are being made on society by groups. He illustrated with the politi-cal claims of the black, the poor, and the elderly. Bell's third framework was the "post-industrial society," a change from a goods-producing economy to a service economy. In a society in which the labor force is

[38] Harold D. Lasswell, "The Future of Government and Politics in the United States," *The Future of Education: Perspectives on Tomorrow's Schooling,* ed. Louis Rubin, Allyn and Bacon, Boston, 1975, pp. 1-21.

primarily engaged in professional and human services, he saw theoretical knowledge as of high importance.

To Bell, in a society marked by these three frameworks, the need to specify the goals and priorities of the society increases. The need for establishing a basic minimum standard of living grows more apparent. Group conflict intensifies. Professionalism grows up alongside the formerly dominant business civilization. Self-realization grows more important.

Bell perceived some educational implications of the emerging society. He concluded that inquiry is more important than amassing subject matter "because subject matter erodes very quickly." He believed that there are societal questions underlying our current problems that have to be explored through education.[39]

Kenneth E. Boulding, an economist and versatile social scientist, stresses "the need for uncertainty" in his chapter in *The Future of Education.* He points out that the validity of projected trends diminishes very rapidly as time passes. He warns that new dynamic patterns often take over, sometimes leading to equilibrium and sometimes toward system destruction. He is even doubtful of current projections of energy scarcity because, though probable, they could be completely reversed by the discovery of new energy resources.

In general, Boulding is skeptical of projections that go beyond a very few years. He differentiates between reliable population projections based on the number of children already born and unreliable population projections based on guesses as to fertility in future years (see Figure 12.4).

Boulding is conscious of the current slackening of demand for education. He points out that if a cheap way of achieving certification could be discovered, the educational system would be in a bad way! However, as Boulding sees it, three possible developments might increase the demand for education. One is better methods of financing education, including publicly underwritten loans to students. A second approach is spreading education throughout the life span, rather than concentrating it heavily on people below the age of twenty. A third possibility is the continued growth in knowledge and the necessity to transmit this increasing knowledge.

Convinced of uncertainty, Boulding is doubtful about numerical measures of educational achievement that could lead to false feedback and bad decisions. Perhaps with tongue in cheek, he says, "My own ideal educational system, therefore, is muddle-headed, full of redundancy, blithely ignorant about its results, careless of statistics, and violating every canon of what is now respectable."[40]

[39] Daniel Bell, "Schools in a Communal Society," *The Future of Education,* pp. 31–48.
[40] Kenneth E. Boulding, "Predictive Reliability and the Future: The Need for Uncertainty," *The Future of Education,* pp. 57–74.

FIGURE 12.4 *Population for School-Age Groups. The traditional school-age populations will continue to decline in size until after 1980, though the number of young adults will grow during those years.*

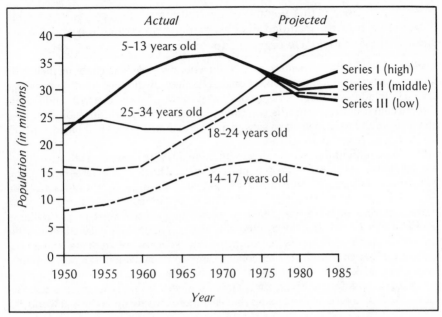

SOURCE: *The Condition of Education,* U.S. Government Printing Office, Washington, D.C., 1976, p. 13.

Louis Rubin, editor of the volume, summarized and compared the views of these social scientists and educators in commentaries that follow each chapter. Each educator contributed his own perspective. Robert G. Scanlon of Research for Better Schools, an administrator, emphasized the importance of policy controls in planning for the future. Robert Glaser of the University of Pittsburgh, a learning theorist, envisioned environments for learning adapted to individual differences in schools of the future. Patrick Suppes of Stanford University, whose specialties include the uses of the computer, described promising technological possibilities, yet persistent problems, in the development and spread of computer-based instruction. Harold G. Shane of Indiana University reminded readers of needed crucial social decisions that must shape social policy. Ralph W. Tyler, director emeritus of the Center for Advanced Study in the Behavioral Sciences, described needed research and development. He summarized the critical unsolved problems that schools of the future must deal with as

(1) providing effective educational opportunities for those not now learning what the school seeks to teach, (2) furnishing educational experiences required for

character development, (3) inducting adolescents into responsible adulthood, (4) educating for occupational life, (5) meeting needs for continuing education, and (6) obtaining financial resources for education."[41]

Rubin, in closing this volume of contemporary projections of possible educational futures, included his observations on curriculum and the organization of schools. He urges the following:

With respect to the curriculum proper, the young are likely to continue their turn toward earlier maturation; subject matter content will need, with increasing urgency, to address the importance of civic awareness, social concern, and citizen responsibility; and (despite the continuing interest in career education) learning and self-growth may come to be viewed more and more as ends in themselves, and less and less as means to an end. . . .

Our most profound need, at the present moment, is to convince both schoolmen and laymen of the need for experimental openness. The dominant imperative of the experiments is that the reorganized school overcome present infirmities without sacrificing present achievements, and without violating the moral obligation of public agencies to serve the common good. The reforms must fit the failings: boredom can be defeated by a more stimulating atmosphere, alienation can be countered by a curriculum better attuned to the concerns of students, childhood anxiety can be reduced by greater compassion, dehumanization can be controlled by a larger respect for human dignity, academic failure can be lessened by perseverance and multiple teaching procedures, and the learner's dwindling faith in education can be reversed by lessons that bear more directly upon the real world.[42]

We should not leave this section on contemporary projections of the future by groups without reminding the reader of proposals already discussed in this book. For instance, the three national reform reports discussed in Chapter 1 are themselves proposals for future community-oriented education. We refer to *Youth: Transition to Adulthood,* the report of the Panel on Youth of the President's Science Advisory Committee, chaired by James S. Coleman; *The Reform of Secondary Education,* a report of the National Commission on the Reform of Secondary Education, chaired by B. Frank Brown; and to *The Education of Adolescents,* a report of a Panel on High Schools and Adolescent Education, U.S. Department of Health, Education, and Welfare, chaired by John Henry Martin and published in full in 1976. We refer, too, to the action-learning movement described in Chapter 9. These community-oriented proposals and practices may have a profound influence on future secondary education.

One alternative future for American secondary education is vocational experiences for all American youth rather than for the present relatively limited few engaged in distributive education and other work experiences. If the momentum of community education continues, the future also may

---

[41] Ralph W. Tyler, "The School of the Future: Needed Research and Development," *The Future of Education,* pp. 179–180.

[42] Louis Rubin, "Observations on Future Schooling," *The Future of Education,* pp. 196, 204.

hold opportunities for community service by all American youth rather than by only those now experiencing opportunities in their communities under the leadership of occasional imaginative teachers.

EDUCATION IN THE YEAR 2000: THREE POSSIBLE FUTURES

In the light of what we can learn from social scientists and educators who are willing to speculate, what are some possible futures of secondary education? In answering the question we must remind ourselves that system breaks in education, as well as in society, must be taken into account. For instance, if the deschoolers had their way, there would be *no* secondary schools. Education for youth would persist, but it would be dramatically different from present school-oriented secondary education. A societal system break such as world war might convert secondary education into a war-support apparatus. Overwhelming computer technology might convert schools into clean factories in which student-workers passed the entire school day at their machines. In the event of such system breaks, all projections as to secondary education would have to be drastically revised or completely discarded—in other words, all bets would be off.

Because system breaks are only partially foreseeable and are completely unpredictable as to time of occurrence, the discussion of possible futures in education that follows is limited to scenarios that now seem to be high among the possibilities. A scenario is a way of probing possibilities for the future by setting forth some hypothetical events. It is a statement of what might possibly happen, not a prediction of what will happen. It does not represent what we want to happen; it is a description of what might occur.

Here are three scenarios for education in 2000 that seem to this author to be within the range of reasonably foreseeable possibilities. One we call "somewhat pessimistic," a second "somewhat optimistic," and a third "most likely." (Bear in mind that the author is not *predicting* that a particular scenario will come about. Nor is he describing what he *hopes* will come about. Instead, he is dramatizing three *possibilities*.)

A SOMEWHAT PESSIMISTIC SCENARIO

1. The American people have lost their traditional faith in education. They now recognize that unemployment is no respecter of educational degrees—the unemployed are as likely to be holders of higher degrees as to be high school dropouts. The weaknesses of public schools as to discipline and teaching the three R's are apparent to the public and continue to be widely publicized by the mass media. People have come to believe what they have been told repeatedly by social scientists at such leading universities as Harvard and Chicago—that, despite the

volume of spending on education and curriculum changes, schooling makes no difference in regard to such American values as achieving equality.

2. School budgets are often rejected by the electorate in a stagflated economy marked by both high inflation and high unemployment. Education is supported at a minimum level. The school day has been shortened in order to accommodate two shifts daily. Electives and extracurricular activities have been dropped from most school programs. Teaching loads are increasing; in junior and senior high schools, pupil-teacher ratios are often thirty-five to one. All school trips have been abandoned.

3. Educators work in buildings constructed much earlier in the twentieth century. A new school building is a rarity; people come from miles around to admire it and to inquire as to how it will be financed. Vandalism and arson continue to be problems in many city schools even though in Boswash, Chipitts, and Sansan there is now one school guard for every two teachers.

4. The highly organized teaching staff is on the defensive. A rash of strikes occurs each September and wildcat walkouts are frequent during the school year. Teachers adhere strictly to the designated hours to be spent on educating students; teachers, like students, report to and leave the school building at the sound of the bell. Seniority and tenure have been maintained by teacher unionism; one result has been an aging teaching staff containing few teachers under age thirty-eight.

5. Specified levels of competency in the three R's are required for high school graduation. Many students from middle- and upper-income groups master the required examinations in the three R's with little difficulty or time expenditure. Many students from disadvantaged backgrounds spend from 25 to 75 percent of their school hours in drill on the three R's in order to achieve the required minimum competencies. Some never achieve the specified competencies and leave secondary schools before graduation. The dropout rate, which had shrunk to less than 25 percent by 1975, rose to almost 50 percent in the year 2000.

6. For the majority of students, the secondary school curriculum is now made up of the separate subjects within the fields of the sciences, mathematics, social sciences, English, and foreign languages. To foster accountability, the New York State system of Regents examinations has been adopted nationally. Courses in home economics, fine arts, music, industrial arts, and similar programs, often termed "fads and frills," are now almost nonexistent. Physical education programs for nonvarsity students are no longer included in the curriculum of schools. However, varsity sports are maintained and, with the added impetus of girls' varsity sports, are prospering. A minority of secondary school students enroll in classes to learn specific trades in out-of-date shops. In an economy of high unemployment, work experience for students is not available through business,

industry, or governmental agencies. Community participation is regarded as irrelevant to the strict academic program. Because of conservative opposition from supporters of back-to-basics programs, textbooks do not deal with conflicting views of controversies.

7. The field of English concentrates on teaching the skills of reading and writing through computerized programs stressing literacy and grammatical usage. Bright students, taught in homogeneous groups, also are taught American and English literary classics.

8. The social science courses required of all students are world history, American history, and right thinking. The last course succeeded courses in economics and social problems after it became apparent that student behavior deteriorated, rather than improved, after schooling. Right thinking includes instruction in patriotism, socially approved values, and correct answers to controversial questions. It is taught through memorization and repetition by both live and machine teachers.

9. The content of the science and mathematics courses are determined by the industrial and military needs of the nation. The life sciences have lost substantial ground in the program.

10. The languages of the allies and the enemies of the nation are taught. Following a period of confusion as to which of the superpowers were more likely to become enemies and which more likely to become friends, the U.S. Office of Education in 1988 mandated instruction in the languages of Russia, China, Japan, and Germany. While USOE could not determine which of the superpowers were most likely to be future allies or enemies, it was considered reasonable to assume that these particular nations would be one of these. Thus study of the languages of these nations was deemed necessary to the national defense. Enrollment in French and Spanish in 2000 diminished to the low level of enrollment in Latin and Greek in 1975.

11. Efforts to replace expensive live instruction with less expensive computerized and televisionized education were largely successful, despite advocates of humanized education and resistant teacher unions.

12. Guidance was abolished in the 1990s as expensive and interference with parental prerogatives. However, some critics of the decision point out that, with the deterioration of family life, parents are ineffective in guiding their children. Juvenile crime rates are rising. Students are confused in their occupational decisions. However, there is no confusion as to choice of school subjects since all courses are required and assignment to the academic or vocational track is through a centralized IQ testing program.

A SOMEWHAT OPTIMISTIC SCENARIO

1. The American people have extended their traditional faith in education. The achievement of virtually full employment through both political and economic processes, a long period of peace

among the superpowers and of diminished regional hostilities, and a steady rise in the GNP accompanied by a low inflation level have contributed to an atmosphere of greater support for education. The demonstrated success of elementary and secondary education with respect to both cognitive and affective education has encouraged the extension of education toward lifelong learning.

2. Recognizing the inequalities in levels of educational support between richer and poorer communities, America relinquished its reliance on local funding and in the 1980s placed heavy responsibility for school support at the state and national government levels. Development of local citizens groups mitigated fears of loss of local control to a faceless bureaucracy. While the costs of education increased to a degree, the climb was not precipitous, since community agencies and business enterprises assumed much of the cost of action-learning. The public and private sector supported student participation because of the economic contribution made to their enterprises by youthful energy. Frequent use of large-group instruction, individualized study, and small-group discussion resulted in better utilization of staff. Teacher-student ratios declined during the 1980s and 1990s (see Figure 12.5).

3. New buildings are being constructed with the union of school and community in mind. New high schools are now equally appropriate for use by adolescents and adults. Though secondary schools are now attended by all the youth population as dropouts shrink to negligible proportions, the growth of action-learning and of alternative schools within community institutions has held the construction of new schools to a modest increase. Comprehensive schools increase in number, but the most spectacular growth is registered by the varied alternative schools.

4. The teaching staff profits from new developments in teacher education that interrelate teacher education programs and public secondary schools in their community settings. The master's degree is now taken for granted as a prerequisite for the beginning teacher. Post–master's degree programs, including doctoral programs, now interrelate theory and practice.

5. The old curriculum quarrels as to whether the curriculum should meet the needs of learners or illuminate social realities or help students clarify, analyze, and arrive at humane values have been resolved. Now it is taken for granted that needs, social realities, and values are each of high importance. It is commonly agreed that the curriculum should include major problem areas or centers of experience. The current curriculum controversy is over how best to teach these problem areas. Some schools rely upon a curriculum divided into broad fields, such as social studies and language arts. Other schools have combined broad fields, such as social studies and language arts, in core curriculums. In experimental schools, careful appraisal programs are under way so that judgments might be made as to the more effective approaches.

FIGURE 12.5 *Pupil-Teacher Ratios in Public Elementary and Secondary Schools. The pupil-teacher ratios for elementary and secondary schools will continue to decline in the immediate future.*

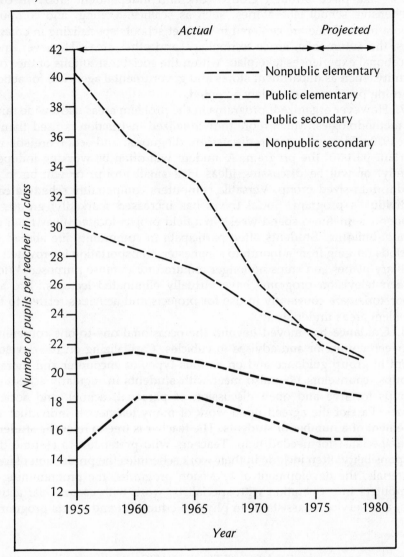

Actual   *Projected*

- – – – – Nonpublic elementary
- – · – · – Public elementary
- – – – – Public secondary
- – – – – Nonpublic secondary

Number of pupils per teacher in a class

Year

SOURCE: *The Condition of Education*, U.S. Government Printing Office, Washington, D.C., 1976, p. 129.

6. In addition to the problem areas that are the heart of the curriculum, all students have preliminary experiences leading to vocations. Some of these take place through group work and independent study in comprehensive school laboratories, such as science, writing, and computer laboratories. Some are centered in magnet schools specializing in creative arts, the automobile, space technology, and other areas. However, most vocational experiences take place within the social institutions of the community, such as department stores and governmental agencies, for action-learning programs are widely accepted.

7. However organized, programs in the problem areas use a wide range of methodologies. Much more individualized instruction is used than in the 1970s. However, group discussion, diagnosis, and action are still important parts of the program. A student will often be working independently, or will be discussing ideas in a small group, or will be in an auditorium-sized group. Versatile computers competently schedule each individual's program. Social travel has increased markedly; groups of students sometimes spend weeks in a field project located away from the school building. Students often participate in community life abroad for periods ranging from a month to a semester; transportation is provided by military planes and ships no longer required for defense purposes. Wide-screen television programs have virtually eliminated lectures. The arts laboratories are constantly in use for projects and activities related to the problem areas under study.

8. Guidance has moved beyond the occasional one-to-one conference between counselor and advisee in cubicles. Capitalizing on the development of group guidance and on various types of encounter and therapy groups, counselors now also meet with students in regularly scheduled groups for free and open discussion of personal, school, and societal issues. Part of the agreed-upon work of many teachers is individual advisement of a number of students. The teacher is free to refer the students to a specialist for needed help. Teachers who prefer not to assume this responsibility often include in their work schedules the production of local materials, the development of television programs, the programming of computers in cooperation with specialists, work with cocurricular activities, and service as assistants in physical education and sports programs.

THE MOST LIKELY SCENARIO

1. The American people continue to believe in the importance of education even though there has been a decline in the number of secondary schools and of secondary school students. (See projection of statistics, Table 12.2.) Parents believe that their children should have more than a high school education. They continue to see education primarily as a road toward economic success. Thus they support practical education. They are respectful of cultural growth, yet doubt that

TABLE 12.2 *High school graduates, by sex and by institutional control, 1963–64 to 1984–85 (in thousands)*

| YEAR | TOTAL HIGH SCHOOL GRADUATES[a] | SEX | | CONTROL | |
		Boys	Girls	Public	Private (estimated)
1	2	3	4	5	6
1963–64	2,290	1,123	1,167	2,015	275[b]
1964–65	2,665	1,314	1,351	2,366	298[b]
1965–66	2,632	1,308	1,325	2,334	298
1966–67	2,679	1,332	1,348	2,381	298
1967–68	2,702	1,341	1,360	2,402	300
1968–69	2,829	1,402	1,427	2,529	300
1969–70	2,896	1,433	1,463	2,596	300
1970–71	2,943	1,456	1,487	2,643	300
1971–72	3,006	1,490	1,516	2,706	300
1972–73	3,037	1,501	1,536	2,737	300
1973–74	3,069	1,512	1,557	2,769	300
1974–75[c]	3,139	1,554	1,585	2,839	300
PROJECTED[d]					
1975–76	3,137	1,552	1,585	2,837	300
1976–77	3,135	1,551	1,584	2,835	300
1977–78	3,146	1,557	1,589	2,846	300
1978–79	3,128	1,549	1,579	2,828	300
1979–80	3,083	1,527	1,556	2,783	300
1980–81	3,033	1,503	1,530	2,733	300
1981–82	2,943	1,457	1,486	2,643	300
1982–83	2,822	1,397	1,425	2,522	300
1983–84	2,728	1,351	1,377	2,428	300
1984–85	2,680	1,327	1,353	2,380	300

[a] Includes regular public and nonpublic schools, residential schools for exceptional children, subcollegiate departments of institutions of higher education, Federal schools for Indians, and federally operated schools on Federal installations. Excludes equivalency certificates. More than 99 percent of public school graduates and 97 percent of nonpublic school graduates are graduates of regular day schools.
[b] Reported data from Office of Education surveys.
[c] Estimated.
[d] The projection of public high school graduates is based on the assumption that for boys and girls separately, the number of high school graduates expressed as a percentage of the population averaging 18 years of age will remain constant at the average of the rates for 1968 to 1974.

The projection of nonpublic high school graduates is based on the following assumptions: (1) the number of nonpublic high school graduates will remain approximately the same throughout the projection period. (2) The percentage of boys among nonpublic high school graduates (48.1 percent in 1964–65) will remain constant to 1984–85.
NOTE: Data are for 50 States and the District of Columbia for all years. Because of rounding, details may not add to totals.
SOURCES: High school graduate data and estimates are based on U.S. Department of Health, Education, and Welfare, National Center for Education Statistics, publications: (1) *Statistics of Public Schools*, annually, fall 1964 through 1974, (2) *Statistics of Nonpublic Elementary and Secondary Schools*, 1965–66, and (3) *Nonpublic School Enrollments in Grades 9–12, Fall 1964, and Graduates, 1963–64*.
Reprinted with permission from *Standard Education Almanac*, 9th ed., 1976–77, © Marquis Academic Media, Marquis Who's Who, Inc., Chicago, p. 266.

academic education is relevant to life as it is lived at the turn of the twentieth century. Although they support a varied curriculum, marked by individualization and multiple options, they wish the schools required higher competencies in the three R's. They believe the schools, the deteriorating family, and such diversions as television and sports all share the responsibility for problems of students in mastering basic skills. They wish somewhat wistfully that the schools could provide the discipline that the nuclear family, now in retreat, formerly provided.

2. The proportion of support for education from local sources has declined from 48 percent in 1976–77 to 30 percent in 2000. State support has moved from 42 percent in 1976–77 to 39 percent in 2000. The sharpest proportional rise in support took place at the federal level, from 9 percent in 1976–77 to 30 percent in 2000. Nonpublic school support remains at approximately the same level, as in 1977. The changes in the proportion of support came about as the local property tax proved to be an anachronistic method of financing schools in an urban society, and as the power of federal government expanded in an increasingly national and centralized society. Supporters of education recognize the necessity for growing federal support, despite their frequent altercations with growing bureaucracies. As to increased federal support, Willie Sutton's insight is frequently cited in justification: "That's where the money is."

3. Contributing to increasing costs of secondary education are the lowered dropout rate, down from 25 percent in the early 1970s to 11 percent in the year 2000; moderate salary increases for teachers; replacement of old buildings and a modest degree of new construction. Contributing to holding costs in check are the decrease in the birth rate, which continued through the last quarter of the twentieth century; the stabilization of the high school population; more effective use of plants, including increased evening use; a decrease in time spent in school buildings by students as action-learning and home study in learning centers in middle-class homes increase. On the whole, education increases in cost beyond the normal increase are attributable to inflation.

4. Growth in school construction is evident on three fronts. Rebuilding of the shattered inner-city areas in the large eastern and middle western metropolises includes the construction of secondary schools designed to serve as community centers. However, older, fortlike inner-city schools are still in use. Prosperous suburbs of the Sun Belt cities from Virginia to Georgia, Florida to Louisiana, and Texas to Southern California, are developing the most elaborate new school plants in America, creative in design and embracing recreational facilities. Small alternative schools, found largely in urban areas, are assuming various dimensions and forms. Elsewhere school buildings look essentially as they did in the 1970s. Although they have been remodeled to house new organizational forms, the boxlike schools built between World War II and President Jimmy Carter's first term are clearly deteriorating.

5. The unified National Federation of Educators (NFE), which grew out of the merger of the NEA and AFT, has substantial power through its membership of more than two million teachers and its ties to labor unionism and the Democratic party. Though the NFE is highly unionized and willing to strike for salaries, benefits, or student welfare, its members as individuals are more conservative than their leaders and do not necessarily vote in accordance with the political endorsements of NFE officials. Many of the older teachers retain the apathetic attitudes toward political action they developed during the mid-1970s, including the election of 1976 in which a bare majority of eligible Americans voted. Even the energy-environment crisis in the mid-1980s did not markedly stir the teaching profession. However, the profession is vigilant in the quest for better salaries and working conditions.

6. Though teachers play little role in curriculum development, they often do modify procedures in their own classrooms. Whereas affective education was infrequent in the 1960s, in the year 2000 the average practitioner is equipped with some skills in this area. However the curriculum is, on the whole, oriented to the development of cognitive skills. Instruction in reading and writing skills on the high school level increased markedly during the last quarter of the twentieth century; the results of the instruction are, however, inconsistent and spotty. Low-income children, in particular, continue to have problems mastering basic skills.

7. Course outlines have been repeatedly updated in the attempt to keep up with the swift social changes of recent years. Some schools focus school programs in broad problem areas such as energy-environment dilemmas. In such schools the broad fields of the secondary school curriculum, such as language arts, the social studies, science, and the various arts, are interrelated in interdisciplinary programs. However, most schools separate the broad fields and their teaching relies heavily upon modern textbooks, television, and computerized instruction.

8. Many more students participate in the community than in earlier decades. The growth in work-related experience has been rapid. The development of service-related experience has proceeded more slowly. Alert school systems expanded into action-learning programs as early as the 1970s. By the late 1980s almost one third of American secondary schools included programs of work experience in the schedules of many students. Recognizing the persistence of problems of financing supervision of action-learning and the reluctance of many cognitive-oriented high schools to foster work experience, the federal government stepped in with financial support. Government-sponsored programs developed, reminiscent of the CCC of the Depression era of the 1930s, the Peace Corps of the 1960s, and the career education movement of the 1970s. Business and industry were granted tax exemptions in exchange for youth employment. In 2000 the majority of adolescents are engaged in either school or federal government programs of work experience. A new group of specialists has

emerged—the community educators. Domestic social travel has increased moderately.

9. Guidance continues to expand at the high school level. The ratio of guidance counselors to students has improved steadily, from 1 to 500 in 1960, to 1 to 300 in 1985, and to 1 to 200 in 2000. Since each teacher is expected to supplement classroom teaching with a chosen work activity, many have chosen to work in the field of guidance.

10. Computerized instruction is a regular part of the secondary school program and is used especially in teaching skills in the language arts and in mathematics. Students also use computerized instruction for independent study in a variety of fields. However, quite contrary to some early predictions, the computer has not revolutionized high school education. Like radio, film, and television, the computer is used as a technological resource in the total educational program.

Which of these possible futures of secondary education do you prefer? What can you do today to bring about the future you prefer?

DISCUSSION

1. In what way is speculation on the future useful in improving the present?

2. What is the distinction between utopians and futurists?

3. What is the meaning of "alternative futures"? . . . of "system breaks"?

4. What are some illustrations of past and future system breaks?

5. What is the distinction between descriptive and normative futurology? Why is it important for futurists to separate in their thinking what they hope will happen from what they think will happen?

6. Discuss Kahn's long-term multifold trend of Western culture. Attempt to illustrate each trend. Do you find any major trend that is omitted from Kahn's list?

7. What does Wiles mean by "analysis groups"? What would appear to be the advantages of such groups? What assumptions about education block educators from establishing widely such groups?

8. What mechanical developments did Wiles depend upon for the acquisition of fundamental skills? Has modern technology brought his vision closer to realization in the years since he wrote?

9. How does Wiles propose that students acquire understanding of the cultural heritage? Do you see any advantages or disadvantages in the use of large classes?

10. What is Wiles's proposed program for the development of specialization and creativity?

11. Which of the commentators on Wiles's conception of the high school of the

future is closest to your own ideas? Which is furthest from your thinking? What is your own reaction to the high school of the future?

12. In Marien's summary of Kahn's long-term trend, do you note any major element that has been omitted?

13. Discuss Marien's closed teaching systems and open learnings systems. What seems to be the advantages and disadvantages of each? Do you agree with Marien that open learning systems are the way of the future?

14. Which of Marien's three scenarios as to rate of transition to open learning systems seems more likely to be enacted?

15. What is the meaning of "future shock"? What are some illustrations of future shock within contemporary education?

16. According to Shane, what should be the new focus of content in secondary schools?

17. Which of the questions raised by Shane and Clift in the 1976 Yearbook of the National Society for the Study of Education seem to you to be most important? Attempt your own answer to the questions.

18. What does Cremin see as significant educative institutions, in addition to schools, existing in contemporary society?

19. In what way is television a "teacher" of all of us?

20. How would education be different if many institutions of society were recognized as educative forces? How would the work of secondary educators be changed? What new responsibilities would secondary educators assume?

21. What might be some new occupations and professions in nonschool educative institutions? What is Toffler's conception of a possible role for students with respect to social problems?

22. What is the distinction between a conventional school trip and social travel?

23. What kind of international travel programs would be appropriate for the future? What problems are in the way of marked expansion of international travel by secondary school youth?

24. What is Lasswell's projection of the future?

25. Talk over Bell's three major social frameworks—a national society, a communal society, a postindustrial society. If these are the emerging frameworks, what are the implications for secondary education?

26. What is the nature of Boulding's skepticism about trends? What kinds of projections seem to him reliable and unreliable?

27. Do you agree or disagree with Rubin's analysis that our greatest need in education is for "experimental openness"?

28. What are the projections of the future implicit in the three national reform reports discussed in Chapter 1?

29. How would you rewrite the "somewhat pessimistic" scenario describing edu-

cation in the year 2000? . . . the "optimistic" scenario? . . . the "most likely" scenario?

30.   For a sustained series of discussion sessions, take comparable items in the three projections and discuss them extensively. Consider, for instance, faith in education, financial support for schools, building design, attitudes of teachers, content of the curriculum, extent of separate subject or interdisciplinary learning, use of the community as educator, methodological changes, the role of guidance. Throughout your discussion, distinguish between what you would like to happen and what you expect to happen. Sum up your discussion with suggestions for what educators must do if the kind of future you prefer is to be realized.

INVOLVEMENT

1.   As a class project, read descriptions of utopias and report upon them to the class as a whole.

2.   Read and report on some of the outstanding futurist publications mentioned in the chapter. Compare and contrast these.

3.   After reading the description of Wiles's *High School of the Future* and of reactions to it, set down in writing your own picture of the desirable high school of the future. Compare and contrast it with the descriptions written by other members of the class.

4.   Develop an adaptation of Marien's chart. On one side list "the teaching I observe" on the other side list "the teaching I advocate." Anticipate that some items will be identical on both sides of the chart, whereas others might be different.

5.   Harold Shane is a prolific writer on the future. Read some of his articles in *Phi Delta Kappan* and in other educational magazines.

6.   Make a list of educative institutions other than schools. Select some for visits. Talk with staff members to determine whether they see their role as educative. Share with them Cremin's concept.

7.   Read Toffler's *Future Shock* and report to the class on its thesis and evidence. Describe some of the methodologies in the volume he edited, *Learning for Tomorrow*.

8.   Develop carefully your own scenario for education in the year 2000. This might well be a major project that summarizes your insights into the future. Try always to differentiate between your hopes and what seems to you most likely to come about. Consider the possibility of attaching your projection to your self-description when seeking employment as an educator.

FURTHER READINGS

Alexander, William M., ed. *The High School of the Future: A Memorial to Kimball Wiles.* Charles E. Merrill, Columbus, Ohio, 1969. Educational leaders react to

Wiles's conception of the high school of the future and emphasize their own projections and preferences.

Cremin, Lawrence A. *Public Education*. Basic Books, New York, 1976. This important book argues that education is much broader than schooling and that other educational institutions such as families and television are an essential part of contemporary education. A challenge to educators to work closely with institutions in the surrounding society.

Ehrlich, Paul R., and Anne H. Ehrlich. *The End of Affluence: A Blueprint for Your Future*. Ballantine, New York, 1974. An argument that we are nearing an "Age of Scarcity" through environmental wastefulness unless individuals and communities act decisively.

Kahn, Herman, and B. Bruce-Briggs. *Things to Come*. Macmillan, New York, 1972. A provocative and exciting exploration of possible futures including projections and scenarios by two outstanding futurists.

Kahn, Herman, William Brown, and Leon Martel. *The Next 200 Years: A Scenario for America and the World*. Morrow, New York, 1976. Consideration of the question of whether industrial growth endangers the future of humankind or promises a higher standard of living. The authors believe in the possibilities of economic growth and widespread affluence.

Kinney, Gloria, ed. *The Ideal School*. Kagg Press, Wilmette, Ill., 1969. Essays on what the ideal school of the future might be. Includes contributions on community involvement and curriculum improvement.

Krug, Mark M., ed. *What Will Be Taught the Next Decade*. F. E. Peacock, Itasca, Ill., 1972. Writings by specialists in various subject matter fields as to the near future of teaching in those fields. Reflects an agreement among contributors that future trends include more attention to student needs and less rigid and structured institutions.

Rubin, Louis, ed. *The Future of Education: Perspectives on Tomorrow's Schooling*. Allyn and Bacon, Boston, 1975. A significant look into the future by three noted social scientists and six able educators who jointly consider current trends and their meaning for public schools of tomorrow.

Toffler, Alvin. *Future Shock*. Random House, New York, 1970. A widely read book that called public attention to the contemporary collision with tomorrow that is creating future shock, "the dizzying disorientation brought on by the premature arrival of the future."

Toffler, Alvin, ed. *Learning for Tomorrow: The Role of the Future in Education*. Vintage, New York, 1974. A book about the ways our schools and universities currently deal with the future. Emphasis is placed on specific ways in which educators are now helping students to understand the future.

Tripp, Maggie, ed. *Woman in the Year 2000*. Dell, New York, 1974. A series of articles on women in American society in the twenty-first century.

Index

Academies, 126–127, 316
Accreditation, of high schools, 164
Achievement
  delinquency and, 105
  sex differences in, 88 (fig.)
Action-learning, 23–24
  community members in, 347–349
  programs in, 276–280
  requirements of, 295, 298
Activism, 70–73
Addams, Jane, 159, 160
Adolescents, 81
  black, 94–99
  common elements among, 81–85
  as critics of education, 8–9
  of European ethnic groups, 101–104
  individual differences among, 85
  Mexican-American, 99–101
  sex roles and, 85–89
  social class and, 89–94
  unemployment among, 46, 108, 321
Adult education, 266
Alcohol, 109–110, 112
Alcott, Bronson, 265
Alexander, William M., 366
Alternative schools
  plants for, 263–264
  private, 10–11
  public, 11–13
American Council of Learned Societies,
  191
American Federation of School Administrators (AFSA), 344
American Federation of Teachers (AFT),
  320, 323–324
Americanization, influence on educational
  goals, 156–158
American Youth Commission, 167
Analysis groups, 240
Anderson, Robert H., 368
Arts
  current programs in, 205–206

in curriculum, 238–239
Audiolingual approach, 200

Back-to-basics movement, 13–18
  in English, 196–197
  in mathematics, 188
Barr, Robert D., 263, 276–280, 348
Beat generation, 64
Bell, Daniel, 379–380
Bestor, Arthur E., 172
Biological Sciences Curriculum Study, 226
Birnie, Howard, 186
Birth control, sex roles and, 86–87
Black(s), 94–99
  unemployment among, 321
Blackburn, Jack E., 302
Black identity, adolescents and, 97–98
Black power, 42
Black studies, growth of, 190
Block-time programs, 287
Bode, Boyd H., 168, 359
Bohemians, 63–64
Boulding, Kenneth E., 380
Brown, B. Frank, 21, 23, 382
Bruner, Jerome S., 173, 185, 227–228
Business cycles, 45
Business education, current programs in,
  211–213

Calculators, mathematics curriculum and,
  189
Calvinism, 61
Campus-type buildings, 256
Capitalism, 44
Career development, 308
Career education, 175
  models for, 212–213
Carnegie unit, 164
Caswell, Hollis L., 229
Censorship, English language arts and, 197
Change, pace of, 32–34
Cigarette smoking, 112

Civil rights movements, black youth in, 97
Clapp, Elsie Ripley, 267
Clift, Virgil A., 375
Clusters, in contemporary school plants, 255
Coleman, James S., 20, 23, 243, 274, 382
Coleman II, 20, 274–275
Collective bargaining, 323–324, 326
College, preparation for, 163–165
College Entrance Examination Board (CEEB), 164
  English program and, 194–195
Collings, Ellsworth, 267
Combs, Arthur W., 367
Commission on Country Life, 160
Commission on the Reorganization of Secondary Education, 165
Committee of Ten on Secondary School Studies, 164
Communication, in curriculum, 243–244
Community living, in curriculum, 241–242
Community members
  in action-learning, 347–349
  evolution of participation by, 345–346·
  power of, 349–350
  responsibilities of, 347
  specifications for, 350
Community-oriented education, 18–25
  projections for, 376–378
Community school movement, 265–272, 295, 298
  emphasis of, 273–274
  reform in 1970s, 274–276
Compensatory education, 174
Competency tests, 188, 196–197, 384
Comprehensive high schools, 262–263
Computer-assisted instruction, 304
Conant, James B., 141, 143, 262
Consumer problems, 45
  in curriculum, 235–236
Contemporary Music Project (CMP), 204
Contracts, 301
Core learnings, criticism of, 172
Core programs, 287–288
  experimentation with, 291–293
  problem areas for, 288–290
  societal developments influencing, 293–294
  team teaching contrasted with, 294
  team teaching within, 298–299
Counseling, 307
Counter-culture, 63–65
Counts, George S., 166, 168
Cremin, Lawrence A., 161, 376–377
Culture
  educational goals and, 156–158

Mexican-American, 100–101
Curriculum
  alternative futures and, 244–245
  arts and esthetics in, 238–239
  communication in, 243–244
  community living in, 241–242
  consumer problems in, 235–236
  economic problems in, 234
  family, peer group, and school in, 240
  governmental processes in, 234–235
  health in, 240–241
  intercultural relationships in, 236–237
  organization of, 245–246
  overpopulation, pollution, and energy in, 233–234
  problem centering of, 229–232
  recreation and leisure in, 237–238
  self-understanding and personal development in, 239–240
  separate subject matter approach to, 225–228
  vocations in, 242–243
  war, peace, and international relations in, 232–233
  world view in, 237
  see also Core programs

Decentralization, 331–332
Delinquency, 104–106
Democracy, 67–69
Desegregation, 41–42
Dewey, John, 162–163, 168–169
Douvan, Elizabeth, 86
Dropouts, 106–109
  race and sex and, 96 (fig.)
Drug abusers, 109–112

Economic problems, 44–46
  in curriculum, 234
  young people and, 46–47
Education
  of Mexican-Americans, 100–101
  sex roles and, 86
Educational attainment, of labor force, 363 (fig.)
Educational Development Center, 303
Educational Facilities Laboratory, 256
Educational goals
  college preparation as, 163–165
  compensatory education and, 174
  current conflict over, 174–176
  Educational Policies Commission's views on, 170–171
  Great Depression and, 166–168
  immigration and Americanization and, 156–158

industrialism and, 155–156
progressive, 161–163, 168–169
projects in subjects and, 173
rural reform and, 160
Seven Cardinal Principles and, 165–166
social reform and, 160
stress on vocational skills and, 158
urban reform and, 158–160
Educational plans, social class and, 91 (fig.)
Educational Policies Commission, views on goals, 170–171
Educators, role and responsibility of, 74–76. *See also* Principals; School boards; Teacher(s)
Eight-Year Study, 169–170
Eliot, Charles W., 132, 164
Emerson, Ralph Waldo, 265
Employment, occupational groups and, 369 (fig.). *See also* Unemployment
Energy use, 39
in curriculum, 233–234
young people and, 40
English language arts, current programs in, 194–197
Enrollment, 318 (table)
declining, 257, 262
Equal Rights Amendment, 43
Esthetics, in curriculum, 238–239
Expenditures, 333 (fig.)

Family
in curriculum, 240
delinquency and, 105
Fingers, in contemporary school plants, 255–256
Fleming, Robert S., 367
Follow-up services, 308
Foreign languages, current programs in, 199–202
Foshay, Arthur W., 227
Foxfire program, 278
Franklin, Benjamin, 151–153
Futurism, 359
rapid development of, 361–362, 364
utopianism and, 360

Goslin, Willard, 171
Governmental processes, 47–49
in curriculum, 234–235
young people and, 49–50
Great Depression, influence on educational goals, 166–168
Greece, secondary education in, 122–123
Greek, stress on study of, 164
Gross, Ronald, 9, 11
Guidance

development of, 306–307
modern, 307–310
Guidance counselors, 308–310

Hanna, Paul R., 268–269, 273–274
Harap, Henry, 229–230
Hart, Joseph K., 265–266
Headmasters, 338
Health
current programs in, 197–199
in curriculum, 240–241
Henry Street Settlement, 159
High school(s)
comprehensive, 141, 143
development of, 127–131
evolution of, 139–141
general, 143
specialized, 143
vocational, 143–144
see also Secondary education; Secondary school plants
High school graduates, number of, 389 (table)
Hippies, 64
Holt, John, 7
Home economics, current programs in, 207–209
Hull House, 159–160

IDEA Materials Center, 303
Immigration, influence on educational goals, 156–158
Income distribution, 44–45
race and sex and, 96 (fig.)
Income tax, 48
Independent study, 305
Individualism, 67–70
modification of, 73
Individualized instruction, 299–300
characteristics of, 300–301
contracts in, 301
goal of, 305–306
independent study in, 305
learning centers in, 302–303
learning packages in, 301–302
teaching machines and computers in, 303–304
Individualized Science Instructional System (ISIS), 186
Individually Prescribed Instruction (IPI), 186
Industrial arts, current programs in, 209–210
Industrialism, influence on educational goals, 155–156
Inflation, 45

Information services, 308
In loco parentis, controversy over, 343
Inner-city schools, problems of, 321–323
In-service, to cope with changes, 374
Instructional staff, number and distribution of, 340–341 (table)
Intercultural relations, in curriculum, 236–237
International Association for Community Educators, 273
International relations, 34–36
  in curriculum, 232–233
  young people and, 36–37
Internships, 278

Jefferson, Thomas, views on education, 153–154
Job expectations, labor force composition and, 370 (fig.)
Job placement, 308
Junior high schools
  development of, 131–135
  purposes of, 135–136

Kahn, Herman, 361–362, 371
Kelley, Earl C., 367–368
Kelley, Florence, 159
Kilpatrick, William Heard, 168
King, Martin Luther, Jr., 71, 97, 302
Kline, Morris, 188
Kuhn, Thomas, 183

Laboratory school, 162
Language arts, current programs in, 194–197
Lasswell, Harold D., 379
Latin, stress on study of, 164
Latin grammar schools, 125–126
Learning alternatives, 300
Learning centers, 302–303
Learning packages, 301–302
Learning styles, 201–202
Leisure, in curriculum, 237–238
Life-adjustment education, criticism of, 172
Life styles
  activist protest and, 70–73
  counter-culture and, 63–65
  individualism and, 67–70
  privatism and, 65–67
  work ethic and, 60–63

McCarthy, Joseph, 171
McClure, S. S., 160
McGuffey Readers, 157
Maher, Trafford P., S.J., 366

Man: A Course of Study (MACOS), 186
Manhattanville Music Curriculum Program (MMCP), 204
Mann, Horace, 154–155
Marien, Michael, 368, 371–374
Marijuana, use by young people, 110–112
Marland, Sidney P., 175
Martin, John Henry, 23, 382
Mathematics, current programs in, 186–189
Melby, Ernest O., 272, 274
Mexican-Americans, 99–101
  unemployment among, 321
Middle Ages, secondary education during, 124
Middle schools, development of, 137–139
Miel, Alice, 366
Migration, influence on educational goals, 156–157
Miller, Richard L., 189
Minority groups, school board representation of, 331. *See also* Black(s); Mexican-Americans
Moore, Hollis A., Jr., 368
Mott, Charles Stuart, 271
Music, current programs in, 202–204

National Advisory Committee on Mathematics Education (NACOME), 188–189
National Aeronautics and Space Administration (NASA), 172
National Assessment of Educational Progress (NAEP), 195–196, 197
National Association of Secondary School Principals, 23–25, 26, 276
National Child Labor Committee, 159
National Commission on the Reform of Secondary Education, 21, 275, 382
National Community Education Association, 273
National Council for the Social Studies, 191
National Council of Teachers of English (NCTE), 195
National Defense Education Act (NDEA), 172–173, 190, 307
National Education Association (NEA), 320, 323–324
National Panel on High Schools and Adolescent Education, 21–23, 275–276, 382
National Society for the Promotion of Industrial Education, 158
New math, 186–187
Normal schools, 319

Olsen, Edward G., 230, 272
Orientation service, 308
Outward Bound, 276

Overpopulation, 37–38
 in curriculum, 233–234
 young people and, 40

Panel on Youth of the President's Science
  Advisory Committee, 20, 274–275, 382
Paraprofessionals, role of, 347
Parker, Francis Wayland, 161–162, 265
Parkway Program, 12, 263
Patterson, Franklin, 366
Peer group, in curriculum, 240
Personal development, in curriculum,
  239–240
Personalized learning, 198–199
Pestalozzi, Johann, 265
Physical education, current programs in,
  197–199
Physical Sciences Study Committee
  (PSSC), 184–185, 226
Pollution, 38–39
 in curriculum, 233–234
 young people and, 40
Prescriptive teaching, 300–301
Principals
 evolution of, 338–339
 power of, 342–344
 responsibilities of, 339, 342
 specification for, 344–345
Privatism, 65–67
Professionalism, of teachers, 319–321
Progressive education, 161–163
 academic criticism of, 171–172
 evaluation of, 169–170
 goals of, 161–163
 right-wing criticism of, 171
 wings of, 168–169
Progressive Education Association, 168,
  169
Project IMPACT, 206
Projections
 of Bell, 379–380
 of Boulding, 380
 community-oriented, 382–383
 of Cremin, 376–377
 of Lasswell, 379
 of Marien, 368, 371–374
 of Rubin, 381–382
 of Shane, 374–376
 of Toffler, 377–378
 of Wiles, 364–366
Prosser, Charles A., 172
Pupil-teacher ratios, 387 (fig.)

Race, definition of, 40
Racism, 40–42

definition of, 40–41
 young people and, 43
Recreation
 current programs in, 197–199
 in curriculum, 237–238
Research for Better Schools, 378–379
Rice, Chandos, 367
Rice, Theodore, 367
Rickover, Hyman G., 172
Rome, secondary education in, 123–124
Rubin, Louis, 381–382
Rural reform, influence on educational
  goals, 160
Rush, Benjamin, 154

St. Paul Open School, 264
Salaries, of teachers, 327, 328–329 (fig.)
Saylor, Galen, 368
Schoen, Harold, 189
Scholastic Aptitude Test (SAT), 164, 187
School, in curriculum, 240
School-age population, 381 (fig.)
School boards
 evolution of, 330
 power of, 332–333, 337
 responsibilities of, 330–332
 specifications for members of, 337
 views of, 334–336 (table)
School Mathematics Study Group (SMSG),
  187
Science, current programs in,
  183–186
Secondary education
 criticisms of, 4–27
 development in America, 125–131
 origins of, 122–124
 possible futures for, 383–392
 reorganization of, 131–144
 statistical data concerning, 144–146
 total setting of, 27–28
Secondary school(s), number of, 317 (table). See also High school(s)
Secondary school plants
 for alternative schools, 263–264
 changing, 280
 nineteenth-century, 252, 253 (fig.), 254
   (fig.)
 projected, 365–366
 team teaching and, 295, 296–297 (fig.)
 twentieth-century, 253, 255–257, 262–
   263, 258–261 (fig.)
Self-understanding, in curriculum, 239–240
Settlement houses, 159–160
Seven Cardinal Principles, 18, 165–166,
  174, 175–176

Sex differences
  in delinquency, 105
  among dropouts, 107 (fig.)
Sex education, controversy over, 197
Sexism, 42–43
  young people and, 43–44
Sex roles
  in adolescence, 85–89
  among Mexican-Americans, 100
Shane, Harold G., 374–376
Silberman, Charles E., 7–8
Size
  of alternative schools, 263
  of high schools, 262–263
Skyline Center, 264
Smith, Vernon H., 263, 276–280, 348
Smith-Hughes Vocational Education Act,
  158
Smith-Lever Act, 160
Social class, 89–90
  adolescents and, 90–94
  among blacks, 98
  delinquency and, 105, 106
Social crisis, teaching during, 50–53
Socialism, 44
Social reform, influence on educational
  goals, 160
Social studies, current programs in, 189–
  194
Social Studies Program, 190
Special Olympics program, 199
Spiral curriculum, 191
Sputnik, influence on educational goals,
  172
Stagflation, 45
Steffens, Lincoln, 160
Student assessment, 307–308
System breaks, 360

Taxes, to support schools, 130, 316, 332
Teacher(s)
  evolution of, 315–316, 319
  power of, 323–326
  responsibilities of, 308–309, 319–321, 323
  specifications for, 326–327
  statistical data on, 327–329
Teacher-advisers, 309–310
Teaching, during social crisis, 50–53
Teaching machines, 303–304
Team teaching, 294–295

within core programs, 298–299
core programs contrasted with, 294
Thoreau, Henry David, 265
Toffler, Alvin, 359, 377–378
Travel, 378
Trump, J. Lloyd, 294, 309–310, 339, 342

Unemployment, 45, 321
  among college graduates, 110 (fig.)
  among dropouts, 108
  among youth, 46, 321
Unified studies, 287
Unionization, of principals, 344
UNIPACS, 303
U.S. Children's Bureau, 159
University of Illinois Committee on School
  Mathematics (UICSM), 187
University of Maryland Mathematics Proj-
  ect (UMMAP), 187
Urban reform, influence on educational
  goals, 158–160
Utopianism, futurism and, 360

Value(s)
  role of educators and, 75–76
  social developments affecting, 73–74
Value confusion, 58–60
Value patterns, see Life Styles
Vars, Gordon F., 289, 309–310, 339, 342
Violence, among students, 322 (fig.)
Vocation(s), in curriculum, 242–243
Vocational education
  current programs in, 213–216
  growth of, 158
Vocational guidance, development of, 306

Wald, Lillian, 159
Webster, Noah, 154
Westinghouse Learning Corporation, 303
Wiener, Norbert, 366
Wiles, Kimball, 364–366
Wilkins, Roy, 97
Willard, Emma, 127
Women's liberation movement, 43
  sex roles and, 87
Work ethic, 60–63
Work stoppages, teacher involvement in,
  325 (fig.)
World views, in curriculum, 237

Zacharias, Jerrold R., 184, 226

ABCDEFGHIJ–H–79876